The
CONSTRAINTS
of
$\mathscr{D}$ESIRE

See how they grow. Woman waters phalloi. *Attic red-figure pelike in the British Museum, E819. (Courtesy of the British Museum.)*

The CONSTRAINTS *of* DESIRE

THE ANTHROPOLOGY OF SEX AND GENDER IN ANCIENT GREECE

JOHN J. WINKLER

ROUTLEDGE
NEW YORK • LONDON

Published in 1990 by

Routledge
An imprint of Routledge, Chapman and Hall, Inc.
29 West 35 Street
New York, NY 10001

Published in Great Britain by

Routledge
11 New Fetter Lane
London EC4P 4EE

Library of Congress Cataloging in Publication Data

Winkler, John J.
  The constraints of desire: the anthropology of sex and gender in ancient Greece / John J. Winkler.
    p.   cm. — (New ancient world series)
    Bibliography: p.
    Includes index.
    ISBN 0-415-90122-7; ISBN 0-415-90123-5 (pbk.)
    1. Sex customs—Greece—History. 2. Women—Greece—Social conditions. I. Title. II. Series.
  DF93.W56 1989
  392.6'0938—dc20

British Library Cataloguing in Publication Data

Winkler, John J. *1943–*
  Constraints of desire : the anthropology of sex and gender in ancient Greece.
  1. Greece. Man. Sexuality ancient period.
  Sociological perspectives
  I. Title
  306.7'0938

  ISBN 0-415-90122-7
       0-415-90123-5 (Pb)

Contents

Preface   vii

Abbreviations   ix

Introduction   1

Part One: *Andres*

Chapter 1.   Unnatural Acts: Erotic Protocols in
             Artemidoros' *Dream Analysis.*   17

Chapter 2.   Laying Down the Law: The Oversight of Men's
             Sexual Behavior in Classical Athens.   45

Chapter 3.   The Constraints of Desire: Erotic Magical Spells.   71

Interlude: Reading Against the Grain

Chapter 4.   The Education of Chloe: Hidden Injuries of Sex.   101

Part Two: *Gunaikes*

Chapter 5.   Penelope's Cunning and Homer's.   129

Chapter 6.   Double Consciousness in Sappho's Lyrics.   162

Chapter 7.   The Laughter of the Oppressed: Demeter and
             the Gardens of Adonis.   188

Appendix One.   Translation of Artemidoros 1.78–80.   210

Appendix Two.   *Phusis* and *Natura* Meaning "Genitals."   217

Notes.   221

Bibliography.   237

Index of Passages Discussed.   255

General Index.   261

Preface

This book is dedicated to the two people who made it happen: to my sister, Cathy Winkler, and to David M. Halperin. It was Cathy Winkler's questions and insights from her work as a feminist anthropologist that shaped much of the inquiry undertaken here, and she has been a source of constant inspiration and help. Her wide-ranging knowledge of the relevant bibliography on women's issues, in particular, has been invaluable to me, and her academic activism sets an example that I would like to be able to live up to. David Halperin first pointed out to me that a number of social and literary essays I had been writing over the years were unified by a common methodology, style, and set of interests—unified enough to be a book. That, as well as his own extremely stimulating work on related areas, has deeply influenced the shape and quality of this project. He has marked almost every page with crisper and more elegant formulations and has probed the substance of the arguments to make them more profound. I owe both Cathy and David an unrepayable debt for their love, support, and generosity.

Many others have read or listened to these pieces in one form or another. Helene P. Foley heads the list, as will be obvious from my reliance on her work in several essays. I'm sure I have absorbed advice from some people whose names I have now forgotten: they should add themselves to this list of those I can remember, and whom I here thank for their advice and criticism: Marilyn P. Arthur, Kenneth J. Dover, Page duBois, N. Gregson Davis, Mark W. Edwards, Christopher A. Faraone, Mark Golden, Michael Herzfeld, Michael Jameson, Ludwig Koenen, Sheila Murnaghan, Dirk Obbink, Josiah Ober, Amy Richlin, Nancy Felson-Rubin, Daniel Selden, Eva Stehle, Susan Stephens, Barry Strauss, and Froma I. Zeitlin.

An earlier version of Chapter Six on Sappho was published in Helene P. Foley, ed., *Reflections of Women in Antiquity* (New York 1981). Abridged versions of three other chapters will soon appear in other publications: Chapter Two in David M. Halperin, John J. Winkler, and Froma I. Zeitlin, eds., *Before Sexuality* (Princeton 1989), Chapter Three in Christopher A.

Faraone and Dirk Obbink, eds., *Magika Hiera* (New York, forthcoming), and Chapter Four in Brenda Silver and Lynn Higgins, eds., *Rape and Representation* (New York, forthcoming).

I have used a modified social science system of reference. Modern authors are referred to by last name alone; full citation of the work in question will be found in the bibliography; first initials and date of publication are added when necessary to distinguish between same-named authors or multiple publications by the same author. Anecdotal or illustrative notes are placed at the foot of the page; the more technical and bibliographical notes are placed at the end. I wish to thank Tasha C. Spencer for compiling the Indices.

This work has been supported by grants from the National Endowment for the Humanities, the Guggenheim Foundation, the American Council of Learned Societies, the Stanford Humanities Center, and the Marilyn Yalom Research Fund of Stanford's Institute for Research on Women and Gender.

Half of the author's proceeds from the sale of this book will be given to the San Francisco AIDS Foundation.

Abbreviations

Books.

CIL = *Corpus Inscriptionum Latinarum* (Berlin 1862–)
DT = A. Audollent, *Defixionum Tabellae* (Paris 1904).
FGrHist = *Die Fragmente der Griechischen Historiker,* ed. Felix Jacoby. (Leiden).
FVS = *Fragmente der Vorsokratiker,* ed. Hermann Diels and Walther Kranz, ed. 14, 3 vols. (Dublin and Zürich).
IG = *Inscriptiones Graecae.*
PCG = *Poetae Comici Graeci,* ed. Colin Austin and R. Kassel. (Berlin 1983–).
PGM = *Papyri Graecae Magicae,* ed. Karl Preisendanz, 2nd ed. by A. Henrichs, 2 vols. (Stuttgart 1973–4).
RE = *Paulys Real-Encyclopaedie,* 24 vols., ed. Georg Wissowa. (Stuttgart 1894–1963).
RGVV = *Religionsgeschichtliche Versuche und Vorarbeiten.*

Journals.

AC = *L'Antiquité Classique.*
AE = *American Ethnologist.*
AJP = *American Journal of Philology.*
AM = *Mitteilungen des deutschen Archaeologischen Instituts, Athenische Abteilung.*
BCH = *Bulletin de Correspondance Hellénique.*
CA = *Classical Antiquity.*
CI = *Critical Inquiry.*
CP = *Classical Philology.*
CQ = *Classical Quarterly.*
CR = *Classical Review.*
CSCA = *California Studies in Classical Antiquity.*

G&R = *Greece and Rome.*
GRBS = *Greek Roman and Byzantine Studies.*
HSCP = *Harvard Studies in Classical Philology.*
HTR = *Harvard Theological Review.*
JEA = *Journal of Egyptian Archaeology.*
JHS = *Journal of Hellenic Studies.*
PCPS = *Proceedings of the Cambridge Philological Society.*
QUCC = *Quaderni Urbinati di Cultura Classica.*
RhM = *Rheinisches Museum.*
RM = *Mitteilungen des deutschen Archaeologischen Instituts, Römische Abteilung.*
SEG = *Supplementum Epigraphicum Graecum.*
TAPA = *Transactions of the American Philological Association.*
ZPE = *Zeitschrift für Papyrologie und Epigraphik.*

The
CONSTRAINTS
of
ＤＥＳＩＲＥ

Introduction

What first attracted me—and many others, I am sure—to the study of ancient Greece was the glamorous combination of exciting myths and beautiful bodies. But on closer inspection the Greece that was presented to me in grade school and high school turns out to have been in part a modern cultural fantasy developed mainly by German scholars such as Winckelmann from the eighteenth century on and in part a fantasy projected by the ancient Greeks themselves. It should have been obvious to me that no real place could have existed where all the men had the bodies of young athletes and all history was so relentlessly noble, tragic, and exciting, but it only dawned on me how constructed was this myth-making when I first visited Greece in 1982. There was, to be sure, youthful beauty aplenty but I also observed numerous instances of behavior that reminded me of scenes from ancient literature.

For instance, the first Gay Pride Day demonstration in Athens, held in the Zappeion Gardens on June 26, was a surprisingly silent gathering which after a short time spontaneously broke up into discussion groups between the demonstrators and the numerous by-standers who were taking their evening stroll. The conversations reminded me of the format of a Platonic dialogue: one person took a stand to defend a proposition and was interrogated by a principal challenger, while a circle of listeners followed the contest and occasionally commented. Beyond the form of their discourse, I began to sense other qualities in the discussants' behavior, particularly a kind of controlled aggression. This is hard to describe but, impressionistically, I would say that all the speakers seemed frank, ironic, guarded, and threatening in ways that I would not expect between strangers.

In the ensuing months I had many similar experiences of the different cultural rules that governed self-presentation in Athens and the Peloponnese. I was fortunate to have, as do most anthropologists, a special informant, Michael, whom I met at that Gay Pride demonstration and whose family also became my friends. But I want to stress that it was not any one person or event that unlocked for me the classical Greek past; rather I filled my

1

mind with scenes of the present and they have over the years affected my sense of how to read ancient texts—how to evaluate their intentions, misdirections, and unspoken premises. I hold no particular brief for the continuity of ancient and modern Greece (in this I follow Herzfeld 1982), but my experiences in modern Greece have cozied up to my reading of ancient Greek texts, nestled next to them, and set up a field around them that has altered my sense of the possible meanings of ancient literature and life.

Since sex and gender are the focus of these essays, let me tell one more story. One afternoon, a cousin of Michael's, a pretty woman in her early twenties, showed up at his apartment. She phoned her father to say that she was spending the afternoon with Michael, and then she abruptly left. As the door closed, Michael made a ferocious gesture: touching his finger tips together into a V he made a slashing gesture towards his own groin. He explained to me that she was sleeping with a married man and that her father was extremely strict, hence the deception. What struck me was the unresolved intersection of several familiar themes: the father vigilant about his daughter's chastity, the woman successfully concealing her affair, the obvious contempt Michael felt for her promiscuity, and his unwillingness to take responsibility for the family violence that would ensue if he told her father the truth. The woman herself was at the center of several force-fields of male violence and passion: dutiful daughter to her father, compliant mistress to her lover, and manipulator of a cousin who despised her. She may not have been typical in playing such a dangerous game, but her case shows both the serious constraints under which women labor and one woman's success in juggling with dynamite.

Turning to ancient Greece, the forms of erotic experience there have long been a contested area in the interpretation of our cultural traditions. One strain of modern thinking has used the vases and luxury literature of ancient Greece to generate an image of hedonistic liberation—satyrs chasing nymphs over the greensward—often supported by a Nietzschean attack on the blighting effect of christian morality.[1] More recently, some feminist scholarship has challenged the innocence of that picture, trying to look at it from the nymph's point of view. Considered as a set of rules and practices that enforced men's sexual control over women, the ancient Greek norms have been attacked as politically oppressive—one more chapter in patriarchy's ongoing war against women (Harrison 1912, Keuls, Lerner, Cantarella). This disagreement about the nature of ancient Greek sex is similar to another longstanding debate about gender: were ancient Greek (which usually means classical Athenian) women treated as little better than chattel, or did they hold an honored, respected, and protected place in society?

Arguments on both those issues—ancient sex and ancient gender—suffer from selective uses of evidence, from framing the questions themselves too narrowly, and even more from the methodology of reading contemporary concerns and politics into texts and artefacts removed from their social context. We cannot, of course, do without contemporary concerns: they generate our questions and energize our work. But both feminist and gay scholarship are now reaching a point where past societies can be studied not for their value in making a political point about the present but for their sheer and surprising difference. As contemporary anthropology more and more incorporates a historical dimension into its analysis, so new techniques are being developed that treat the distant past as "real" society, rather than as some kind of exotic Never-Never-Land.

Unlike modern anthropologists, working as participant observers, we cannot interview ancient Greek men or women to discover their categories and concerns. But the techniques of social and cultural anthropology, particularly as practiced by feminists, can elicit from those texts and pictures a richer and more complex understanding of sex and gender. "Recent work in the anthropology of women does what cultural anthropologists do best—namely, it heads full tilt at culture-bound assumptions in our own thinking. Since the formative years of the discipline, anthropologists have effectively challenged a long list of pre-conceived notions about human nature and human institutions. Mystifications of race, religion, and nationalism, among others have been targets. One reason, perhaps, that feminism and anthropology have taken well to each other is that feminist anthropologists have continued this tradition by tackling hitherto unquestioned assumptions about sex and gender" (Atkinson 238).

The successes of this ongoing project have been stronger in analyzing the cultural constructions of gender than those of sex. After the groundbreaking work of Pomeroy and the material collections of Lefkowitz and Fant, several important anthologies of essays have established women's studies as one of the most exciting growth points in the field of Classics (Foley 1981b, Cameron and Kuhrt, Peradotto and Sullivan, Skinner 1987a), but only very recently has serious attention been turned to sex. Sex itself in the social sciences is generally treated as an unanalyzable given, the province of biology or perhaps psychology, but not subject to cultural investigation. As Rosalind Coward puts it, "Why is the study of sexuality when it appears in the social sciences frequently subsumed under studies of institutionalised (social) forms of sexual regulation, like marriage? Why is there no theory of forms of domination and inequality in the dynamic of sexual relations? Why is there no understanding of the construction of sexual identity or consideration of the distribution of power and status which this identity might entail?" (4).

For ancient Greece the questions about sex itself were very excitingly posed by Michel Foucault, one of the great thinkers of our age, who died of AIDS in 1984. His series title, *The History of Sexuality,* sounds at first rather grand and definitive, but that is a false impression. I once heard him refuse to sign a copy of one of his books on the grounds that one should only sign works of art and that his books were to be taken as working papers. As a series of working papers, Foucault's arguments have been taken up by a number of Classicists, whose essays have been collected in Halperin, Winkler, and Zeitlin. The key Foucauldian thesis is that "sexuality" is a distinctively modern construction, a new nineteenth- and twentieth-century way of speaking about the self as organized around well-defined (and therefore catalogable) sexual characters and desires. It is impossible therefore to have, say, a history of homosexuality, since neither it nor heterosexuality nor even sexuality are timeless facts of human nature (Halperin 1989). Since "sexuality" in this sense is a recent invention, Foucault's first volume, setting out this thesis about the nineteenth-century's obsession with speaking about sex, had no reference to the ancient world. The next volumes, however, reflect his growing curiosity about how individuals came to inspect their own states of desire as if their desire were a central problem, and about the Greco-Roman context in which problems of desire had not yet been seen as problems of the *self*. The introduction to Halperin, Winkler, and Zeitlin sets out many of the critical themes in this new study of ancient sexual behavior, above all the need to suspend our sexual categories (including the importance and centrality of sex) when studying another society, particularly a pre-modern one.

The essays in the present volume, composed over the last eight years, take up some of these issues, using methods and observations inspired by my casual observations of modern Greek behavior and also from my reading in contemporary social and cultural anthropology, especially of the Mediterranean area. It is clear that posing our questions in terms of the "status" of women is inadequate, and that our knowledge of women's lives is largely refracted through the gnomic utterances of men. The first priority, therefore, must be to recover the usually unspoken premises or protocols governing the force of public utterances, and it appears that much of men's talk about women *and about themselves* was a calculated bluff. The study of women in the ancient world cannot proceed very far unless it is accompanied by an equally penetrating examination of men and how they constructed their practices of sex and gender-identity. Hence this sequence of essays begins with three on men (*Andres*) before going on to the lives and representations of women (*Gunaikes*).

By calling the fundamental conventions "protocols" I mean to avoid two false emphases. On the one hand, like the preliminary definitions and agreements within which the terms of a specific treaty are hammered out, fundamental conventions such as androcentrism in ancient Greece would not generally have been regarded as negotiable items. A public world that was not androcentric, such as that imagined in Aristophanes' *Ekklêsiazousai*

(*Congresswomen*), in which women take charge of public affairs, was by that very fact marked as not a real public world but a fantasy.

On the other hand, androcentrism is an utterly conventional arrangement, not a natural order—an arrangement limited in many ways to the public realm of business between competing households. Androcentrism functioned in some ways like Native American sign language: it allowed public communication between competing households, potential enemies, enabling them to negotiate on terms mutually understood and with continual reference to the possibilities of aggression and defense. As such the convention of androcentrism is a limited language of men in certain conditions; it does not adequately represent the entire social world, as we would like to describe it, but rather serves to mark off a restricted area of importance (that of public transactions) and to speak of it in absolute terms as if it were the whole.

A social protocol such as androcentrism is therefore somewhat paradoxical: its meaning is both never seriously questioned and yet never taken literally. Mediterranean androcentrism is both an unquestioned truth and a universal fib: each man acknowledges its force, nodding sagely and silently, with his fingers crossed behind his back. We must learn to read our texts from several angles, seeing in them both honest pretensions and cover-ups, just as informants try to manipulate an anthropological observer by presenting themselves in the best light. Instead of snipping opinions from their context, like the famous remark in the speech *Against Neaira,* * and treating them as objective dogma, we should learn to see the various kinds of spin and misdirection that qualify the meaning of such pronouncements in their full social context, the unspoken stage directions that are understood but not voiced by the social actor. Not infrequently we can detect in them a simultaneous denial and recognition of ideologically inconvenient social realities.

In studying the limitations of prescriptive statements concerning sex and gender, women occupy a central and crucial role. Most of our surviving documents simply cannot be taken at face value when they speak of women. As long as the discussion is centered on *gunaikes,* citizen-wives, there is a large interference in the data from male speakers' sense of social propriety: even to mention the name of a citizen-wife in the company of men was a shame and an insult, implying an intrusion into another man's symbolic privacy (Schaps 1977, Sommerstein, Gould 1980: 45, Bremmer, Skinner 1987b). The speaker of Demosthenes 57 has been attacked because his mother was a wet nurse. He responds, "You will find many citizen women who at

---

* "We have courtesans for our pleasure, concubines for the daily service of our bodies, and wives for bearing legitimate children and keeping faithful watch over the goods in our houses" ([Dem.] 59. 122).

the present time are wet nurses, and if you like I will actually (*kai*) mention them by name" (Dem. 57.35).

The busyness of metic (non-citizen) women, by contrast, can be discussed without danger of insulting anyone but the woman herself: thus, a certain Zobia hid Aristogeiton from the police, gave him money, was beaten for her trouble, and then, "typical meddling woman, she went around to her acquaintances and complained of what he had done."[2] Outside forensic contexts, there is a slightly greater likelihood that the responsibilities and agency of women will receive some acknowledgment. Aristotle appears to notice the *de facto* independence of Athenian wives in managing their households: "The husband rules concerning the things which a husband should rule; what is appropriate for a wife he assigns to her."[3] (More on Aristotle below.)

The modern study of women's place in men's ideologies and their perspective on men's ideologies has had an extraordinarily beneficial effect on our comprehension of ancient societies. The more we learn about comparable gender-segregated, pre-industrial societies, particularly in the Mediterranean area, the more it seems that most of men's observations and moral judgments about women and sex and so forth have minimal descriptive validity and are best understood as coffeehouse talk, addressed to men themselves.[4] Women, we should emphasize, in all their separate groupings by age, neighborhood, and class, may differ widely from each other and from community to community in the degree to which they obey, resist, or even notice the existence of such palaver as men indulge in when going through their bonding rituals.* To know when any such male law-givers—medical, moral, or marital, whether smart or stupid—are (to put it bluntly) bluffing or spinning fantasies or justifying their 'druthers is so hard that most historians of ideas—Foucault, for all that he is exceptional, is no exception here[†]— never try.

Let us take just one example of the revealing gap between prescriptive discourse and social reality. In *Politics* 1.12 Aristotle devises a threefold comparison of household authority-relations to forms of political authority. The relation of the patriarchal master to his slaves is like a political tyranny:

---

*Some of the variables—economy, settlement and residence, inheritance, ritual, associational life—are surveyed by Rogers 1985 in a study of two French towns, in one of which male dominance is a sort of social myth, while in the other it is a reality. For Athens, religious ritual seems the strongest candidate as a factor that might have allowed women a sphere of independence and psychic distance. "While the deme in its narrowly political aspect necessarily remained an all-male preserve, the sphere of religion and cult operated under a different, older set of imperatives, and 'in the sacred and ritual activities of the community the active presence of women in the public world [was] not merely tolerated but required'": Whitehead 79, quoting Gould. See also Dubisch 1983, Cole 1984b, and Chapter Seven below.

†As he acknowledges: Foucault 1985: 12.

the master gives commands in his own interest and the slaves must obey (S. Clark 184, Smith). The relation of the father to his children is like that of a king to his subjects: the king rules unilaterally in the interests of all. The children must, of course, obey his commands but those commands are intended to be in their interest. The relation of husband to wife, says Aristotle, is like a democracy. In a democracy all citizens are equal in rights and are equally eligible for office. Those elected to office are invested with insignia marking their temporary and purely conventional difference from the rest of the citizens. When the period of office is over, they take off those insignia and return to a state of equality. The only difference, says Aristotle, is that in the case of husband and wife the distinction is permanent. This is mind-boggling. Given Aristotle's other conceptions of the inherent, definitional inferiority of the female,[5] there was no need for him to compare the relation of husband and wife to democratic equality, no need to raise the thought that wives might, if elected, govern the household in turn with their husbands, and no need to conjure up the paradoxical image of a democratic system in which the same citizens always hold office.

One way to comprehend what has happened here is to say that Aristotle is caught in the very act of processing descriptive data into his legislative system. Women's work with children, food, and clothing inside the *oikos*, all their contribution to the administration and prosperity of the household, is a feature that Aristotle almost entirely ignores and notices only to misrepresent. I suggest that in Aristotle's text we momentarily see him off guard, caught in the act of referring obliquely to women's capacities for administrative independence and not fully digesting that fact into his scheme of social legislation. We should at least keep our minds open to the possibility, which studies of some comparable societies have documented, that Athenian wives had a considerable degree of practical independence in managing their households. If we do entertain the notion that Athenian citizen-wives had at least certain kinds of informal power, we must also be clear that it was socially necessary for men not to acknowledge it*—to deal with it at most indirectly through myths of Amazons and through their cultural fantasies of rebellious wives in tragedy or comedy.[6]

But if the strength and independence of Athenian women constituted a sort of guilty secret, it might also be alluded to on occasions of indiscretion as a guilty pleasure. I have in mind here an interchange in Aristophanes' *Lysistrata* (885–8) where Myrrhinê berates her husband Kinesias for not taking proper care of the baby. While she comes down from the fortress to attend to the baby herself, he remarks, inappropriately, that she seems to

---

*Xenophon describes the honorable role of women as remaining indoors, the shameful role for men as staying inside rather than tending to affairs outside: to do otherwise is an unnatural act, literally "against what god made natural," *par' ha ho theos ephuse* (*Econ.* 7.31).

look much younger and milder than he remembers; and "I just love it when she talks so harshly and haughtily to me."[7] Kinesias, of course, is portrayed as a man under considerable pressure and his situation as amusing, but the social historian can still glean something useful from his predicament: if Athenian wives had been powerless and dominated *in the same way as* (say) their slaves, Kinesias' remark would not have made the audience smile.

As guilty secret or as guilty pleasure, women's practical autonomy in certain spheres may well have been the sort of fact that in the company of men was known but never acknowledged or discussed, for in such company to do so would have brought shame.[*] Aristotle should here be understood as engaging in the perfectly natural (that is, perfectly conventional) prevarication of masculine discourse about the role of women in his day, a prevarication which we may simply dub the androcentric protocol. In the sex–gender system constructed and experienced by citizen males, the first unwritten rule is that men are the important agents, while women are properly dependents rather than agents. Men count as significant, women do not signify.[†] When women are active, they are trouble. Since a man does not want to invite trouble, it is prudent for him and other men to assume, until forced to do otherwise, that the women of his household are invisible, obedient, and industrious.

Anthropology and the Classics

Whereas Classics is a rather conservative field and has cultivated an image of its own continuity for almost two hundred years, anthropology tends to attract more adventurous souls and that discipline has undergone several sea-changes in its half-as-long history. Thus, although earlier generations have sometimes paired anthropology and the Classics, the anthropology in question has been very different from what now passes under that name. At the turn of the century Sir James G. Frazer, Jane Ellen Harrison (Peacock 1988), Francis M. Cornford, and Gilbert Murray studied Greek religion and literature in the light of the anthropology of their day, which essentially meant reading about so-styled primitive tribes. The experiment to look for the primitive roots of Greek literary forms (tragedy and comedy: Murray

---

[*] du Boulay 1983 gives an excellent analysis of the muted correlative to laments over the birth of a daughter: girls in their original families are destined to leave and to take with them some of the family's wealth just at the moment when they become most valuable, whereas brides entering into a family are highly valued and admired for their character, skills, and dowry.

[†] So sexual relations between women are virtually without significance in Artemidoros' classification, and can only be formulated in words by using the language of male agency: see below, p. 39.

in Harrison 1912; Cornford 1934), of social practices (the Olympic games: Cornford in Harrison 1912), and of religious ideas and rites (Harrison 1903, 1912; Murray 1912) was received with great distaste by many of their contemporaries. Finley 1975 describes, in his Jane Ellen Harrison Memorial Lecture, the frank revulsion felt by Classicists, one of whom spoke of Harrison's work as having "tipped over to the slimy side" (103). (This reaction says at least as much about the white-washed, romantic, and racist image of Greece, which was so useful for pedagogical purposes in the North Atlantic states, as it does about anthropology itself. See the groundbreaking work of Bernal.)

Anthropology then turned, under the influence of Malinowski and Boas, from being an arm-chair study of primitives and progress to being a more first-hand analysis, based on the observer's participation in an actual culture, and this has remained the standard practice, rather like an initiation rite into the field. The decades of this century have seen important innovations in styles of analysis, principally functionalism and structuralism and their sometimes cooperative alliance, and more recently semiotics and feminism. Above all anthropology has lost its exclusive concentration on "primitive," pre-literate, tribal societies and now studies contemporary social and cultural groups of all sorts. At their best, anthropologists no longer condescend to their informants as backward but develop an appreciation for the distinctive styles of meaning and practice of another culture.

Anthropologists, starting with Friedl and Campbell, have done excellent studies of the regions of modern Greece.* More recently the provocative and insightful work of Michael Herzfeld has made Greece a centerpiece of Mediterranean studies,[8] though he would be one of the first to raise critical questions about that term ("Mediterranean") as a unit of analysis (Herzfeld 1984, 1987b). The interaction between North Atlantic anthropologists (among others) and Mediterranean cultures has involved many prejudices on both sides: Greece, Turkey, Spain, Egypt, Algeria, especially in their rural areas, may all be taken to represent technologically backward, or exotically Oriental, cultures. These stereotypes can in turn be used as a manipulable mask against the North Atlantic tourist, anthropologist, colonialist (Herzfeld 1982, Alloula). Herzfeld has been particularly shrewd in noting among modern Greeks the difference between a public ("Hellenic") face and a private, familial ("Romeic") reality (Herzfeld 1986), in which gender roles are seen to be rhetorically manipulable, rather than fixed and static.

---

*There are, of course, great differences between the regions, e.g. between herdsmen and farmers (Denich), and between what each observer notices: Handman is so struck by the violence and deception of Greek social life that she wonders why any Greeks bother to live together (194).

But let me make very clear that the issue of continuity between ancient Greek and modern Greek culture is a red herring. It is not that cultural ways have survived intact and can be taken as evidence for ancient life. My own observations in Greece were a fillip to reflection, not the basis of an interpretation. It is simply the case that certain deep premises (protocols) about social life, widely shared and with very significant variations around the Mediterranean basin, can be used to frame and illuminate ancient texts, bringing out their unspoken assumptions. Even that is too strong as a description of my methods, for I try never to place real weight on contemporary parallels. Rather, my readings in ethnography from various parts of the world, but especially the Mediterranean, have opened up avenues of thought about the richer and more complex meanings of ancient Greek oratory, vases, politics, magic, poetry, and religious rites. My studies have not been systematic, but have proceeded rather by what Apuleius in the *Golden Ass* called a "desultory science" (*desultoria scientia* 1.1), perhaps better translated as "equestrian academics," a metaphor derived from circus acrobats who leap from one horse to another. Anthropological methods have provided me with particular techniques of reading, of supplying implied meanings, and with specific interpretive stances. From time to time I have quoted illustrative parallels, as at the end of Chapter Seven, but for the most part I have used my anthropological reading as an artist's penciled outline, which is erased when the picture is finished.

A true anthropological description of an ancient Greek community is, of course, impossible. The ancient material data and literary texts are drawn from no single community and no single time. A meaningful ethnography would require at the minimum not only a social object well defined in space and time but the possibility of interviews, observations and counting, which our resources cannot provide. My methods, then, and questions and observational style have been influenced by contemporary social studies, and the data is sometimes similar enough to warrant citation, but the analysis of ancient material should stand on its own terms.

The Shape of this Book

Instead of artificially forcing these essays to speak with a single voice, I have let each of them follow its own logic, so that together they reproduce the variety of perspectives and experiences which single approaches tend to simplify and iron out. This is in keeping with the insight that both a traditional history-of-ideas approach and a structuralist approach fail in certain ways to do justice to their object. The former does not capture the practices of real people, intellectuals included, while the latter, with its emphasis on system and regularity, misses the contest and conflict of a society with multiple centers of authority and a high sense of bluff and the unspoken.

Nevertheless, the arrangement of the essays has been dictated by a cumulative argument, which could be outlined as follows. Out of all the meanings and facets of sexual behavior that might be singled out for special attention, Greeks insistently focused on dominance and submission, as constituted by phallic penetration. Our best witness to this is Artemidoros, a dream analyst, who spent years investigating the social meanings which average people saw in their dreams. His theory and practice of interpretation uniquely qualify him as a witness to common conceptions because he sees his role as one of letting the social meanings held by his clients speak for themselves. Those meanings turn out to be structured by the three protocols of androcentrism, phallocentrism, and invasion (Chapter One). As appendices I have included a translation of Artemidoros' text on erotic dreams and a short study of an undervalued meaning of *phusis* ("nature") as "genitals."

Sex, so understood, was basically a way for men to establish their social identities in the intensely competitive, zero-sum formats of public culture. The rigor of this sexual ethos was applied to individuals when citizens were about to enter political office in Athens: each underwent a public scrutiny of his personal life, including his sexual conduct. Yet from the records of challenge and defense it becomes clear that the standards of rigor had virtually nothing to do with actually regulating men's sexual behavior, but were a means of insuring a certain image of public authority and allowed the elite to attack each other out of motives that were essentially political rather than moral (Chapter Two).

If men's procedures for self-regulation were thus a kind of façade, concealing a laissez-faire attitude to actual practice, this suggests that women too, for all the strictures uttered by men, might have exercised a degree of autonomy insofar as they remained out of the light of public scrutiny. But the understanding of the social meaning of sex in terms of dominance requires that we look more closely at the issue of violence against women. The erotic spells, found in great numbers in the Greek magical papyri, are full of violent imagery in which the lover performs a ceremony aimed at making the woman he desires burn and suffer until she gives herself to him. Yet the underlying scenario of these performances suggests that it is the lover himself, alone at night and feeling victimized by a helpless passion, who is symbolically projecting his own distress onto his putative victim (Chapter Three).

Moving from social practice to its representation in literature, I next treat Longus' novel *Daphnis and Chloe* as a study of the unequal social violence experienced by two teenagers in love. This is still a male text, but one that introduces disturbing perspectives into its treatment of erotic socialization, particularly of the heroine (Chapter Four). The author's treatment of violence seems to be deliberately ambiguous, which requires us to "read against the grain," coordinating Longus' uncertainties and silences with his culture's outspoken norms. This chapter is a kind of fulcrum between Parts One and Two, suggesting both the seriousness of the issues of violence and their conventionality, that is to say, their purely arbitrary character as social procedures that could have been arranged otherwise. Violence focused on women is presented as both an unavoidable fact of life and as an unnatural and repugnant vise which slowly closes around the maturing Chloe.

After analyzing the distinctive quality and character of men's pretensions about sex and gender, the second phase of the investigation is an attempt to restore the circumscribed dignity and autonomy of Greek women, undervalued both by ancient Greek men in their public pronouncements and by victimage theorists in modern times. This part of the project, *Gunaikes,* is much more difficult because the evidence is fainter, more scattered, and usually refracted through masculine lenses. Here there is considerably less latitude in choosing access points that will be as revealing of women's lives as the topics in Part One illuminate men's. However, Homer's Penelope, Sappho's lyrics, and women's rituals in honor of Demeter and Aphrodite can tentatively be made to yield some muted alternatives to the men's coffeehouse talk that so dominates the ancient record.

Readers have always sensed something distinctively feminine about Homer's *Odyssey,* with its emphasis on the workings of a household and its portraits of strong women. Penelope, in particular, seems to be central to the interlocking stratagems of the competing players, but it is unclear to what extent she is a victim of the social constraints that bind her, to what extent an agent capable of maneuvering within them. I argue that Homer presents both aspects of her situation, but that his own narrative cunning as a story-teller leads him to diffuse and obscure Penelope's master-plot, building up to the surprising moment when she tricks Odysseus in order to assure herself of his identity. According to this reading Homer is paying tribute to the usually concealed but powerful operations of a Greek wife in maintaining an estate jointly with her husband (Chapter Five).

But we would of course like to get closer to Greek women's representations of their own experience, and this is possible in two ways, individually through a female author and collectively via the religious rites conducted exclusively by women. The fragments of Sappho's lyrics contain significant traces of an alternate perspective on the cultural construction of sex and gender. In her deliberate contrast of men's and women's values she partly reproduces the common understanding of the separateness of the sexes, but she does so with a difference. In distinguishing women's perspective from men's she necessarily shows a double consciousness of the two systems and their putative relation to one another as dominant to submissive. But, like linguistic minorities forced to be bilingual, Sappho understands more about the "dominant" practices of men than they do about the "submission" of women (Chapter Six).

Sappho, however, was a member of the elite, living at a time (c. 600 B.C.E.) when the details of social life are almost entirely undocumented. Her perspective might be that of an exceptional individual, unrepresentative of citizen-wives in general. The final chapter is an attempt to locate in the symbolism of two festivals celebrated by citizen-wives (the Thesmophoria) and by women generally (the Adonia), an alternate understanding of men's and women's contributions to the reproduction of the household. Marcel Detienne, in his *The Gardens of Adonis,* portrays the meaning of those festivals in an androcentric fashion by equating men with productive work and women with transitory pleasure. But the comparison of a mythic pattern attested several times in Sappho with the ritual pattern of the festivals suggests the opposite—that women saw their own work as sustaining and globally encompassing that of men, whose contribution to the production of children and crops is, though indispensable, relatively brief and short-lived (Chapter Seven).

I hope that the particular readings offered here will stand on their own, knowing that several are quite controversial. But even more I hope that these methods of anthropologically informed reading will help to discredit the ethnocentric interpretations which have dominated the English and German traditions of Classics for the past two hundred years. The rather cool culture of NATO Classicists has been a poor premise for interpreting the emotional and political protocols of Mediterranean people. I hope these essays will show how much more interesting the Greeks really were.

Part One:
Andres

1
Unnatural Acts:
Erotic Protocols in
Artemidoros' *Dream Analysis*

For "Nature," Read "Culture."

If sex were simply a natural fact, we could never write its history. We would have then to abandon what has become one of our favorite modern projects—describing the sex/gender systems of the varied societies we know, their development and periodization and dialectical interaction.[1] But sex is not, except in a trivial and uninteresting sense, a natural fact. Anthropologists, historians, and other students of culture (rather than of nature) are sharply aware that almost any imaginable configuration of pleasure can be institutionalized as conventional and perceived by its participants as natural.[*] Indeed what "natural" means in many such contexts is precisely "conventional and proper." The word "unnatural" in contexts of human behavior quite regularly means "seriously unconventional" and is used like a Thin Ice sign to mark off territory where it is dangerous to venture. Such warnings may be couched in absolute terms, but all such claims have been eroded by time: like the geological changes over millennia in the earth's surface the moral land-masses and "natural" boundaries can be shown to have undergone radical shifts.

There certainly was a time when the contrast of nature and convention, of *phusis* and *nomos,* as applied to sexual activity and to everything else, was not exploited, a time before that particular contrast was developed as a linguistic or ideological turn. In our records the contrast of nature vs. culture seems to be a product of the sophistic enterprise of the fifth century B.C.E.[2] Before that time there were no doubt other ways of condoning and con-

---

[*]"A Manchu mother, for instance, would routinely suck her small son's penis in public but would never kiss his cheek. For, among the Manchus, fellatio is a form of sexual behavior except in the context of mother and small son, whereas kissing of any kind is always sexual. We are perplexed because, in our culture, fellatio is always sexual, whereas cheek-kissing among kin never is" (Henderson 1988: 1251).

17

demning sexual behavior,* but the use of "nature" appears not to have been among them. It is important to underline that the contrast of *phusis* and *nomos*, of nature and culture (if you will), is itself a cultural item, a format of thought once newly discovered, which thereafter spread and eventually was enlisted as a weapon in a historically specific cultural struggle (now called the Enlightenment). Over time it has become an automatic cliché, a deeply imbedded habit of the sort that is almost (as we say) a second nature, such that we can hardly imagine not thinking in those terms.[3] This is to say that although it seems natural to us to discuss sex in terms of nature and "unnature," the "naturalness" of these categories is itself a sort of cultural illusion. Like sexuality, "nature" (as applied to sex) has a history.

History of Ideas/History of Practices

But how should we write such a history? It certainly will not do (though it is often done) to latch onto isolated bits of moralizing texts, snip them from the page and pin them to a drawing board so that they form a "systematic" narrative—Plato to Philo to Paul to Plotinos.[4] Above all it is a methodological mistake to invest such clippings with a cultural authority derived only from projections into their future.

Consider the example of cultural attitudes to paederasty, and the implications of one famous text that seems to inaugurate a condemnation of the practice. Plato's spokesman in the *Laws* (835B–842A) toys with the idea of inventing a social order that would conform to "nature" as Greek society supposed it was before Oidipous' father Laios invented paederasty. To do so would require a massive restructuring of common belief and practice, placing paederasty on a par with incest so that everyone acquired a horror of it.† Plato's legislator confesses his idea to be a pipe-dream. Yet even though that dream, or rather nightmare, came true—and did so in the very terms employed in the *Laws,* with paederasty coming to be stigmatized as "unnatural"—what should stand out about Plato's text is the despair there felt about the impossibility, almost the inconceivability, of the project. It was clearly a thought-experiment on the same order as censoring traditional poetry in the *Republic,* one that went utterly against the grain of the values, practices, and debates of Plato's society. These speculations of Plato are

---

*Peisistratos had sex with Megakles' daughter *ou kata nomon,* "not in the conventional way," Herodotos 1.61.1; Pindar calls Ixion's intercourse with a cloud who was not his wife "an uncustomary bedding" (*eunai paratropôi, Pythian* 2.35) and advises that one should both lust and concede to another's lust "in due season" (*kata kairon;* frag. 112 Bowra = Athenaios 13.601C).

†For an example of high-level ignorance concerning the history of sexuality, one may cite the U. S. Supreme Court decision in the case of Bowers v. Hardwick (the Georgia sodomy law): 478 U.S. 186 (1986). See Sedgwick 102–4.

unrepresentative—not the opening move in a new game of moralizing sex—and hence only obliquely useful for writing the history of a society's sexual mores and practices.

But our critique must go further. Aside from the issue of treating philosophical or theoretical texts as if they possessed prophetic weight, we err in a more general way when we reconstruct cultural history simply or primarily in terms of ideas, no matter whose, rather than in terms of the competing variety of social practices. Philosophers and moralists offer primary material for the history of ideas, only inadvertently for the history of practices. This is particularly true in the case of classical Greece. We know what kinds of person possessed cultural authority in a typical assembly of Athenian citizens in Plato's day because we know who is constantly appealed to by those delivering political speeches and courtroom arguments: Homer, Hesiod, Tyrtaios, Solon, Sophokles, and Euripides have such authority, along with various culture-heroes from history.[5] Sokrates, Plato, Aristotle and the like count for nothing—in this context. Athens was a society in which philosophers were often ignored and when noticed were easily represented not as authority figures but as cranks and buffoons.[6] If we focus our attention not on that eccentric côterie but on the citizen body (in its own way an elite in the population of Athens), we get quite a different picture, one in which the debates of philosophers have no discernible impact. *

After demoting philosophers from the privileged position sometimes assigned to them in reconstructing a picture of ancient society, we must go on and apply a similar critique to other texts. It cannot be said too strongly or too frequently that the selection of book-texts now available to us does not represent Greek society as a whole. The social and editorial conventions within which most public speaking and published writing took place tended to give voice to a select group of adult male citizens and to mute the others—female, adolescent, demotic (working persons with a minimum of leisure), metic (non-citizen). Further, as we shall see in Chapter Two, the public proprieties could also misrepresent the interests and feelings of even the adult male citizens who sponsored them. Those conventions of male prominence and competition between households are well known and roughly correspond to proprieties still broadly observable in the family of cultures around the Mediterranean basin. But inasmuch as our current intellectual interest is not to pay allegiance to the values or pretensions of that hegemonic group (and thus indirectly to support its equivalent in our own society), we must not allow these conventions to represent "everyone."

---

* "But in order to understand [Aristophanes' *Clouds*] we must make an imaginative effort to adopt an entirely different position, the position of someone to whom all philosophical and scientific speculation, all disinterested intellectual curiosity, is boring and silly" (Dover 1968: lii).

More than that, we are not simply trying to "map" a culture and find its system or complex of competing systems. As Bourdieu has shown for the conflicting genealogies, calendars, and other sorting systems of the Algerian Kabyle, the very act of drawing a map, insofar as it implies an established and unarguable regularity and system, falsifies important uncertainties, smoothes out the wrinkles, and regularizes all matters that are still to be negotiated between actors in the social conglomerate (Bourdieu 1977: 2, 37, 105). Rather we would like to make some statements about that social conglomerate which manage both to characterize the fundamental conventions or protocols and to show the limits of their application to real lives. The first part of this goal is the subject of the present chapter, in which Artemidoros' *Dream Analysis* is used to reveal the basic principles of meaning employed by Greek-speaking men around the Mediterranean basin in ancient times to interpret sexual acts. The second part, the estimation of how strongly or lightly those principles weighed on individual lives, is the subject of the next chapter. This approach or interest, which may be designated anthropological, is one way of reading ancient texts and it does not, of course, preclude other uses of the same texts. One may still decide to study the history of ideas: what one should not do is misrepresent those ideas as having a weight, a power, a dominance which they did not possess.[7]

What Was "Unnatural"?

If it is indeed the case that the nature/culture contrast, as it applies to sex, was not exploited before the sophistic movement of the fifth century B.C.E., it is also the case that, when it *was* exploited, it did not possess the same valence that it does today. The terms "natural" and "unnatural," in other words, did not function (as they have since the Enlightenment) as equivalents of "normal" and "abnormal," "healthy" and "diseased," "ordinary" and "monstrous." A glance at some of the contexts in which the contrast between nature and culture was applied to sex clearly reveals that the content assigned to "natural" behavior in the ancient world is surprisingly different from that assigned to it today, and further that its mode and range of application (that is, who comes under its restrictions) are far from universal. Thus, Thoukydides' description of open class warfare in Korkyra (Corfu), the wives support their husbands' struggle by throwing tiles from the roof onto the heads of the oligarchs: their endurance of the din of battle is "unnatural," *para phusin* (3.74). In this case "unnatural" is a term of praise, as the wives transcend their socialized reticence and engage in open violence in support of their families' interests. What *we* can call Greek women's "socialized reticence," Thoukydides terms their "nature," meaning a conventional or expected limitation which they can heroically rise above. He does not mean that the Korkyran democratic women are perverts, acting in violation of the universal laws discovered by science or theology.

If we juxtapose the passage from the *Laws,* quoted earlier, which seems an anticipation of later condemnations of unnatural sex, to some passages from other texts (less favored by historians of ideas), a new picture starts to emerge. Seneca, for example, inveighing against luxury in *Epistle* 122.7–8, declares the following items to be *contra naturam:* hot baths, potted plants, and banquets after sunset (requiring wakefulness at night and sleep in the daytime, both unnatural acts). When he goes on to treat sex between men in the same passage, he makes it clear that what he condemns is either men dressing in clothing appropriate to women or men making themselves look youthful—both of which suggest to Seneca the wish to serve as the sexual object of other men. * "Contrary to nature" means to Seneca not "outside the order of the kosmos" but "unwilling to conform to the simplicity of unadorned life" and, in the case of sex, "going AWOL from one's assigned place in the social hierarchy." This Stoic view, though articulated as universal, is obviously directed at a very small and wealthy elite—those who can afford the sort of luxuries Seneca wants "all mankind" to do without.

The world view that frames Seneca's diatribe against luxury is nicely drawn by the Greek orator Dio Chrysostom in his idealized depiction of Euboian hillbillies (*Oration* 7), two families who live directly from their own farming and hunting, pay no taxes, buy no goods, and are unfamiliar with the normal amenities of urban life. It would be better if barber shops and house paint were forbidden altogether, Dio argues (117–8), so that people would not have their minds turned from a simple life in accordance with nature (103). Dio contrasts this simple life in the mountain wilds with city life, where brothels flourish, adultery is tolerated, the wealthy seduce one another in private, and men tired of their easy conquests of women corrupt boys contrary to nature (134–6, 149). The content given to this use of "nature" has more to do with the general thematic of expenditure and loss, of thrifty and prudent behavior in a scarcity society, than it does with modern conceptions of universal law based on the paradigms of natural science. Dio wants to argue in favor of simplicity and against lavishness: the life of the poor can, believe it or not, be "dignified and natural" (81). Farmers, hunters, and shepherds are induced by their poverty to lead lives that are "better and more useful and more natural" (*mallon kata phusin*) than those of the urban wealthy.

Dio's "nature" has also laid down moral rules about sex: the non-reproductive is unnatural (134–36, 149). But again if we look closely at the

---

*That is not what Plato was calling unnatural in the *Laws.* What is exceptional, indeed unparalleled, about that passage is its condemnation of the desire of the typical adult *erastês* or "active lover" as unnatural.

argument it appears that "unnatural" refers not so much to behavior which contravenes the necessary order of the world but to behavior which is self-indulgent, luxurious, and exceedingly appealing. His principal target is urban prostitution, since it provides a luxury market of boys and women for sale, and encourages the sexual desire of male consumers to wax wanton, reaching out to ever more exquisite and refined forms of satisfaction. When human appetite is restricted to basic needs, as it is for the simple mountaineers, life is stable—and this is Dio's image of human good. But when markets are introduced, stimulating but never satisfying desire, the consumer becomes restless, acquisitive, never at peace with himself. Using a slippery slope argument, Dio describes how "the man who is never satiated with such desires" (151) progresses from buying the services of prostitutes to seducing honorable women by offering them money, and finding that there is no challenge there, "no scarcity, no resistance," moves on to rarer game still, namely, the young men of good family who will soon be holding city offices. Nature, in this world view, has set a "sufficient and clear boundary" to masculine lust, declaring that males are off limits (149). But this "nature" is not a cosmic principle of physical and generational order, it is a voice crying in the wilderness— or rather in the cities—a preacher's diatribe against self-indulgence brought on by wealth. The ultimate crime against nature, according to this argument, is to treat the city's future leaders as if they were slaves available in a common brothel. It is really an offense against class, an upsetting of the social hierarchy. "Nature" turns out to mean "culture."

There were many moral authorities like Seneca and Dio in the first and second centuries C.E. recommending one program or another, and none of them is very useful for reconstructing a rounded picture of sexual life in the ancient world. Let me offer just one more example, before turning to the uniquely valuable information of Artemidoros. In depicting their vision of the simple, "natural" life, such moralists often turned to animals for examples. * Claudius Aelianus (c. 170–230 C.E.) composed seventeen books *On the Characteristics of Animals* in Attic Greek. The elephant, he reports, is extremely sensitive to the sanctity of marriage. On one occasion in the reign of the emperor Titus an elephant noticed that its trainer's wife was having an affair with another man, so it ran them through as they lay together in bed, one on each tusk, and then covered them with a cloak. What this fantasy tells us is that men could attribute their anxiety over their wives' adultery to a sort of higher and unarguable authority, the simple and unsullied instinct of nature. It does not tell us about the countervailing attitudes, the temptations to commit and admire adultery—such as the comments of

---

*Aristotle investigates the natural characters of animals in *Hist. Anim.* 9, ranging from the "frankly fabulous to the acutely observed" (Lloyd 1983: 20). Obviously an appeal to the animal world is a very old trope of folk morality.

Apollo and Hermes when they see Ares and Aphrodite caught *in flagrante delicto* in Hephaistos' net—that to enjoy Aphrodite in bed it might be worth the embarrassment of getting caught (*Odyssey* 8.335–43).

The most succinct and terrifying script that I know for this morality play is given by Philo, an Alexandrian Jew of the first century C.E.

> Not only among animals domesticated and reared by us but also among the other species there are those which appear to have self-restraint. When the Egyptian crocodile . . . is inclined to copulate, he diverts the female to the bank and turns her over, it being natural to approach her [when she is] lying on her back. After copulating, he turns her over with his forearms. But when she senses the copulation and the impregnation, she becomes malicious in purpose and pretends to desire copulation once more, dislaying a harlot-like affection and assuming the usual position for copulation. So he immediately comes to ascertain, either by scent or by other means, whether the invitation is genuine or merely pretense. By nature he is alert to hidden things. When the intent of the action is truly established by their looking into each other's eyes, he claws her guts and consumes them, for they are tender. And then unhindered by armored skin or hard and pointed spines, he tears her flesh apart. But enough about self-restraint. (Terian 89–90)

There is a *lot* of culture packed into this one exemplum from nature: male initiative ("when he is inclined to copulate") and control ("he turns her over"), one natural position for intercourse (did the crocodile learn it from missionaries or vice versa?), wanton female desire for repeated intercourse even after she has conceived (the whole point of the operation as far as her legitimate interests are concerned), her seductive activity ("harlot-like affection") in the service of her essential passivity ("assuming the usual position for copulation"), patriarchal suspicion and condign punishment meted out on the spot. The crocodile does not tolerate female self-indulgence in his own wife, much less in himself, and in this he is a lesson to all men. Philo does not go so far as to maintain that human adultery or a wife's desire for intercourse is against nature, but his projection of a patriarchal image onto the screen of the animal world illustrates the same moral gambit as Seneca's or Dio's use of "nature" to authorize one facet of culture.

Artemidoros, Participant-Observer.

There is one ancient text, however, that deals significantly with basic issues of sex and gender and yet largely escapes the limitations of a Plato, Dio, or Philo. It is the *Oneirokritika (Dream Analysis)* by Artemidoros of Daldis,[8] a studious and practicing dream analyst who traveled through the major Greek cities of the Roman Empire in the second century C.E.: "in Greece, both in the cities and at festival assemblies, and in Asia and Italy and the largest and most populous islands I patiently listened to old dreams and their outcomes" (1.proem: 2.17).[9] Artemidoros' *Dream Analysis* continually puts on exhibit common social assumptions, shows the operation of androcentric and other sex-gender protocols, and yet itself stands outside them.

To justify the claim that Artemidoros escapes the usual biases of moralistic or elite texts and is of enormous value in reconstituting the parameters of ancient sexual practice, I shall first show how his interpretative methods put him in a unique position for recording other people's rules, both general and individual, without endorsing them himself (Foucault 1986: 9, 16). Once that foundation has been carefully laid, I will be able to assert with some confidence that Artemidoros' categorization of sexual acts corresponds to widespread and long-enduring social norms—that is, to the public perception of the meaning of sexual behavior.

A close scrutiny of the five books of Artemidoros' text shows that both his theory and practice are remarkably—one may even say uniquely—free of those pre-judgments and biases that normally are brought to bear by any ancient author who reports and evaluates social information. The singularity of his perspective is a rigorous consequence of his theory of what dreams are and how they have meaning. There are two Greek words for "a dream"— *enhupnion* (literally, "something in one's sleep") and *oneiros*. Though they may be used interchangeably in ordinary speech, Artemidoros uses them to distinguish two types of sleep event. Many things seen while sleeping are merely expressions of present physical states, such as satiety or lack of food, or emotions, particularly desire or fear, and hence are not informative about the future. Such dreams he calls *enhupnia:* "a lover necessarily sees himself with his beloved in his dreams and a frightened man sees what he is afraid of, the hungry man eats, the thirsty man drinks" (1.1). These dreams are significant, but only in a very limited sense: they signify the present state of the soul or body.*

A small class of dreams, however, does contain true information about the dreamer's future, and these are referred to as *oneiroi*. The information in such predictive dreams is not just any old future fact but items that will more or less seriously affect the dreamer's health, wealth, status, or livelihood. For instance, "a man dreamed that he was feeding bread and cheese to his penis as if it were an animal; he died miserably; for the nourishment that should have gone to his mouth went instead to his penis, hinting at the absence of a face and mouth" (5.62). "A man dreamed that he overheard someone say that his staff had cracked; he became sick and was paralyzed; the support of

---

*Dream interpretation has always been a matter of discerning not so much the message of a dream but, in the first place, whether the dream is a valid one or only a wish/illusion. Thus Penelope distinguishes between dreams that will be fulfilled from those that will not (*Odyssey* 19.560–9), clearly hoping that her dream is more than merely her personal desire for the suitors' slaughter. (For more on that dream, see Chapter Five, pp. 153–4.)

his body, that is, its strength and good condition, was indicated by the staff. The same man, distressed and depressed by his long paralysis, dreamed that his staff was broken; he immediately recovered, for he no longer needed a support" (5.51). "A man dreamed that he had three penises; he was liberated from slavery and acquired two more names from his former master, so that he had three names instead of one" (5.91). "All-night vigils and nocturnal festivals and joyous occasions of staying up late are good dreams for a marriage or a partnership; they signify wealth and increase of property for poor men" (3.61).

Ancient belief in the significance of dreams was not only nearly universal—dream interpretation being already an art, if not a profession, in Homer (*Iliad* 1.62–3, 5.149–50)—but also quite varied (Dodds 102–34; Kessels), and by Artemidoros' time there was a very extensive literature on the subject, now almost entirely lost (Corno 1969). Medical literature took some dreams quite seriously, understanding them to be the soul's intuition of what diet or therapy would be good for its sick body. * It is clear from Artemidoros' own references to the throngs of diviners in the marketplace (1 proem, cf. Cicero *de div.* 1.132) and from the criticism that his own book received (4 proem) that the subject was a very contentious one, torn by professional rivalry, by competition between different kinds of prognostic systems (astrology, palm-reading, incubation [e.g., Strabo 14.1.44], liver inspection, augury, physiognomy, necromancy, and the reading of sieves, cheese, or dice: 2.69), and challenged by skeptics who doubted or despised the whole enterprise.[10]

In this welter of conflicting claims and appeals to the authority of various gods and systems, Artemidoros' dream theory is pointedly empirical and naturalistic. He repeatedly insists that significant connections are only knowable after the fact, from observation (*têrêsis*) or experience (*peira*), though a practiced interpreter will accumulate a fund of observed cases that will enable him to make shrewd diagnoses of the likely meaning of people's dreams. †

Not only is this an empirical theory, it is a naturalistic one. The agent who constructs the dream and sends it as a useful message is the dreamer's own soul, *psuchê* (1.2). Artemidoros' language varies between "the dream says" and "the soul says": "This dream warns a slave to obey his master" (2.33); "the soul brings a story to our attention whenever it wishes to

---

* Kessels 414–24. Physicians were concerned to exclude two types of dreams that were not significant for their purposes—the mere reflections of bodily or mental states (Artemidoros' *enhupnia*) and dreams from the gods or from the precognitive nature of the soul itself.

† Artemidoros frequently contrasts general opinion, whether from books or other professionals, with his personal observations (*egô de etêrêsa*): 1.32; 2.12, 18, 58, 65, 66. After describing the correspondence between gladiatorial weapons and the type of wife a man will marry, he remarks: "These are not conjectures or mere probabilities; I have often observed (*etêrêsa*) these actual outcomes in my experience (*peira*)" (2.32).

announce beforehand that something resembling the story in its content is about to take place" (2.66). * Without discussing the nature of the soul or mind and its kinds of conscious or unconscious knowledge,[11] Artemidoros assumes that the *psuchê* of its own nature is prophetic: it is directly aware of important future events that will affect the dreamer. The point of the communication is to arouse (*oreinein*, 1.i, a pun on the root *oneir-*) the dreamer and make him alert to the prospect of benefit or danger. †

These elements of his theory can be put into an interesting mirror relationship with Freud's (Price). Both divide the mind into a waking or conscious sector and an unconscious element that contains much more than the waking mind is aware of. For both, dreaming is a natural activity of the psyche and consists in veiling significant events or feelings by condensation (1.4) and displacement into a symbolic language whose elements are drawn from the dreamer's immediate associations. The difference is that Artemidoros' soul is looking to the immediate future, Freud's to the distant past. ‡ The mental operations, apart from the future- or past-directedness, are much the same in both systems. What distinguishes them is not so much their theories of the soul's structure or operation, nor their practices of interviewing clients, but the culturally determined value assigned to sex.

The significant messages from the Artemidoran soul concern external matters of fact, not internal feelings, whereas the Freudian soul is trying to talk about supressed wishes. Freud focuses on repression and the censorship of intimate feelings; for Artemidoros the discovery that the real content of a particular dream is the client's desires or fears serves to disqualify it as a signifier of a hidden signified. There are times, Artemidoros says (in a remark that will remind us of cigars), when in a dream having an erection simply means having an erection and times when it means something else (4.1: 241.17). How the dreamer felt during the dream may be very important to

---

*Freud (n.d.: 385–6) detected the reason why a young man dreamed he attended a performance of *Fidelio:* certain lines from the libretto could be understood as referring to his suppressed love for his opera companion.

† "One man dreamed he was riding on the back of a ram and fell off in front of it; he was engaged and about to celebrate his wedding; the interpreter advised him that the dream foretold his wife would be unfaithful (*porneusei*) and would place the proverbial horns on him. And so it happened: because of the dream's forewarning he broke his engagement, but his friends eventually prevailed upon him to marry the woman; in fear of the dream he guarded his wife and she remained perfectly secure; after a year she died blameless; then he married another woman, thinking he had isolated the determinate meaning of the dream, and fell into the predicted misfortune, for she turned out to be the ultimate in wantonness" (2.12: 120.11–25).

‡ At times one may wonder which is the stranger supposition—that the unconscious mind is aware of momentous changes in the offing or that it is obsessed with the remote events of one's childhood; Plutarch argues from the strangeness of our powers of memory to the reasonableness of precognition, *defect. orac.* 432B.

determining its meaning (1.12), as it was for Freud, but the goal of the transaction is not to explore character or reveal childhood trauma or allay hysterical anxieties but to determine whether or not the dream contains notable information about imminent changes in the dreamer's social or physical circumstances.

That is, for Artemidoros sexual acts are not a matter of real concern, either on the manifest or latent level of dream content. He assumes that people engage in sexual activities of all sorts just as they eat and exercise and bathe once a day. Sex, like food and clothing, provides material with which the soul can talk to us about the truly important things in life, such as whether we will come into money, whether my son will recover from an illness, whether my wife will be faithful and hard-working, whether I will win or lose a lawsuit. These are issues that matter.* It may take some effort of the imagination to think ourselves into this world view, and I have found that a good way to begin is to read the ethnographies of contemporary rural societies around the Mediterranean. The paramount concerns are generated within a framework of scarcity, competition, and intense mutual inspection. This is a primary sense of the "constraints" in my title. Sexual behavior is, indeed, extremely important for what it says (is taken to say) about the stability and integrity of households. Instead of repressing a knowledge of sex, Mediterranean cultures tend to employ it freely and even centrally as a way of structuring community relations. But sex in itself is not regarded as an elusive key to the personality or as an area of personal confusion or exceptional tension. Because sex is (and was) a matter so public, it is not invested with the same aura of mystery and concern that we tend to bring to it.

We shall return to this topic later. Now we must lay out some other basic features of Artemidoros' system. If the portended event is imminent, the soul communicates its warning directly and literally. Since there is no time to lose, the soul in effect shouts out an unmistakable message, showing what will happen (1.2).[12] A man at sea dreamed that he was in a shipwreck; after he woke up the ship actually sank (1.2). But if there is time for the waking mind to ponder a dream and no urgency about the outcome, the soul reckons that it is a beneficial exercise for us to contemplate the dream and figure out

---

*A measure of the anxiety attached to such affairs is the following comparison to crucifixion: "Alexander the philosopher dreamed that he was condemned to death and that he barely escaped crucifixion through his entreaties. But he was living an ascetic life and was not involved in any of the things that are signified by crucifixion—marriage, business partnerships, wealth. On the following day he got into an argument with a Cynic, who hit him over the head with his wooden club. This is what his mind was prophesying to him—that he would come close to dying as a result of a wooden object" (4.33).

its possible meanings for ourselves. * Such dreams come to us in coded symbols,[13] and most of the *Dream Analysis* is devoted to explaining how those symbols work, alone and in combination, for different dreamers and in different circumstances.

The most important feature of Artemidoros' interpretive system is his working principle that the symbols and associations of a coded dream are drawn by the soul from the individual dreamer's own cultural experience, not from a universal Book of Meanings or from the language of the gods. †

Of course, the commonalities of experience are such that many people have the same obvious associations, a fact which generates the misleading appearance for long stretches of Artemidoros' text (as it does for Freud's *Traumdeutung*) that he is transcribing from a cosmic and impersonal decoding manual. ‡ As with many such points, the more detailed theoretical statements and examples occur in Book Four. Seven different pregnant women each reported dreaming that they gave birth to a serpent; the observed outcome of each dream was different, according to the associations each one had with a serpent (4.67). One man had the same dream—that he lost his nose—at three different times in his life: when he was a perfumer, it meant that his business would fail; when in desperation he forged a signature, he was disgraced and exiled, "for anything missing from a face disfigures and degrades it;" when he fell ill and had the same dream, he shortly died, "for the skull of a dead man has no nose" (4.27).

The principal statement of this interpretative axiom is at 1.8–9 (cf. 4.4), where Artemidoros distinguishes between conventions (*ethê*) that are universal and those that are specific to a local culture. Thracians who dream of tattooing are telling themselves something different from Getai who dream of tattooing, since among Thracians tattooing is a sign of noble birth, whereas among the Getai it is a sign of slavery. The well-qualified dream-interpreter must therefore know the customs of different lands if he travels

---

* "It is a favorite device of the powers above to whisper at night what the future holds—not that we may contrive a defense to forestall it (for no one can rise above fate) but that we may bear it more lightly when it comes. The swift descent of unforeseen events, coming on us all at once and suddenly, startles the soul and overwhelms it; but when the disaster is expected, that very anticipation, by small increments of concern, dulls the sharp edge of suffering" (Achilles Tatius 1.3).

† The fact that philologically sophisticated dreams only occur to educated persons is one more proof that "*oneiroi* are the work of the soul and do not come from anything outside" (4.59: 284.6).

‡ A type of dream handbook familiar from many ages, the oldest being from the early second millenium in Egypt (Gardiner 9–23). Its format consists in listing dreamed acts, followed by "good" or "bad" plus a short reason; for instance, "if a man sees himself in a dream binding fast his own legs,—good; it means sitting among his townsfolk" (4.14) and "if a man sees himself in a dream copulating with a pig—bad; being deprived of his possessions" (9.16).

or if his clientele is drawn from more than a single city (which in most large cities of the Eastern Mediterranean and at festivals, such as the Olympic games, would have been normal).

He must also know what is specific to the identity of each individual dreamer—wealth, social and marital status, occupation, health, age, and so forth. As Ephesians dream in the cultural language of Ephesos, so fishermen dream in the language of tackle and bait. "Marshlands are a good dream only for shepherds; for everyone else they signify unemployment and for travelers they mean obstacles" (2.28). "Someone dreamed that he became a bridge: he became a river ferryman, serving the same function as a bridge. . . . However, a rich man dreamed he became a bridge: he was despised by many and thus was (as it were) trampled on. If ever a woman or a handsome lad sees this dream they will become prostitutes and receive many onto themselves. A man involved in a lawsuit who sees this dream will rise above his adversaries and the judge himself, for the river is like a judge in that it does what it wants with impunity, but a bridge is above a river" (4.66). Hemp is a bad dream for most people, but not for hemp-makers (2.59), and cunnilingus and fellatio between husband and wife are terribly ominous dream-acts—but not for two particular men of Artemidoros' acquaintance who merely liked that sort of thing. "They simply saw what excited them" (4.59: 283.8–17).

This last example clearly illustrates the axiom that dream-images are determined in principle by the individual's own contingent experiences and associations, rather than by universal or divine connections laid down ahead of time, and it also exemplifies Artemidoros' non-judgmental stance. For him to be able to give accurate readings of dream-meanings, he must know the relevant facts and practices of the client, even if they are intimate, embarrassing, or peculiar. Thus at 4.2 (243.4–12) he distinguishes publicly shared conventions from private idiosyncracies: "but each person decides for himself what way of life (*enstasis*) he will adopt, and similarly what clothing and footware and food and haircut and other bodily ornament and practices and personal choice (*prohairesis*)—whatever an individual most approves: 'different people have different rules, and each one approves his own way as right,' as Pindar says."[14]

Freud misunderstood this crucial point about Artemidoros, criticizing him for treating dreams "as a kind of cryptography in which each sign can be translated into another sign having a known meaning, in accordance with a fixed key."[*] The status of the individual dreamer is already important in

---

[*] Freud (n.d. 97, beginning of Chapter II). "The essence of the decoding procedure [in Artemidoros] . . . lies in the fact that the work of interpretation is not brought to bear on the dream as a whole but on each portion of the dream's content independently, as though the

the earliest texts known to Artemidoros,[15] but he carries the principle much farther and justifies it by a theory of the dream's origin in the language and experience of the individual soul.

To be sure, Artemidoros does not anticipate that such individual traits will often interfere with the process of interpretation, much less that they are the object of the inquiry. The goal of decoding the soul's premonitory messages about the future is largely directed at external changes of wealth, health, and social status, not at understanding or addressing interior emotional states. But it is crucial for the success of Artemidoros' project, on his understanding of it, that he identify the appropriate tool-kit of meanings, which may be quite individual, and that he not impose his evaluations or associations on those of the client.

Some dreams are virtually impossible to interpret because their symbolism is so particular that no general theorem can be laid down ahead of time which would cover it. For instance, a military commander dreamed that the letters iota, kappa, and theta were inscribed on his sword (4.24). The outcome of the dream was that he performed brilliantly in the campaign to suppress the Jewish revolt at Kyrene. The letters stood for "death (*thanatos*) to the Jews (*Ioudaioi*) at Kyrene." Artemidoros offers this example with a degree of self-congratulation because he succeeded in guessing this outcome, but he admits that such happy strokes must be chalked up to luck (*epituchês*, 259.16), which explains a similar story recorded of the famous prophet Aristandros, who told Alexander the Great that his dream of a satyr (*saturos*) playing on top of a shield was a coded sentence, "Tyre will be yours," (*sa Turos*, 4.24). This too was a lucky interpretation (260.6). The practical advice in the face of such very particular dreams which do not fall under the theorems of dream analysis is "Don't lose heart" (259.15).

Artemidoros is therefore in the business of translating people's messages to themselves, not of influencing the content of those messages, let alone "correcting" that content. In most cases, apart from unique and individual dreams, he naturally finds himself dealing with the whole range of common, public associations and evaluations, which makes him an excellent source for information about daily life in the ancient world (Riess; Laukamm). But

---

dream were a geological conglomerate in which each fragment of rock required a separate assessment" (99). This is a false verdict, based perhaps on a hasty and partial reading; it is explicitly contradicted at *Oneirokritika* 4.28: "I have recorded this dream for you so that you will learn that you must not devote your attention solely to the first images that appear in a dream but rather that you must consider the systematized totality of the dream images." In a footnote added to the same section in 1914, Freud carried his misguided attack on Artemidoros still further: "A thing in a dream means what it recalls to the mind—to the dream-interpreter's mind, it need hardly be said. . . . The technique which I describe in the pages that follow differs in one essential respect from the ancient method: it imposes the task of interpretation upon the dreamer himself" (Freud n.d.: 98 n.1).

he always does so with a shrewd eye for the differences of status, morality, and behavior (*ethê*) that may characterize individuals. It is methodologically unthinkable for Artemidoros to *impose* any significance on the dream and still maintain the naturalistic and objective premises of his work.

This amounts to saying that Artemidoros stands in relation to Greek society in the role of a participant-observer. Like an anthropologist he shares the life of the people he studies, trying at once to get inside people's feelings and behaviors and also to stand outside them. Though Artemidoros did not try to write an ethnography, virtually any material or social fact in his clients' world might turn out to be relevant information, and he must, for his own professional success, have a capacious knowledge of cultural facts and a shrewd awareness of individual and regional peculiarities.

But should we rely on his mere protestations of theoretical objectivity, or should we not rather suspect that there must have been the normal gaps between his theory and his practice? As it happens, we have a control on what he really thinks about his practice in Book Four. Books One to Three, dedicated to Cassius Maximus,[16] were written for general circulation; Book Four and the collection of dream outcomes assembled in Book Five were written for Artemidoros' son, also called Artemidoros, to help him become an unchallenged master of the craft, and contained the initial warning "to keep it for your own use and not to share copies of it with many people" (4.proem: 238.1). In that fourth book Artemidoros reveals many trade secrets, giving a sort of insider's view on the practical difficulties a working dream-analyst may encounter.

One of the realities of the business is that, though the dream-analyst is an ordinary, non-visionary person like the rest of us, he must deal with clients in whom credulity and wariness are mixed.* At one and the same time they expect some supernatural display and distrust it when it happens. Without ever doubting the fundamental validity of his professional knowledge, Artemidoros admits that certain forms of quasi-fraudulence are sometimes appropriate. Clients like a display of scientific knowledge and technical learning: when you are sure of a dream's meaning on empirical grounds, you may satisfy the client's desire to be impressed by adding some specious causal explanation:

> Try in every case to come up with an explanation (*aitiologein*) [of why the dream content points to a certain outcome] and add on to each interpretation some rationale and some plausible arguments. For even though what you say [about the outcome] may be perfectly true, if it is given out as a bare, unadorned conclusion,

---

*The credulous is emphasized by Theophrastos, describing the type of man who "when he has a dream, goes to the dream-analysts, to the prophets, to the bird-watchers, to ask them which god or goddess he should pray to" (*Characters* 16.11).

you will be thought of as rather inexperienced. But do not fool yourself that the explanation you give really determines the outcome (4.20).

There were several mumbo-jumbo techniques that could be employed to give an air of authority to the analyst's pronouncements, such as anagrammatism* or isopsephism.†

In Book Four Artemidoros' commitment to an empirical and objective theory of dream decipherment is still strong and unequivocal. The correspondences between dreams and outcomes are for him an empirical fact; supplying the reasons why individual souls make the associations they do is a more challenging task, always revisable and never wholly secure. "Many dream outcomes regularly occur as discrete patterns and we know from their uniform regularity that they come true according to some rational rule (*logos*), but to discover the causal explanation (*aitia*) of that pattern is beyond our powers. Therefore we maintain that the patterns of outcome have been discovered by experience but the rationales come from ourselves and vary according to each interpreter's ability" (4.20). This admission of his own limitations, which provides a justification for improvising false explanations, also strengthens our confidence in the fairness and accuracy of his practice.

So, too, does his observation that not all clients have predictive dreams. By far the majority of dreamers who come to him, he believes, report simple *enhupnia,* not predictive *oneiroi* (4 proem: 240.25), though here too the art of decoding associations can be useful, since the soul of a person who knows something about dream analysis uses allegorical associations in *enhupnia* as well as in *oneiroi.* "A man who can discern such connections, whether he has read them in dream books or learned them by associating with dream-analysts or knows them because he simply has a talent for figuring such things out—such a man, when he is in love with a woman, will not see her but a mare or a mirror or a ship or the sea or a female animal or women's clothing or some other thing that signifies a woman" (4 proem: 239.20).

---

*Anagrammatism refers to rearranging or supplementing the letters in the name of an object in a dream; the technique is mentioned as normal at 1.11 but criticized in the private writing at 4.23: "I mentioned anagrammatism at the beginning of my treatise, and now I recommend to you that you use it whenever you want to generate the impression that you are wiser than another interpreter, but on no account should you use it in arriving at interpretations for yourself, since you will only be misled."

†Isopsephism refers to the substitution of one word for another when the sum of their letters' numerical values is equal. "Use isopsephism when the meaning of the dream itself, apart from the numerical equivalence, already shows you what the isopsephism points to. For instance, when sick persons dream of a *graus* ["old woman"] it is a symbol of death. The words *graus* and *hê ekphora* ["funeral"] both have the value of 704. But (you would know this) even apart from the isopsephism: an old woman is indicative of burial inasmuch as she is not far from death" (4.24). On isopsephism, see Dornseiff 98–104, 181–2; Skeat.

Presumably many of Artemidoros' regular clients were of this type, and the bulk of the allegorical dreams they brought to him had no significance for the future but only restated in symbolic form the dreamer's current anxieties. At the other end of the social scale, perhaps as an ideal type, some few persons of perfect virtue are said to have mainly or only predictive dreams. Since *enhupnia* are the product of emotional or physical turmoil, people who maintain perfect control over their emotions and their diet tend to have only *oneiroi:* "for their soul is not clouded with fears or hopes, and they control their body's pleasures."* Note in both these cases that it is the individual soul which is responsible for the nature and quality of the dream: people who know how to see analogies in dreams have dreams which use such analogies, people unfamiliar with symbolism do not have symbolic dreams; men whose souls are unclouded by unsatisfied desires do not have wish-fulfillment dreams.

Behind the scenes, therefore, Artemidoros is very alert to the different classes to which dreamers belong and the different orders of psychology that are likely to be manifested in their dreams. Like the participant-observer he both enters as deeply as possible into the mind and behavior of his informant and at the same time interprets his informant's words and deeds in terms not necessarily shared by or even accessible to the informant. Artemidoros' interpretation in effect fits the informant into a larger behavioral pattern.

This lengthy discussion of Artemidoros' methods and principles has been necessary to lay the groundwork for my reading of his pronouncements about sexual events in dreams. The value of his text for us depends on our confident realization that it represents not just one man's opinion about the sexual protocols of ancient societies but an invaluable collection of evidence—a kind of ancient Kinsey report—based on interviews with thousands of clients.

The Social Meaning of Erotic Dreams

Turning to the subject of erotic dreams, it might be useful first to note the frequency with which, throughout the ancient world, people did dream of their sexual desires. Herophilos has a category for instinctive dreams, "whenever we see what we want, as occurs in the case of those who see their girlfriends (*erômenas*) in their sleep" (Aetios *Placita* 5.2.3). Many dreams obviously reproduce daily cares, which include sexual anxieties, such as "The prostitute writes a note to her lover; the adulterous woman yields

---

*4 proem: 239.18. Plato advises sober meals and temperate behavior to promote the more rational dreaming of the soul's highest faculty (*Republic* 571D). He shares the belief that a small class of men can either entirely or virtually eliminate the wayward desires that are manifested in sleep (571B).

herself."[17] Plato's Sokrates observes that every soul contains both respectable desires and shockingly unconventional (*paranomoi*) desires, which like satyric selves prance about when the ruling part of our soul is asleep.[18] These fantastic escapades include a man having sex with his mother, or with any and every human being, god, or beast; murder; and eating shameful foods.

But so far from being an object of interest to any ancient dream theoretician, sexual desires, when detected, serve to disqualify a dream as significant. "If a man dreams that he has intercourse with a woman who is familiar to him, and he is in a sexual mood and is attracted to the woman, the dream foretells nothing: the tension of his own desire exhausts its meaning," says Artemidoros (1.78: 88.12). Popular language actually referred to genitals as "nature," indicating that their needs and activities are to some extent just the unproblematic way of things (see Appendix Two).

Some dreams whose outcomes were observed by Artemidoros refer to hidden sexual events. "A man dreamed of shitting into a bushel basket. He was caught having sex with his own sister. The bushel is a measure, and a measure is like a convention (*nomos*), so in a sense he was breaking the conventions" (5.24). But the events disclosed are in the proximate future, not the remote past, and they are contingent facts, not deeply embedded formations of the personality. Thus, one woman's dream of wheat stalks emerging from her chest and entering into her vagina referred to the fact that she would unknowingly, "by a turn of events" (*kata peristasin*), have sex with her own son (5.63), and one man's dream of bed-bugs in his clothing came true the following day when he learned that his wife was committing adultery (5.64).

Though genital organs and social-sexual behavior occur on both sides of the Artemidoran equation, both as signifier and as signified, as dream[*] and as outcome[†] (or as both[‡]), the real meaning of dreams for the future has little to do with the dreamer's psychology, with his or her personal or sexual

---

[*]An iron penis signified patricide (5.15); a man having intercourse with himself signified desperate need (5.31); bearing and nursing a child signified for an athlete that he would give up competing with other men (5.45); also in Book 5: 62, 65, 68, 86, 87, 91, 94, 95.

[†]A man who dreamed that he butchered and sold his wife later turned her to prostitution (5.2); a horse sent by a friend to a man's bedroom signified that the man would lose access to his friend's daughter, who was his mistress (4.46); many items may signify a wife, a prostitute or a mistress: balls (1.55), horses (1.56), apples (1.73), bedrooms (2.10), seagulls (2.17), trees (2.25), etc.; marriage is indicated by gladiatorial fights (2.32); adultery is signified by falling off a ram (2.12: 120.15), a serpent in one's bosom (2.13), a river flowing from the house (2.27: 149.7), etc.

[‡]A man who dreamed that his penis became extremely hairy all the way to the tip became an open *kinaidos* [see my discussion of this term below, pp. 45–54], "who enjoyed every unregulated pleasure and stopped using his penis in the way conventional for men; that part was so unused, from not being rubbed against another body, that it could grow hair" (5.65); also 1.79: 95.11.

life. In all the cases just mentioned what the dreamer is concerned about is the shame that will accrue to the family and the consequent lowering of its fortunes when a sexual misdemeanor becomes publicly known.

In interpreting the probable meaning of predictive dreams, Artemidoros relies on six basic elements (*stoicheia*) or categories of analysis—nature, convention, habit, occupation, name, and time (1.3, 4.2)—and two modal qualifiers in each category—"in accordance with" (*kata*) or "against" (*para*). These categories, he proudly claims, exhaust the types of meaning generated in dreams, in contrast to some other interpreters who listed dozens or even hundreds of such categories (1.3).

The two principal elements are nature and convention, *phusis* and *nomos:* "of all things that exist, some are by nature, some are by convention [*nenomistai*]; these are the first and ruling categories" (4.2: 242.19–21). Things conventional are further divided into the unwritten social rules (*ethos*) and written laws (*nomos*): "of things conventional some have been established by general agreement among humans and imposed as rules on themselves; *ethos* is the name for such, and it is—as Phemonoe says— an unwritten *nomos*. But the rules people have written down out of fear that they might be transgressed are known as *nomoi.*" The *unwritten* social principles (as opposed both to written rules and natural laws) are spelled out twice: "People have reached common agreement on mystery rites and initiations and all-night festivals and competitions and warfare and farming and the settlement of cities and marriage and the raising of children and everything else like this" (4.2: 243.4). "The common *ethê* are these: to respect and honor the gods . . . , to raise children, to be attracted to (literally, "to be defeated by") women and intercourse with them, to be awake in the daytime, to sleep at night, to eat, to rest when tired, to live under a roof rather than under the open air" (1.8).

Although, as a general rule, things which are out of place, unconventional (whether explicitly or implicitly), or unnatural tend to signify bad outcomes for a dreamer,* there are many exceptions. A man who dreamed of beating his mother, which would have been an extremely grave offense against convention (*paranomon*), came into a profit since he was a potter and beat clay (mother earth) for a living (4.2: 245.9). A man dreamed that he took pleasure in sexually penetrating his sick son, again an extremely grave offense against convention, but the dream signified the son's recovery since the man took pleasure in "having" his son. Artemidoros contrasts this outcome with that of a man who dreamed that he had intercourse with his sick son and

---

* "Snow and frost seen at the proper season signify nothing, for the soul is mindful of the day's cold even when the body is sleeping; when seen out of season it is a good dream only for farmers; for the rest it foretells that their undertakings and imminent projects will turn cold, and it hinders travel" (2.8: 109.7).

did not like it; the son died because being the object of a sexual act (*peraines-thai*, literally "to be penetrated") is, like death, called "corruption."* The discrimination between these two clearly indicates how attentive Artemidoros is to the whole texture of a dream experience and how non-judgmental he is about what is represented in it.

Books One and Two are arranged according to the human span of life from birth to death, with intercourse (*sunousia*) at the center (1.78–80).† "The best set of categories for the analysis of intercourse is, first, intercourse which is according to nature and convention and habit, then intercourse against convention, and third, intercourse against nature" (1.78). It is an amusing game at parties to ask people what acts they think Artemidoros might have placed in each category, given that he is not legislating the matter but recording common perceptions in the Mediterranean world of the second century C.E.

"*Natural and conventional*" acts are all those in which a man penetrates a social inferior (wife, mistress, prostitutes in brothels, streetwalkers, vending women in the marketplace, female or male slaves, other men's wives), is penetrated by another man, or masturbates. Though the acts are natural and conventional, the outcomes of the dream are sometimes good and sometimes bad. Having and enjoying one of these sexual acts tends to indicate a future profit, since, as Artemidoros charmingly puts it, "people enjoy sex and they enjoy making a profit."[19] Penetration usually indicates that the penetrator will receive a future good (or ill) since he is (or is not) receiving pleasure, but from the point of view of the penetrated person penetration means receiving something good (or bad) from the penetrator.‡

It will raise some eyebrows to note that the sameness or difference or the anatomical sexes of the persons engaged in a sexual act is not a factor in the analysis of dreams. "Having intercourse with one's female or male slave is good, for slaves are the dreamer's possessions and therefore signify that he will take pleasure in his own possessions as they increase in number and value" (1.78: 88.5). The congruence of social status and sexual hierarchy is a good sign; gender does not factor into the equation, except insofar as women are all social subordinates to men. For the dreamer to imagine

---

*4.4: 248.5–15. The client's feeling about dreamed events must be carefully enquired after (1.12). A man dreamed that he had been sexually penetrated by the god Ares and that he enjoyed it. He later underwent successful rectal surgery. "The pleasure in the intercourse indicated that the surgery would not be fatal" (5.87).

†Chapters 78–80 are translated in Appendix One.

‡ "To be penetrated by an acquaintance is profitable for a woman, depending on what sort of man is entering her. For a man to be penetrated by a richer, older man is good, for the custom is to receive things from such men. To be penetrated by a younger, poorer man is bad, for it is the custom to give to such. The same meaning applies if the penetrator is older but poor" (1.78: 88.25).

himself penetrated by another man may be good or bad, depending on whether the penetrator is older and richer than the dreamer (which signifies that the dreamer will receive something good) or poorer. For a man to be penetrated by his household slave is inauspicious, not because of the slave's gender or the sexual act itself but because a social inferior is represented as a sexual superior, and so the soul of the dreamer regards such a sexual contact with repugnance.

The relations of pleasure are never perceived as mutual—or, rather, the *significance* of such relations is always interpreted *asymmetrically* in terms of a calculus of profit—in terms of who is giving pleasure/money and who is taking it from others. The significance of dreamed sexual acts rests on a perception or interpretation of them as forms of invasion, injury, profit-taking, superiority, and command.* These relations of domination are regarded as "natural and conventional," meaning that the actors represented in them, when taken in pairs, can be ranked in both the social and the sexual realms. The very fact of considering social and sexual relations together provokes the question, "Who's on top?"

"*Unconventional*" acts fall into two broad categories—incest and oral-genital contact. The variants of each are listed in some detail, again according to a calculus of profit determined mainly by the relative status of the parties involved and the relative degrees of pleasure accruing to them. "It is good for a poor man to have sexual intercourse with a rich daughter, for he will receive great assistance from his daughter and, in this way, take pleasure in her" (1.78: 90.22). Gender, as in the previous category, is not a signifier (though sexual relations are in a different sense deeply gendered, insofar as they are constructed for and around men's bodies, not women's—Halperin 1989: 35). Thus, incest with son or with daughter has the same general meaning. The age and wealth of the child affects the outcome, not his or her anatomical sex. "To have sex with one's grown son is good for a man

---

*Injury: "He who penetrates a male friend will develop an enmity with him after inflicting some prior injury" (1.78: 91.3).

Profit-taking: "If a poor man who lacks the essentials has a rich mother [and has intercourse with her in a dream], he will receive what he wants from her, or else he will inherit it from her when she dies not long after, and thus he will take pleasure in his mother" (1.79: 92.9).

Superiority: "To penetrate one's brother, whether older or younger, is good for the dreamer; for he will be above his brother and will look down on him" (1.78: 90.29).

Command: "To have sex with one's own wife when she is willing and desirous and not resistant to it is good, equally for all who dream it. For the woman is either the dreamer's professional skill or business which he uses to provide himself with pleasures, or it is that which he manages and controls as he would a wife" (1.78: 86.21). "(A dream of intercourse with one's mother) is good for all office-holders and politicians, for the mother signifies the fatherland: so just as he who has sex according to the conventions of Aphrodite (*kata nomon Aphroditês*) controls the entire body of the woman who is obedient and willing, so too the dreamer will have authority over all the business of the city" (1.79: 91.21).

sojourning abroad; the dream signifies coming together (*sunelthein*) and returning home because of the name 'intercourse' (*sunousia*); but if they are both at home and living together, it is bad: they are bound to separate since the intercourse of men usually takes place with one turning his back on the other" (1.78: 89.29).

Dreams of a man having sex with his mother are treated in great detail according to the position assumed and other variables. This speaks perhaps to the mother's central symbolic role in the household and to the ambiguities of a grown son's control over her. (More on this in the next section.)

One of the side effects of having established Artemidoros' non-judgmental stance as a recorder of common beliefs is that it enables us to affirm, on the basis of his testimony, that there was evidently in his world a very deep apprehension about fellatio and cunnilingus, which were treated somehow on a par with incest as forbidden, shocking, unspeakable. "To do the un-speakable" (*arrhêtopoiein*) is precisely the word for oral-genital activity. There are, of course, many stray references to fellatio and cunnilingus in classical literature and they tend overwhelmingly to be pejorative.[20] But we could not properly assess the weight or representativeness of such comments without the framework supplied by Artemidoros. For instance, claiming that Manichaeans ceremonially eat a fig dipped in semen, Cyril of Jerusalem exclaims, "Who would accept instruction from such lips? Who would, under any circumstances, kiss him on meeting? Quite apart from the sin against religion that that would involve, will you not shun such defilement and men worse than mere profligates and more abominable than any prostitute?" (*Catecheseis* 6.33). Artemidoros' evidence suggests that Cyril was mobilizing a widely shared disgust for the purpose of slandering his religious enemies.

"*Unnatural*" acts are an apparently heterogeneous assortment: necrophilia, sex with a god, sex with an animal, self-penetration and self-fellatio, and "a woman penetrating a woman." Some of these signify good things to come: "To have sex with Selene (the moon) is very favorable for sea-captains and navigators and importers and astronomers and men who love to travel abroad and vagrants; for the rest it signifies dropsy" (1.80: 97.25). But as usual it depends on who does what to whom: "If someone dreams that he mounts an animal, he will receive a benefit from that species, whatever it is. . . . If he is mounted, he will have some violent and awful experience" (1.80: 98.12).

What idea or ideas of nature generate this heterogeneous list of things *para phusin*? Not reproductive potential, since both the natural-conventional and the unconventional categories contain acts that are not reproductive (anal intercourse is conventional, fellatio is unconventional). The basic idea seems to be that unnatural acts do not involve any representation of human social hierarchy. Relations with sheep and gods, though they are interpreted (like the rest) in terms of the dreamer's positioning of himself in an anthropomorphic hierarchy, do not involve two human beings, but cross over species boundaries. Bestiality is not "unnatural" in the sense of being what modern psychology calls a perversion; rather it is outside the conventional field of social signification. If a man gains advantage over a sheep, so what? Nor do transitive activities conducted without a partner (anal intercourse with oneself—signifying "serious illness or incredible torture, for a man could not have sex with himself without great torture"—or auto-fellatio), or with a corpse (necrophilia), fit into a system of hierarchical social meanings. The soul may use an image of such acts to say something, but the acts themselves are not ones that carry social signification in their own right.

The most revealing item on the list is "if a woman penetrates a woman." The phrase must not be domesticated by a soft-focus translation, such as "lesbianism," for that would be to gloss over the very point where ancient Mediterranean sexual significations diverge from our own, hence the point where they are most revealing. Sex between women is here viewed as not intrinsically equipped to display the hierarchy of its participants. The act should be interpreted along the same lines as the others in the section as containing a socially anomalous image. To formulate a more exact statement of what that means, let us specify two further protocols operative in these chapters.

In addition to its androcentric* focus, its orientation around male agency and concerns, sexual significance is both phallocentric and invasive. The privileged terms for sexual activity in the *Oneirokritika* are *perainein* and *perainesthai*, to penetrate and to be penetrated. "If she does not know the woman she *penetrates,* she will undertake useless projects. If a woman *is penetrated* by a woman, she will be separated from her husband or will be widowed; however, she will nonetheless learn the secrets of the other woman" (1.80: 97.9). Sexual relations between women can only be articulated here in the significant terms of the system, penetrator vs. penetrated, not as what we would call lesbianism. Sexual relations between women are here classed as "unnatural" because "nature" assumes that what are significant in sexual activity are (i) men, (ii) penises that penetrate, and (iii) the articulation thereby of relative statuses through relations of dominance. These three protocols determine the field of significance. Woman–woman intercourse† is "unnatural" only and exactly insofar as it lies outside that

---

*Artemidoros reports dreams of women, as he does of slaves, and the changes of social status or health he looks for in them are the same as for men's dreams. Women's dreams: 1.16, 26, 28, 30, 41, 44, 56, 58, 76, 77; 2.3, 5, 6, 7, 18, 20, 30, 65; 3.16, 23, 32, 65; 4.59; 5.63, 80, 86. One should leave open the possibility that a female analyst would see things differently, such as the Isis devotee at Athens who was both a lamp-lighter and an *oneirokritis* (IG III.162, dated to 127/8 or 128/9 C.E.).

†This awkward, unnatural phrase is meant to keep alive the non-translatability of Artemidoros' category.

determinate field of meaning.* The "unnatural" is the meaningless: "nature" once more turns out to stand for "culture."

The third protocol bears special watching since it sums up the other two and gives them a very anti-romantic twist. Many of us may like to think that sexual activities involving two people will be mutually pleasurable, but *erôs* in Artemidoros' cities more often traveled along one-way streets.† Artemidoros in his programmatic opening chapters has a list of activities that do not affect one's neighbor and concern only the agent, and he includes sexual penetration among them: speaking, singing, dancing, boxing, competing (*agônizesthai*), hanging oneself, dying, being crucified, diving, finding a treasure, sexual activity (*aphrodisiazein*), vomiting, defecating, sleeping, laughing, crying, speaking nicely to the gods. It is not that second parties are not present at some of these events (speaking, boxing, competing, having sex, being crucified, flattering one's favorite divinity), but that their successful achievement does not depend on the cooperation, much less the benefit, of a second party. The invasive protocol restates the principle that sex (like competition) makes reference chiefly to the self by treating it as a way of expressing hierarchical movement, up or down the ladder whose rungs are marked by levels of wealth and prestige. To penetrate is not all of sex, but it is that aspect of sexual activity which was apt for expressing social relations of honor and shame, aggrandizement and loss, command and obedience,‡ and so it is that aspect which figured most prominently in ancient schemes of sexual classification and moral judgment.

It would of course be wrong to read this interpretative system as a phenomenology of actual desire and behavior. There are traces even in Artemidoros that mutuality was sometimes a perceived feature of intercourse, albeit a muted feature. "To have sex with a son already grown is good for a man who is out of the country, for the dream signifies coming together and

---

*And it is sometimes brought into that sphere of intelligibility by medical discourse, which postulated enlarged, penis-like clitorises on some women (Philoumenos *ap.* Aetios 16.103, Paul of Aigina 6.70), or by fictional accounts, such as the fifth of Lucian's *Dialogues of the Courtesans,* in which one shaven-headed prostitute straps on a dildo to mount another woman.

†For the general tendency, see Halperin 1989: 29–36.

‡Competition was so deep-seated a cultural reflex that Galen recommends a program of self-control in these terms: when we practice moderation in food, drink, and sex, "we should not compare ourselves to the undisciplined; it is not enough to surpass them in self-control and moderation; rather we should first of all strive competitively to outdo people committed to the same moderation—for such competition is an excellent thing—and next we should strive to surpass ourselves" (*de propriorum animi cuiusque affectuum dignotione et curatione,* vol. 5, pp. 32–3 Kühn). Also revealing on the connection between pleasure and dominance is Aristotle's remark: "Winning (*nikân*) is sweet—for everyone, not just for those ambitious to win (*philonikois*); it produces a feeling of superiority, for which all people have a desire (*epithumian*), either moderately or more so" (*Rhet.* 1.11: 1370^{b}32, cf. 1371^{b}28 on the pleasure of criticizing one's neighbors).

abiding together, by the name 'sexual union' (*sunousia*)" (1.78: 89.29). The limits of the meaning-system revealed by Artemidoros are that it does not take us very far into the domestic sphere, in which husbands and wives and lovers negotiated their relationships (like the two men who enjoyed fellatio and cunnilingus respectively), nor into the sphere of luxury living, in which passive and sometimes mutual sensuousness found cultural expression (lyric poetry, romantic novels). But it is an excellent description of the *public meanings attached to sexual relationships*. Artemidoros' testimony thereby helps to explain the shame of adultery* and the corresponding pride in successfully controlling a substantial family and appearing to others as a man of power. And as such it provides a ground plan for most men's (and presumably many women's) behavior *whenever that behavior was regarded as possibly coming under public scrutiny*.

We might refer to this set of protocols as "what will the neighbors think." They are not moral rules determining one's own conduct, except insofar as that conduct will be available to and assessed by the community. Knowing them gives us a firm idea of community values, but not necessarily an account of individual or private behavior.

Artemidoros, Ventriloquist

One final section of these chapters, in which Artemidoros suddenly and strangely sounds like a fundamentalist preacher, requires a closer look in order for us to draw some lessons concerning Artemidoros' systematic use of *phusis*. His writing often slips into a ventriloqual mode, when he supplies the voice of the dreaming soul itself explaining why it symbolized x by y. "Dogs often indicate a fever because of the star Seirios, which is a cause of fever and is called by some the Dog" (1.11 end). "Bed bugs symbolize depression and anxieties, since like anxieties they keep us awake; they also indicate displeasure and disgruntlement on the part of some members of the household, as a rule among the women" (3.8). "Walking on the sea is a good dream for a man who wishes to go abroad, particularly if he is going to sail: the dream foretells a high degree of safety; it is also a good dream for a slave and for a man who has decided to marry: the slave will control his master and the man will control his wife, since the sea is like a master because of its power and like a woman because of its wetness" (3.16).

Such supplied connections belong to the realm of *aitiologia*, which as we have seen is always a difficult and relatively uncertain operation. Without necessarily endorsing the associations and evaluations behind the connection,

---

*A distinguished prophet in Rome had amassed wealth and prestige but it did him no good, for the outcome of a dream was that his wife stopped loving him and betrayed him with another man, so that he left the city in shame (5.69).

Artemidoros frequently reports some common belief available for the *psychê* to play with. It is this feature which makes Artemidoros such an invaluable window onto popular lore and perceptions. The multiple associations available for the penis are a case in point, and it is worth quoting in full:

> The penis is like a man's parents since it contains the generative code (*spermatikos logos*), but also like his children since it is their cause. It is like his wife and girlfriend since it is useful for sex. It is like his brothers and all blood relations since the meaning of the entire household depends on the penis. It signifies strength and the body's manhood, since it actually causes these: for this reason some people call it their "manhood" (*andreia*). It resembles reasons and education since, like reason (*logos*), it is the most generative thing of all. . . . It further suggests surplus and possession since it sometimes opens out and sometimes is relaxed and it can produce and eject. It is like hidden plans since both plans and the penis are called *mêdea;* and it is analogous to poverty, slavery, and imprisonment since it is called "necessity" and is a symbol of constraint. It is like the respect of being held in honor, since it is called "reverence" (*aidôs*) and "respect." (1.45)

In his long analysis of mother-son incest he distinguishes the various positions and modes of copulation—face to face, from the rear, both standing upright, mother on her knees, mother on top "riding cavalry," many different positions in succession, not omitting fellatio. In evaluating the sense of these he remarks that "some say the frontal position is according to nature (*kata phusin*)" (1.79: 91.12).

That overheard legislative voice, dictating proper sexual activity, speaks again at greater length in the discussion of the "many and various positions," which essentially means treating one's mother like a prostitute.[21] "That the other positions are human inventions prompted by insolence, dissipation, and debauchery and that the frontal position alone is taught by nature is clear from the other animals. For all species employ some regular position and do not alter it, because they follow the rationale (*logos*) which is according to nature," etc. (1.79: 94.13). This is not Artemidoros speaking in his own person but rather his reading of some common values and attitudes that must be supplied to support his empirical observation that when sons dream of whoring around with their mothers no good follows. When he calls the use of any other position than the frontal unnatural, he is making use of a "found" piece of thought, an item circulating in the discourse of his day. He may also happen to have believed it himself when thinking about his own practices, but this is not something we can know; and the significant fact is that his interpretive system is not based on this use of "nature," but rather on an understanding of "nature" to mean the conventionally bounded field of human hierarchy. Once again, "nature" stands for "culture."

There are three conclusions to be drawn from the study of Artemidoros' *Oneirokritika* in regards to things erotic in the second century C.E. First, it is uniquely informative about the perceived public meanings of sexual activity. Artemidoros' empirical stance allows us to grasp a general semantics of sex in the ancient world usually obscured by the tendentious treatment of the moralists. The protocols are that sexual contact is understood in public contexts as male-initiated, phallos-centered, and structured around the act of penetration; all acts that conform to those protocols are relatively non-problematic (*kata nomon*); the only acts for which a general horror could be assumed are incest and oral-genital contact; and, lastly, there is an implicit presumption that sexual identity does not organize the person but is peripheral to the central goals and worries which are focused on survival, public status, jockeying for place in social hierarchies at the expense of fellow competitors, the stability and prospering of patriarchal families in a hostile environment.

Second, Artemidoros uses the word "nature" not as a value judgment but as a category term to mark an important boundary in this field of social signification. By "unnatural" he simply means that certain acts are either impossible or irrelevant, that is, they are insignificant within the terms of the social meaning of sex. Thus, Artemidoros in his own way illustrates once more the theme that "nature" means culture, but with the interesting twist that culture (his "nature") includes both the conventional (*kata nomon*) and the unconventional (*para nomon*), for both those categories fall under the "natural" (*kata phusin*). But at the same time that Artemidoros' "nature" is used to organize fundamental social values and disvalues in the public domain, his quotation of a sermon on nature's law concerning the only proper position for human sexual intercourse reminds us that his contemporaries could draw the noose with varying degrees of strictness. Moralists intending to legislate proper behavior regularly and easily appeal to "nature" when they want to mark one of their recommendations as fundamental and unarguable.

Finally, it may be suggested that Artemidoros' survey escapes not only the usual charges we bring against moralistic writers but also the elite and intellectualist biases which typify so much ancient writing. Artemidoros' *Dream Analysis* "lets us see certain generally accepted schemas of evaluation. And one can affirm these are very near to the general principles which already in the classical period organized the moral experience of *aphrodisia*. Artemidoros' book is therefore a landmark. It testifies to a scheme of thinking that was long-enduring and current in his day" (Foucault 1986: 15). Over against these perennial evaluations we may plot the degrees of deviance contained in the arguments, critiques, and utopias of various philosophers and moral historians.

Along the same lines, the impression is worth recording that our modern impetus to locate changes, to write all kinds of history as a story of development and transition, has probably led to deep falsifications at least in the study of Mediterranean cultural patterns. The fourth century B.C.E. and the second century C.E. are two periods from which numerous written documents are extant, and this contingent fact offers an almost irresistible temptation to scholars of those periods to manufacture stories about social changes supposedly brought on by sophists and christians, respectively. We should at least keep in mind the possibility that the debates of philosophers and the soap-box oratory of moralists, while they may tell us much about the formation of a class of intellectuals and about competition for ideological hegemony, are of little consequence in describing the beliefs and practices of the population at large.

2
Laying Down the Law:
The Oversight of Men's Sexual
Behavior in Classical Athens

Simply knowing the protocols does not tell us how people behaved. We must attempt to see through and beyond social prescriptions, however widely held and publicly unquestioned, to that usually unspoken fund of knowledge about their application, their bending, their observance "in the breach," and the hidden agenda they sometimes concealed.

There is a relatively dense record of literary and social data for the Athenian polis in the years 430–330 B.C.E., and its sexual prescriptions have been read to good effect against the honor/shame system of morality in a scarcity economy by Alvin Gouldner, though he is not good on things sexual, by K. J. Dover in his *Greek Popular Morality,* and by Michel Foucault in *The Use of Pleasure.* I propose to take a closer look at the social operations by which deviance was articulated, inspected, and managed in that community during the period when the *nomos/phusis* contrast was supposedly well established, paying attention not to the statements of its intellectuals but to the everyday functioning of the community and in particular to its practices of "self-control" (or control of selves).

The exposition is in three sections. I begin with the cultural images of right and wrong manhood, and try to illustrate how they are at times loose-fitting hand-me-downs that do not reveal the shape of individual behavior. The fundamental protocols are personified, positively, in the figure of the hoplite (citizen soldier, wealthy enough to provide himself with a set of armor) and, negatively, in the *kinaidos.* The latter constitutes a powerful image—whether for serious reproach or humor—of a socially and sexually deviant male. The meaning of the term will be explored below. It is important, however, to note at once that the meaning of *kinaidos* is distinct from that of "homosexual" in modern parlance. Scholars of recent sex-gender history have asserted that pre-modern systems classified not persons but acts and that "the" homosexual as a person-category is a recent invention.[1] The *kinaidos,* to be sure, is not a "homosexual" but neither is he just an ordinary guy who now and then decided to commit a kinaidic act. The conception of a *kinaidos* was of a man socially deviant in his entire being, principally

45

observable in behavior that flagrantly violated or contravened the dominant social definition of masculinity. To this extent, *kinaidos* was a category of person, not just of acts. (Of course, it is quite another question whether outside the amusing or vituperative arenas of discourse where the image of the *kinaidos* is found there actually were any real-life *kinaidoi*.)

Neither of these ideal types is frequently or obsessively spoken about in fourth-century prose yet, like training wheels on a bicycle, they are there whenever a man begins to lose his proper balance. While the hoplite warrior is the ideal self to which every well-to-do citizen looks, the *kinaidos*, mentioned only with laughter or indignation, is the unreal, but dreaded, antitype of masculinity behind every man's back.

In the second section I go on to ask how that image was brought to bear on individuals. Both public scrutiny by the state and privately initiated lawsuits could charge a male citizen with fundamental derelictions of his social responsibility. The laws having to do with sexual morality were framed, of course, not in terms of sexual deviance, which was never as such actionable in court, but in terms of prostitution. The crime was to have confused incompatible categories—those of male citizen and male prostitute (Halperin 1989: 94–8). The *kinaidos* is a scare-image standing behind the more concrete charges of shaming one's integrity as a male citizen by hiring out one's body to another man's use. The three components of the accusation are promiscuity, payment, and passivity to another man's penetration.

Yet the evidence suggests that such surveillance and punitive actions were only employed by a very restricted class of elite players in the high-stakes game of the city's policy management, where they were used as a weapon to knock opponents out of the game. The rules, that is, and the enforcement procedures against social deviants were a public fiction normally held in abeyance and only put into operation as a political strategy within a relatively tiny—though conspicuous—fraction of the social body.

In the final section I turn to the popular languages of moral evaluation, those of comedy and public speaking rather than that of philosophy. In these domains there was a rich appreciation of individual characteristics—personal styles, predilections, and bents—and here *phusis* indicates not a universal norm but the personal difference. Even in a text of specialized scientific discourse which analyzes *kinaidoi* as having an "unnatural" constitution, a contradictory analysis is found alongside it, maintaining that *kinaidoi* are not so because their nature is unnatural but because habit and its attendant pleasures are more powerful than nature—are, in fact, a kind of second nature.

Hoplites vs. Kinaidoi

I am astonished, Demosthenes, that you dare to criticize Philôn—in the presence of the most reputable citizens of Athens, who have assembled here to pass judgment on the city's policy and who are now noting and weighing our lives rather than our rhetoric. Which do you think they would rather pray to have—ten thousand hoplites like Philôn, with bodies as well-made as his and souls so disciplined, or thirty thousand *kinaidoi* exactly like you?

Aiskhines 2.150–1

Aiskhines' alternatives—hoplites sound in mind and body or *kinaidoi* like you, Demosthenes—are not very common expressions in Athenian public speaking but they pinpoint the boundary conditions within which ordinary public discourse and behavior always took place. Its structure is that typical polarization between extreme opposites (Lloyd 1966) which found its social correlative in ancient Athens in zero-sum competition. The cultural understanding of competition was not simply that winners gained rewards and honor, but that losers were stigmatized with shame and penalties in proportionate amounts, or, to put it another way, winners won at the direct expense of losers.* The logic of a zero-sum calculus underlies many of the most characteristic predicates and formulae that were applied to issues of sex and gender. Thus, not to display bravery (*andreia*, literally "manliness") lays a man open to symbolic demotion from the ranks of the brave/manly to the opposite class of women. †

The heft and weight of a problematic term like *kinaidos* cannot be estimated in isolation; it has to be measured within the system of cultural images used in public discussions about the proper behavior of citizen-soldiers. Each time there was an official gathering of the men who held citizen rights in Athens, whether in a full assembly of the entire body (held four times a month, one of which was principal) or in smaller representative groups such as juries, the self-definition of the community as a vigorous elite ran close to the surface (Dover 1974: 41, 160–7).

In calling that group an "elite" I mean to emphasize that a majority of the actual *population* of Attika did not have the rights to attend the Assembly, sit on juries, or be elected to office.[2] It was a "vigorous" elite in that the proper citizen-soldier saw himself as a householder defending the interests of the dependents in his *oikos* (household) and ready to face danger in person by standing in the ranks of a phalanx and meeting the external enemy in honorable, rule-bound combat, a kind of corporate-duel between cities, on

---

*Gouldner 45–55; an explicit statement of the "zero-sum" rule is found in the sophistic extract known as the *Anonymus Iamblichi* in FVS 89.2 (vol. 2, p. 400): "People do not find it pleasant to give honor (*timân*) to someone else, for they suppose that they themselves are being deprived of something." Plato *Laws* 1. 626B is close: "All the goods of the vanquished become the victors'. " It is implied at Hesiod *Works and Days* 341 (Millett 95).

†The alternate title to Eupolis' comedy *Astrateutoi*, concerning those who avoided military service, was *Androgynoi* (men who are partly women). See also Plato *Timaios* 90E, where cowardly males are reincarnated as women. Dover 1974: 95–102.

the plains of Greece (Pritchett, chapters 7–9; Connor). All citizens were soldiers, and were subject to military service on a rotating basis during each summer from the ages of eighteen to sixty, though the twenty- to forty-year olds were called before the older and younger (Andrewes). For all that the military reality was more complex, with heavy dependence on the navy and the strategic use of mercenaries, the community image consistently evoked in public speaking was that of the hoplite-citizen. * All the private discipline exercised by the household administrator over his body, his luxuries, and his dependents, so well traced by Foucault 1985, was framed and justified by this public discourse on the necessary manliness of each responsible, duty-sharing citizen.

Citizen-soldiers must support each other when fighting a common enemy, but within the polis the competition between citizens, particularly the enterprising or the conspicuous or the young, is fierce enough to require rules about the physical person. The speaker of Demosthenes 22 makes it clear that according to the laws the body of a citizen is sacrosanct: in certain situations his property may be confiscated, but his physical person may in no case be touched (Dem. 22.53–55, cf. Dem. 21.178, 180). Inviolability of the person is a marker separating slaves from citizens: slaves may be manhandled in any way, citizens are literally untouchable. To put your hand on a citizen's body is to insult him profoundly, implying that he is a social inferior. † Included in the body-language of social position is sexual dominance; physical contact with a citizen that expressed a "master's" touch was a deadly serious gesture. Enslavement of free-born women and youths, which was punishable by death, implied the possibility of sexual aggression as one component of a social dominance.³

In Athens, according to one editorializing observer ([Xenophon] *Ath. Pol.* 1.10), free persons and slaves and metics dressed so much alike that in a crowd one might not be able to tell them apart, which made it difficult for citizens properly to chastise insolent slaves who did not show due deference on the street. ‡ The fact that slave/free or citizen/metic status was less visible

---

*Ridley. Thouk. 8.97.1–2 regards the rule of an unremunerated hoplite class as ideal; similarly [Arist.] *Ath. Pol.* 33.2. Navy service, as corporate and not personally confrontative, did not have the same glory; cf. the contemptuous analysis of [Xen.] *Ath. Pol.* 1.2: bosuns and deckhands have more political power in Athens than "the hoplites and the noble and the good." The general Philokles sponsored a law that prisoners of war should have their right thumbs cut off "so that they could not wield a spear, though they could still ply an oar," Plutarch *Lys.* 9.5.

†It is not the gesture itself but the social meaning of the gesture that counts: "If a man has struck someone, it does not necessarily imply that he has insulted (*hubrisen*) him, but only if he has done it for a motive such as dishonoring (*atimasai*) that man or gratifying himself," Aristotle *Rhet.* 1.13: 1374a13–5. On physical abuse as a marker of status, see Golden 1985: 101ff. [As Prof. Golden reminds me, a citizen can be guilty of *hubris* against a slave: Aiskhines 1.17.]

‡In the ultimate democratic city, according to a Platonic fantasy, not only do slaves and

in Athens as compared to other Greek poleis meant that such status distinctions had to depend all the more heavily on invisible markers: the privileged citizen class was defined as a group by their untouchability as persons who could throw their weight around to intimidate metics and slaves.[4]

Of course, insulting behavior between citizens occurred aplenty, particularly in the conspicuous echelons of the ambitious and well-to-do. Inviolability of the person may have been the rule, violence was not infrequently the practice. Lysias 3 documents two street-fights, with stone-throwing and broken heads,[5] between rival lovers of a Plataian boy.[*] The regulations for social clubs (eranoi) contain long passages dealing with fights, assaults, and disturbances.[6] Perhaps the most revealing such incident left in the records is a grudge fight in the agora one evening in which Konon and his sons not only knocked down their opponent but held him upside down in a mud-puddle while Konon put his hands under his arm-pits, flapped his arms like a victorious rooster in a cock-fight and crowed (Dem 54.7–9).[†] It would be wrong to overemphasize the lines of tension among citizens. Daily life in Athens for the average citizen was surely not a perpetual, near-violent squabble. But for the conspicuously wealthy (the speakers of Lysias 3 and Demosthenes 54 belong to the liturgical class[7]) and for young men (Konon's sons were the principal actors)—i.e., those for whom honor is a leading concern—life could certainly be lived by hair-trigger rules of contentiousness.

The enemy was also within. Plato's Laws opens with a general characterization of social life in terms of zero-sum competition: "according to nature" (kata phusin) there is a perpetual war between equivalent units at all levels— city versus city, village versus village, household versus household, male versus male, and person versus self (625E–626E). That last item is not a Platonic peculiarity but a faithful reflection of the common moral language

---

women behave with insolence as if they were the equals of free men, but "the horses and jackasses walk along the streets freely and proudly, bumping into people who don't get out of their way," Rep. 8.563B-C.

[*] The youth is Plataian, and probably free (Bushala 33), but does not have Athenian citizenship since he can be tortured to give evidence (33). Rivalry for boys was so common an occasion for fighting to break out (e.g., Xen. Anab. 5.8.4) that one tradition was able to maintain that Oidipous killed Laios because both of them were in love with the same boy, Chrysippos (Scholiast on Euripides Phoinissai 66). On hubris (insolent behavior which dishonors another), see MacDowell 1976, Fisher.

[†] Cock-fighting took place in taverns and gambling shops (Aiskhines 1.53) and is depicted on either side of the central throne in the theater of Dionysos, a sign that theatrical performances were organized as a competition according to the same canons of manliness that are found in public speaking (Winkler 1985b, Zeitlin 1985). Cock-fighting was a supremely clear representation of zero-sum competition: "You'll never see a cock that is a kinaidos," said an unidentified comic playwright (Com. Adesp. 1213 in Kock); Aristophanes Birds 70–1; Plato Laws 7.789B-C; Aelian Var. Hist. 2.28; Lucian Anakharsis 37. K. Schneider, Hoffmann.

which praised a good man as "stronger than himself" (*kreittôn heautou*), that is, able to manage[8] and control his various appetites, and a bad man as "weaker than himself" (*hêttôn heautou,* Foucault 1985: 63–77). The temptations in question are food, drink, sex, and sleep. At all levels of practical morality and advice-giving we find the undisciplined person described as someone mastered or conquered by something over which he should exert control, usually conceived or conceivable as part of himself. Whether choosing a general to save the city (Xen. *Mem.* 1.5.1) or a bailiff to manage the farm (Xen. *Econ.* 12.13), one wants a man who is the honorable master of his pleasures, not—by the logic of zero-sum competition—the shameful slave of them (*tais hêdonais douleuôn aischrôs,* Xen. *Mem.* 1.5.5). The polarized expressions strike us as odd, particularly when the transformation from self-mastery to lust-slavery is said to be instantaneous: "'Miserable wretch,' said Sokrates, 'are you reckoning what will happen to you if you kiss a beautiful youth: instantly (*autika mala*) to be a slave instead of a free person . . . ?'" (Xen. *Mem.* 1.3.11).

Such cautionary attention to behavior is premised on the beliefs that male life is warfare, that masculinity is a duty and a hard-won achievement, and that the temptation to desert one's side is very great. This odd belief in the reversibility of the male person, always in peril of slipping into the servile or the feminine, has been noted by Stephen Greenblatt, who observes that for the ancient world the two sexes are not simply opposite but stand at poles of a continuum which can be traversed. Thus, "woman" is not only the opposite of a man; she is also a potentially threatening "internal émigré" of masculine identity. The contrast between hoplite and *kinaidos* is a contrast between manly male and womanly male, and therefore rests on a more fundamental polarity between men and women. The cultural polarity between the genders is made internal to one gender, creating a set of infra-masculine polarities between the hoplite and the *kinaidos*.

One can find rare instances in which the class of women is similarly divided into the feminine and the manly. Aristotle refers to dark-skinned women as masculine and light-skinned women as feminine (*Gen. Anim.* 728[a]3–5). The author of the Hippokratic treatise on *Diseases of Women* notes that the healthiest sort of woman is masculine, and less given over to maternity and conception (1.6). But the vast preponderance of anxious attention and thought in our surviving texts was directed to men. One axis along which masculinity could be measured was hardness/softness. "'Tell me, Charmides, if a man is capable of winning a crown at contests and thus being honored in his own person and making his fatherland more renowned in Greece but does not wish to compete, what kind of person do you think this man would be?' 'Obviously a soft (*malakos*) and cowardly one'" (Xen. *Mem.* 3.7.1).[9]

In daily life the contrast of hard men and soft women was more often assumed than expressed, hence we find most of our proof texts in the more speculative and editorial forms of composition, including comedy.* For instance, the appropriate social relations between the hard and the soft are illustrated on a unique red-figure oinochoe of 465–460, which shows a young, short-bearded Greek man, wearing only a cape and holding his erect penis in his right hand, approaching a Persian soldier in full uniform who is bending over away from the Greek and looks out at the viewer with his hands raised in horror. The inscription identifies the about-to-be-buggered soldier as a representative of the losing side in the Athenian victory over the Persians at the battle of Eurymedon (465 B.C.E.): "I am Eurymedon, I am stationed bending forward."[10] Outside of such cartoons, the hard-male-hoplite/soft-female-*kinaidos* polarity does not frequently surface in our extant documents, but the pressure it could exert on reality was surely felt when Peisistratos' son Thessalos, having failed to win Harmodios' special friendship, insulted him as *malakos* (*Ath. Pol.* 18.2; Lavelle).

But, having described this broadly shared self-image of the righteous citizen as hoplite rather than *kinaidos*, we have only assembled prescriptive utterances, utterances which did not have the force of law. How can we specify their force? When Foucault (1985: 12) announces that he will deal with prescriptive texts, he means "as opposed to theoretical ones," but we need to take a further step to comprehend the limits of such prescriptive texts as public fictions. Beyond such images and recommendations we need to know whether they were obeyed like homicide laws (almost universally), like traffic regulations (when the police are watching), or like Vatican pronouncements (in Italy, not at all). So let us now notice some ways in which these rules of men for themselves might be circumvented, ignored, or teased.

First a pair of snapshots from Plato's *Republic*. The opening gives us Sokrates walking home from Peiraeus. A group of friends comes up behind him and asks him to stay the night at their house. A close look at the style and tone in which the invitation is delivered shows that we are not dealing with simple hospitality, but with a mock-kidnapping. First, a slave catches up with Sokrates and makes him wait for Polemarchos and his friends to saunter along. When Polemarchos arrives, he says, "You see how many men I have with me? You have to choose between showing yourself stronger than we are (*toutôn kreittous*) or else remaining here." Sokrates plays along with the joke, saying meekly, "But isn't there another option? I might

---

*The agôn of Aristophanes' *Clouds* contrasts the manly discipline of a well trained soldier's body with the physical laxness of sophists. At *Clouds* 529 Aristophanes refers to his *Banqueters* (produced 427 B.C.E.), which featured two young men in a similar opposition, called *ho sôphrôn* (responsible, mature, and self-controlled) and *ho katapugôn* (lax of body, pleasure-bent, and anally receptive).

From comedy or perhaps some other byway of heroic narrative comes the story that Philoktetes suffered the "female disease" after killing Paris: he left for shame and founded a city called Malakia (Softness), Schol. Thouk. 1.12.

persuade you to let us go." "How could you persuade us if we chose not to listen?"

In a culture where issues of strength are continuously being put at stake, the threat of violence does not lie very far beneath the surface. But the interesting fact is that Polemarchos is playing, not uttering a "real" threat. At least among intimates a certain skating near thin ice is not only possible but likely, for it is a way of sharing the pressure of constraints. Thus it is even possible for Sokrates, among friends, to allude to what was most unspeakable for any man, namely, softness (*malthakia*). In the face of a very difficult argument, Sokrates begs to be allowed to relax, to fantasize a bit about his desires as men do when they're on holiday or just walking alone along the road. It's reprehensible, of course, but Sokrates says *malthakizomai:* "I succumb to this softness" (458B). Again, it is only a playful touch to the argument, but significant for all that.

As meetings of friends and the private symposium were occasions at which men might play and tease each other about the rules of decorum, so the City Dionysia was in some respects like a symposium for the entire polis. Although we do find in the comedies of that festival some grumpy criticism of contemporary youth and their effeminate art-forms as degenerations from the military rigor of the Good Old Days, such enunciations are amusing rather than editorially serious. At least, they are no more serious than an equally typical gag in which the actual members of the audience are surveyed and declared to be *euruprôktoi* (literally "wide-anused") to the last man (*Clouds* 1083–1104). * In assessing the image of personal discipline held up for themselves by Athenian citizens, we should never underestimate the home-truth that "most men enjoy joking around and teasing more than is proper." † The City Dionysia was surely not the only occasion on which soldiers grumbled about going to the field (*Peace* 1127–90) or entertained the fantasy of peace for one's own *oikos* while the generals went on patrol and came back battered (*Akharnians* 1071–234).

Since I have suggested that men could adopt an insouciant attitude to the ideology of self-mastery, let me also underscore the real horror that could

---

*To spell out the implications, *kinaidoi* were automatically assumed, according to the protocols that polarized penetrators and penetrateds, to desire to be penetrated by other men, which assimilates them to the feminine role.

†Aristotle *Eth. Nikom.* 4.8: 1128ᵃ13–4. In an academic study of proper behavior, we should never forget the obvious fact that, as Aristotle reminds us, serious things are not pleasant, unless one is accustomed to them, whereas jokes and naps and carefree behavior are pleasant (*Rhet* 1.11: 1370ᵃ12–6). One man who had it both ways was Autolykos, a dignified member of the Areopagos, who in speaking to the Assembly used some uproarious double-entendres but gravely pretended not to notice his own jokes (or else he was so virtuous that he did it innocently and, like Margaret Dumont in the Marx Brothers movies, could not figure out what was funny) (Aiskhines 1 *in Tim.* 81–3).

be felt, especially in competitive contexts, at the possibility of being assimilated to *kinaidoi*. The scene is in Plato's *Gorgias* (494C-E). Kallikles has urged that the good life is one in which a man regards his desires as all-important and does not try to check them. Sokrates refutes him with an argument about itches.

"Well said, my good friend; now go on as you began and see that you don't give in to shame. I too will have to face down my shame. Now if a man felt very itchy and had unlimited opportunities of scratching himself, happiness for him would be a life of perpetually scratching his itches, yes?"

"You're ridiculous, Sokrates."

"Well, I managed to shame Polos and Gorgias, but don't you give in to shame. Be a real man and give me your answer."

"O.K. I admit that the scratching man would have a pleasant life."

"And if it's pleasant, it's also happy?"

"Yes."

"Now if he were to scratch only his head . . . — do I have to take the questions any farther? You see what your answers will be, Kallikles, when I lead you along the entire series that starts here? The end point to which such questions are directed, the life of the *kinaidoi*, isn't that a terrible and shameful and awful thing? Or would you dare to say that such people are happy when they have unlimited access to what they want?"

"Aren't you ashamed of yourself, Sokrates, taking the argument in that direction?"

"Such people," "the life of the *kinaidoi*"— the references seem quite well defined in the speakers' minds, and become even more so when we understand Kallikles' horror within that Athenian framework of rigorous body-obsession I outlined. Sokrates and Kallikles know what they're talking about and they don't want to talk about it. [*]

We are clearly in a different realm from the romantic pursuit of young men in their teens by young men in their twenties known as paederasty, an activity well illustrated on Athenian vases of the late sixth and early fifth centuries and portrayed in Plato's dialogues as an experience sometimes heartbreaking, [†] sometimes delicious, but always of general interest and approval. In paederasty, as Dover 1978, Golden 1985, and Foucault 1985 have carefully demonstrated, a variety of conventions combined to protect the junior partner from the stigma of effeminacy, of being a *kinaidos*. Kal-

---

[*] "I have heard that this man practiced misdeeds and insolence on the body of Timarchos of such a kind that—by Olympian Zeus—I would not dare to mention them to you. The acts that this man was not ashamed to do in very fact—I could not bear to live if I uttered them clearly before you," Aiskhines 1.55.

[†] Aristotle describes the bittersweet feeling of falling in love and thinking about an absent boyfriend: *Rhet.* 1.11: 1307^{b}15–29; *Eth. Nikom.* 8.3: 1156^{a}31–^{b}6.

likles' *ho tôn kinaidôn bios* ("the life of the *kinaidoi*") is not just a joke or a possibility without reality for him; it is a way of life that he and Sokrates can imagine being led in fourth-century Athens, and their imagination is horrified at the prospect.

The protocols explain why. Since sexual activity is symbolic of (or constructed as) zero-sum competition and the relentless conjunction of winners with losers, the *kinaidos* is a man who desires to lose. Contrary to all social injunctions prescribing the necessity of men to exercise their desires in a way that shows mastery over self and others, the *kinaidos* simply and directly desires to be mastered. Women too, in this ideology, are turned on by losing, a perception which is at the core of Greek misogyny (Halperin 1989: 133). Women are cast as the necessary supporting players in that social script. The quite different fact of *male* desire to be penetrated simply could not be accommodated as a legitimate actor's role in the public sexual categories.* Note that Sokrates' argument to Kallikles implies that even a man could find being a *kinaidos* pleasurable if he were to seek pleasure alone and weigh no other consideration. In other words, male pleasure at penetration is a social, but not a sexual, impossibility. Honor, not *erôs,* is offended.

Anecdotes of this sort add an elusive holographic texture to our sense of how some Athenians lived with the boundary marker of *kinaidia.* But as long as we stay in the universe of cultural *images,* that is, vituperative or amusing talk, we still cannot say very much about the prevalence of the horror or the humor so far documented. Instead we must turn to the procedures for social enforcement. What was the relation between this image of self-mastery and the real-life behavior of citizens in public forums? When was that corporate fiction brought to bear on individuals, whether by the state or by other individuals or by themselves?

Anus-Surveillance

> Kleon: I put a stop to the fornicatees, erasing Gryttos from the rolls.
> Sausage-Seller: Well, isn't that amazing! You practiced anus-surveillance and put a stop to the fornicatees! The truth is, you were envious and would stop at nothing to prevent them being Speakers.
>
> Aristophanes *Knights* 877–80

The procedure by which Kleon successfully booted "Gryttos" and others out of the citizen body was probably that known as *dokimasia* ("testing" or

---

*Halfway between humor and horror we should place the use of the extended middle finger, known as *katapugôn* (= *kinaidos*): Diog. Laert. 6.34 and *Priapea* 56.6 illustrate the gesture, Pollux 2.184, 6.126 records the name. Sittl 101–2; Courtney 459.

"scrutiny"). * There were two types of regular occasion when the corporation of Athenian men clarified their community self-definition by applying it to individuals: entry into the group (new citizens, ephebes) and emergence into the limelight of public administration (men allotted to the annual magistracies and to the Council) (Lipsius 269–85; MacDowell 1978: 167–9). The interrogation was officially conducted by two groups representative of the citizen body, first the Council, then a jury, but as symbolic forums where communal identity was figured and confirmed they were also open to the public and were attended by citizens at large. † The numbers involved annually—500 prospective Council-members, several hundred public officers and probably that many ephebes (A. Jones 150 n.28)—must have prevented any detailed inspection of private lives, but the apparatus was certainly in place and seems to most observers to have come down from archaic times.[11] The impression of antiquity is based on the questions put concerning ancestry, family cult (Apollo Patrôos and Zeus Herkeios), family tombs, and care of parents. Candidates were also asked whether they had made their proper contribution to the defense and welfare of the polis through taxes and military campaigning.[12] At the *dokimasia,* perfunctory as it must often have been, any candidate could be challenged by another citizen: the formula was "Does any one wish to accuse this man?" ([Aristotle] *Ath. Pol.* 55.4). Since rivalry and enmity were the electricity of that social machine, particularly at its top level, challenges did occur[13] and, as at any Athenian trial, they could easily expand from a single issue into a review of the opponent's entire life.

Generals and Speakers (*rhêtores*), according to Deinarchos (1.71, cf. 2.26), could be held to even higher standards: they must own land in Attika and have legitimate children.[14] These are the men who "manage" the citizen body[15] and must therefore in a more visible and representative way than the rest be seen to have managed their own, to have acted the role of prudent patriarch and ready warrior—the symbolism described in the previous section. Although the role of Speaker (*rhêtôr*) was not an elective or formal

---

*It may also have been a *graphê hetairêseôs* ("indictment for prostitution"), which was not an indictment for prostitution as such but rather for trying to exercise citizen rights after conducting oneself as a prostitute. The penalty for that was theoretically death (Lipsius 436–7), and Gryttos has merely been removed from the rolls, so *graphê hetairêseôs* might seem to be out of the question; however, the loss of citizen-rights was sometimes spoken of as civic death. Timarchos was deprived of civic rights (*êtimôsetai,* Dem. 19.284), Aiskhines "killed" him (285); Timarchos "died and was insulted" (287). Full *atimia* included a ban on entering the Agora (Hansen 1976: 62). In general, penalties depended a great deal on the type of legal process set in motion, rather than on the offense itself (Hansen 1976: 120).

†Rhodes 1981: 619. Philokleon likes to attend the *dokimasia* of ephebes because he gets to see their genitals (*Wasps* 578); he may be attending as a member of the general public or, more likely, as a jury-member.

office, the men who frequently spoke in the citizen Assembly (and were, hence, so named) were readily recognizable* by their conspicuous activity in the city's affairs—proposing legislation† and delivering major speeches to the Assembly. Speakers do not as such constitute an official category; they are simply the men with political interests and experience who regularly address the Assembly (Hansen 1974: 22–3). In their case, it was possible for individual citizens to introduce a special challenge known as *dokimasia rhêtorôn*, questioning the fitness of any citizen who chose to play that role.

The only surviving example of a *dokimasia rhêtorôn* is the speech of Aiskhines *Against Timarchos* (28, 32), a case heard in the archonship of Archias (346/5), probably in the early spring of 345, not too long after the the rural Dionysia at which a joke was made on "big Timarchan sluts" (157, cf. Wankel). This is the text which K. J. Dover used as the basis of his excellent study, *Greek Homosexuality*. As we can infer from that speech, the law governing the scrutiny of Speakers contained four qualifications on anyone who would address the people: (1) he must not have abused or neglected his parents; (2) he must not have refused military service or deserted the ranks ("thrown away his shield") in battle; (3) he must not have sold himself for the sexual pleasure of another man, either in a stable relationship (*hêtairêkôs*) or to multiple partners (*peporneumenos*); and (4) he must not have "eaten up" his patrimony or any inheritance (Pollux 8.44–5).

Each of these charges picks up a different light wave refracted through a single prism—the image of the stout-hearted citizen who can be trusted to exercise his military duties and to control the pressure he may feel from his dependents, his circumstances, or from his own needs. The man who kisses Alkibiades' beautiful son will instantly become a slave instead of a free man and will expend vast sums of money on harmful pleasures (Xen. *Mem.* 1.3.11).‡ Timarchos, according to Aiskhines, originally controlled property sufficient to put him in what we might call the highest tax bracket, the liturgical class (1.97), but in his mania for erotic pleasure (with the most expensive flute-girls and *hetairai,* 75) and for all forms of self-indulgence he turned to consuming his paternal real-estate (95–105).§ The key element in

---

* "The customary and established Speakers," Dem. 22.37.

† Hypereides 4 (*For Euxenippos*) 9: "the first part of the law applies to all citizens . . . , the latter part to the Speakers alone, for it is their task to draft decrees."

‡ The hyperbolic features of this cultural image make it easier for us to detect its unreality and to see its use as a weapon of self-discipline. In modern American culture a similar scare-figure is the psychopathic sex-maniac: Freedman.

§ Davies 84. The significance of this dereliction only becomes apparent when one realizes that the military budget of Athens in the fifth and fourth centuries was supplied annually by a fairly restricted class. Rhodes 1982 estimates 1200 for the trierarchy, somewhat more for the *eisphora,* war levy (except for what we might call their "Reagan years," 357–340, when the

this accusation is not that Timarchos' sexual desire itself was wayward or exorbitant but that his lust for luxury became an addiction that destroyed his sense of careful accountancy: "He didn't even sell his pieces of property for their fair market-value: he was unable to wait for the better offer or the advantageous deal but sold each for what it would instantly fetch—so impetuously was he driven to satisfy his pleasures" (1.96). Can such a man be entrusted with advising and managing public affairs? Stability of land and property was a deeply rooted caution: each citizen swore in the archaic oath of the ephebes to "hand down the fatherland [to the next generation] not diminished but enhanced and improved" (Tod, no. 204)—a corporate ideal reflected in the somewhat trickier but no less fundamental goal of keeping one's individual patrimony intact.

Obsessive indulgence in the wild life[16] will obviously lead one to other fundamental crimes of the gravest sort, such as slighting one's parents or betraying the state, since addicts and maniacs will violate *any* fundamental rule that we reasonable people observe: "their impulsive bodily lusts and their insatiability—these are what drive men to mugging, to piracy on the high seas, these are the Fury that drives them to slit the throats of fellow-citizens, to enslave themselves to tyrants, to subvert the democratic constitution" (1.191).

The point that people like Timarchos are potential traitors is made by Aiskhines in his gloss on the law forbidding citizen-prostitutes to be Speakers: the person who has sold himself will be ready to sell out the common good of the city.* It might seem that the sex-addict who sells his property cheap to get ready money is rather different from the calculating politician who amasses a fortune by accepting consulting fees from foreign clients.[17] The former is an image of treachery through fiscal irresponsibility, the latter of treachery through calculating profit. But the point is that Athenian ideology did not employ our more careful distinction of sex from politics; instead it assumed that good men were those who in the cause of social solidarity exercised control over all their various personal impulses to acquisitiveness.

The defendant in Deinarchos 2 is on trial for taking a bribe but the prosecution manages to mention everything in his past that might be held against him, including his refusal to pay for his father's funeral and his temporary *atimia* (loss of citizen rights) because he has inherited his father's

---

wealthiest were substantially remitted much of that burden: so argues Davies 19; see also Thomsen 140–3.

*1.29. If it can be proved that an Athenian has taken pay for sex, all the normal ambiguities are resolved and his disenfranchisement is certain. "But which of the citizens have I *hired* for sex, as you have done, Phormio? Show me. Whom have I deprived of the city . . . and the freedom of speech enjoyed in it, as you have done to this man whom you disgraced?" Dem. 45.79.

debt to the state treasury. Similarly, in the surviving *dokimasiai* for Council-membership and magistracies, men are attacked for a range of basic faults, often supported only by rumor or innuendo: Philôn mistreats his mother and was a cowardly soldier (Lysias 31; Feraboli, Weissenberger). Mantitheos tries to defend his military service, his managing of his estate, and alleges his distance from the young men who gamble and drink, from which we may infer that he was accused of the same rowdiness that common knowledge held against Timarchos (Lysias 16). These performances are not so much trials in the modern sense as they are showcases for criticizing or defending an entire career, including all the rumor and gossip that circulates through such a community. They are specialty displays of the tactics of innuendo that may be employed in any mustering of public opinion against a political enemy.[18]

Aiskhines is quite explicit about the role of rumor or common knowledge (*phêmê*, 129). He tries to make a virtue of necessity by claiming that Timarchos is so well known and has such a reputation as an easy lay that common knowledge itself dispenses him from the need for witnesses or proof (44). The notoriety of Timarchos' companions and their open display of sympotic luxuries have only one possible meaning (73–6).* The *de facto* certainty is as great as when one sees a male prostitute in front of his brothel take a client inside and close the door: "Now if someone were to ask you when you were right there on the street what that prostitute was doing now, without seeing it happen and without knowing who the client was but only knowing the prostitute's chosen profession, you would know for a fact what he was doing" (74).

Gossip, rumor, and common knowledge are very intense in a community like that of ancient Athens, even though it was a comparatively large polis. But Timarchos was well known to the audience for other reasons. He belonged to that small circle of public Speakers who were clearly distinct, in numbers, in prominence, and often in wealth, from the "private citizens" (*idiôtai*).[19] Demosthenes contrasts "the speakers" (*hoi legontes*) with "the majority" (*hoi polloi*) who are *idiôtai* (Dem. 22.37). Hypereides answers a prosecutor: "You treat Euxenippos, who is an *idiôtês*, as if he were in the rank of a *rhêtôr*" (4.30).[20] Those who enter as Speakers into the political arena, as into a cock-fighting ring, are playing a high-stakes game: "the life of private citizens (*idiôtai*) is safe and free from care and danger, while that of the politically active (*politeuomenoi*) is subject to censure, and risky, and full of confrontations and problems every day" (Dem. 10.70).†

---

*Since sexual *desire* is excluded as a motive, being an "easy lay" means being willing to *sell* oneself, which may be prompted by any number of motives besides desire.

† The small class who strove to be part of the city's affairs thought of themselves as exemplifying the highest standards of masculinity: "The pursuit of honor (*philotimia*) is not a

Though Speakers derive honor and gain from their activities, they also are continuously exposed to risk (Hyp. 4.9)—not least from the watchful gaze of their enemies, who will jeer at them and try to expose their every fault. "Mr. X—I won't mention his name since I don't want to make him an enemy—was not a private citizen but one who attended to the city's business and (therefore) subject to abusive remarks (*loidoriai*)," (Aiskhines 1.165). Personal enemies, that is, competitive Speakers, are always standing nearby and watching every move a political player makes (*echthrôn ephestêkotôn*, Aiskhines 1.108). This could be touted as a virtue of the system: "What is commonly said of public trials is no lie—many public affairs are rectified by private enmities."[21] The role played by gossip and common knowledge in the *dokimasiai rhêtorôn* is so great because Speakers are not just citizens, they are featured players in the public spotlight—star performers on the political stage.*

We have an interesting paradox here. On the one hand the regular *dokimasiai* were an apparatus of public scrutiny applying to all citizens and provided an opportunity for challenges to the moral fitness of citizens and officials. The hoplite vs. *kinaidos* ideology could have been brought to bear against any individual—the apparatus was in place for doing so. But, on the other hand, it appears that no significant application of that cultural image was made to the citizen body as a whole but only to the conspicuous representatives of it who managed public affairs.†

Aiskhines employs a feint at the beginning of his speech against Timarchos, promising to cite rules of decorum that will apply "not only to private citizens but also to Speakers" (7, 8). But when it comes time to redeem that promise, all he can cite are laws concerning *eukosmia*, "orderly conduct" in the Assembly, such as speaking in order of seniority (22–4). He does this to give himself an opportunity to refer to Timarchos' flamboyant and undignified speaking style (26). Aiskhines himself is our best witness to the gap between ordinary *dokimasiai* and the political weapon of *dokimasia rhêtorôn*: "The law scrutinizes not those who mind their own private business (*idiôteuontes*) but the politically active (*politeuomenoi*)" (195).

The same distinction is made in a speech against another Speaker accused, among other things, of *hetairêsis*:

---

natural component (*emphuetai*) of the irrational animals nor of all human beings; those who have a natural desire in them for praise and honor are at the greatest distance from cattle—they are considered to be men, no longer merely human beings," Xen. *Hiero* 7.3.

*In the case of families whose wealth is old rather than new, their preeminence can be perceived as "natural": Aristotle *Rhet.* 2.9: 1387ª17.

†". . . if an Athenian citizen made no secret of his prostitution, did not present himself for the allocation of offices by lot, declared his unfitness if through someone's inadvertence he was elected to office, and abstained from embarking on any of the procedures forbidden to him by the law, he was safe from prosecution and punishment" (Dover 1978: 29).

[Solon's law] forbade citizen-prostitutes to speak in Assembly or to propose decrees. For he saw that most of you, though you have the right to speak, do not speak—so that this law, he reckoned, was not burdensome. If he had wanted to punish such people, he could have imposed a much harsher law. But he did not lay any stress on that [sc. the existence of citizen-prostitutes], rather in the interests of you and your political order he specifically forbade them to be Speakers, for he knew, yes, he knew that men whose lives are shameful cannot flourish in a political order in which anyone may openly criticize their vices. What political order is that? A democracy! (Dem. 22.30–1)

This is a remarkable passage, for it is at once a justification of applying a rigorous scrutiny to the sexual behavior of the politically active, with an implied endorsement of the mechanism for doing so through watchful enemies, and a statement that laissez-faire about the private lives of "private citizens" was a long-standing (Solonian) tradition.[*] The crucial point seems to be not sexual behavior in itself but rather some notion of preserving the political order by restrictions placed on its directors at the top. Demosthenes goes on to argue that if a sufficient number of such "shameful" Speakers were to be active at the same time they would not only be bad administrators of the commonwealth but they would overturn the democracy (in which they can be criticized) and set up an oligarchy (in which they would be free to do as they pleased without fingers of shame pointing at them).

It begins to look as if the entire procedure had very little to do with sex and everything to do with political ambitions and alliances in the high-stakes game of city leadership according to the rules of honor/shame competition. This impression is confirmed by the fact that Aiskhines' prosecution took place many years after the events in question[†] and was unabashedly motivated by a desire to remove Timarchos from the ranks of the prosecutors who had indicted Aiskhines for treason.[‡] The case was not brought forward as a sexual charge on its own merits. It just happened that Aiskhines, looking for a way to disqualify one of his opponents, found a potential weak spot

---

[*]Dionysios of Halikarnassos contrasts Greek tolerance of private behavior with Roman censorship of private morals: though the Athenians punished those who were publicly lazy and the Spartans commissioned their elders to strike any undisciplined persons with a staff, "still they paid no need or watchfulness to things that took place inside the house, considering each one's courtyard door to be the boundary of life's freedom, whereas Romans drew back the curtain on every household even to the bedchamber" *Antiquities* 20.13. (I owe this reference to Daniel Selden.)

[†]The only one mentioned as of recent occurrence is Timarchos' speaking to the Assembly in an undignified style with his arm outside his cloak (26).

[‡]Dem. 19.284, 286. Similarly, Hegesandros was presenting himself as a Speaker (*parêiei epi to bêma*) and was "waging war" (*prosepolemei*) with one Aristophon; Aristophon apparently got Hegesandros to back off by threatening to challenge him to a *dokimasia* focusing on his sexual behavior (Aiskhines 1.64).

in Timarchos' public reputation and attacked it with all his might. In general, it appears that all aspects of a Speaker's private life were open to scrutiny and that his erotic self-management was not a special locus of danger. That such charges were both restricted to politicians and were politically motivated makes sense of the earliest reference we have to such an action, that of Kleon against Gryttos in 424 referred to in the epigraph of this section. Kleon boasts of having removed a *binoumenos* ("a fucked male") from the citizen rolls. The saucy hero of the play, an unnamed *idiôtês* whose trade is selling sausages, replies that Kleon was in fact envious (*phthonôn*) and wanted to get rid of competitors, literally, "to stop them becoming Speakers." The chafing of interpretations that occurs between Kleon and the Sausage-seller neatly frames the paradox of sexual surveillance. On the one hand, the Speaker who tries to foment public indignation against another Speaker does so on the basis of "fundamental" values, the contrast of hoplite and *kinaidos*. Although the technical charge would have been that Gryttos had confused the roles of prostitute and citizen, calling him a *binoumenos* shows that the force of the charge resides in the application of the hoplite/ *kinaidos* imagery. On the other hand, as the Sausage-seller points out, the prosecutor's indignation is largely a fiction. It is not really concerned with either sex or surveillance as such but is simply a maneuver to attack a political opponent. *

In such attacks, prosecutors no doubt tried to muster the audience's moral indignation against the defendant in the grandest terms. A fragment of Hypereides (215), which survives only in Latin translation, calls Nature herself to witness that a kinaidic man has forfeited his very manliness, becoming in effect a woman.

> What then if we were conducting this case with Nature as judge—Nature who has distinguished male and female so that each performs his/her own proper duty and office—and what if I were to show that this man has misused his own body in a feminine way? Surely Nature would be shocked and astonished that any man would not think it a most blessed gift for him to have been born a man and that he had spoiled Nature's kindness to him, hastening to transform himself into a woman?[22]

---

*In general, "a blind eye was often turned to *atimoi* [disenfranchised persons] who behaved as *epitimoi* [full citizens]" (Hansen 1976: 59–60). Prof. Mark Golden has remarked to me on this point that citizen-wives were not treated so lightly. The sanctions against proven sexual misconduct on the part of women could be enforced by any member of the community: a Solonian law against women caught in adultery forbade them to wear finery or to appear at public events and allowed anyone who saw an adulterous woman violating this ban to rip her clothes and beat her, short of maiming or death (Aiskhines 1.183). Presumably this would be done in part to shame her *kyrios* as derelict in his control of her. The clansmen involved in Neaira's case did not turn a blind eye to her sexual misconduct, refusing to acknowledge the marriage of her daughter ([Dem.] 59.85–7).

What the preceding social analysis reveals is that such fulminations were heard in a context that gave them a very different force from identically worded fundamentalist appeals in more recent societies. At the moment of utterance, of course, the Athenian audience would have temporarily misrecognized that force, led by the rhetoric to think literally in terms of universal law. * But they also knew that "law" to operate differentially in social practice.

The Sausage-seller had earlier alluded to the possibility of his own youthful prostitution. His trick as a boy was to distract the butcher, swipe a piece of meat and hide it between his buttocks, swearing that he was innocent: "one of the Speakers who saw me doing this said, 'Undoubtedly this boy will grow up to govern the people.'" To which the Chorus replies: "A good guess, and it's clear how he reached that conclusion: you swore a false oath after embezzling, and your anus held onto the meat" (*Knights* 425–8). The series of jokes in Old Comedy characterizing both Speakers and the liturgical class in such crude terms has been interpreted as the average Athenian's criticism of practices he does not share—the plain man's sneer at the lifestyles of the rich and famous (Henderson 1975: 209–10, 216–8). But the orators' references to the limitations on sexual surveillance and the interchange between Kleon and the Sausage-seller support a somewhat different reading. It is not that active players in the political game—a class that considerably overlaps that of the wealthy—have a different lifestyle, but rather that because they move in the limelight they are subject to more intense viewing and to more widespread talk, both favorable and unfavorable. The young, in particular, are watched: they are subject both to the erotic praise of being called *kalos* (Robinson and Fluck) and the erotic abuse of being called *katapygôn* or *pornos*. † As potential players in the fiercely competitive game of Athenian city-management, where friendships and alliances must be assiduously courted, the young are particularly interesting, because their futures are still uncertain, and particularly vulnerable, because convention casts them in the chased-but-chaste role (Vlastos 95–6).

There is no record that anyone was ever prosecuted simply for prostituting himself, nor even that such a legal action was even conceived. The cases we

---

* Such misrecognition is a normal feature of the social regulation represented by talk of "nature." "Every established order tends to produce (to very different degrees and with very different means) the naturalization of its own arbitrariness. . . . Schemes of thought and perception can produce the objectivity that they do produce only by producing misrecognition of the limits of the cognition that they make possible, thereby founding immediate adherence . . . to the world of tradition experienced as the 'natural world' and taken for granted" (Bourdieu 1977: 164).

† Two of the five *katapygôn* graffiti found in the agora are also *kalos* names: Milne and von Bothmer; Fraenkel; *pornos* has been added near the name of Enpulos on a rock covered with erotic graffiti near the archaic ephebes' gymnasium on Thera (IG XII.3.536, cf. 537, 542).

know of were framed not in terms of sexual behavior but in terms of political participation. The alleged crime was not that a citizen sold his body but that, having sold his body, he then presumed to act as a policy manager for the *polis*. The penalty, fitting the crime, is loss of the citizen-rights to participate in corporate deliberations—in the Assembly, on juries, as a Council-member or magistrate. This raises an interesting question about citizens who were not politically active. *Philotimia,* of course, should impel all capable men to exert themselves to the maximum in garnering honor and recognition for themselves in the service of their city, but reality must have occasionally whispered to some that the tests of action in the sudden-death arena were not worth it. Were there any citizens whose predilections led them not to seek prominence in legislative debates?

Xenophon constructs a little dialogue between Sokrates and the pre-Epicurean Aristippos at *Memorabilia* 2.1. Aristippos, available to us largely in unfriendly reports (Giannantoni; Mannebach; Guthrie 1971b: 170–9), is there characterized as "rather undisciplined" in regards to "practicing self-mastery (*enkrateia*) over the desire for food and drink and sex and sleep and cold and heat and hard work" (2.1.1). The argument is focused on the issue of fitness to rule (*archein*), taken in a very general sense to include masters overseeing slaves (chastening their wantonness with starvation and blows, 16), one nation conquering or dictating policy to another (10), and conducting the government of Athens (*ta tês poleôs,* 2). Aristippos unabashedly declares that he does not put himself in the ranks of those who wish to govern the city (8), agreeing with Sokrates' division of people into the self-mastered who can rule others and those without self-mastery who have no pretensions to rule (7).

Perhaps we might have looked to Aristippos, if the sources were not so antipathetic, for a serious critique of the zero-sum protocols underlying the honor-shame system; but, as it is, the best our conventional sources can do is to portray his position in terms that make it fundamentally unacceptable. In the terms available to Xenophon, Aristippos' declining to compete for eminence in the city's ruling class is fully explained by his preference for self-indulgence and personal comfort over the culturally approved style of toughness.

Aiskhines mentions a group of men who, in contrast to the chaste and honorable lovers known to the city at large (155–7), are notorious for "sinning against their own bodies" (*eis heautous exhamartanontas,* 159)— Diophantos, who sued a resident-alien for non-payment of his prostitute's fee, Kephisodoros the Beautiful, Mnesitheos the Butcher's Boy, and "many others whose names I would willingly forget." They seem to represent a class of citizen little studied in Athenian politics, men who freely and deliberately chose not to live by the fictions of self-mastery for reasons that in some cases approach what we might nowadays formulate in terms of life-style preference (not sexual preference, since Aiskhines never suggests that *desire* could be a motive for prostitution).*

It is at least clear that Aiskhines recognizes the possibility that some young men will choose a life of prostitution that entails their voluntary apostasy from the arena of political warfare: "[Solon] commanded that whoever engaged [in prostitution] should not participate in the common affairs of the city; for he thought that anyone who *as a young man stood aside (apestê) from the competitive struggle for high honors* should not as an older man receive such honors" (160). When Aiskhines says that some young men who are eligible for leadership roles may choose not to compete, he does not say that they do so because they like being *kinaidoi* or that they have a personal inclination towards that type of activity (often called "passivity"). We may ourselves wonder whether anyone in that group felt so inclined, since our modern notion of a sexual identity is constructed around that issue, but the salient fact about Aiskhines' charges is that they do not include the *desire* to submit oneself sexually to other men.

If it is correct to regard the forum of Athenian politics as a closely watched arena where the comparatively few—who enjoy rhetorical training, family connections and all the subtler splendors that come from wealth and breeding—dueled for pre-eminence, and if the actors were watched with all the enthusiasm and partisanship that we associate with sports and entertainment, then perhaps it would be right to detect a note of peevish disappointment in the case of Kephisodoros (158): "Which citizen was not peeved (*eduscheraine*) at Kephisodoros, called Molon's son, who wasted his magnificent beauty in a life without honor (*kallistên hôran opseôs akleestata diephtharkota*)?" The translation could be adjusted to yield different emphases, but it is worth suggesting that the popular attitude toward Kephisodoros, as a young Robert Redford or "magnificent beauty" of his day, was not one of outrage at his sexual behavior but rather mild regret that his personal choices barred him from that public stage where it would have been a pleasure to watch him. That pleasure in watching the Young and Beautiful make their way through the minefield of political friendships, patronage, and enemy traps is the other side of Old Comedy's barbed remarks about the unmanliness of ambitious young Speakers.

Different Strokes

To round off the picture drawn in the previous section of a society in which a certain idea of male sexual deviance was strongly articulated but only very selectively enforced, let us briefly notice that common language

---

*For a unique case in which desire is taken to be the motive for a man wanting to be penetrated, see section 3 below.

used *phusis,* which some time later became an "enforcement" word, on the opposite side of the issue. In comedy and public speaking *phusis* could readily and unselfconsciously be employed to name not a common denominator that everyone had to obey but rather one's own unnegotiable bent.

There was no lack of expressions for personal predilections and individual character in fourth-century Athens.[23] *Tropos* ("turn," "manner"), *êthos* ("character"), *phil-* compounds, *prohairesis* ("choice"), and *phusis* could all be used to say that someone just was a certain way or just happened to like a certain class of objects.[24] In Alexis' comedy *Linos,* Herakles is invited to pick a book from the library; "for thus you will display your *phusis,* what it has a special tendency towards." (Herakles chooses a cookbook.) "All of human life . . . is regulated by nature and by laws: *nature* is disorganized (*atakton*) according as each man has his own, but the laws are common and organized and the same for all" (Dem. 25.15). When old Philokleon, who used to have an unwonted passion for juries and for Kleon, starts to enjoy the finer things in life, the chorus comments that he is learning new ways and will undergo a major transformation in the direction of softness and luxury: "but perhaps he won't want to, for it is hard for any man to depart from his individual *nature (physeôs . . . aei),* whatsoever it is" (*Wasps* 1456–8). People differ by age but even more by *phusis,* says Lysias (19.18).[25]

Of course individuating characteristics are not unique: many such uses of *phusis* refer to types, such as the stubborn farmer (*Peace* 607) or the unscrupulous wheeler-dealer (Dem. 25.30; 45; 50; 96, and his supporters, 45), including body-types (Isok. 15.115). Political sympathies are also traceable to one's personal nature ("Old Solon had a pro-democratic nature," Aristophanes *Clouds* 1187), an assertion which is just as easily denied ("No one is naturally oligarchic or democratic," Lysias 25.18). Isokrates goes so far as to praise Demonikos' father for paying more attention to his serious (presumably political) friends than to his relatives, "for he considered that when it came to allies a man's nature was far more important than convention, his behavior more important than blood relation, his chosen convictions more important than necessity."[26]

One can sometimes be proud of one's *phusis.* Xenophon asks what kind of nature Kyros had that gave him such special power for ruling men.[27] Demosthenes frequently refers to the admirable *phusis* of the young man who is the subject of his *Erôtikos* (6, 24, 29, 32, 51, 55). Neaira had a *phusis* skilled to discern which little girls would grow up to be beautiful ([Dem.] 59.18). Themistokles "displayed the force of his nature" (Thoukydides 1.138.3). Or it can name something of which one ought to be ashamed: Theramenes was a traitor by nature (Xen. *Hell.* 2.3.30). Men summoned before the Areopagos abide by the conventions and restrain their base natures (Isok. 7.38). Demosthenes calls Aiskhines a tragic ape, a counterfeit Speaker, a *kinaidos* by nature (*phusei,* 18.242). Kimon was highly erotic by nature

(Plutarch *Kimon* 4.3). The argumentative purpose often latent in the use of *phusis* rather than another word to describe a person's character or life-style may be defensive ("It's my *phusis*—I cannot do otherwise") or dismissive ("It's his *phusis*—what else can we expect?"). These locutions tend to cast personal character as inevitable ("He couldn't change his *phusis*, he was and remained a gentleman," Isok. 15.138).

The point of noticing that *phusis* sometimes occurs on the side of what needs to be regulated is simply to underscore the variety of actual discourse in fourth-century Athens and to suggest that when speakers or writers shifted into natural law language ("Nature lays down that all men should . . .") it would have been relatively easy to perceive the pretense. Perhaps the principal missing rubric of those which once governed the comprehension of ancient Greek discourse is the expectation that people will stake out as much territory as they can, making assertions with confidence and unshakeable personal authority. (Directions are given to travelers this way in modern Greece.) The friendly description of this is that a man's *aretê* is shown by his decisiveness; the unfriendly description is that they are all bluffing. Correlative to this agonistic rubric for speakers, an Athenian listener's response was properly guided by doubt, by a reluctance to acquiesce in any man's claim to anything.

> There is one quality that the nature of sensible people intrinsically possesses as a common protection—a good and saving quality for all, but most especially for citizen bodies against tyrants. And what is this? Distrust! (*apistia*) Guard this, hold on to this; if you preserve this, you will surely suffer no calamity." (Dem. 6.24)

Note the characteristic use of "nature" to indicate a fundamental cultural rule, of which one should not need reminding.

The selective enforcement of manhood rules, analyzed in the previous section, is not the same as a laissez-faire attitude. On the contrary, parallel to the procedures for public inspection, social control is exercised by gossip, close observation, reading suspicious signs, and imagining the worst. Of special interest in this connection is the informal practice of reading people's "natures" by the observation of their physical characteristics and style—the science of physiognomy (Gleason). The *phusi-* in physiognomy is not a completely individualized "nature"—people fall into types—but it is the unarguable substratum that shapes each person's character. Though later writers said that Pythagoras was the first to use physiognomy,[28] the earliest document to discuss it was probably *Zôpyros*, a work by Sokrates' disciple Phaido.[29]

The elementary notion that people's character can be seen in their look and behavior is not new: Idomeneus gives directions for spotting a coward before battle (Homer *Iliad* 13.275–87). But the first surviving manual for the practice is probably a work of the fourth century, collected with the writings of Aristotle.[30] One of the "natures" that can be detected in the [Aristotelian] *Physiognomonics* is that of the *kinaidos*: "The signs of a *kinaidos* are an unsteady eye* and knock-knees;† he inclines his head to the right;[31] he gestures with his palms up and his wrists loose; and he has two styles of walking—either waggling his hips[32] or keeping them under control. He tends to look around in all directions. Dionysios the sophist would be an instance of this type"[33] (808ᵃ12–6).

If common language was labile in its use of *phusis,* so were fourth-century attempts to think systematically about the fixity and flexibility of behavior-patterns. Another Aristotelian text that tries to establish that *kinaidoi* are physically unnatural ends up by proclaiming that habit is stronger than nature. It is the 26th Problem in the fourth book of the Aristotelian *Problems,* and it begins by asking, "Why is it that some men enjoy being acted upon sexually, whether or not they also enjoy being active?" The word I have translated as "acted upon sexually" is simply the passive participle *aphrodisia-zomenoi*—they enjoy being aphrodite'd. What is puzzling to this author is the enjoyment: this text strives to find possible connections between two concepts that conventionally never overlap—"man" (*anêr*) and "the enjoy-ment of being aphrodite'd."

The first point to make is that the author is not just idly speculating, not wondering if such a thing *were* to occur what he *would* say (the future less vivid construction) but rather he wonders why it is that they do. It is not a question of appearances alone or a pretense of enjoyment. They *enjoy* it, and inquiring minds want to know "Why?"

This text contains the most complex and many-sided theory of "natural" sexual desire known to me from ancient sources. The factors involved are nutrition and its dispersal throughout the body into natural places, also fantasy (which is assigned a co-equal role in prompting desire), natural ducts leading to the testicles or the anus, and finally habit (*ethos*), which has nothing to do with *phusis* and may even replace it and become (as this author says) *phusis.*

It is normal in problem-literature for multiple explanations to be advanced; what is worth noting here is that we have a unique opportunity to watch a highly articulate analyst assert first the all-dominant power of nature to distinguish the proper from the improper, and then abandon that line of thought and assert that mere habit has just as strong an explanatory value. What is more, this author does not simply forget that he had employed earlier on the same page an argument based on physical nature, he maintains that habit itself is as powerful as nature, saying it three different ways.

---

* Also a sign of cowardice, 808ᵃ7–11.

† All female animals have knock-knees, 809ᵇ8.

Let us review the main points of the text. The first answer is that there is a natural place (*kata phusin*) for every excretion that is separated out from our nourishment.[34] Urine goes into the bladder, dehydrated food into the bowels, tears into the eyes, mucus into the nostrils, blood into the veins, and sperm into the testicles. Another factor in the process is the *pneuma*, the hot breath, which is the result of exertion, the cause of that digestive separation and also a concomitant of any desire that is aroused.[35] *Pneuma* rushes to the natural place where any excretion has gathered and hastens its expulsion. Now, desire may arise from two causes, the accumulation of an excretion in its natural place (holding it in is unnatural*) or from thinking—*dianoia*. As he puts it, "desire is felt both as a result of food and as a result of thinking," for which we might put the marginal gloss "fantasy."

So much is laid down in nature. But it happens in this case, as in every other, that what is natural is not always realized. There are men whose internal conduits are not arranged *kata phusin:* those leading to the testicles may be dead-ends, in which case alternate channels exist leading to the *hedra* (literally, "seat"). In some cases men have both sets of channels open. "Those whose conduits end exclusively in the seat desire to be acted upon sexually, those whose conduits terminate in both places desire both to act and to be acted upon, and whichever place has more is the locus of greater desire." So the system is flexible (which in theory is a virtue) but at the same time unfalsifiable (which is not).[36]

The notion of spermatic fluid going to the seat might seem a weak point in this theory, but the author has at least thought about it.[†] He has a notion that in some people the excretions may tend to be thin and airy, hardly noticeable because dispersed rather than gathered together and expelled in a mass. But excretion there is: here he actually appeals, as an observable proof of his theory, to the fact that there is "a colliquescence of the area around the seat" during anal intercourse. The thinness and dispersal of this fluid is, in his view, comparable to female sexual response. "Thus it is that they are insatiable, like women, since the fluid is very little and is not ejected and loses heat quickly."

In this text nature is both the norm and the culprit, for it is nature who (in one way of speaking) has made certain men unnatural: "Men who are naturally womanish," *phusei thêludriai*. The explanation of their observable behavior is that "their constitution is *para phusin*." The most interesting part,

---

* "The friction [of sexual activity] is pleasurable, being the emission of pneumatic fluid which has been unnaturally enclosed," [Arist.] *Prob*. 4.15.

† Not only is the labor of the buttocks during intercourse essential to the act, and hence thin buttocks are one of the most revealing signs of too much indulgence in *aphrodisia*, "it is impossible for a man to ejaculate without constricting the region around the seat and keeping the eyes open" [Arist.] *Prob*. 4.2.

however, is the conclusion. "This situation comes to be true for some men out of habit (*ethos*), since whatever they regularly do they come to enjoy, even emitting their fluid in this fashion. So they desire to do whatever it happens to be that brings this pleasure, and actually habit (*ethos*) becomes, as it were, their nature (*phusis*). Therefore any man who not before *hêbê* (adolescent maturity), but at *hêbê*, develops the habit of being acted upon sexually, since memory follows the experience and pleasure follows the memory,* because of the habit they, as it were naturally (*hôsper pephukotes*), desire to be acted upon. The repetition and the habit become for them a sort of nature. And if a male is both hypersexual and effeminate (*malakos*), all the more so."†

The doctrine that habit becomes a second nature is good Aristotelian opinion (*Rhet.* 1.11: 1370^{a}6–9), as is the notion that some naturally occurring characteristics or even whole species are unnatural (Lloyd 1983: 40–3). The subject of unnatural pleasures in general is analyzed at *Eth. Nikom.* 7.5 (1148^{b}15–49^{a}20), where Aristotle speaks of plucking hairs, biting fingernails, gnawing coal or earth, and *aphrodisia* with males as unnatural.‡ Again, either nature or habit may be the explanation.

One could say much more about this text and about the subject, but let me close this chapter by underlining the strategy of reading that I mean to promote. Behind sentences that begin "The Greeks believed . . ." there lies a fairly small set of elite canonized texts. Many of them are what I would broadly call legislative rather than descriptive. One culturally specific turn of language developed on a small scale in the fifth century was the contrast of nature and convention. "Nature" in that usage, though it can be made to sound impressively absolute, refers precisely to convention: it is norm-enforcing language.

---

*Speaking of both boys and girls at about the age of fourteen, Aristotle warns that early sexual experiences promote wantonness, both because the channels are widened and lubricated and because "the memory of the accompanying pleasure produces desire for intercourse" (*Hist. Anim.* 7.1: 581^{b}19–21). Adolescent males have to be doubly on guard—against penetrative and receptive sex (*ean t' epi thatera ean t' ep' amphotera,* 581^{b}18).

†The strategy of labeling something "against nature" is deployed from time to time in Plato's dialogues, when his characters offer a radical critique of contemporary ethical assumptions. Thus Kallikles in *Gorgias* 484A asserts that all democracy's *nomoi* are *para phusin.* The notion of one's practice becoming second nature is found at *Republic* 395D: "When men persist in imitations long after youth is past, that imitative behavior becomes their established habit and nature."

‡We can tell that the subject here is really *kinaidoi* rather than the desire of men for young males for three reasons: he refers to the persons as having been "aggressed upon from boyhood"; he compares their morally inculpable state to that of women, "whom no one would blame for being penetrated rather than penetrating"; and his other casual references to paederasty (see 53n.) show that it was unproblematic for him as it was for most (Dover 1978: 169). On the flexibility of Aristotle's "nature" in political contexts, see Michelakis.

Further, the content assigned to standards of proper sexual behavior (whether or not they are designated as "nature") is dramatically different from our modern conventions (Davidson, Halperin 1989). The calculus of correctness operated not on the sameness/difference of the genders but on the dominance/submission of the persons involved. Sex was perceived, as Halperin (1989: 30) says, in terms of "either act or impact," giver or receiver, doer or done to. "Nature" busies herself about hierarchies and dependence, not about peripheral matters like hair-color or gender. As Aristotle put it, nature gave us warfare so that we could sort out the natural masters from the natural slaves (*Pol.* 1.8: 1256^{b}20–6).

Finally, even when the correct protocols have been identified so that we can see exactly why our current sexual categories do not translate into Greek, we must further notice the many limitations on the enforcement of or obedience to those protocols. The texts we study are, for the most part, rather like men's coffeehouse talk. Their legislative intent contains a fair amount of bluff, of saving face: they regularly lay down laws which are belied by the jokes those same men will later tell.

What we do not have written down are the stage directions (as it were) for those texts—the crossed fingers, the knowing nods of conspiratorial agreement. Yet there are revealing moments—hesitations, refusals to speak, backtracking—that can be assembled into a more convincing ethnography— one that posits a plurality of norms, of practices and authorities, some more vocal than others and all busy ignoring or outlawing the rest. Within such a (typically Mediterranean) ethnography, impartiality, scrupulous objectivity, and fairness to opposing views are not to be expected. They would be unnatural acts.

3

The Constraints of Desire: Erotic Magical Spells

Once on the island of Samos while a wedding procession moved through the streets to the groom's house, a bystander announced to his friends that the bride would be kidnapped before she reached her new home and on that very night another man would make her his wife. And so it happened: a group of armed men descended on the crowd, killed some who resisted and scattered the rest as they fought their way to the bride in the center and made off with her. The shrewd observer was no magician but Polemo, a second century detective of the heart's secrets through the science of physiognomy, who continues his account: "I later learned from people discussing the events that it had happened with her consent. And now I will explain to you the signs on which I based my judgment."[1] Polemo had noticed near the bride a young man whose face and bearing revealed the forces that had mastered him: audible breathing, sweaty spots on his clothes, a palpitation in the nose, color shifting back and forth from pallor to blush and an overall trembling as if from fear of disgrace. The bride's eyes were unusually liquid though her gaze was sharp, and a certain sorrow hovered over her features.

This scene contains most of the social and psychological traits that characterize relations of amicable association (*philia*) and sexual desire (*erôs*) in the Mediterranean family of cultures. Where the previous two chapters have been restricted to the world of men, jockeying for position amongst themselves, we begin in this chapter to take seriously the impact of such protocols on women. The subject requires exceeding care and a large view, for the material contains much that is humorous and much that is horrifying.

Let us begin (in section 1) by looking at this event's telltale signs and, like Polemo, analyzing the character that informs its cultural surface. In this way we will be able to place the symbolic and tangible techniques for manipulating *erôs,* known from a wide variety of practical handbooks as well as literary scenes, into a living context of intelligible purposes rather than mystify what would, to the original purveyors of and clients for "love spells," have been no mystery at all: a problem perhaps, but not a mystery.

At the same time, though much of what we loosely call "erotic magic" can be seen to conform to Mediterranean common sense, the confrontation between actual erotic spells and the masculine literary fantasies about erotic witchcraft will illuminate some dark corners of personal anguish and interpersonal spite (section 2).

Indeed it is the presence of so much venomous and malicious feeling in many of the erotic magical rites that offers twentieth-century readers such a jolt. "Love" is certainly not le mot juste for the scenes of bondage and humiliation that are acted out in the central group of procedures aimed at bringing a desired person to one's bed; we can speak of this as "passion," "lust," or "desire," but hardly as "love" (Halperin 1985). The vanilla connotations of "love" for us include mutual delight and consent, harmonious and balanced tenderness, perhaps a certain loss of self in the great mystery of the beloved other; they do not include wishing discomfort, annoyance, profound inner turmoil, and pain on the body and soul of one's beloved, as do the bulk of erotic incantations, both generic and prescription, found in the major collections of ancient "magic"—the *Papyri Graecae Magicae* (PGM) and *Defixionum Tabellae* (DT).[2]

When we further note that the norm for such procedures is male agency and female victimage, we clearly have much to be concerned about. Do we have here one more concerted assault on women as a class, comparable to foot-binding, clitoridectomy, witch-burning, and similar institutions of historical misogyny?[*] The answer (in section 3) is a complex one, involving experiences of projection and desire symbolized in a Mediterranean setting where the whole question of access—whether to divine powers through magic or to anything else—had a rather different weight than it does in twentieth-century capital economies.

Each of the three sections of the present essay contains a field of data, an argument about it, and a subtext on the relation of that ancient material to our conditions of understanding. The last requires a word of comment. I take it that some such awareness should be present in any hermeneutically sophisticated account, but it is particularly necessary in the case of a "distanced" subject like magic. "Magic" is a relative term: we only call something "magic" if we do not (or no longer) accept the premises of its meaning or operation.[3] The term thus reveals—or may be used to reveal—as much about the speaker as it does about the object. The perspective adopted here has something in common with Polemo's as a participant-observer in the wedding on Samos, that is, it neither exclusively identifies with the observed field nor pretends to stand wholly outside it, but tries to understand what the actors themselves experience and intend and also, where possible, to see more than they do. Let me here make explicit the tendency of my subtexts, in case the defensive reader would like to design a phylactery against them.

---

[*]Calling such institutions "historical" is not meant to rule out their currency: Russell and Van de Ven.

(1) First I present some of the ordinary technologies for managing *erôs* and explain them as relatively unproblematic actions, given the social setting of Polemo's captured bride, with its typically Mediterranean cultural patterns of agonistic dramatization. The only reason to call these "magic" is that our modern reliance on impersonal sciences and other centralized disciplines of the state and university has deprived us of the crafty resourcefulness in regard to available materials and symbols that flourishes in a more face-to-face and self-reliant society.

(2) Then I explore the twilight world of *agôgai,* rituals designed to lead a desired person to one's house and bed. These provide an unusually intimate picture of private and heart-felt anxieties, as staged in one's *psuchê* by persons more experienced in self-dramatization, and in entertaining themselves, than are the creatures of our relatively passive consumer culture. The bed at night, or the rooftop nearby, is the imagined location of most *agôgai,* their place of performance and the goal of the rite; and it is in the fantasy world of half-sleep that the desperate, sometimes suicidal passions grow strong. Some of the violence of language and gesture in the *agôgai* is due to the projected intensity of the performer's own sense of victimization by a power he is helpless to control. My subtext takes the risk here of romanticizing Mediterranean passion (as Stendhal and Browning did for Italy) as something exquisite and vital, missing in our drier and paler culture. The reader's phylactery for this might be to gloss my phrases such as "intensely dramatized anxieties" with a less friendly description such as "self-pity" or "petulance."

(3) Finally, I dwell on the implications of a disturbing terracotta statuette in the Louvre, using the anthropological common sense of section 1 and the passionate psychology of section 2 to graph some of the deep tremors of hatred of women that seem to seethe in the symbolic actions of the *agôgai.* It should not be possible in the late twentieth century to continue to ignore the institutions of terror that have circumscribed the experience of women over the centuries, but the more seriously we take this question the harder it is to give a single answer.

I will suggest, among other things, that the victimage models enacted in *agôgai* paradoxically incorporate rather than suppress women's desire, but that they do so only within the models of family competition and male fantasy in which any desire is a dangerous irruption into one's autonomy and women's desire in particular must be thought of—that is, by men—as submitting to the pretensions of masculine control.

1. Home Remedies for *Erôs*

A public drama

The Samian wedding witnessed by Polemo would not have been perceived as a tale of true love triumphing over opposition. It was rather an unmitigated

social disaster for all concerned. The two families, putting their alliance on display in the open streets by a procession from house to house, have been shamed before an audience that watches, evaluates, spreads the tale, and keeps it in long remembrance. In the zero-sum competition between families a fall in the stock of one group means a rise in the value of others. * The social force of prescribed enmity, manifested in competition, gossip, and envy, is so strong that its deleterious effects can even make themselves felt unconsciously and unwittingly, as in the case of the evil eye.[4] The two principal terms that articulate this perpetual jockeying for position are honor and shame, represented respectively by the men and the women of a family. †
The behavior of men in controlling the reputation of a household and in prudently administering its resources has been brilliantly analyzed from fourth-century sources by Michel Foucault (1985). The experience of Mediterranean women is considerably more difficult of access (appropriately enough) and falls outside the scope of Foucault's project, which is to trace the archaeology of certain practices of self-discipline, but modern analogies provide a consistent framework within which the ancient evidence fits snugly and comfortably.

Young women are the passive actors whose cooperation is essential in the highly unstable process of transmitting property through the re-creation and re-definition of family units. As the bearers of a tremendous symbolic weight determining the good or bad reputation of two families, virgins, brides, and young wives are often perceived as the point of maximum vulnerability in a household's integrity. "A woman's status defines the status of all the men who are related to her in determinate ways. These men share the consequences of what happens to her, and share therefore the commitment to protect her virtue." ‡

An emphasis on protecting the vulnerable, of course, installs the vulnerability of women as a permanent and necessary part of the system—a bar to

---

*Gouldner 45–55. The economic metaphor is natural to us but should not mislead: the value in question is precisely not one that can be quantified and exchanged but depends on personal assertion, vindication, and negotiation in the intimate forums of a small-scale society. Good examples of misreading the honor code as an exchange relation in Bourdieu 1965.

†Peristiany shows that the values are not a uniform system throughout the area, a point well made by Herzfeld 1980; cf. Dover 1974: 95–102, 205–13, 226–42; Pitt-Rivers.

‡J. Schneider. The charge of adultery brought against Lykophron was supported by an allegation that he had followed the mulecart on which a bride was riding during the wedding procession and had openly begged her not to consummate the marriage. Since her brother, an Olympic wrestler, was there, "could I have been crazy enough to utter such shameless words about a free woman in the hearing of all present and not be afraid of being strangled to death on the spot? For who could have endured to hear such words about his own sister . . . and not have killed the man who uttered them?" (Hypereides *In Defence of Lykophron* 6). See also the anecdote in Plutarch *mul. virt.* 244E (quoted in Chapter Six, p. 181n.) and Lavelle.

the crossover of women, should any aspire to do so, into activities of the public and male realms. This is the first key point at which we must invoke a sophisticated awareness of the interplay between our values and our evaluations. A naive reliance on the public pronouncements of ancient men would lead us to think that their wives and daughters were objectively weak in mind and body, both light-headed and prone to passion. Such statements should be taken seriously as a social move in the competitive game but should not be taken literally. An equally naive assumption that ancient women were much the same in character and aspirations as modern women would lead us to dismiss most ancient texts as patriarchal propaganda and even to resent their automatic classification of women as counters in an exclusively male game.*

To counteract these temptations we must not only weave together various types of evidence—in this essay mainly literary productions and medical self-help procedures—but we must be aware of the historical, cultural, and material premises of their utterance.[5] Chief among these, and one very difficult for us to grasp, is the prevalence of lying (du Boulay 1976, Walcot 1977). Duplicity is not just a cultivated skill, useful in special circumstances, but a permanent state of defensiveness against intrusive enemies who will use any knowledge about the private affairs of a family to bring it down. Hence with every affirmation of family honor we must also posit the unspoken comments of neighbors doubting its truth; by the same token every aspersion on a family's integrity must be understood as an "interested" comment. In short, every statement implies a plethora of competing and opposing evaluations in a network wherein no allegation is disinterested and every assessment is a strategic move in the collective maneuvering of public opinion concerning the relative prestige of family-units.

These comments on duplicity serve, first, to underscore the high stakes of a public performance like a wedding, which stages the outcome of delicate negotiations between families entering into an alliance in the presence of numerous well-wishers who undoubtedly entertain concealed thoughts of at least low-grade hostility. In 1968 Manoli, an eighteen-year-old man from a socially prominent family on the island of "Nisi" fell in love with a girl from a poor family. "As Manoli had eaten at the girl's house, his family felt that someone there must have put a love potion into his food." Resisting all the advice and pressure from his family, Manoli eloped with the girl and after a few days returned and went through a formal wedding ceremony.

---

*In the Cretan mountain village of "Glendi," card games in the coffeehouse are an emblematic male contest in which the cards themselves are frequently given feminine names, successful players are spoken of as sexually charged ("he's hot," "he's ploughing straight" = "he is copulating"), and unlucky players are taunted as having had recent sexual contact, which polluted them. Herzfeld 1985a: 152–62.

"The groom was unable to consummate the marriage. It was believed that when the best man passed the wedding crowns over the couple's heads three times, someone present had uttered magic words and had tied three knots in a string, thereby acquiring power over the couple. . . . The groom took ill and was bedridden for four months. He began to waste away, and the priest was summoned daily to bless him and the house. A relative suggested that a witch in Athens be consulted and he, his parents, and his wife went to Athens. The witch performed a curing ritual and instructed them to return to Nisi and be remarried at an outlying chapel. This was done. At this service, known as reversing the crowns, the magic was broken." The intense disapproval of the bride's parents at her elopement and of the groom's family at Manoli's folly gives ample grounds to reconstruct the network of "social forces" at work—gossip, defamation, dirty looks, and other covert symbolizing activities such as knot-tying and muttered words of power—influencing and correcting the young couple's improper behavior. A few years later the couple was divorced after Manoli became convinced that his original love "must have been witchcraft. Otherwise, he would have listened to his father and waited. He added, 'Why else would I have married during the best years of my life?'"[6]

The transition from the protected inner sanctum of one house to that of another along public thoroughfares exposes the symbolically vulnerable family members, bride and groom, to malignancy which is both inevitable and invisible.* (Playing out this line of thought, we might maintain that many forms of what we call ancient "magic" are simply our way of representing "social forces," equally inevitable and invisible, "forces" that no longer prevail with us.)

Second, the assumption that hostility will be present but masked goes a long way towards placing techniques of erotic influence where they belong in the extensive infra-red penumbra surrounding public events, usually unrecorded by conventional public discourse but undoubtedly present in unguessably large amounts. Thus it is only the more conversational or unpretentious or deliberately outrageous works of classical literature that allude with any regularity to the covert acts of symbolic influence which most citizens are constantly practicing—and always denying that they practice—on their fellows. How did Perikles come to have so many cooperating allies (*philoi*)? "One hears" and "they say" that it was due to spells (*epôidai*) and love charms (*philtra*).† Playfully, Sokrates can explain the faithful devotion of his friends Apollodoros and Antisthenes to *philtra* and *epôidai*, and

---

*See the discussion of the customs of disguising the bride in J. G. Frazer 410–1.

†Themistokles, a less lovable character, must have used an amulet (*periamma*), "attaching (*periapsas*) some good thing to the city" (Xenophon *Mem.* 2.6.10–3).

the drawing of Simmias and Cebes all the way from Thebes to the even stronger attractive power of *iunges* (Xenophon *Mem.* 3.11.16–8).

Recipes for Success

The later handbooks of self-help procedures record many such devices for (in the words of a modern magus) "winning friends and influencing people." Those that are focused narrowly and exclusively on sex will be considered in section 2. Here we must first note the texture of the social fabric into which such private practices are woven, for *erôs* cannot be neatly detached from the total world in which these actors try to upstage each other. The ideal of personal success for men in an agonistic, duplicitous, self-dramatizing culture includes the items requested in a prayer to Helios (*PGM* III 494–611): "Come to me with your face gleaming, at the resting-place (*koitê*) you choose yourself, granting me, So-and-So, life, health, safety, wealth, fine children, knowledge, ready hearing, good disposition, good counsel, good reputation, memory, charm (*kharis*), looks (*morphê*), beauty (*kallos*) before all persons who see me, and make my words persuasive, you who hear everything without exception, great god" (lines 575–81).

The petitioner would like to shine in his community not only with external marks of physical success but most particularly in personal qualities, because the truly significant interactions in which his value is continuously judged and rated by others are those where he shows his individual excellence. To get the edge on competitors often means charming or outfoxing them rather than fighting or insulting them, so generalized prayers for success frequently include what may seem to us a rather peacock-like pride in looking good and being seen as sexually appealing. The social implications of radiating *kharis* in the eyes of the community are brought out in spells specifically directed to acquiring or reinforcing one's charisma, such as XII 397–400, which promises the bearer of an inscribed wormwood root that "you will be charming and befriended and admired by all who see you."[7] Part of such a person's total influence as a force in his society is his outright sexiness, as in the recommendation to carry the right eye and first tail-joint of a wolf in a gold container to make the bearer "well thought of and successful and honored and victorious and sweet and desirable in form and loved and desired by women."[*]

Competitive success is regularly joined not only with personal charisma

---

[*]Kyranides 2.23.21–8. Similarly, the right eye of a seal wrapped in deer skin makes one successful and desirable (*axierastos*)—Kyranides 2.41.9–10, 4.67.14–6. The seal's tongue brings victory and its whiskers and heart are a *kharitêsion megiston,* guaranteed to bring success. I cite the Kyranides by book, chapter, and line numbers in the edition of Kaimakis 1976.

but with power to soften and restrain the anger of one's enemies.* A prayer to Helios under the rubric "Spell to restrain anger, win victory, gain charisma" (XXXVI 211–30) asks not only for "sexiness (*epaphrodisia*) and charm before all men and all women" and for "victory over all men and all women" but also for protection against failure, plots, harmful drugs, exile, and poverty. These latter eventualities are seen as the outcome of other people's *thumos* (anger, resentment) which must be restrained, hence the name *thumokatochon* (anger-restraint).

Exuding charm and warding off anger are equally necessary and co-implicated strategies in the project of maximizing personal success.[8] Anger-restraining techniques range from reciting lines of Homer (IV 831–2)[†] to saying prayers (XXXVI 161–77) to carrying inscribed pieces of metal or papyrus (VII 940–68, IX, XII 179–81).[‡] The last three are designed so that the name of a particularly dangerous person may be inserted according to the needs of the wearer. We have one such prescription spell on an ostrakon asking Kronos to check the anger of Hori, son of Maria, and not let him speak to Hatros, son of Taeses (O.1 in PGM, vol. 2, p. 233). This is mild. Others beg the god to subject, silence, subordinate, enslave, and trample on So-and-So (VII 940–68, IX); that intention is acted out by placing a tablet in one's right sandal inscribed with mystic vowels and angels' names: "Just as these sacred names are being trampled, so also let So-and-So who hinders me be trampled" (X 36–50).

The systematic interlacing of violence and charm, which we may find puzzling and even repugnant, is simply the necessary shape given to aspirations for success in that agonistic, masked, and duplicitous society. The *philtrokatadesmos* of Astrapsakos (VIII 1–63) is obviously "a spell for some shopkeeper to ensure good business," as its translator notes.[9] But the blessings prayed for So-and-So and his workplace (*ergastêrion*, line 63) include

---

*Or, in some cases, one's friends: Antigone reminds her angry father that "Other men too have terrible sons and a sharp anger (*thumos*) against them, but assuaged by the spells (*epôidai*) of friends their angry nature is dis-spelled (*exepaidontai*)," Sophokles *Oidipous Kol.* 1192–4. According to Myrsilos of Lesbos (FGrHist 477 F 7) the original function of the Muses, who were actually seven Mysian maidservants bought by Megaklo, queen of Lesbos, was to sing enchanting (*katepaidousai*) melodies to soften the anger of her husband Makar with his mother-in-law.

[†] = IV 467–8. Empedokles once saved his host Anchitos from being murdered by the son of a man who had been executed in a capital case brought by Anchitos: as the young man rushed forward with sword drawn and in a state of terrible anger (*thumos*), Empedokles struck a soothing and restraining (*katastaltikos*) chord on his lyre and recited *Odyssey* 4.221 ["without sorrow or anger, forgetful of all ills"] (Iamblikhos *Vit. Pyth.* 113 = FVS 31 A 15). For other uses of Homeric and Vergilian lines cf. Heim 1892: 514–20.

[‡] "Restraint" is the first of many points of contact between two fields usually kept separate in modern accounts—erotic rites and binding spells, e.g. "Hermes Restrainer, restrain Manes . . . ." R. Wünsch *Defixionum Tabellae Atticae*, IG III Appendix, no. 109.

not only victory and wealth but charisma (4, 27, 36), sexiness (*epaphrodisia*, 5, 62), a handsome face and body (*prosôpou eidos*, 5; *morphê*, 27, 30; *kallos*, 27). Our analytic surgery should not sever the nexus of triumph and seductiveness in this shopkeeper's social personality, for they are constantly juxtaposed in its litanies.[10] Both his charm and his strength serve the same goal in the wary game of life: "Humble all before me and give me power and beauty, etc." (30–1). Hence, the title *philtrokatadesmos*, which equally invokes violent restraint (*katadesmos*) of one's competitors and friendly alliance (*philtro*), is not misleading, as the translator claims, but expresses the diffusion of a visible, low-grade *erôs* throughout the competitive structure.

The serviceableness of such *erôs* is most vividly portrayed in the rite for constructing and empowering a wax image of Eros to be an all-purpose Assistant (*Parhedros*) in XII 14–95. When it has absorbed the life-breath of seven strangled birds, the Eros statue will serve its master in bearing powerful messages of compulsion to all men and women whom the owner wishes to influence. "I call upon you, in your beautiful resting-place (*koitê*), in your house of desire, serve me and always convey whatever message I tell you" (40–1). Among other things, this Assistant can "make all men and all women turn to desire me" (*ep' erôta mou*, 61–2) and can "grant me charisma, sweet speech, sexiness towards all men and all women in creation, that they be subject to me in all things that I wish, for I am the servant of the most high god who controls the kosmos, the ruler of all" (69–72). The power of this Eros Assistant to enter people's houses (82), to appear in their dreams or as a divine visitation in the midst of sleep (15–6, 41–2, 83–4), to "afflict them with fear, trembling, anxiety, mental disturbance" (54–5, 84) assimilates this serviceable or "social success" *erôs* to the more focused *agôgai* of the next section.

Before turning to those, however, we must round off this treatment of simple self-help therapies by taking a brief look at aphrodisiacs and antaphrodisiacs.

Erotic pharmacology

The terms *philtrokatadesmos* and *kharitêsion* covered not only prayers and amulets but more directly material technologies for stimulating and managing sexual feelings, such as penis ointments[*] (VII 191–2) and love potions: the penis of a lizard caught copulating produces indissoluble affection in the woman who unwittingly drinks a potion made from it, and if you can throw your handkerchief over lizards copulating it will be a *kharitêsion mega* (great

---

[*]Cf. XXXVI 283–94; PDM xiv 335–55, a fish-oil to be applied both to phallos and to face before intercourse. PDM xiv contains eight other penis ointments plus an erotic fish-oil just for the face (355–65).

spell to produce charm). The tail worn as an amulet promotes erection (Kyranides 2.14.10–3).

This is useful knowledge and it circulated in massive quantities along informal channels on the ground, leaving but few traces in the stratosphere of dignified writing.[11] Before the compilation of handbooks it resided with families and individuals who might share it as they chose.[12] Plato's *Charmides* shows how a cure for headache (consisting of a leaf and a recited spell) could be passed on; Achilles Tatius' novel *Leukippe and Kleitophon* does the same for a bee-sting remedy (2.6). But note that both cures are incorporated into the narrative as tricks to seduce a desirable person (*Charmides* 155B) rather than as straightforward home-remedies.

The antiquarian and medical literature that picks up information about aphrodisiacs tends to set it in a symposiastic context.[13] The "Playful Tricks of Demokritos" include lamp illusions, oinoprophylactics, and sexual stimulants. * Athenaios' experts on cultivated dining know a good deal about what foods rouse desire. † They cite treatises in prose and poetry from classical and hellenistic times (Philoxenos *Dinner*, Herakleides of Tarenton *Symposion*, Terpsikles *Concerning Aphrodisiacs*) which included equally useful advice on which foods cause gas (53C) and which promote sperm (bulbs, snails, and eggs: 64A). But this material is obviously much older and more widely available; most of Athenaios' aphrodisiacs are cited from fourth-century Attic comedy (63E–64B, 356E-F). He might have added Aristophanes *Ekklêsiazousai* 1092, where the crones demanding sex from a young man advise him to gulp down a potful of bulbs. ‡

Theophrastos records, with varying degrees of skepticism, the claims of fourth-century herb merchants §: ointment of snapdragon produces good

---

* VII 167–86. Wellman. Hippolytos *Refut. Haer.* 4.28–42 interprets all magician's performances as tricks: Ganschinietz.

† Bulbs are prominent (*Deipnosophists* 1.5B, 2.63E–64B, 64E-F, 8.356E), evidently from their resemblance to testicles (especially those that grow in pairs, cf. Pliny *nat. hist.* 26.95, Dioskorides *Mat. Med.* 3.126). Satyrion, frequently cited as an aphrodisiac, has a "bulbous root like a fruit, ruddy with a white inside like an egg" (Diosk. *Mat. Med.* 3.128). Sometimes the aphrodisiac effectiveness resides not in the shape but in the significant name, as in the case of scallops (*ktenes*, also meaning "vaginas") and the sea creatures known as *fascina* and *spuria* (Apuleius *Apologia* 35; Abt 223–4 = 149–50). The words also mean male and female genitals, respectively (sources cited in Abt).

‡ What works for humans, works for animals. Squill and deer's tail will stimulate reluctant bulls (*Geoponika* 27.5, Varro *Re. rust.* 2.7.8) and "this same procedure works for humans too" (*Geop.* 19.5.4). Red mullet is an antaphrodisiac for men, a contraceptive for women and birds (Athenaios 7.325D). The root of all-heal (*Ferulago galbanifera*) is good for birthing, other gynecological problems, and flatulence in cattle.

§ Literally, "root-cutters", *rhizotomoi*, on which see Lloyd 1983: 119–35. *Rhizotomoi* was also the title of a play by Sophokles concerning Medea, cf. Sutton 117–8.

reputation (*Hist. Plant.* 9.19.3), mandrake root in vinegar is a love-potion (9.9.1). Hipponax evidently referred to a love potion to be drunk when one saw the first swallow in the springtime (172 West; Degani). The simplest ways are sometimes best: the Aristotelian *Problems* 3.33 recommend a big breakfast and light dinner to promote sexual desire.

Many of these ingredients are explicitly conceived in a system of balances, since the prudent householder needs to control *erôs* both in its arousal and in its dispersal, both for male and for female. The plant known as "rocket" (*Eruca sativa, euzômon*) eaten green prevents erection and wet dreams, [*] but its seeds mixed with pepper and honey produces an erection two fingers long and is especially recommended for "older men whose part is relaxed."[14] The weasel's right testicle is conceptive, the left is contraceptive (Kyranides 2.7). The right molar of a small crocodile worn as an amulet guarantees erection in men, the left produces "equally powerful pleasure in women" (Kyran. 2.29). [†] The testicle-like double bulbs of the orchis and satyrion have opposite effects (*adversantur altera alteri,* Pliny *nat.hist.* 27.65), stimulating or depressing desire,[15] producing male or female children.[16]

Some ingredients are directed specifically against women, such as crane brain (Aelian *nat. anim.* 1.44) and sparrow's gizzard, which given secretly in a drink promotes pleasure and *erôs* in the maiden who swallows it (Kyranides 1.18.42–4). Evidently most of this popular-technical writing was composed for men, yet in literature and historical anecdote suspicions are regularly directed to women as foodhandlers who might add secret ingredients to affect men's *erôs.*[17] Here too the network of competition and suspicion motivates the action. Aretaphila, married to the hateful tyrant of Cyrene, tried to poison him; detected in her food-tampering, she defends herself by claiming merely to be preparing antidotes to the drugs and devices of other women, so that her husband's affection (*eunoia*) will not be drawn away and her honorable position will continue to be secure. (Plutarch *mul. virt.* 256A–C.) Deianeira, in Sophokles' *Trakhiniai,* is similarly motivated: she hates "bold women," presumably those who use erotic charms to gain lovers, but uses Nessos' blood to keep Herakles faithful to her (575–87). [‡]

---

[*] Hence it is eaten regularly by temple attendants—Kyran. 1.5.13–4, preferable perhaps to the three cold baths per day described by Chairemon *ap.* Porphyry *de abstin.* 4.6–8. Hemlock is consumed for the same reason by the hierophant at Eleusis (Hippolytos *Refut. haer.* 5.8). Also useful are red mullet (Terpsikles [a pseudonym if I ever heard one] *ap.* Athenaios 7.325D), associated with Artemis (Plato comicus *ap.* Athenaios 7.325A), and water-lily root (*nymphaia:* named for a nymph who was hopelessly in love with Herakles—Pliny *nat. hist.* 25.75; cf. 26.94, Dioskorides *Mat. Med.* 3.132).

[†] The wearing of a crow's heart (male by man, female by woman) ensures affection (*eunoia*) forever—"an unsurpassable miracle" Kyran. 1.2.14–9.

[‡] A woman accused of using aphrodisiacs to gain the love of Philip was brought before Olympias who, seeing her beauty and hearing her intelligent conversation, said "The accusa-

These self-help procedures, in their very ordinariness, do not constitute a reliable system for managing the deepest and most disturbing problems of passion, particularly the deeply unwanted experience of falling helplessly and hopelessly in love. Let us turn then once more to Polemo's wedding to study the medical and psychological aspects of such invasive, anti-social *erôs* and the covert, symbolizing activities used by lovers on unwilling subjects.

2. Remedium Amoris

Polemo's detection of the truth concealed in two lovers' hearts was couched in a specifically medical idiom.[*] In effect, he was diagnosing an illness on the basis of signs visible in the face and bearing of the bride and her lover. The belief runs deeply through ancient medicine, social practice, and literature that intense desire is a diseased state affecting the soul and the body, an illness which up to a point can be discerned and analyzed, but which is remarkably difficult to treat. The pathology is fundamentally melancholic: "Those who possess a large quantity of hot black bile become frenzied or clever or erotic or easily moved to anger and desire."[†] Nowadays, free associating on the word "love" would not elicit "frenzy" and "anger" as primary responses. Since the premises we bring to "love stories" are somewhat different from those of the ancient Mediterranean, we must always be on our guard against misreading such narratives. For instance, when Herodotos begins a dynastic tale by saying "Kandaules fell in love with his own wife" (1.8), his audience knew from the word *erôs* itself, as well as from the ominous conjunction of *erôs* with marriage, that desperate events were in the offing.

If falling in love is, in many co. .xts, much the same as falling ill,[18] this is particularly the case for those whose desire has been roused for someone they may not associate with or marry. Of course, it is true for young lovers in general: "What is sweeter for a human being than the desire for a woman, especially a young man's desire? . . . Yet griefs and toil follow close behind."[‡] If the lover's desire is not reciprocated, or is not sanctioned by his

---

tions are baseless, you have aphrodisiacs in yourself" (Plutarch *conj. praec.* 141B–C). A similar story can be found in a discussion of misogyny in Satyros' *Life of Euripides* (a dialogue in which at least one of the three speakers was a woman), P. Oxy. 1176, frag. 39, col. xiv: "When he saw her stature and beauty, he said 'Hail, lady; the accusations are false, for you have drugs in your face and eyes.'" The trope is reversed at Lucian *Dial. Meretr.* 8: "His wife told everyone that I had driven him crazy with drugs, but the only drug involved was his own jealousy."

[*] As in the detective stories of Hippokrates visiting Demokritos, Diog. Laert. 9.42. For an ancient drawing of two hearts, or what Audollent saw as such, see the "valentine" at DT 264.

[†] [Aristotle] *Problems* 30.1: 954^a52, cf. 954^a25: "when black bile is overheated, it produces cheerfulness accompanied by song, and frenzy, and the breaking forth of sores."

[‡] Antiphon Soph. *On Likemindedness*, FVS 87 B 49. "A sign of the onset of *erôs* is not delight

or her family, the situation is desperate indeed, often expressed in taking to bed, wasting away and, if untreated, death. * Suicide is a common end to stories of hopeless love, as in the old Greek folk-song of Kalyke, who leaped from a cliff rather than live without the young man who rejected her. † *Erôs* in such circumstances is felt to be the sort of constraint or external pressure that may make life simply unlivable. The moral justifications for suicide in classical philosophy refer generically to god-sent constraints, among which *erôs* counted as one in popular opinion, if not in Aristotle's. ‡

Since *erôs,* for all its beauty, loosens the limbs and dominates one's better judgment (Hesiod *Theogony* 120–2), it is crucial to be able to diagnose and treat the affliction. § Polemo's demonstration belongs to a long line of claims and stories showing the limits of ordinary medicine to cope with the devastating and disruptive power of *erôs*. He can detect it but he cannot control it. A few such narratives (proving the rule) do manage to have happy endings. The famous physician Erasistratos not only correctly analyzed the cause of prince Antiochos' sickness as unfulfilled *erôs* but detected the object of his

---

in the presence of the beloved, which is only normal, but rather the sting and pain felt in the beloved's absence" (Plutarch *quomodo quis suos in virtute sent. prof.* 77B). "These signs—groans and tears and pallor—indicate nothing other than *erôs*" (Lucian *Jup. Trag.* 2).

* Some famous literary cases: Euripides' Phaidra, Kallimachos' Kydippe, Chariton's Kallirhoe. Lesser known sufferers are the son of Diogenes (*Souda* s.v. Diogenes) and the rich young man who fell in love with a farmer's daughter (Athenaios 12.554C-E, from Kerkidas' and Archelaos' *Iamboi*).

† Athenaios 14.619D-E (from Aristoxenos); traditionally attributed to Stesikhoros (Page 1962: 277). Dimoites, cursed by his wife, falls in love with a corpse washed up on the shore; since it is in an advanced state of decay, he buries it and kills himself on the grave (Parthenios 31). When Antiope gently but firmly refused the suit of Soloeis, he leaped into a river and drowned himself (Plutarch *Theseus* 26.2–5). After Enalos' beloved was hurled into the sea to satisfy an oracle, he leaped after her but was saved by a dolphin, who carried him to Lesbos— evidently a folktale told about a dolphin-rider image on Lesbos (Myrsilos of Lesbos, FGrHist 477 F 14). Daphnis' mother is afraid he will commit suicide (Longus 3.26.3). Phidalios of Korinth (FGrHist 30 F 2) states the general principle: "it is natural for lovers to cling to the beloved and to die for her . . . ; for they are made savage by desire and do not use their minds to reason with." So common is the motif that Lucian makes fun of it: in a check-list of those entering Hades are "seven who slew themselves for *erôs*" (*Kataplous* 6).

‡ "Some constraint (*anankê*) sent by god" Plato *Phaido* 62C; "constrained (*anankastheis*) by an unbearably painful and inescapable misfortune or meeting with a hopeless and unlivable shame" Plato *Laws* 9.873C; "to die to escape poverty or *erôs* or some anguish is the mark of a cowardly rather than manly person" Aristotle *Eth. Nikom.* 3.7: 1116^{a}12–4. (Prof. Elise Garrison drew these to my attention.)

§ Plutarch recommends that the old practice of public diagnosis of illness be applied also to emotional disorders, imagining the following comments from bystanders: "'You're suffering from anger; stay away from x.' 'You're feeling jealous; do y.' 'You're in love; I was in love once but I recognized my mistake (*metenoêsa*)'" (*lat. viv.* 1128E).

love by feeling his pulse as various members of the household entered the sickroom.[19] (Galen believed the story and claimed to have done the same.[20])

But more typically *erôs* confounds social expectations and medical expertise. People who lived near the river Selemnos in Achaia told Pausanias that bathing in its waters cured *erôs* for men and women alike, but he comments wryly: "If there is any truth in the tale, the water of the Selemnos is more valuable than great wealth" (7.23.3). The continual, quasi-medical complaint is that there is no drug to cure that disease—except the beloved in person. *

The core experience represented in Greek erotic literature is that of powerful involuntary attraction, felt as an invasion and described in a pathology of physical and mental disturbance. There are many well-known examples from Sappho[†] to *Daphnis and Chloe,*[‡] but let us rather give to the lovely Sosipatra, from the pages of Eunapios' *Lives of the Philosophers* (Wright 398–417) the attention her case deserves. Trained from the age of five in religious and philosophical lore by two old Chaldaian magi, Sosipatra acquired the powers of prescience and telepathy that were the aim of many iatrosophists in the fourth century of the common era. Her kinsman Philometor, "conquered by her beauty and her speech," falls into a state of *erôs,* which "was constraining him and doing him violence." He begins to ply unspecified arts at which he is adept to make Sosipatra feel the same and she begins to be aware of his attempts. As she describes her *pathos* to her confidant Maximus, "When Philometor is present, he is just Philometor. . . ; but when I see him leaving, my heart inside me is stung and twists about at his departure." Philometor perseveres in his rites and Maximus struggles against him, "learning by divinatory sacrifices what Power Philometor had summoned to help him and then invoking a more violent and forceful Spirit to dissolve the spell of the lesser one."[§] Sosipatra is freed from her unwelcome feelings and Philometor stops his plotting.

---

*Plato *Phaidros* 252A-B; orderly education will moderate other desires, but as for *erôs,* the source of a million evils for individuals and whole cities, "what herbal drug can you cut to liberate these people from so great a danger?" *Laws* 8.836B; "O King, there is no other *pharmakon* for *erôs* but the beloved in person," Chariton 6.3.7; a magus declares that he can command the moon and sun and sea and air, "but for *erôs* alone I find no drug" (PGM XXXIV, a novel fragment). Theokritos declares that there is no cure except poetry (*Idyll* 11.1–3); Kallimachos accepts the point and adds starvation as another cure (*Epigram* 47). Philetas advises Daphnis and Chloe, "There is no remedy for *erôs,* nothing to drink, nothing to eat, nothing to chant in a song, except a kiss and an embrace and lying down together without clothes" (2.7).

†Plutarch nicely observes that the physical symptoms described in Sappho 31 are exactly those of *erôs* (*Demetrios* 38).

They are also unwelcome, involuntary, and perhaps the result of a spell; see Chapter Six, pp. 173–4.

‡Chloe tentatively diagnoses her own symptoms as a spring fever, 1.13–4.

§So the love spells of Canidia were countered, she imagines, by "the incantation of a more scientific witch," *veneficae scientioris carmine* (Horace *Epode* 5.71–2).

What covert symbolizing activities did Philometor practice? Many low-tech devices are known from PGM, such as words to whisper over a wine-cup before giving it to someone to drink,[21] or ingredients to add to the drink itself.[22] A sun scarab properly boiled in myrrh and with just a touch of vetch ("the constraining plant," *katananke botane*[23]) enables you to compel a woman to follow you once you have touched her, presumably with a dab of the wonderful oil.[24] Eye-contact is powerful even without pharmaceutical or spiritual assistance,* but the effect can be enhanced by saying the secret name of Aphrodite to yourself seven times while looking at her (IV 1265–74) or by saying a formula and breathing deeply three times while you stare at her: if she smiles back it is a sign that the spell has worked![†]

But Philometor was not fooling around with amatory *jeux.* The compulsion he tried to project, *because he felt it himself,* belonged rather to the far more extensive and expressive set of rites known as *agogai,* spells to lead or draw a person to one's house and bedroom. The compelling power, if it works ideally, knows no resistance. I will use two literary pictures of perfectly effective *agogai,* albeit both contain a measure of authorial irony, to frame an account of the rites and procedures known from PGM.

The first occurs in Apuleius' *Golden Ass* (2.32 and 3.15–8). Fotis, servant to the witch Pamphile, is directed to filch some hairs from a handsome Boeotian youth while he is sitting in the barbershop. The barber prevents her, so, to cover her failure, she brings her mistress some hairs of the same color taken from goatskins recently shorn and hanging up, inflated, to dry. Pamphile takes them at night up to her rooftop, where she has her laboratory stocked with herbs, engraved metal tablets, pieces of shipwrecked wood, parts of human corpses, and animal bones. With fire and incantations and various liquids she knots and burns the hairs, which causes the bodies from which they came, not the Boeotian youth's but the inflated goatskins, to come bouncing along the street and beat at Pamphile's housedoor.

Before the recovery of the rituals in PGM one might have thought that Apuleius' picture was so much fantasy. But everything in it, with the stunning exception of the untypical gender of the magician (on which more below), belongs to the regular procedures for drawing a person helplessly out of her house and into one's bed. At VII 462–6, for instance, a copper nail from a shipwreck is used to write characters on a tin plate which is then

---

*As Hippodamia says of the beautiful Pelops in Sophokles' *Oinomaos:* "Pelops has such a magician's implement to capture *eros,* some lightning in his eyes; it warms him, it scorches me entire" (frag. 474). "As fire burns those who touch it, so beautiful people ignite a subtle fire in those who see them even from a distance, so that they glow with *eros*" (Xenophon *Kyropaidia* 5.1.16. Halperin 1986: 63 n.5.]

[†]X 19–23. Surely, friendly eye-contact from an admirer for the space of three deep breaths is an unmistakable message in its own right: the formula serves more for self-confidence.

bound with *ousia*—some real material from the body of the person being enchanted, typically hair[25]—and thrown into the sea. The inscription reads, "Make Miss So-and-so love me." CXVII (from the first century B.C.E.) requires "two strands of her hair." XVI, XIXa, and LXXXIV, all prescription love spells, were actually found wrapped with hair.[26] The progressive power of a spell to force its victim from her house and along the streets to yours can be watched in the flickering of seven wicks made from the hawser of a wrecked ship at VII 593–619: "If the first flame sputters, know that she has been seized by the demon; the second, that she has come out; the third, that she is walking; the fourth, that she is arriving; the fifth, that she is at the gate; the sixth, that she is at the doorlatch; the seventh, that she has entered the house."

Many *agôgai*, like Pamphile's, employ fire; *empuron*, "in the fire," is even used as a rubric.[27] The obvious symbolism of burning passion felt as internal heat and fire occurs also in the commands ("may the soul and heart of Miss So-and-so burn and be on fire until she comes loving to me So-and-so," XXXVI 81–2) and in the act of placing the inscribed papyrus (with *ousia*) in the dry-heat room of a public bathhouse (XXXVI 75; Kuhnert).

But in some ways a more revealing aspect of the spell-worker's fire is not its heat but the fact that it is specifically lighted at night. For *agôgai* are fundamentally generated not by a belief in some thermal technology as such but from a dramatic scene of nocturnal isolation with well-defined psychological features and a consistent strategy of duplicitous projection. If we look not at the pre-scientific *beliefs* (such as the power of "sympathetic magic") that may be extrapolated from the procedures but rather at their rhetoric, drama, and social psychology, we will be able to reach a much more authentic understanding of their tenor and function in the lives of ancient lovers.

A night scene. When the setting for an *agôgê* is specified, the time is night, the place is ordinarily a high room or rooftop from which the agent may speak to and observe the moon or the planet Venus, and the equipment includes a lamp or fire and sundry materials. There are twelve secure examples of such rites in PGM and PDM: IV 1716–870 (Sword of Dardanos), 1496–595 (= XXXVI 333–60), 2006–125 (Pitys' *agôgê*), 2441–621, 2708–84, 2891–942, VII 862–918 (Lunar spell of Klaudianos), XII 376–96, xiv 1070–7, XXXVI 134–60 (a night-rite at one's own house door), lxi 112–7, and LXI 1–38. Other *agôgai* involving lamps (VII 593–619, LXII 1–24) are almost certainly to be performed as night scenes, even though darkness and stars and sleep are not mentioned. In order not to misperceive the psychological and social relations implied in this scene, it must be divided into two aspects: the ritual scene of the agent, typically a man about to go to bed, and the imagined scene of the victim, typically a woman asleep in her own house.

The agent. "Keep the offering (a mixture of drowned field mouse, moon beetles, goat fat, baboon dung, two ibis eggs, etc.) in a lead box, and whenever you want to enact it, remove a little and build a coal fire and climb up onto a high house and offer it saying the following formula at moon-rise" (IV 2466–70). The agent stands facing the night sky, looking at the moon (or the planet Venus), addressing a long prayer to her and watching for the goddess' reactions: "If you see the star (Venus) glowing, it is a sign that she (the victim) has been hit; if you see it scattering sparks, she has begun to walk along the road; if it assumes an oblong shape like a lamp, she has arrived" (IV 2939–42).[28] Certain preliminary steps may be required during the preceding day, such as placing an inscribed ass' hide under a corpse at sunset (IV 2038–41) or burying a wax Osiris under her doorsill (lxi 116), but the dormant power of such preparations is only awakened to life in the dead of night.

The victim. The person to be affected by an *agôgê* is usually sleeping in her own bed and what the agent wishes for her is an increasingly powerful feeling of restlessness and inner torment so that she cannot sleep. "Take sweet sleep away from her, let her eyelids not touch and adhere to each other, let her be worn down with insomniac anxieties focused on me" (IV 2735–9).[29] "Isis is twisting and turning on her holy bed. . . . Make So-and-so, daughter of So-and-so, have insomnia, feel flighty, be hungry and thirsty, get no sleep, and lust for me So-and-so, son of So-and-so, with a gut-deep lust until she comes and makes her female genitals adhere to my male genitals. If she wants to sleep, put thorn-filled leather whips underneath her and impale her temples with wooden spikes" (XXXVI 142, 147–52). The anxiety wished upon her is variously elaborated in terms of physical and mental symptoms such as burning ("burn her psyche with a sleepless fire," IV 2767), disorientation ("make her dizzy, let her not know where she is," LXI 15–6), and frenzy ("let her be terrified, seeing phantoms, sleepless with lust and affection for me," VII 888–9).

Between the agent and the victim, as depicted in these scenarios, there is a curious transference. The rite assigns a role of calm and masterful control to the performer and imagines the victim's scene as one of passionate inner torment. But if we think about the reality of the situation, the intended victim is in all likelihood sleeping peacefully, blissfully ignorant of what some love-struck lunatic is doing on his roof, while the man himself, if he is fixated on this particular woman, is really suffering in that unfortunate and desperate state known as *erôs.* The spells direct that the woman's mind be wholly occupied with thoughts of the lover: from the evidence of the ritual we can say rather that the lover himself is already powerfully preoccupied with thoughts of the victim.[30]

The experience of *erôs* as a victimization by unwanted invasive forces requires powerful therapy. The method of behavior modification employed in these rites is to make the lover go through motions that are masterful and dominating, with a text that suppresses all reference to his felt anxiety and conjures up instead an image of his love-object experiencing the torments that he is actually feeling: "Let her mind be dominated by the powerful constraint of erôs" (IV 2762–3). The texts, of course, are technical manuals for professional (or at least expert) use and they do not provide us with information about the clients who consulted the expert. But it fits better with what we have seen of the psychology and type-scenes of Mediterranean erôs to imagine that the typical client for such a rite was not a Don Juan who wanted to increase the sheer number of his conquests but rather some young male who needed it rather desperately. Philometor, for instance, resorted to such rites because he was first "conquered" by the beauty and speech of Sosipatra. His attempt to project erôs onto her was a calculated response to his own miserable plight.

Just such a client is featured in the second literary picture of an agôgê (as promised above). Allowing again for a certain authorial irony affecting the tone of the narrative, it presents an altogether more credible and realistic context for the actual employment of professional expertise in a problem of lovesickness. Young Glaukias, who is eighteen and has just inherited his father's estate, has fallen in love with Chrysis, the wife of Demeas, and it throws him into utter helplessness so that he can no longer study philosophy. His teacher comes to his rescue by bringing in a Hyperborean mage who can summon demons, call stale corpses to life, and send erôtes to get people. The mage expects four minas up front to buy materials and sixteen more if the rite works. He waits for the waxing moon and at midnight, in an area of the house open to the sky, first summons the shade of Glaukias' father, who reluctantly gives his blessing to the affair, and then makes Hekate come up from the underworld and the Moon come down from the sky. Finally he fashions a little statue of Eros from clay and tells it to go fetch Chrysis. It flies off and after a little while she knocks at the door and rushes in to embrace Glaukias "like a woman absolutely mad with lust." At cockcrow Hekate, the Moon, and Chrysis herself all return to their proper places.*

Under the Lucianic icing of irony there is a substantial and perfectly plausible rendition of the real-life concerns and motives that led people to use PGM rites. By looking at the fuller social context of their performance we can see that agôgai are structured as a system of displacements. The first displacement, presumably of therapeutic value in itself, is the intense imaging of the client's illness as a thing felt by someone else. It might be very healthy for a self-conceived victim of love to act out a scene of mastery

---

*Lucian *Philopseudes* 13–5. The narrator comments: "But I know that Chrysis; she is a lusty and forward lady, and I don't see why you had any need of a clay ambassador and a magus from the Hyperboreans and Selene herself when for twenty drachmas one could lead (*agagein*) her all the way to the Hyperboreans."

and control, and to see from the outside and at a psychic distance what those torments look like. An *agôgê*, too, is the kind of last-ditch therapy made necessary by a certain cultural conception of *erôs*, and as such it is a therapy that not only proclaims its own extremity but even in a certain sense its own impossibility. For the implied message of the rite is that home-truth enunciated on p. 84 above—there is no cure for *erôs*—except the beloved herself/himself.

The control exercised by the agent is in some part a control over his own desperation, summoning chthonic powers to do terrible things, and puts him in a role opposed to that of the erotic victim he "actually" is. The spiritual authority assumed by the lover is a second kind of displacement, for he speaks with the backing of and sometimes in the person of a mighty Power: "for I have about me the power of the great god, whose name cannot be uttered by anyone except by me alone on account of his power. . . . Hear me because of the constraint, for I have named you on account of So-and-so, daughter of So-and-so, that she have affection for me and do whatever I want" (LXI 23–9). Within this displaced authority—"it is not I the helpless lover who command you but I the god or friend of gods"—we can also detect the real authority of the expert who has designed and administered the rite. Desperate lovers like Glaukias are helped by their friends and also by experts, whose wisdom about personal problems may be couched in language very different from that now current but which was surely effective in its way (a point not appreciated by Lucian).

A third, and particularly revealing, displacement is that which occurs in the diabolic strategy occasionally adopted to enlist the aid of the goddess. To inflict so awful a condition as *erôs* on an unwitting human, the goddess must be persuaded that the intended victim deserves to be punished.

> Let all the cloudy darkness part asunder and let the light of the goddess Aktiophis shine forth for me and let her hear my holy voice. For I come announcing the slander (*diabolê*) of the foul, unholy woman, So-and-so. For she has slandered your holy mysteries, making them known to mortals. It was So-and-so who said this, it was not I who said "I saw the greatest goddess descending from the celestial pole, walking on earth without sandals, carrying a sword, naming a disgusting name." It was So-and-so who said, "I saw the goddess drinking blood." So-and-so said it, I did not: "Aktiophi Ereschigal Neboutosoualeth Phorphorba Satrapammon Choirixie Sarkobora." Proceed to So-and-so and take away her sleep and make her psyche burn; give her mental torment, sting her out of her mind, chase her from every place and every house and bring her thus to me, So-and-so (IV 2471–92, cf. XXXVI 138–44)

The procedure is remarkably duplicitous, and therein lies its resonance with the larger patterns of Mediterranean social relations and with the cultural configuration given to *erôs*. The projection of the lover's *diabolê*, like the similar transfers of his own victimage onto another and of another's commanding power onto himself, can also guide us in interpreting the deep dissonance that exists between the literary creations and the material artefacts in this field.

There are two contrasts to be drawn. First, in literature lovesick clients are usually female and the ritual experts whose help they seek in learning how to counteract or fulfill *erôs* are usually male,[31] whereas the prescription papyri and tablets are predominantly composed by (or on behalf of) men in pursuit of women.[32] The generic rites in manuals, too, regularly and unselfconsciously assume that the client will be a man aiming at a woman.[33] The second contrast is that poetry and novels are fascinated by the powerful crone, often in groups like Macbeth's weird sisters.[34] Yet gangs of ugly women raiding cemeteries and swooping down on handsome young men do not figure in the papyri or tablets. In real life the persons famous for their "magical" powers and knowledge are regularly men, not women (Apuleius *Apologia* 90; Abt 244–55/318–29).

Both contrasts make sense as part of a cultural habit on the part of men to deal with threats of *erôs* by fictitious denial and transfer. When weakened by invading *erôs,* men could seek help through a personal ceremony that reassigned the roles of victim and master and, in the more generalized forum of literature, through the construction of public images which relocated both the victimage (in young women—Theokritos' Simaitha *et aliae*) and the wickeder forms of erotic depredation (in older women—Horace's Canidia *et aliae*).

Women, for all we know, might have resorted to the same ceremonies; in a few cases (p. 81) we know that they did, and this is testimony to the cultural belief that women are potentially victims of Erôs and agents of demonic *erôs* in the same way that men are. But they certainly did not do so in the tangible materials that are left to us in anything like the numbers of men who did so.[35] At a guess, I would say that insofar as women's conceptions of *erôs* as a problem for family politics overlapped with men's, their activities were more likely to take the form of vigilance and direct intervention in their immediate neighborhood. Young women who might fall into lovesickness are considerably more watched and guarded and disciplined than their brothers, and presumably had less easy access to the male experts with their books and to the money required for hiring them. The "old women who know incantations" (Theokritos 2.91) have expert knowledge but tend not to leave much behind them in the way of papyrus, lead, and published poetry. Clement of Alexandria imagines that rich ladies, carried in their litters to public temples, associate with old women and mendicant priests who teach them whispered spells to gain lovers (*Paidagôgos* 3.28.3).

It might be tempting to identify such old women, wrinkled and dressed in black, as a source for the witch fantasy in men's imagination, but they are at most a Rorschach blot onto which men projected facets of their own behavior. One more paradoxical conclusion to be drawn from the confrontation of real *agôgai* with literary fantasies is that Horace's Canidia behaves in a masculine style, and not only because she is energetic in going after what she wants (*mascula libido, Epode* 5.41).

The conceptual or imaginative source of the witch fantasy in men's erotic rituals is revealed in the poetic *diabolê* at IV 2574–601, where the agent accuses his victim of distinctly witchy behavior: Miss So-and-so offered to the goddess an unholy brew—fat of dappled goat and blood and filth, gore of a dead virgin, heart of one untimely dead, *ousia* of a dead dog, a human fetus.[36] He goes on in the same creative vein to paint a picture of a recognizable witch, an unholy, dangerous outcast from the goddess' true worshippers. Yet no secret is made to us of the fact that this is a lie, deliberately concocted as a strategy to discredit the victim and to enlist the goddess' dread powers on the side of the lover. Further, the lie is a version of the lover's own truth, for the macabre handling of charnel material that regularly figures in witch fantasies is all of a piece with the *agôgai*, which require a good deal of animal mutilation, contact with cemeteries, and converse with the violent dead (more on this in section 3).

A Dream of Passion

credimus? an qui amant ipsi sibi somnia fingunt?
"Do we believe? Or do lovers make up dreams for themselves?"

Vergil *Eclogue* 8.108

A final facet of the lover's therapeutic procedure has yet to be disclosed in order to appreciate the many-sidedness of these highly (and in some ways deliberately) misleading texts. He frequently employs a compelling go-between—an Eros, an unquiet corpse, the goddess herself, or any messenger chosen by her.[37] The imagined scenario is that the demonic assistant will literally fly to the victim's house, enter her bedroom and torment her until she comes to the agent's house. The most physical version is "Drag her by the hair and by the feet" (VII 887).[38] The visitation of the compelling Assistant is acted out in a puppet-show at IV 1852–9: after making a clay statuette of Eros to be your Assistant, "go late at night to the house of her whom you wish, tap on her door with the Eros and say to it, 'Look, here is where Miss So-and-so dwells; stand above her and say the words I have chosen, assuming the appearance of the god or demon she worships.'"

But that last clause introduces a notion which, at least in our categories, is something completely different. The Power who will stand over her head in the likeness of a revered deity is a dream. The classic descriptions of significant messages received in sleep represent the dream-speaker hovering over the head of the dream-receiver. The erotic Assistant in *agôgai* accomplishes his mission in a psychic form indistinguishable from influenced dreaming.[39] Indeed, the same ritual is frequently employed for dream-sending (*oneiropompê*) and for love-drawing (IV 2443, VII 877, xiv 1070, LXIV). It is not a question of redeploying the same procedure for a different purpose, rather an *agôgê* is inherently a nocturnal drama set in or near the lover's own bedroom; the imagined narrative of what happens to the victim is a projection of the lover's own disturbed sleep and erotic dreaming.* "Put the leaf (inscribed with an *agôgê*) under your head while you sleep" (xiv 1070–7). "(The Assistant you summon) will stand by you in the night *in your dreams*" (IV 2052–3).[40]

The interlacing of dreams and sex could be explored in some detail, but let me here cite only a few intriguing texts. Dio Chrysostom interprets Paris as a man who fantasized about a perfectly beautiful woman in a daydream. The entire story of Helen was originally Paris' dream, based on his erotic desire, but then he had the status and wealth to carry it out in waking life (20.19–23). In Diktys of Krete's journal of the Trojan War 6.14–5, Ulysses was frightened by powerfully erotic dreams, which interpreters saw as a warning against incest with his own son. The omen is fulfilled when Telegonus and Ulysses kill each other. Apollonios' Medea is entranced at the sight of Jason: as he leaves his image stays in her mind as if she were dreaming and it remains there as a second level of reality during her waking moments (*Argonautika* 3.442–58). Best of all, "when night came on again, Artaxerxes was on fire, and Erôs reminded him how beautiful were Kallirhoe's eyes, how fine her features. He praised her hair, her walk, her voice, how she had entered the courtroom, how she had stood and spoken and kept silent, how she had showed modesty and how she had wept. He kept awake most of the night and only fell asleep long enough to see Kallirhoe in his dreams" (Chariton *Kallirhoe* 6.7).

These literary elaborations are based on a widespread, but little studied, association of dreams and sex which is summed up in the verb (*ex*)*oneirôttô*, noun (*ex*)*oneirôgmos* or *oneirôxis*. The verbal suffix -*ôttô*/-*ôssô* indicates a physical disturbance, usually of an unhealthy sort (Kühner-Blass 328.9). Observations concerning such dreams are plentiful in Hippokrates, Aristotle, Galen, and similar writers. The term applies not only to the dreams of men accompanied by seminal emissions but also to women's erotic dreams: Aristotle *Gen. Anim.* 739ᵃ21–7, *Hist. Anim.* 10.6 (637ᵃ27–8), 10.7 (638ᵃ5). The most striking case I know of its use occurs in Celsus' charge that Mary

---

*Aristotle *On Dreams* 2 has a very acute analysis of the parahypnotic fantasies of emotionally aroused people: the timorous man seems to see his enemy approaching, the amorous man his beloved (460ᵇ1–15).

Magdalene's encounter with the resurrected Jesus was only the *oneirôgmos* of a sexually excited (*paroistros*) woman.[41]

To give a rounded account of this erotic therapy one should also include (though there is not room to do it here) the rites of dream-sending (Eitrem forthcoming). In Pseudo-Kallisthenes' *Alexander* the Egyptian pharaoh-in-exile, Nektanebos, meets Olympias and agrees to help her with his knowledge.

> Nektanebos went forth from the palace and quickly picked and gathered a plant which he knew suitable for provoking dreams. And having rapidly done this, he made a female body of wax[42] and wrote on the figure Olympias' name. Then he made a bed of wax and put on it the statue he had made of Olympias. He lit a fire and poured thereon the broth of the plant, until the spirits appeared to Olympias; for he saw, from the signs there, Ammon united with her. And he rose and said, "My lady, you have conceived from me a boy child who shall be your avenger." And when Olympias awoke from her sleep, she was amazed at the learned diviner, and she said: "I saw the dream and the god that you told me about, and now I wish to be united with him." (Wolohojian 27)

The same disturbing, malevolent imagery occurs both in *agôgai* and in dream-sending rites, such as that of Agathokles (XII 107–21): "Take an all-black cat who died a violent death, write with myrrh on papyrus the following inscription with the dream you want to send and place it in the mouth of the cat." With this we should compare two erotic *agôgai* in which papyrus inscriptions are to be placed in the mouth of dogs who died a violent death (XIXb, XXXVI 361–71) and one which requires that a skull fragment of a man who died violently be placed in the mouth of a wax dog (IV 1872–926). The symbolic and gestural language is similar because the cultural configuration of classical and later Greek *erôs* is shaped with elements of violence and dreaming that our culture keeps at arm's length.

There are many *agôgai* like these two that do not happen to contain explicit references to the night scene which I sketched above. If we correctly place the typical enactment of such rites in the lamp-lit world of a lovesick man alone with his feelings and about to enter the powerful underworld of his own psyche, then *agôgai* again turn out to make sense as psychodramas in which intensely disturbing emotions are manipulated and treated. Taken together, they give us a uniquely vivid view of personal anxiety in a Mediterranean cultural setting, with their characteristic self-dramatization, suicidal intensity, and masking procedures.

3. The Torments of Psychê

A tiny but deeply disquieting terracotta statuette in the Louvre shows a woman on her knees, hands behind her back, pierced with thirteen nails.[43]

Instructions for such an artefact are given at IV 296ff., where a wax or clay image of a kneeling and bound woman is to be accompanied by a statuette of Ares standing over her and plunging a sword into her neck. Each body part on the female is to be inscribed with a magical phrase and pierced with one of thirteen copper needles while the agent says "I pierce such-and-such part of Miss So-and-so, in order that she have no one in mind but me, Mr. So-and-so."

The purpose expressed in the words is psychological—the lover aims to create in his victim a state of mental fixation on himself—but the imagery is physically violent, even sadistic. A contrast between psychological "bonding" and physical torment is even clearer in the spell known as the Sword of Dardanos (IV 1716–870), in which a magnet is engraved on one side with Psyche being ridden by Aphrodite above and burned by a torch-holding Eros below and on the other side with Eros and Psyche embracing.

The problem can be posed in more general terms by noting that a good deal of covert erotic ceremonial employs the objects, methods, and language found in the procedures against enemies known as *katadesmoi* or binding spells.* The statue instructions cited above are entitled *philtrokatadesmos,* which might seem to be a simple contradiction in terms—at least on a certain understanding of affection and desire and the desirability of mutual affection. The fundamental idea behind binding spells and *agôgai* alike is constraint. Compare to the Louvre figurine the procedure at V 304–69: an iron ring is wrapped inside a sheet of papyrus or lead, inscribed "Let his mind be bound (*katadethêtô*)," pierced with the pointed stylus, tied round with knots while saying "I bind (*katadesmeuô*) So-and-so to such-and-such an action," then placed either in an unused well or in the grave of one untimely dead. Or the colorful "I bind you, Theodotis daughter of Eus, by the tail of the snake and by the mouth of the crocodile and by the horns of the ram and by the venom of the asp and by the whiskers of the cat and by the penis of the god, that you may not be able to have intercourse ever with another man either frontally or anally, nor to fellate[44] nor to take pleasure with another man except me alone Ammonion Hermitaris."[45]

Audollent rather indiscriminately bundles together incantations designed to curse love-rivals, divorce couples, make a pimp's business decline, and bring a desirable person to one's door.[46] It is only the last that interests us here. Lead texts, rolled up, frequently pierced with a nail and often found

---

*Klearkhos offers a variety of explanations for the popular notion that men whose wreath comes undone at a symposium are suffering from *erôs,* one of which is that it is only the bound who come undone: "for men in love have been bound," *katadedento gar hoi erôntes* (Klearchos frag. 24 Wehrli = Athenaios 15.670C). Other instances of unbound or slipping wreaths signifying love: Asklepiades *Anth. Pal.* 12.135 (18 Gow-Page), Kallimakhos *epigram* 44, Ovid *Amores* 1.6.37–8.

in tombs, contain commands to powerful spirits identical to those in papyrus texts—to take away the sleep of a named woman, to make her burn with love for a named man, to make her think constantly of him: *coge illam mecum coitus facere* (DT 230).[47] Operations for bringing about a divorce or enmity between friends naturally invoke Typhon,[48] but he also figures prominently in *agôgai,* both by name and symbolically in the use of ass' blood (VII 467–77, XXXIIa, XXXVI 69–101). Like binding spells, erotic rites employ the violent and untimely dead as agents.[49] The first effect of some *agôgai* is to send the affected person to her bed feeling ill;[*] to this we may compare CXXIV, a spell designed specifically to cause illness (*kataklitikon*), which uses a wax doll pierced with bones and placed in a pot of water.[50]

The forces brought to bear for erotic constraint are in principle deadly: the *agôgê* demonstrated to Hadrian "evoked in one hour, sickened and sent to bed in two hours, killed in seven."[†] Hence both binding spells and *agôgai* can employ animal mutilation to strengthen their point. A test for the reader: which of the following procedures is used for love and which for hate? (A) Smear an inscribed lead tablet with bat's blood, cut open a frog and place the tablet in its stomach, stitch it up and hang it from a reed. (B) Take out a bat's eyes and release it alive, put the eyes in a wax or dough figurine of a dog, pierce the eyes and bury it at a crossroads with an inscribed papyrus. The former (XXXVI 231–55) requests the supreme angels that your enemy Mr. So-and-so drip blood as the frog drips blood, the latter (IV 2943–66) asks Hekate that Miss So-and-so lie awake with nothing on her mind except you.

The Louvre figurine raises thoughts of system-wide female victimage and male dominance. Is this what *erôs* meant (or means) to men—women's bondage, pain, humiliation, submission? The answer is complex. In the previous section I sketched the pretensions of male control and the patterns of gender-transfer used to hide men's vulnerability and erotic agency. The

---

[*] Indicated by (*kata*)*klinein:* IV 2076, 2442, 2624. "Caligula was unhealthy both in mind and body . . . . He was believed to have been drugged by his wife Caesonia with a love potion that sent him mad. He was most of all tormented by sleeplessness" (Suetonius *Calig.* 50).

[†] IV 2449–51; "Be sure to open the door for the woman who is being led by the spell, otherwise she will die," IV 2495. Cp. Theophrastos *Hist.Plant.* 9.11.6 on the effect of different doses of strychnine. Pitys' *agôgê* "attracts, sickens, sends dreams, restrains, answers in dreams" (IV 2076–8). Is XII 376–96 an *agôgê* or a recipe for death by insomnia? It compels a woman to lie awake, day and night, "until she consent" (*heôs sumphônêsêi,* 378), but the words command her to lie awake until she die (*heôs thanei,* 396) and directions promise that she will die without sleep before seven days have passed. In recommending that lovers not use drugs and spells, Ovid argues both that they do not work and that they harm the psyche and the sanity of young women: *nec data profuerint pallentia philtra puellis; philtra nocent animis vimque furoris habent* (*Ars Amat.* 2.105–6). A humorous statement of the death brought by a love potion (metaphorically for love itself): *si semel amoris poculum accepit meri eaque intra pectus se penetravit potio, extemplo et ipsus periit et res et fides* ("property and credit") Plautus *Truc.* 42–4.

Louvre image, existing within a cultural system that assumed and demanded a woman's submission to the controlling male of her family, could certainly not escape that network of meanings. But the submission in question is a social protocol, not a sexual practice, and we should at least be cautious about assuming a perfect isomorphism between the public stance and the private posture. Ancient texts are not as chatty and revelatory about personal and sexual histories as modern writers, but what we can see of personal psychology in the *agôgai* (section 2), framed by the social constraints depicted in section 1, points to four other facets of the bondage imagery that should be given weight as well.

(i) Insofar as the operations are a wish that Miss X come to feel *erôs* as deeply and disturbingly as the operator himself feels it, the binding and piercing represent not a will to dominate but a replication in her of his own experience. The submission in this case is portrayed as a submission to Eros itself, to a painful state of being in which one is afflicted by "affection, desire, pain" (XVI 5–6), though willing someone into that state is of course selfishly motivated. The problem here is one of translating emotions and gestures from one cultural system to another. We—or at least some of us—lack the categories, and hence the experience (except perhaps via nineteenth century opera), to say "I bind you Nilos with great evils: you will love me with a divine *erôs*" (XV).*

(ii) Some of the torments—insomnia, loss of appetite, dizziness—are temporary phenomena, inducements to act rather than ends in themselves. That at least seems to be implied by the frequent stipulation that she feel those things "until she comes to me."[51] This instrumental view of erotic torments runs contrary to the previous one, which sees them as constitutive of *erôs,* but it shows in the agent that same quality of radical self-centering and indifference to the needs of others, which somehow remains innocent of malice. The aseptic distance and respect for persons that are fundamental to some modern social ideologies make it difficult for us to see the petulant bravado of these private rites on its own terms. In a modern context they would be *simply* malicious; in an ancient context they are that and other things as well. In order not to misinterpret the significance of rites of erotic compulsion, we have to grant that they grow organically and naturally in a

---

*Similarly in the Coptic *agôgê* published by Smither, the speaker conjures Iao, Sabaoth, and Rous "that even as I take thee and place thee at the door and the pathway of P-hello the son of Maure, thou shalt take his heart and his mind and thou shalt master his whole body. When he stands, thou shalt not allow him to stand; when he sits down, thou shalt not allow him to sit down; when he sleeps, thou shalt not allow him to sleep; but let him seek after me from village to village, from city to city, from field to field, from country to country, until he comes to me and becomes subject under my feet—I Papapolo the son of Noah, his hand being full of every good thing, until I have fulfilled with him my heart's desire and the longing of my soul, with a good will and an indissoluble love."

culture that assumes a far higher degree of self-serving activity in every sphere of social relations, on the part of every agent and counter-agent, individually and in groups.

(iii) The erotic rhetoric reckons little with days and months: its units of measurement are now and forever.[52] When Pamphile casts her eye on a handsome youth, she aims to bind him with "eternal bonds of profound love" (*amoris profundi pedicis aeternis alligat, Golden Ass* 2.5). The agent in at least some of these cases seems to be aiming at the bondage of marriage, or the equivalent, praying for continuous, life-long love: "all the time of her life" (VII 913–4); "let him continue loving me until he arrives in Hades" (XVI 24–5); *usque ad diem mortis suae* (DT 267). In one case this is explicit: Domitiana adjures the demon to bring the tortured and sleepless Urbanus to her and ask her to return to his house "to be his mate" (*sumbion genesthai*). Her prayer concludes, "Yoke them as mates in marriage and desire, for all the time of their lives; make him subject to her in desire as her slave, desiring no other woman or maiden" (DT 271). Bondage in this event means permanence and stability. From the last text quoted, it might also seem to mean dominance, but I take that to be a private metaphor for Domitiana's real aim, which is not that her husband be publicly known to be her devoted slave but that he be faithful to her.

(iv) Finally, and most importantly, we must look at the real social context of these covert operations. *Agôgai* are a kind of sneak attack waged in the normal warfare of Mediterranean social life. Plato's Diotima generalizes in calling Eros a crafty hunter and a bold plotter against the beautiful (*Symp.* 203D); in fact *agôgai* are aimed as a rule at women and maidens, who are constantly guarded and watched by their own families and by all the neighbors. The means of eliciting consent and independent action on the part of these "passive actors" in the dynamic game of inter-family competition is to rouse their sexual desire. Let us return a final time to the Samian bride observed by Polemo: "And I later learned that it had happened with her consent" (cf. Herzfeld 1985b).

Covert erotic rites operate on exactly the same protocols as parental vigilance, namely, that young women are quite apt to have sexual feelings and minds of their own and might well act on them even though it results in social tragedy and a calamitous fall in the fortunes of a house. Thus, not only are such rites of use to lovelorn swains, they are very useful for the face-saving needs of families whose daughters have actually eluded parental control. If they can claim that some devil made her do it, family honor is not so deeply hurt as it would be by her voluntary wantonness. *Agôgai*, viewed from this angle, are a back-handed tribute to the potential power of female sexual autonomy, though their language is that of divine compulsion, not that of *Our Bodies, Ourselves.*

If the heat of this last analysis properly brings out the invisible writing on love spells—their implied social script—then we have the paradoxical result that these wishes for bondage are a discourse (of sorts) about women's desire; and they speak of women's desire as an experience that will seem to be not forced on them by the expressed choice of a parent or suitor but rather to spring up from within. They are one of the few categories of ancient text that speak at all of female pleasure, and they do so persistently and with a wide range of expression. "May she come melting with *erôs* and affection and intercourse, fully desiring intercourse with Apalos" (XIXa 53). "May she accomplish her own sexuality (*ta aphrodisiaka heautês*)" (IV 404). "Bring her loving me with lust and longing and cherishing and intercourse and a manic *erôs*" (CI 30–1). The social implications of this autonomous desire are alluded to in the neighboring clauses that request forgetfulness of parents and relatives, husband and children.[53]

These four considerations do not—and are not intended to— dispel the anguish roused in us by the Louvre image. Rather they are baby-steps on a methodological path that has not yet been widely followed in studying classical and later Greek culture, particularly the subjects of sex, gender, and magic. These terms and practices are bundles of complex, historically specific meanings which are socially constructed according to the interests of cultures and economies very different from our own and hence difficult to translate without losing not just their savor but their very soul. There is no magic phrase, such as "Anthropology!," that will guarantee success to our hermeneutic project, any more than earlier slogans worked to unlock all secrets: "Fisher King," "Mother Goddess," "Class Conflict," "Structuralism." But cultural and social anthropology does at least raise questions and provide comparisons that illuminate much of the ancient material, letting us see much more clearly just how familiar and how strange it really is.

Interlude:
Reading Against the Grain

4
The Education of Chloe: Hidden Injuries of Sex

A Pastoral Experiment

The Egyptian pharaoh Psammetikhos (as Herodotos tells the tale, *Histories* 2.2) wanted to confirm the common opinion, at least among Egyptians, that they were the oldest people on the face of the earth. Historical records not being available, he devised the following test: he placed two new-born babies, chosen at random, in the care of a shepherd with instructions to keep them isolated in a remote hut and see to it that they heard no human speech at all. They were to be fed directly from nanny-goats, perhaps because a wet-nurse could not be trusted not to croon to them in her arms. The purpose was to determine what articulate and identifiable words babies so raised would first utter. After two years of this nurturance, if one may call it that, the shepherd entered the hut one day and both infants reached out their little hands and said "bekos." Since, upon inquiry, it was learned that this is the Phrygian word for "bread," Psammetikhos announced that the Phrygians must be the oldest people in the world; he remained confident without further testing that the Egyptians still held at least second place.

It is customary to think of Longus' *Pastorals of Daphnis and Chloe* as a pastoral romance, a sport among the several dozen ancient novels, * both the first of its kind and the last until Boccaccio's *Ameto* (1341) and the spate of sixteenth-century imitations. But the practice of reading backwards in literary history, from later works in a tradition to earlier ones, can produce a dyslexic perception of the distinctive characteristics of the earlier ones, not

---

*Only seven novels survive (five in Greek, two in Latin) and two of those are seriously fractured (Petronius and Xenophon of Ephesos). Fragments of some two dozen other Greek novels are known from papyrus (see Stephens and Winkler, forthcoming). For a brief but powerful justification of the term "novel" in relation to Longus' text, see Turner 1968.

written to be the founding instances of a "tradition."* In Longus' case what is often missed is the interesting fact that Daphnis and Chloe, the two exposed infants who grow up on the island of Lesbos to be suspiciously handsome teenagers ("a beauty more than rustic," 1.7[1]), are not raised from childhood as goatherd and shepherdess. On the contrary, their foster-parents, who are subsistence farmers of dependent (though not servile) status (3.31), have given them an education and a nurturance above the usual level of peasant life, banking their hopes for the future on the foundlings' beauty and the expensive recognition tokens that were discovered with them. If Dryas and Lamon had their way, the children would serve as an economic step up for their households, either through their intrinsic value in the bartering process of arranged marriages or (less likely) through a re-union with their natural, and evidently wealthy, parents.[2]

Erôs has other ideas. He appears simultaneously to the two fathers in a dream and directs them to send Daphnis and Chloe, now fifteen and thirteen years old respectively,[†] out into the fields to tend the goats and sheep.

> On seeing this dream they were upset at the prospect that their children would be shepherds and goatherds, for their swaddling clothes and tokens had held out hopes of a better lot. For that reason they had been rearing them with more delicate food and care, and had been teaching them letters and providing them with every good thing that was available in a rural environment. But they decided that they had to obey the gods . . . , so they sent them out to tend the herds and taught them the routine—how to graze their flocks before noon and to rest them when the heat was oppressive, when to lead them to water and when back to sleep, in which cases to use the crook and in which the voice alone. (1.8)

This unexpected event decisively shapes the plot by re-shaping the paternal intentions.[3] The playful and powerful godlet Erôs, like Psammetikhos in his own way, is conducting a pastoral experiment. What will happen when two adolescents are set apart from the enculturating influences not only of urban society in Mytilene but of the ambitious foster-parents who want to rear them to a higher station in life than that of rural peasantry? Their education in letters cut short, what will they learn in the open fields?

The short, abstract answer is that Erôs' experiment will display in turn the relative contributions of nature, culture, and happenstance to the erotic development of two attractive teenagers. Some readers dwell on the charm

---

*Halperin 1983 shows how this backwards reading has infected our current readings of Theokritos.

† Since they were nursed by a sheep and a nanny goat who were also nursing their own kids, Daphnis and Chloe were born at about the same time that the herds drop their young—late winter, early spring (J. Campbell 21–3). Eros' pastoral experiment begins in spring (1.9), so Daphnis and Chloe have just had their thirteenth and fifteenth birthdays.

of *D&C*,[4] others on its rustic comedy (Anderson) or its "aesthetic cogency of plot and symbol" (Heiserman 140) or its place in the bucolic tradition.[5] Calling it a *pastoral experiment* is my attempt to do justice both to its artifice and to what I perceive as its serious intellectual play with social reality. Longus and Erôs, designing authors both, have fashioned episodes as theorems to test (as it were) the interplay of instinct and learning, of nature and convention.[6] At some points they seem to suggest the possibility that without certain forms of schooling human beings might not succeed in being sexually active at all but would sit in helpless frustration like Daphnis at 3.14: after lying with Chloe in a naked embrace and then vainly imitating the sheep's position for copulation, "Daphnis sat down and cried to think that he was more ignorant (literally, more uninstructed, *amathesteros*) than the rams in the works of *erôs* (desire)."[*]

D&C is not about the natural growth of erotic instinct but about the inadequacy of instinct to realize itself and about the many kinds of knowledge, education, and training required both to formulate the very meaning of spontaneous feelings and then to express them in appropriate action.[7] Longus' tentative and exploratory fiction is, we might say, more about culture than about nature, and at times it seems to lead us in the direction of the thesis that sex itself is in no recoverable sense a natural fact but is through and through a social reality. Insofar as that is true, we must wonder why the mythos of Chloe is a tale specifically of rape repeatedly escaped and yet continually and disturbingly re-surfacing.[8]

My central topic in this chapter is the inherent violence of the cultural system discovered by Daphnis and Chloe as a necessary supplement to their untutored impulses ("they wanted something but did not know what they wanted," 1.22) and the unequal impact of that violence. As will appear below, the novel begins by positing an innocent equality between Daphnis and Chloe, explores her dawning and unclouded consciousness of *erôs*, but thereafter undertakes a serious and repeated inspection of the forms of sexual violence to which Chloe—and to a certain extent Daphnis—is subject. The

---

[*] "In the always diagnostic area of sex, where control of behavior proceeds phylogenetically from gonadal, to pituitary, to central nervous system prepotency, a similar evolutionary trend away from fixed activity sequences toward generalized arousal and 'increasing flexibility and modifiability of sexual patterns' is apparent; a trend of which the justly famous cultural variation in the sexual practices of man would seem to represent a logical extension. Thus, in apparent paradox, an increasing autonomy, hierarchical complexity, and regnancy of ongoing central nervous system activity seem to go hand in hand with a less fully detailed determination of such activity by the structure of the central nervous system in and of itself; i.e., intrinsically" (Geertz 75–6). Geertz goes on to cite in a footnote the fact that adult male rodents reared in isolation copulate normally the first time they are offered an estrous female, where similarly inexperienced adult male chimpanzees usually do not understand what to do and have to be taught to copulate.

sweetness of the novel's overall tone cannot hide—perhaps does not try to hide— the pain of sexual acculturation. In some ways I would compare Chloe's (and the reader's) experience to that of noticing a bruise on one's body and not being able to recall the moment of actual injury. (This happens to me a lot.) There may be plausible ways to explain how one can discover, after the fact and yet for the first time, an *already inflicted wound*: sometimes the shock of a collision focuses us on the persons or objects involved rather than on the actual physical pain, particularly in minor scrapes and embarrassing bumps. But the traumatic notion that adult female sexuality is a kind of inescapable vulnerability is more troubling by a quantum leap. The notion itself, discovered in the course of Chloe's education (which is conducted largely in terms of Daphnis' more explicit education, Chloe becoming more and more a problematically mute pupil), feels like a deep, discolored bruise whose moment and manner of infliction have been erased.

Longus' controlled experiment, placing the youngsters in an artificially "natural" environment, seems designed to test whether there was ever a "natural" period before that wound was inflicted, either in the individual's consciousness or in the history of our culture. Given that Chloe begins her adolescence with such liveliness and zest, what brings it about that she is increasingly cramped and constrained? (There is no mention of menstruation in the book, but Chloe increasingly suffers what we might call social cramps.) The answer is directly tied to the threat of violence against her: the restraints gradually imposed on her earlier freedom come at her in hints and waves, as she learns that the world about her is organized around the *idea* of female vulnerability. But Longus' picture of a natural state in which *erôs* instinctively hums and gambols and flourishes (1.9, 23) makes the education of Chloe into the "realities" of violence seem a thing to be regretted. Could Longus be inviting or at least allowing his readers to wonder at the arbitrariness, the unnaturalness, of a sexual order that inexorably transforms females into victims?

It is not entirely clear to me how far Longus deliberately raises that question, and my framing of it may reflect the normal anachronism that exists between a twentieth-century urban readership and second-century Mediterranean constructions of the countryside. That is why I call this exploration "reading against the grain." My aim is not to be Longus' ideal second-century novel-reader but to infiltrate his text with questions, like those of a visiting anthropologist, who notices problems which native experiences raise without directly addressing.

Allusion, Ellipsis, and Displaced Authority

Before analyzing the recurring shadow of sexual violation in Chloe's education, the larger issues of interpreting this allusive and elliptical fiction have to be confronted and its relation to social ideology clarified. We cannot charge into the themes of violence and women's (or men's) sexuality in an antique text without first establishing what kind and style of discourse we have before us.

"Second Sophistic" is the (to us, rather misleading) name assigned by its first historian, Philostratos, to that brilliant period of Greek literary renaissance under the Roman Empire, centered in the second century C.E.[9] Its stellar figures—Lucian, Herodes Atticus, Pausanias, Achilles Tatius, and many others—employed various styles and produced literary projects of great originality but all acknowledged the authority of a by then classicized tradition of Greek letters.[10] For instance, when Daphnis, after being granted Chloe's hand in marriage, climbs up an almost bare fruit tree to pick the single apple remaining "highest on its high branches" (3.33) and gives it to Chloe, he is enacting a simile found in a three-line fragment of a wedding song by Sappho (fr. 105a Lobel-Page):

> like the sweetapple ripening to red on the topmost branch,
> on the very tip of the topmost branch, and the apple-pickers
>   have overlooked it—
> no, they haven't overlooked it but they could not reach it.

It is as if Longus' characters, living as they do on the island of Lesbos, now and again just happen to come across the same scenes which Sappho saw. The location (Lesbos), the occasion (hymeneal), and the language (*akrois akrotaton : akron ep' akrotatôi*) make the allusion certain, though the loss of Sappho's context makes it difficult to assess the tenor of the allusion.* It is not far-fetched to maintain that if we had more than our meager extant flotsam of earlier Greek literature concerning the socialization of *erôs*, especially lyric poetry and New Comedy, we would be much better equipped to appreciate that stratum of Longus' fiction which is a deft collage of earlier texts.

The same deftness and allusiveness are also characteristic of other sophisticated writers of texts on rustic subjects,[11] which help us date Longus to the late second, early third century C.E. But such brevity, understatement, and appeal to a common fund of high-literate tradition also cause deep problems of interpretation. There is no real doubt nowadays that Longus has fashioned and faceted his novel like a careful gem-cutter and that its mirroring of multiple poetic traditions is in some measure to be taken "seriously," in

---

*In particular whether the bride compared to the unreached fruit remains unplucked in the rest of the wedding song: see Chapter Six, pp. 183–4. The distinctive feature of Longus' scene is that Chloe is sad and angry at Daphnis' attempt to pluck the apple.

contrast perhaps to the more rhinestone quality of Aelian's and Alkiphron's *Rustic Letters*.

Longus' allusion and ellipsis make the temptation particularly strong to supply *D&C* with a framework and interpretive perspective not explicitly vouched for in the text. * The temptation is real—and it is not simply to be resisted, for Longus wants us to supply a good deal of information not there, such as our knowledge of Sappho's hymeneal song and indeed of the large body of New Comedy, forensic rhetoric,[12] pastoral poetry, and earlier love novels. This means that in tracing the thematics of violence in Chloe's education and socialization we ought on the one hand to be cautious not to fill in those deliberate gaps with fantasies of our own making (a well-worn warning) and on the other we must be alert to the possible significance of the almost-said, the discretely understated, the meaningful gestures left incomplete.

The narrator (who is unnamed and not automatically to be identified with the author Longus) complicates the hermeneutic issue by sidestepping responsibility for his story. His compact proem posits a doubly displaced origin for the ensuing narrative.

> While hunting game on Lesbos I saw in a grove of Nymphs the most beautiful vision I ever saw—an image inscribed, a narrative of desire . . . . As I watched and wondered a yearning seized me to counterscribe the painting;[13] I searched out an exegete of the icon and I carefully crafted four books, an offering to Eros and the Nymphs and Pan, a joyous possession for all human beings, which will heal anyone who is sick with desire and will console anyone who is sorrowing, will remind anyone who has loved and will educate in advance anyone who has not loved. For it is a universal truth that no one has escaped or will escape Erôs (Desire) as long as there be beauty and eyes to see. And may god grant us soundness of mind as we write the experiences of others.

Note the gaps: the narrator, an unnamed hunter, almost says that the following tale is a record of what the local tour-guide[14] told him in explanation of the figures in an admirable painting. He certainly implies that the literary elaboration of it is his own (*exeponêsamên*), a claim borne out by the text's sophisticated techniques—clausular rhythms, isocola, avoidance of hiatus.[15] But the material itself, he seems to say, is not his creation; rather it is a narrative already laid out in its essential lines in the painting and explained

---

*The rich and (for us) often non-specific suggestiveness has led some modern readers to see more than is there, fancying that *D&C* alludes to religious mysteries, to initiatory scenarios of Dionysos, even to precise though otherwise unattested rituals of Erôs: Chalk, Merkelbach 1960, 1962, 1988; refuted by Berti and Geyer. Mystery-uncodings have also been claimed for Lollianos and Apuleius: these are answered by, among others, Sandy, C. Jones, Winkler 1980 and 1985a.

in more detail by a local authority. Both the painting and the exegete are assigned a prior responsibility for the shape and content of the narrative, designated as *ta tôn allôn,* "the (experiences) of others."

This is surely the author's fiction about his fiction, one that we may come to recognize as a characteristic irony (in its original sense of false modesty) on the author's part. The narrator adopts an attitude of innocence about the fundamentals, as if he could bear no responsibility for the hard data, the basic facts made beautiful in the painting and then even more beautiful in his text. As far as he is concerned, the effects of *erôs* are universal, inescapable, not subject to questioning. *

But the *narrator's* irresponsibility in the proem and elsewhere should be recognized as a pose and should not be misread as the *author's.* This is to say that the order and construction of events, the delicate and allusive style, the saying more by saying less, belong to Longus and are intentional, however little the narrator's voice calls attention to them. These premises are important for our assessment of the forms of social violence portrayed in *D&C* as "facts of life," deliberately chosen for a certain kind of inspection.

The Constrained Life

The allusive style, we might even argue, is really a high refinement of the reserve of ordinary Mediterranean discourse—a reserve based on the caution felt to be necessary in a scarcity economy. For rural Greeks the facts of life *are* fairly harsh and they themselves have regularly said so in ancient literature as in modern times. Anthropologists who have lived in the countryside of Greece describe a scarcity economy in which predation, calculation, and suspicion are paramount features. Many reactions and behaviors in *D&C* are recognizably drawn from the ordinary dangers and difficulties of that culture—or from prior literary treatments of those dangers.[16] A piece of rope is hard to find in Longus' landscape (1.12) and when a hawser is left unguarded it may be stolen (2.13). Property and person are always at risk from marauders coming from the other cities of one's own island, whether they are high-class rowdy youths (2.12) or low-class bandits (1.28, the Pyrrhaian pirates[17]). The possessions of even well-off peasants are cheese and wine and bread (1.16.4). When a foundling baby is rescued, the goatherd

---

* Analogous to the notion of an unchanging "human nature" invoked by Thoukydides (1.22) to justify his recording of the Peloponnesian War. The narrator's reference to his composition as a *ktêma,* as all commentators have noticed, echoes Thoukydides' famous programmatic statement.

waits until cover of darkness before bringing it home (1.3). Chloe is valuable to her future in-laws' household as an extra hand "for the chores" (3.31). *

Though families must save and scrimp they are most reluctant to appear dependent. Favors may be accepted but always with some kind of repayment or gratuity given to show that one is not in need of handouts, that one is not known in the community as poor or unfortunate (1.2.5; Millett 98–100). The community's unwritten accounting system of family status constantly monitors speech and behavior, looking for signs of defect, treachery, or concealed goods.[18] When Daphnis tries to find an excuse to visit Chloe during the depths of winter he imagines himself being interrogated by her father about the plausibility of his cover story (3.6). Dionysophanes similarly tests (*ebasanize*) Lamon's claims about Daphnis (4.20). Questions and suspicion are the permanent backdrop against which all social interactions take place.[†] We might call lying and detecting lies the native equivalents of the hermeneutic demanded by the book itself, insofar as its deliberate program of understatement, as described in the previous section, calls for judicious supplement. The kind of reader demanded by the novel is represented in the novel by the characters who suspect the adequacy of what they are told and who try to ferret out the hidden design.

The classic scene of such canny tact in action is the interview between Lamon and Dryas about the possible marriage of their children: both appear friendly, both are trying to maximize their profit from the transaction, and both are lying through their teeth (3.30–2). The style of communication, of playing cards close to the vest, corresponds on one side to the pressures of peasant life and to Mediterranean norms generally, as observed in modern times, and on the other side to the restraint and understatement which are Longus' own chosen mode of discourse.

The set-up is as follows. In the long, hot summer of Chloe's fifteenth year, suitors come buzzing about her, bringing gifts to her father Dryas. Daphnis, depressed at this development, wants to join their number, but his family is poor and cannot compete with wealthier shepherds. He is afraid even to broach the subject to his father Lamon, but approaches his mother and she discusses it with Lamon at night. He refuses to consider the possibil-

---

*du Boulay 1983 offers a superb analysis of the laments for the birth of a daughter, balancing them off against the rejoicing over the acquisition of a good daughter-in-law. The laments are motivated not by simple misogyny but by the thought that if all goes well and the daughter is raised to be a good, charming, thrifty, and hard-working member of the household she will then be given away and become a valuable resource for someone else's household.

†Little conspiracies occur throughout the book: Chloe does not tell Daphnis about Dorkon's dying kiss (1.31), Daphnis and Chloe lie to their parents about his falling into an animal pit (1.12), Daphnis seconds Lykainion's lie by telling Chloe that he recovered her goose (3.20), the master's son agrees to blame the garden's destruction on the horses (4.10).

ity of marrying his foundling son, whose secret identity might someday be discovered and bring a measure of fortune to them, to a poor shepherdess. Daphnis' mother, however, fearing that her son might commit suicide at this outright denial, conveys to him a different message—that if he can persuade Dryas to give him Chloe with no substantial presents or offerings in return, they would not object to the marriage (3.26). She holds out the hope, without believing it for a moment herself, that Dryas might allow his daughter to choose a poor but handsome goatherd whom she loves rather than force her to marry an older, wealthier man with the face of a baboon. Her sympathetic deception is predicated on her belief that Dryas, who is receiving so many rich offers, would never consent to forgo any profit from the marriage of his only daughter. (Dryas is influenced by his wife's advice that if they accept a handsome offer for Chloe's hand they can use the money for the benefit of their own legitimate son, Chloe's little foster-brother, born not long ago, 3.25.)

Her deception keeps Daphnis from total despair and encourages him to hope for a miracle, which the Nymphs provide by showing him where to find three thousand drachmas in a money-bag from a shipwreck, covered in seaweed and lying near a rotting dolphin. Dryas immediately accepts Daphnis' proposal, even with the condition that he not tell Lamon about the three thousand drachmas. The loops of interconnected lying grow more complex, now that Daphnis is using Dryas to deceive his parents, based on his mother's lie that they would approve a marriage to Chloe that did not cost them anything. Dryas now takes an active part in the cycle of deceit by approaching Lamon "to sue for a groom—an unheard of novelty" (3.30). He finds Lamon measuring his recently winnowed barley and grousing that the year's yield is so small, and Dryas joins them in their sour attitude—"crops have been bad everywhere this year." Dryas asks for Daphnis as his son-in-law, on the grounds that the youngsters love each other. Once again, as with the lie told by Daphnis' mother, adolescent romance is only acknowledged by the grown-ups when it serves as a cover for their intentions to profit ("he said this and much more, knowing that the reward for his persuading Lamon would be the three thousand drachmas" 3.30).

Lamon is nearly checkmated but he manages to postpone accepting the offer by making the excuse that he must consult his landlord, who will visit the estate in the fall. The friendly rounds of drinks that follow this agreement hide both farmers' true states of mind. The mental processes of Dryas are reported in some detail, as he walks back to his own threshing floor and picks over all he knows about Daphnis' history, wondering whether Lamon might be harboring a secret about Daphnis comparable to his own about Chloe (3.32).

The assumption underlying all these interchanges is that people are regularly not telling each other the truth, whether their motives are kindly (Daphnis' mother), romantic (Daphnis), or mercenary (Lamon and Dryas).[*] This is a fundamental feature of much ancient discourse, one which is particularly difficult for modern readers to accept. It flows from an entirely different sense of life's constraints, of the danger one runs in divulging intimate knowledge, since any knowledge is a precious resource in the serious game of protecting and augmenting one's limited family goods.

Dryas and Lamon are not hostile to each other, nor are they merely polite: they enjoy drinking together in the shade when their negotiations are for the moment concluded. Our emphasis on the competitive conditions under which they operate should not mislead us into thinking of Greek social agents as being like the characters in Samuel Beckett's How It Is, slithering through a universe of mud and armed with can-openers to fight each other off. Gilmore 1987a has emphasized that the merciless psychological aggression he found in Andalusia was not incompatible with an extraordinarily gracious charm and politeness, and Herzfeld 1987a has stressed that the entire system summed up under the rubric "honor/shame" might be grasped in a more positive and critical fashion by approaching it with an understanding of the conventions governing hospitality. Yet once these cruder misunderstandings have been eliminated it remains true that some observable Mediterranean behavior appears to be marked by caution, guardedness, and sensitivity to the unspoken.

As a style of communication such deviousness is not only adapted to the conditions of a life conceived to be economically precarious, it also sets up positive values. Lamon and Dryas and their wives and children grow skilled in reading each other's minds and in using their unspoken knowledge in a shrewd and sensitive way to further personal or family goals which might be difficult to discuss openly. Let me compare two other scenes from earlier Greek literature which show a similar delicacy and restraint in dealing with a family's dispositions concerning young love. The first is the very familiar interchange between Nausikaa and her father at the beginning of Odyssey 6. She is reaching the marriageable age, as a dream reminds her (27), and should of course be prepared for that event by having the finest and cleanest clothes in readiness. But to her parents she mentions other motives for her washing expedition, "since she was embarrassed to mention the subject of marriage to her own father. But he understood it all" (66–7). The interchange between Nausikaa and her father is almost telepathic. It is not that she is speaking in a code or misrepresenting her feelings, rather she allows him to see what is on her mind without forcing him to acknowledge her initiative in a matter where the prerogative is nominally his.

---

[*] Zeitlin 1985b has shown how Hippolytos' transition from the naivety of youth requires that he learn the necessity and cost of keeping secrets, the mark of a socialized adult being that he or she experiences the gap between the inner and outer, or true and displayed, selves.

The second is a scene of exceeding charm in Dio's Seventh (Euboian) Oration, partly analyzed above (pp. 21–2). The narrator has come to the remote mountain dwellings of two families who live together. His host has a daughter of marriageable age (*hôraia gamou,* 65), who is serving the food when his brother-in-law returns from hunting with his son, "not a bad-looking young man." The narrator notices that the maiden blushes. He later turns the conversation to the father's plans for her marriage, and both the young people turn red. "The father remarked, 'She will have a poor man for a husband, a hunter like us,' and he smiled as he looked at the young man" (70). The narrator asks when the marriage will take place and the father notes that a good day for that requires a full moon and a clear sky. Shortly after that the narrator begins talking about hunting skills, and the young man enthusiastically volunteers the information that he caught a rabbit in his nets last night, "for the sky was beautifully clear and the moon was as big as it has ever been. At that point both fathers smiled, the maiden's and the youth's, but he was embarrassed and fell silent" (71–2). The scene continues with more teasing[*] and indirect negotiation between the two sets of parents, abetted by their children, and the upshot is that the marriage is set for the day after next.

The apparent reticence and indirection of these three scenes of communication are directly related to the social constraints of fixed and well-defined familial roles, which in turn are a function of (or coordinate with) the real or supposed constraints of material subsistence and the consequent imperative to competition—Phaiakian wealth notwithstanding. Such narrow (to our experience) limits on self-expression represent the matrix within which individuals come to maturity and articulate as best they can their aspirations and desires. Longus' allusive style, which does not reveal the author's intentions, replicates the normal caution and restraint of Mediterranean social intercourse.

It is an appropriate style, too, for a theorematic novel, in which the author may have no single intention but rather experiments with a variety of possibilities and perspectives, shifting from scene to scene. Though Longus is clearly thinking in terms of a social geometry of desire, it is not clear (and may not be true) that he is commited to a single Euclidean system. We should not assume that even he knows how ultimately to coordinate the varied scenes into one grand dogmatic scheme. Instead of privileging in our analysis the author's intentions, which may be imperfectly integrated and

---

[*]The girl's father teases the young man by suggesting that he might want to wait until "the pig is fatter," referring in the first place to the sacrificial victim, but he exclaims that the pig is about to burst with fat. They then further tease him by alluding to the physical effects of lovesickness which they have noticed—his thinness and his restlessness at night. "Be careful lest, while the pig gets fat, this boy gets thin" (78). The lad persists in deflecting this unwelcome attention to his personal behavior, and they finally let him off the hook.

opaque to himself, we should think of the second century's range of sexual attitudes and practices, its set of tropes, and watch Longus turn the kaleidoscope from one to another.

A Conventional Lover

Returning now to the theme of erotic education and what it is that Daphnis and Chloe learn, let us look at some of the gaps between untutored desire and its fully socialized forms. We may begin by comparing the passion of the novel's most conventional and fully realized lover with the "natural" feelings of Daphnis and Chloe as they enter their adolescence.

The conventional picture of a tormented lover, like those encountered in the previous chapter, is best instantiated in *D&C* in the fascinating character of Gnathon. He comes to the country in the entourage of the young master Astylos ("City Boy"). He is a *parasitos* (4.10), a regular dinner guest and hanger-on whose only contribution to the household is his ready tongue and conviviality. From the point of view of working farmers and shepherds, this is not "real" work and Gnathon is scornfully described as a parasite in the modern sense of the term: "a man who had learned how to eat and to drink to inebriation and to have sex while inebriated, and who was nothing other than a gaping jaw (*gnathos*) and a stomach and the parts below the stomach" (4.11). Other predatory lovers, such as Dorkon, Lampis, and Lykainion, are not described in this contemptuous tone, because they work for their living in the recognized country ways. Gnathon represents the full flowering of erotic culture made possible by the accumulation of wealth in the city. "He was educated (*pepaideumenos*) in all love's mythology at the symposia of wanton men" (4.17), as his subsequent lush speech on the beauty of a shepherd and slave shows.

In the fashion of New Comedy, from whose milieu Gnathon seems to be drawn, his passionate love is humorously presented in a set speech as overcoming even his passion for food:

> Your Gnathon is dead and done for, master. I who till now was a lover only of your table, I who formerly swore that nothing was more lovely than a cup of aged wine, I who said that your delicacies were better than the ephebes of Mitylene—now I confess that Daphnis alone seems lovely to me. I no longer taste rich food, even though each day so many dishes of meat, fish, and sweets are prepared; and I would gladly become a nanny goat, eating grass and leaves, if I could listen to Daphnis' syrinx and be guided by him. You must save your Gnathon and overcome unconquerable Erôs. Otherwise, I swear by you, my god, that I will take a dagger and fill my stomach with food and kill myself in front of Daphnis' doors—and you will never again be able to call me your sweet little Gnathon, in your joking way. (4.16)

As with all the other blocking figures, Gnathon's passion itself (apart from the question of his relation to the means of production) is presented in an essentially sympathetic fashion. The response of Astylos, "who was not without his own experience of erotic sorrow" (4.17), is to promise to ask his father to bring Daphnis to the city as Astylos' slave and Gnathon's boyfriend (*erômenos*). It is important to understand why and how this plan is blocked, since the outrage felt by Daphnis and his father at this possibility, although it is in fact based on the principles and protocols I have described in Part One, probably strikes a casual or uncritical modern reader as a perfectly "natural"—that is, heterosexual— sort of revulsion. Most readers take the response to Gnathon to be unequivocally homophobic, and therefore of signal importance in the history of sexual "attitudes." Nonetheless, the strenuous objection of Lamon to Gnathon's plans for Daphnis is not based on moral reservations about same-sex contacts but on more prudential considerations having to do with social disparity. Astylos had earlier (4.17) twitted Gnathon about the fact that he was in love with a stinking goatherd, who should be beneath him. But Lamon knows that Daphnis' true birth is from a higher class and feels forced to reveal that secret in order to prevent Daphnis becoming the "party plaything" (*emparoinêma*, 4.18) of Gnathon. As long as Gnathon seemed to be a station above Daphnis, he could at worst be kidded for his choice. Once it is known that Daphnis is probably the offspring of a free and wealthy family, Gnathon's intentions seem deeply reprehensible. In neither case does anyone object to sex between man and adolescent boy, only to sex between equals in status. Presumably, if Daphnis had really been a simple slave and goatherd, no one of his elders or masters would have seen any unfitness in Gnathon's design: in fact, Astylos and his father agree to transfer Daphnis to their city house "since he is beautiful, better than rustic, and can quickly be taught city ways by Gnathon" (4.19).

One other passage is relevant to this issue. When Gnathon first fell in love with Daphnis, he befriended him and then in the evening came up to him, kissed him, and asked him to present his backside as the nannies do to the billies. Daphnis is slow to understand because, as he says, he has never seen a billy goat mount a billy goat or a ram a ram or a cock a cock. He is unwilling to suffer violence from Gnathon, who is already drunk, and easily knocks him down and runs away "like a puppy" (4.12). I imagine that any casual observer of animal behavior in the lower orders would know that Daphnis' remark is at best a half-truth. It is not that mature males never try to mount other males, which is standard dominance display, but that other males refuse to let them. As with the human society described in Part One, male desire is fairly rambunctious and often indifferent to the gender of its object: the one strict rule is that the exerciser of male desire must not allow himself to be the object of another's. Daphnis is concerned not about his "nature" but about maintaining his identity as an up and coming billy rather than a nanny.

Gnathon is introduced as "naturally a lover of young men" (*phusei paiderastês*, 4.11), a nature or type which as such raises no eyebrows in this fictional universe. But what is found (at least fictionally) offensive about Gnathon's style is his self-indulgence in food, drink, and sex, with its consequent insolence towards the proper boundaries separating classes of people. Actually Gnathon's self-indulgence, which already shows its innocence by its essentially comic presentation, is further rendered innocuous by his ignorance of Daphnis' true identity, and it is finally redeemed by his heroic rescue of Chloe (4.29). Our own sexual categories, constructed around matters of sexual object-choice, make the moral and social meanings of Longus' world somewhat hard to recover. *Its* focus is on Gnathon's lack of restraint and self-discipline, on his social identity as a non-laboring parasite of an extremely wealthy family, in a context where basic goods for most people are severely limited and the appropriate behavior is determined by an ethics of constraint. (The irony, however, is that Longus' own text is evidently a luxury product, and its attitude of shock at city indulgence and the overwrought culture of urban love is itself a pastoral conceit.)

But to play Longus' game and follow the theorems of his pastoral experiment, let us contrast this conventional lover—a lover, for all his faults, through whom we can follow the operations of the protocols and conventions—with the "natural" or instinctive lovers whose discovery of them, though supposedly inevitable, requires a many-sided education in order to bring their instincts into a socially acceptable form.

Natural Lovers

Daphnis and Chloe are unconventional lovers—not only in being (through their own ignorance, in part) outside conventional patterns of seduction and courtship—some of which they re-invent on their own*—but in being examples of what worried Greek culture about early adolescence. Thus, Chloe's earlier sexual maturity and curiosity dramatize aspects of girlhood that a patriarchal order carefully guarded, while Daphnis' energetic explorations as a sixteen-year-old, when he is technically still a *pais* or "boy," represent the sort of precocity in young males which the Greeks acknowledged but preferred not to take seriously. Indeed, against the projected image of conventional courtship, what is truly remarkable about *D&C* is the

---

*Such as the kiss via a drinking cup, 3.8.

sensitive portrayal of the lovers' equality, confirmed by their later indifference to city living even when when they are entitled to indulge in its freedoms.

Equality is not exactly the right word, though the balancing of episodes between Daphnis and Chloe gives some such impression. Rather Chloe is the leader, reaching sexual adolescence at thirteen—she is the first to feel *erôs* and to try to act on it—whereas Daphnis, though he is spurred into feeling a competitive affection for Chloe against the rivalry of Dorkon, does not become fully active in his sexual feelings until he turns sixteen: "Inasmuch as he had reached adolescence (*hêbê*) during the winter months when he was housebound and at leisure, Daphnis now was swelling with eagerness for their kisses and he was avid for their embraces and he was very curious and bold as to all they might do" (3.13).

Chloe, though younger, is ahead of Daphnis in experiencing the mysterious and painful stirrings of *erôs*, and Longus devotes some of his most stunning early pages to exploring her consciousness, leaving Daphnis pretty much on the periphery. When Daphnis has fallen into an animal trap, she helps him to bathe:

Going to the Nymphs' cave with Chloe, Daphnis gave her his chiton and wallet to guard while he stepped into the spring and washed his hair and his entire body. His hair was black and thick, his body was darkened by the sun: one might have conjectured that it took its color from the shadow of his hair. As Chloe watched him, Daphnis seemed to her to be beautiful; because that was the first time she noticed his beauty she supposed that the bath was the cause of it. And as she washed his back his flesh felt soft under her touch, so that she secretly and repeatedly touched herself, testing whether he was the more tender. Then, for the sun was already setting, they drove their flocks home, and Chloe suffered nothing worse than that she desired to see Daphnis bathing again.

The next day, when they came to pasture, Daphnis sat under their accustomed oak tree and piped on his syrinx while he watched his goats at rest and as it were listening to his melodies. Chloe, sitting near by, kept an eye on her flock of sheep but even more was watching Daphnis. Again he seemed to her beautiful as he piped, and this time she supposed that the music was the cause of his beauty, so that she took up the syrinx after him, to see whether she too might become beautiful. She persuaded him to bathe again, and she watched as he bathed, and she touched him as she watched, and she left there still admiring him—and that admiration was the beginning of *erôs*.

She did not know what it was she was suffering—a young maiden raised in the country and not even having heard anyone mention the word *erôs*—but a stressful disquiet claimed her soul, she could not control her eyes and she often said the name "Daphnis." She ignored her food, lay awake at night, forgot her flock. Now she was laughing, now crying; then she was sitting, then leaping up; her face turned pale, then again it burned with a blushing red. Not even a cow stung by a gadfly (*oistros*) was so frisky and active. (1.13)

This indirect presentation of her thoughts and feelings is followed by a long and charming monologue in which she tries to analyze her sickness by its symptoms—pain and burning that cannot be physically located—and begs the Nymphs to help her recover.

Her aggressive experiments are worth noting. She tests (*peirômenê*) the softness of her skin against his, she takes over his syrinx, she maneuvers him into the spring again. Chloe, as some country person might put it, is coming into heat, and she is innocently determined to find out what to do about it. Since sexual aggression was conventionally attributed to married women but denied to maidens, Longus' sympathetic (and always slightly ironic) description of her feelings and her expression of them is somewhat outside the social conventions.

Though Daphnis is made to feel something too, prompted more by rivalry with Dorkon for Chloe's kiss* than by his own slower puberty, Chloe is still leading him by a considerable margin. Longus, I think, underlines her activity by contrasting the story of the ring dove with Chloe's rescue of Daphnis from cattle-rustling pirates at the end of Book One. The ring dove myth (1.27) tells how a beautiful maiden who loved to sing tended cows. She needed no staff or goad to control them since they responded to her songs. But a boy who also tended cows not far away, "beautiful too and musical like the maiden," charmed away eight cows from her herd. The maiden was depressed so the gods turned her into a songbird.

But if that story represents female inferiority ("he entered into competition with her song, and his voice was louder because it was a man's and sweeter because it was a boy's"), Chloe herself has not yet learned that lesson. When Daphnis is kidnapped along with Dorkon's herd of cows—kidnapped because of his beauty (1.28)—it is Chloe who takes Dorkon's syrinx and blows the proper melody as loud as she can. The cows respond to the tune and jump off the ship, drowning the armored pirates and freeing Daphnis.† In contrast to the ring dove, Chloe does not lose but recovers cows and, morover, she does so by virtue of her music, which is loud and effective. The sweet, sad myth of metamorphosis is deliberately set at odds with Chloe's reality.

Chloe's heroism, however, along with her sexiness and spunk, are facts of nature that will in the course of the novel be constrained by culture, that is, by the habits and beliefs of adult society. The naive promptings of desire in both Daphnis and Chloe are repeatedly thwarted until they come to terms with the competitive and hostile economy of adult Greek culture.

---

*She does not wait for him to take it but leaps up and kisses Daphnis, 1.17.

†This heroic intervention had already been anticipated in Chloe's rescue of Daphnis from the animal trap: she had summoned assistance, used her sash as a rope, and helped haul him out (1.12).

"Protocols" remains a useful designation for these fundamental terms, particularly in relation to the agonistic quality of Mediterranean life. Technically speaking, protocols are the conventions and principles of precedence laid down to facilitate the interaction of opposing parties. Literally, they are the first (*prôto-*) sheet of writing glued (*col-*) to a scroll, the primary agreements laying down the terms on which enemy parties will negotiate or which contain fundamental concessions. As framed by the protocols, the energy of sex is conceived not as something that relates friend to friend or equal to equal but more as a dynamic that clarifies a relation between enemies, opposites, unequals. Chloe is made to learn that she can only relate to Daphnis on a permanent and adult basis within a framework that dictates for her an unnatural role as pursued, weaker, and vulnerable to assaults of many kinds. So far from being about innocent hormonal energy, *D&C* is about the painful confrontation of unsocialized youth with the hostilities of real life.

"Real life," however, as I would like to argue, is itself made to seem problematic in this novel, not least by the charm and sympathy with which Longus depicts Chloe's consciousness in the first book. The retraining of that consciousness and its gradual erasure is the theme I will follow in the next sections. To some Greek readers of the second century C.E., the fundamental theorems of Chloe's education probably appeared universal and beyond question, * perhaps even continuous with "nature," but I believe Longus' narrative brings out elements of dissonance as well as harmony between "nature" and "culture." Androcentrism, phallocentrism, and the threat of sexual violence do not turn out to be merely unhappy accidents which might be avoided, rather they combine to form a destiny written into the very premises of human reality—"reality," that is, as it was socially constructed in Longus' day (and for a long time before and since). Daphnis, to be sure, experiences some of this violence but Longus has made Chloe the silent center of the plot: it is she of whom Eros wants to make a *mythos* (2.27) and it is she whose body is discovered to be "essentially" (that is, conventionally) vulnerable to sexual wounding. The lesson Chloe is taught is that "nature" itself (which I take to be a name for those *cultural* imparities that are usually regarded as unquestionable) seems to endorse the painful conventions of male-prominent, phallocentric society. That lesson delivers a blow which the narrator apparently does not feel or notice, and which the reader may not feel at first, but as the discoloration of the bruise spreads across the serene surface of the novel's dénouement, the reader will be hard put not to recognize that the designer of this pastoral experiment (Erôs/

---

*My study of Artemidoros was originally undertaken (in 1980) in tandem with this essay on *D&C* in the hopes of determining what framework of social values about sex and gender readers would typically bring to the work.

Longus) has orchestrated its outcome in ways that seem to imply a greater awareness than either narrator or reader may be prepared to embrace.

Erotic Protocols and Prior Violence

Let us consider some of the crucial moments at which Chloe experiences the shadow and reality of her supposed vulnerability.

"While Daphnis and Chloe were thus playing (*paizontôn*), Erôs devised the following serious event (*spoudên*)" (1.11). In the pastoral world of protected experiment, there is a constant threat of dangerous violence intruding from the wild. The external threat is a mother wolf hunting sheep to feed her young, the internal threat is the attempt of Chloe's other would-be lover, Dorkon, disguised in a wolf-skin, to rape her.* The wolf's predation is made to seem natural (a mother feeding her young), while his imitative predation is by contrast a cultural contrivance. The contrast with the wolf-predator is further signaled by his name, which means "gazelle," as the similarity is underlined by his disguise ("thus turning himself into a beast," hiding in the thickets where "a true wolf" might hide, 1.20). The wolf's intelligence outsmarts human craft, spotting the traps dug to catch her: she sees that they are artful imitations (1.11). Dorkon by contrast is trapped by his own device: the herd-dogs surround him and bite him before he can leap out of his hiding place in the brush and terrify Chloe into submission.

Yet this "serious" intrusion is easily—and significantly—forgotten. "Because they had no experience of erotic assaults, they thought his donning the wolf-skin was a shepherd's joke [*paidian,* childish playfulness]" (1.21.5). Their misperception of his attempted rape is just that—a misperception due to their lack of education. Chloe already knows that men are dangerous; she walks the fields less briskly than Daphnis because she is female (*hôs korê*) and she is keeping a watchful eye out for macho shepherds (*phoboi tôn agerôchôn poimenôn,* 1.28). But she does not know what specifically sexual violence is.

The children's ignorance should not be taken as a model for the reader, which is in effect what those critics recommend who see the various kinds of violence in *D&C* as a simple rejected alternative to the blissful harmony which is Daphnis' and Chloe's "natural" birthright.† Rather, the novel assumes that Chloe's virginity and beauty will be the object of male desire, that men will offer her (later, her parents) gifts to obtain them, and that if gifts fail men may resort to violence. Dorkon's wolf strategem was a fall-

---

*He had first tried to seduce her with gifts (1.15), then to seduce her father with gifts (*thelkhtheis,* 1.19.3) to give her to him in marriage. Force, as a systematic alternative to persuasion, was in Dorkon's mind from the beginning (*dôrois ê biai,* 1.15.1).

†Pandiri; on hunting and predation as a standard erotic trope, see Halperin 1985: 168; 1989: 172, n. 21, and 202, n. 148.

back plan: "after he had failed a second time and had lost good cheese in vain, Dorkon decided to attack Chloe physically when she was alone" (1.20). Dorkon is a "recently bearded young man who knows the works of *erôs* and the meaning of the word" (1.15) whereas Daphnis and Chloe have passively experienced some of the effects of *erôs* but do not know the word, that is, the culturally elaborated forms of courtship, seduction, and love-making.

From the moment he falls in love with her, Dorkon decides that he will have his way with Chloe "either by gifts or by force" (1.15). Chloe does not understand the lover's code, and so she is prepared for neither alternative. Her tentative experience of *erôs* is so unenculturated ("since she was inexperienced in the arts used by a lover," 1.15) that she does not hesitate to accept Dorkon's numerous and expensive gifts—she passes them on to Daphnis. When his attempts at seduction fail, he tries giving gifts to her father for her hand in marriage, and only when that fails does he revert to the second of his original alternatives—violence. This too Chloe misunderstands, even when she looks right at it. Happenstance (the dogs' attack on Dorkon) protects her this time, as the gods do at other times, but the novel's insistence on her innocence about her own victimage stands in an uneasy tension with its repeated focus on such violence, the absence of any moment when Chloe realizes that this is a part of socialized *erôs,* and her caution about walking alone when rough shepherds might see her (1.28).

At an impromptu celebration for Chloe's rescue from enemy soldiers, all the traditional forms of a Greek festival are displayed—feasting, an all-night stay in the fields, religious songs and sacrificial offerings, stories of the old days, tales of the gods, musical competition, imitative dancing (2.32–8). The last three form a complex triad in which the younger generation (Daphnis and Chloe) absorb and adopt from the local patriarchs some of the accepted social meanings of *erôs.* Lamon tells the myth of Pan and Syrinx, in which Syrinx is a maiden singing, playing, tending her flock of goats, whom the goat-god approaches. When she rejects his advances, Pan pursues her to do violence (*es bian*), that is, rape. "Syrinx tried to escape both from Pan and from his violence (*bian*)" (2.34). When she is transformed into reeds, he cuts them down in anger trying to find her. Finally he binds together reeds of unequal length, symbolizing that "their *erôs* was unequal." "She who was then a beautiful maiden is now the musical syrinx."

This tale is closely integrated into the immediately ensuing action. Philetas' son returns carrying an enormous syrinx, so much larger than the ordinary panpipes of shepherds that "one would think this was that very one which Pan first constructed" (2.35). On this syrinx Philetas plays many melodies, including a Dionysiac song to accompany the harvest and vintage while Dryas mimes the actions of the vintage in a dance. Then Daphnis and Chloe too perform a mimetic dance: the narrative they enact is that of Pan and Syrinx. But the sinister and essential elements of force, so vivid in the mythos just related by Longus, are missing from the young lovers' imitation. Daphnis pleads, Chloe smiles her indifference; his pursuit is described by focusing on the charming detail of his tip-toe imitation of goat's hooves. What happened to the rape? Chloe feigns to be tired of the race, she does not pretend that she is terrified of the rapist. Daphnis then takes Philetas' great syrinx and plays three kinds of love-melody—sad longing, persuasion, and invitation to return—none of them violent.

So excellently does Daphnis perform on that old man's syrinx that he is given it as a present, for he is a sort of successor to Philetas and is directed to pass it on to the next worthy successor. Longus thus notices the continuity from generation to generation of the cultural forms which enshrine erotic violence and at the same time conceal it. The role of sheer force is unmistakably central—no other erotic threat or tension could replace rape in such a myth—and it is just as essentially erased from the present-time enactment in mimetic dance. The whole occasion is a celebration for Chloe's rescue from violent men by the saving god Pan: Pan had personally panicked the sailors who had carried her off and he had forced her release. Yet the celebration of this rescue now features a story of the rescuer as arch-enemy of the pastoral woman, Syrinx. The pupils are not forced or cajoled into imitating the myth but spontaneously volunteer, and in their performance they unthinkingly do what we have just been told is an act of violence, do it playfully and cheerfully.

The entire scene then is structured around the initial positing of a point of view (Syrinx' pastoral happiness before the irruption of Pan) and the gradual effacement of all traces of her consciousness. All that remain are, so to speak, the rough marks on the page where the eraser has scraped the surface of the paper. Syrinx is eliminated from the world by a process both narrative (the tale) and imitative (the dance) which both repeats and forgets her suffering. Like children saying a word without knowing what it means Daphnis and Chloe play at rape without taking it seriously. Their imitation on tippy-toe is very pretty, their obliviousness is potentially more serious.

As Chloe was the object of a predator in wolf's clothing, so Daphnis is later watched by a rather more benign predator named Lykainion, "Little She-wolf." Like Dorkon she lies in wait in the thickets for her prey to pass by. Yet she appears not as an apparition of strange horror and violence but as a messenger from the gods. She is able to divine (*katamanteuomenê*) Daphnis' love for Chloe by watching his behavior. She then puts her own desire to acquire him as a lover into action by telling a series of unscrupulous and wholly charming lies. Her first lie is to her aged husband, that she must go off to help a neighbor in labor; her second is to Daphnis, that she needs his help in rescuing one of her geese from an eagle; her third lie is that the Nymphs have appeared to her in a dream and have bid her be Daphnis' teacher, saving him from his frustration by teaching him the works of *erôs*.

Her motivation is distinctly sympathetic as well as erotic: when she had spied on them and seen their sexual difficulties "she felt with them in their sorrow and thought that the time was doubly right—for their salvation and for her desire" (3.15).

Where Gazelle had appeared as a wild wolf, Little She-wolf appears as a sweet, saving teacher sent by the benign goddesses. "Give yourself to me as a pupil," she offers, "and as a favor to those Nymphs I will teach you" (3.17). Daphnis' response is piously enthusiastic: "Daphnis could not hold out against his pleasure but as one might expect of a country boy, a goatherd, a lover, a youth, he threw himself at her feet and supplicated Lykainion to teach him as quickly as possible the art (technê) whereby he could do what he wanted with Chloe, and just as if he were about to be taught something important and truly god-sent he promised to give her a weaned kid and soft cheeses from the first milking and the nanny herself" (3.18).

Here is a first hint of inequality to come: Daphnis is to learn the workings of erôs before Chloe. No premium is to be placed on *his* virginity, although the charm of the relationship between the teenagers as it had been depicted in the early books of Longus' romance had consisted precisely in their mutual, exactly mirroring ignorance of the facts of life. If one of them has to be taught by an outsider before the other, why should Chloe not have been taught by Dorkon how to make love to Daphnis? The very possibility is unthinkable, apparently, but Daphnis' prior initiation is not only thinkable but, it would seem, perfectly "natural." "Nature," then, of her own accord acts to reverse the order in which the lovers had awakened to erôs (Chloe first, Daphnis second), initiating Daphnis into the workings of erôs so that he may gain ascendancy over Chloe. What is a source of pleasure in its own right for Lykainion is to Daphnis only a training exercise in phallocracy.

This scene of mock epiphany reaches its apparent conclusion when Lykainion shows Daphnis that the secret of sex is penetration. But the real lesson is to follow. Daphnis wants to run quickly back to Chloe to practice what he has just learned, lest he forget. But she holds him back to add a footnote to this "erotic education" (erôtikês paidagôgias).

> You must learn this also, Daphnis. Since I am a *gynê* (wife/woman-not-maiden) I did not suffer now. Long ago another man educated me, taking my virginity as his payment. But when Chloe wrestles with you in a bout like this, she will scream and she will cry and she will lie in a large pool of blood as if slain.[19] You should not fear the blood, but at the time when you persuade her to offer herself to you, bring her to this place, so that even if she cries aloud, no one will hear, and even if she weeps tears, no one will see, and even if she is bloodied, she may wash herself in the spring. And remember that it was I who have made you an *anêr* (husband/man-not-boy) before Chloe. (3.19)

This graphic image of a slain victim, crying with pain and bleeding profusely, is very striking: its three elements are repeated as if in a chant first by Lykainion and immediately thereafter by Daphnis. "But Daphnis began thinking about what Lykainion had said and therefore tempered his former zeal, reluctant to trouble Chloe beyond kisses and embraces, not wishing her to shout aloud as against an enemy nor to weep tears of pain nor to be covered with blood as if butchered" (3.20).

We must not, of course, take Lykainion's words as an authoritative revelation.[*] She has shown no scruple about lying in various ways to suit her purposes, and one might see in her warning to Daphnis both a friendly counsel, based on her genuine sympathy for the two youngsters, and a certain exaggeration, designed to encourage Daphnis to keep coming back to her for a while. Daphnis' concern for Chloe is also highlighted here, perhaps for the charm of its naivete. Nevertheless, the content of Lykainion's warning, even if the context shifts it into an ironic mode, is still grim: even the loving, protecting, and tender male falls inevitably into the category of Chloe's enemy (*polemios*). If he thinks about it, Daphnis must recognize that Chloe's pain is inextricable from his own desire: he has to acknowledge his desire as, *inter alia,* a desire to hurt her.

Is that inevitable? The unexamined though ever more problematic protocols of male initiative, phallocentrism, and invasive penetration seem to require it.[†] This troubling thought governs the behavior of Daphnis for the rest of the novel: his fear of her blood/wounding/pain is what keeps the plot from being consummated then and there (3.24). But it is *his* secret. Lykainion's revelation with its dreadful addendum is not imparted to the intended victim, and Daphnis and Chloe continue their relation as more and more distinctly unequal partners, like Abraham and Isaac journeying up the mountain.

Daphnis' feeling of responsibility to protect Chloe, not only from predators but from painful knowledge and from his own desire, is a sign of his growing maturity in conventional terms. He is acting more and more as a

---

[*]To unpack further the constructed notion of female vulnerability, one would have to investigate male jealousy of menstruation, a loss of blood which naturally keeps the body healthy (Dem. 54.12: a spontaneous loss of blood saved the speaker's life) and in jokes such as that about the fool Margites, a man so ignorant that he had to be tricked into having intercourse with his bride: she told him that she had a wound between her legs and that only the application of his penis would cure it. Sources for the homeric *Margites* in Allen 158–9.

[†]Some readers take the author's point to be that Daphnis must learn "to accept the element of masculine aggressiveness" (Turner 1960: 122); "Longus does not shrink from recognising as fundamental in life, and in Eros, the elements of violence, pain and contradiction" (Chalk 46). These readers, philosophically resigned to the "necessity" of male aggressiveness and violence, reproduce in their reading of *D&C* the very ideology of domination that Longus' text renders problematic.

Greek male was expected to act towards women, burdened with the knowledge of his power to injure them. He takes another step along that path in the "highest apple" scene toward the end of Book Three. Spotting the lone apple on a dangerously high branch, he shinnies up the tree, ignoring Chloe when she warns him and tries to prevent him. For one of the last times in the novel we have a flash of Chloe's consciousness: "she was angry at being ignored and went off to the herds" (3.34). Though he manages to charm her by putting the apple in her bosom and speaking sweetly, Daphnis has clearly shown himself a Greek man—one who does not listen to the words of women when they try to restrain his bravado.

Book Four opens with a scene of gardening. In preparation for the arrival of the lord from the city, Lamon tends the lush garden of trees, shrubs, and flowers. It is designed according to the satisfying model of a proper household: the fruit-bearing plants are in the center, stockaded and defended by the non-bearing plants (4.2). The sensuous artistry of nature and the gardener work in perfect cooperation with each other, though in the center of it all is a frozen image of violence. A temple of Dionysos is decorated with paintings of some of his famous myths, each of which recalls death, mutilation, or loss of self—Semele's giving birth, Ariadne abandoned, Lykourgos in bondage, Pentheus in pieces, the defeated armies of India and the Tyrrhenian sailors who tried to kidnap Dionysos. The garden is a microcosm of the pastoral world[20]—protected, fertile, flowering, with a structure of recollected and institutionalized violence in the center. Within the protected sphere memories of danger and force hover like ghosts, and leave a slight chill in the very experience of safety and love. Thus Chloe, worried about the implications of the master's arrival, kisses Daphnis often "but the kisses were fearful and their embraces anxious" (4.6).

There is a rapist here too. A rejected suitor named Lampis plans to make the lord upset with his tenants so that perhaps he will not approve their plans for Daphnis and Chloe to marry. Knowing that the master cherishes this garden he decides to ravage it. It would be too noisy to chop down the trees "so he concentrated his attention on the flowers . . . . Some he rooted up, some he twisted and broke, some he trampled on like a boar" (4.7). The devastation is obviously wanton, and produces long laments from Daphnis and Lamon when they discover it, since their bodies will feel the master's blows. And yet, Daphnis is in a sense Lampis' double. For over against the violent intruder, there is a figure of nurturance and good tending. "There was a spring, which Daphnis discovered for the flowers; the spring was used exclusively for the flowers, and it was called Daphnis' Spring" (4.4). The gentle waterer, the male who found and opened the natural source of water for the flowers, is Daphnis.

Longus makes a symbolic contrast between the rejected suitor, who crushes tender blossoms, and the accepted suitor, who permanently and gently waters them. Daphnis is further placed on the side of gentleness and goodness by the threat of physical punishment to his own body. In this theorem of his longer calculus the author displays one familiar tactic for interpreting sexual violence: bad men do it, good men do not. But this proposition itself is at least obliquely called into question by the concluding scene of the book.

Not a Wedding Song

The wedding night of Daphnis and Chloe is described in the novel's closing paragraph. All the living characters in the novel reappear at the bridal feast, and all are forgiven their transgressions. Lykainion too is there, but the trauma which she foretold and which shaped the course of the action from 3.20 on both is and is not there. Lykainion had said, "*Remember* that it was I who made you a man before Chloe." May we presume that Daphnis and the reader have not forgotten that, nor her careful description of defloration as trauma—the screams, the tears, the pool of blood? "Daphnis and Chloe lay down together naked, embracing each other and kissing, awake during that night more than owls; and Daphnis did some of what Lykainion had taught him; and then Chloe for the first time learned that the things which had taken place in the woods were only the playful games of children" (4.40).

If it were not for the mention of Lykainion and her instruction in the center of that sentence, we could take the image of Daphnis as Chloe's unwilling slayer to be truly forgotten. But there is yet more here to suggest that Chloe's education is presented not as a fact but as a problem. (i) The phrase "playful games of children" circles back to Erôs' original intervention, bringing something "serious" to their pastoral "play" at 1.11. "Serious" there referred to incursions by a predatory wolf and a wolf-clad rapist. The last sentence has a curiously elliptical quality, not saying what happened but only that it was *not* childish and that it was *not* play.

(ii) "Then as night fell everyone accompanied them to the bedroom, some playing on syrinxes, some on flutes, others holding aloft great torches. And when they were near the doors, they were singing *in a harsh and unpleasant voice, as if breaking up the earth with tridents, not singing a hymenaion.*" Again a negative, "not a hymenaion" (wedding song), but this time Longus gives us the positive, "breaking up the earth." This amazing detail of attendant discord, unexplained roughness in the song, is mysterious and unexpected. *

---

*It may be formally compared to the mysterious sound of the pan pipes heard by the Methymnaian marauding expedition: "but it did not gladden them like a syrinx, rather it frightened those who heard it like a war trumpet" (2.26). But that displaced effect is immediately obvious and appropriate: as the narrator says, "these events were intelligible to all who had their wits about them," namely as manifestations of the anger of Pan.

The allusion to sowing fields is perfectly appropriate, since Greek marriage was conventionally said to be for the "sowing" of legitimate children,[21] but the harsh unpleasantness and the explicit contrast to a wedding song are exceedingly odd in such a carefully controlled composition.

(iii) The structure of the entire plot is based on the series of scenes seen by the narrator in the Nymphs' grove in the proem. There too there was a missing element. "In the painting there were women giving birth and others wrapping the infants in swaddling clothes, babies exposed, herd animals nursing them, shepherds taking them up, youngsters coming together, an incursion of brigands, an attack of enemies, many other things and all to do with *erôs.*" The implied narrative is a familiar one in Greek story-telling: infants exposed and nursed by animals are born from maidens raped. Pelopia, raped by her father Aigisthos, Tyro raped by Poseidon, Auge raped by Herakles, Akakallis raped by Apollo. Even when animal-nannies are not part of the story, an exposed infant can often be assumed to be the unfortunate result of a maiden's rape or seduction. If the picture seen by the narrator is indeed a representation precisely of Daphnis' and Chloe's story (a fact hinted at but not quite said), then the circle is complete. Or rather, its lines almost touch but just fail to do so, leaving a carefully designed gap just at the point where the unarguably harshest blow of socially constructed sexuality falls on Chloe. This in turn lends an ominous tone to the last sentence of the novel, which focuses precisely on her and what she then experienced, always through negation rather than by explicit specification: "And then Chloe learned for the first time that the things which had taken place in the woods were only the playful games of children" (4.40)."

(iv) The divinities, in addition to the special figure of the cosmic infant Erôs, who preside over the book are arranged in a revelatory series. They are, by its own testimony, four in number: "He sacrificed to the gods who are in charge of things rustic—Demeter and Dionysos and Pan and the Nymphs" (4.13). The Nymphs are present from the beginning, Pan is introduced to the youngsters as a new object of veneration in Book Two (2.23), Dionysos is patron of the autumn vintage.* But, though there are

---

*D&C is structured in two movements by the seasonal progression from spring to autumn of one year (Books One and Two) and from winter to autumn of a second year (Books Three and Four). Dionysos' vintage is the backdrop of the whole of Book Two, in which the ripening sexual attractiveness of both Daphnis and Chloe is recognized by the community at large: the women tease Daphnis, the men flirt with Chloe (2.2). It is also the backdrop of Book Four, though by a typically deft sidestep Longus describes other Dionysan events, not the vintage itself. The cycle of two movements is demanded in part by the belief that females reach adolescence earlier than males: Chloe, at thirteen, is the first to feel desire and does so spontaneously, where Daphnis is prompted more by competition with a male rival (1.15.4). Sixteen is the age at which boys first reach *hêbê* (the bloom of youthful maturity) and are enrolled in the civic corporation. So it is only in the second year of the novel, when Daphnis has turned sixteen

wheat fields on the estate (1.1) and the wedding guests sing what sounds like a song for the sowing of seed (which occurs in the fall just as the winter rains are beginning*), Demeter seems to be invisible. Or rather, she was there all along in Chloe, whose name is a well known cult title of the goddess[22] whose daughter was seized by Hades and whose thesmophoric ceremonies were fundamental to the well being of every Greek polis (see Chapter Seven). The experiences of Demeter Chloe are allusively present, an absent presence placed at the crucial climax of the autumnal wedding night.

Reading Against the Grain

And what does it finally mean? I find it hard to determine whether the well-concealed Longus had a fundamentally patriarchal attitude to Chloe—that she is to be simultaneously protected and made to undergo a painful rite of passage—or the more critical stance I have outlined here. The former reading is implied by most of the modern critics who have noticed the violence at all.[23] A sophisticated version of the critical issue is proposed by Helene Foley (in a private letter) who sees Longus as "taking a very conscious and polemical stance towards the question of violence and sexuality."

But the larger methodological issue is whether readers should simply be trying to reproduce the author's meaning (if he had one—that is, if he had *one*) as the goal. Should we concede that much authority to the writers we read?[†] If our critical faculties are placed solely in the service of recovering and reanimating an author's meaning, then we have already committed ourselves to the premises and protocols of the past—past structures of cultural violence and their descendants in the bedrooms and mean streets and school curricula of the present. This above all we must not do. The ambiguities and contradictions within the sexual ideology of *D&C*—whether they derive from the author's intention or from internal inconsistencies in the dominant cultural discourse of his age—afford us an opportunity to become resisting readers in the complex guerilla fighting of cultural studies (Fetterley; Flynn and Schweickart) and an occasion to struggle against the tacit, conventional, and violent embrace in which we are held by the past.

(*enhêbêsas* 3.13.4), that he "swells" with lust. At 3.30.4 the fathers acknowledge that their children have now reached the proper age for sleeping with each other.

*Farming is given less prominence in the novel than pasturing, but it is decidedly there: e.g., 3.29.2, 3.30.3.

†Many of the ancient novels, to be sure, are problem texts rather than authoritative texts, designed to provoke rather than to declare, so that the whole question of finding authoritative theses or perspectives may not arise: Winkler 1982a and 1985a, Bartsch.

Part Two:
Gunaikes

5

Penelope's Cunning and Homer's

While reading the *Odyssey* during a sojourn in Sicily in the summer of 1891, the English novelist Samuel Butler got to the description of Circe, who controlled her island without the help of men, and suddenly realized in a flash that the book had been written not by a man but by a woman. He was so taken by this inspiration that he devoted most of the next decade until his death in 1902 to studying and translating the *Iliad* and *Odyssey*. In 1892 he made the further discovery that the *Odyssey* had been written at Trapani, a seaport at the northwest tip of Sicily. The significance of these two discoveries together was that they provided an answer to the burning Homeric question of the day, which was whether the epics had been written by one person or many. For if the *Odyssey* showed a feminine sensibility throughout and was based on close observation of people and places in the port of Trapani, then it must be the work of a single author—since there could not have been two such brilliant women in a small Sicilian seaport at the same time.[1]

Butler published his theories in letters to English journals and in Italian articles and eventually in a book entitled *The Authoress of the Odyssey* (1897). The only favorable response he records came from George Bernard Shaw, who said after Butler lectured on the subject to the Fabian society that he had earlier heard of Butler's notion and had initially thought it was a mere fancy, but that he had re-read the first hundred lines of the *Odyssey* and was convinced that it was certainly true.[2]

What Butler hoped for was, if not approval, at least serious discussion of his ideas by the established Classicists, and this he did not get[3]—a fact about which he complained bitterly in the preface to his book. Perhaps I should apologize to the shade of Samuel Butler, because I too will not be discussing his ideas in any detail. Rather I want to focus attention on what I take to be a much more interesting aspect of his work—namely, his two assumptions about how to read the *Odyssey,* assumptions which squarely blocked his understanding of the epic, both its style of representation and the nature of the society portrayed or created. I will refer to these interpretive premises of Butler's as the anthropological (concerning the nature of the society described) and the narratological (concerning Homer's narrative practice). Butler reads the *Odyssey* as if were an English novel of manners; he treats it as a nineteenth-century written book, not as an oral composition performed for an audience, and he assumes that its point is to describe characters and ways of life. Of course the *Odyssey* does in passing describe characters and ways of life but they are not nineteenth-century English characters or ways of life.

After dwelling a bit on Butler's two assumptions and then taking a short detour to visit a little known scholarly satirist of the ancient world, I will argue that if we view the *Odyssey* not as a novel describing English social conventions but as a story about Mediterranean social practices, then we may see that Homer—whether man or woman—has given Penelope a rather stronger and more cunning role in the plot of Odysseus' homecoming than is often attributed to her. The recognition of this depends largely on a reading of the epic in the light of modern feminist anthropology, which is learning to see the resourcefulness of women in cultures where they had hitherto been reported to be passive victims of male manipulation. But the ambiguities of Penelope's situation and the double bind placed on Greek women generally are captured in the *Odyssey* not only in what the poet represents but on a second level—by the author's own cunning in deliberately avoiding too close a look at what Penelope might be thinking and scheming. This is an intentional sleight of hand on Homer's part, making possible the extraordinary epiphany of Book 23 in which Odysseus and we the audience simultaneously realize that we had underestimated Penelope and that she has richly earned her reputation (*kleos*) for cunning (*mêtis*).

These two interpretive frameworks, comprising Penelope's cleverness and the poet's, together produce a double duplicity, which I take to be necessary for a just appreciation of the normal complexity of women's lives as represented in the poetry and theory of Greek men. Duplicity will also be a key concept in the analysis of Sappho's poetry in the next chapter, as it was in the discussion of *dokimasia* and love spells in Chapters Two and Three.

S. Butler, Critic

It is clear that Butler imagines the conditions of production and dissemination of the *Odyssey* as rather like those of book-publishing in the nineteenth century, and that the purpose of fiction, then and now, is to describe daily life and social manners in a faithful and artistic fashion. He regards the royal family scenes on Phaiakia as "drawn from life" (p. 7). He confesses himself aghast at the rudeness of the young men who compete in games there in Book 8—they boast and swagger and hurl insults: such behavior would not be appropriate on the playing fields of Eton. But if we think instead, as Butler did not, of the behavior of young Greek males, the Phaiakian princes are not so much rude as overzealous, according to their own cultural ideals of manliness and gentlemanliness. In general Butler finds that in the *Odyssey* "the men often both said and did things that no man would say or do, (but) the women were always ladies when the writer chose to make them so" (p. 8). For comparison he brings in Jane Austen, whose "young men . . . are seldom very interesting," though no one "will feel any wish to complain of her for not understanding young men as well as she did young women" (p. 11).

Realizing that Butler conceives, or rather assumes, that the *Odyssey* was produced and circulated in much the same way as a nineteenth-century English novel, it becomes easy to see how he arrived at the notion that it was written by a woman. The nineteenth century in England was not only a great period for women's writing, it was an age in which pseudonyms were widely used by women, writing under men's names. Butler's acuity in reading the gender of the *Odyssey*'s author was honed by the practice of detecting telltale signs of femininity in supposedly masculine literary works. For instance:

> Book vi. is perhaps the loveliest in the whole poem, but I can hardly doubt that if it were given to a *Times* critic of to-day as an anonymous work, and he was told to determine the sex of the writer he would ascribe it to a young unmarried woman without a moment's hesitation. Let the reader note how Nausicaa has to keep her father up to having a clean shirt on when he ought to have one (vi. 60), whereas her younger brothers appear to keep her up to having one for them when they want one. These little touches suggest drawing from life by a female member of Alcinous' own family who knew his little ways from behind the scenes. (p. 145)

Butler regards the practice of sex-detection as normal and claims that "as often as an anonymous work is published," and "even when women are posing as men," the careful reader will have little difficulty in determining the sex of the writer. "I have heard say that a celebrated female authoress was discovered to be a woman by her having spoken of a two-foot *ruler* instead of a two-foot *rule*" (p. 10). This habit of shrewd reading which put all novel-writing under suspicion and investigated it for signs of female authorship is the background out of which Butler's reading of the *Odyssey* sprang.

Nowadays we can easily notice that his assumptions, particularly about social life and the roles of men and women, are anachronistic, when applied to Homer (if not to contemporary writing as well).[4] His list of female traits that supposedly give away the *Odyssey*-writer's sex include severity against women who have disgraced their sex, love of small religious observances,

of white lies and small play-acting, of having things both ways and of money
(pp. 115–24). These are the very traits, though described in less pejorative
terms, that emerge from the sketch of Mediterranean culture presented in
previous chapters, only there they apply not to women but to men. Butler,
unfortunately, did not adjust his interpretation to an anthropological framework. Hence he expresses no qualms about illustrating social life in Homer's
day by contemporary anecdotes, such as:

> I was at an inn once and asked the stately landlady if I could see the landlord.
> She bridled up and answered, "We have no landlord, sir, in this house; I cannot
> see what use a man is in a hotel except to clean boots and windows." There spoke
> Circe and Calypso, but neither of them seem to have made even this much
> exception in man's favour.
> Let the reader ask any single ladies of his acquaintance, who live in a house of
> their own, whether they prefer being waited upon by men or by women, and I
> shall be much surprised if he does not find that they generally avoid having a man
> about the house at all—gardeners of course excepted. But then the gardener
> generally has a wife, and a house of his own. (p. 105)

Butler understands the homeric and Mediterranean past in terms of his
own present. When he translates the advice that Athena gives to Telemakhos,
he hears the voice of his "dear kind old aunt who when I was a boy used to
talk to me just in this way" (p. 121). One of the most glaring of these social
anachronisms is his conclusion that the author must be specifically a *young*
woman because she portrays the suitors of Penelope simultaneously as ardent
lovers and as spongers. "[T]he writer who can tell such a story with a grave
face cannot have even the faintest conception of the way in which a man
feels towards a woman he is in love with . . . ; I conclude, therefore, that
she was still very young, and unmarried" (pp. 127–8). It is tempting to say
that Butler epitomizes the imperial insularity of nineteenth-century Britain,
that radical insensitivity to cultural differences which stands behind the
image of the Englishman abroad who, when the natives do not understand
him, just speaks louder—in English.

But my concern here is not to dwell on Butler's faults. Rather, I would
like to take a positive approach to the strength and subtlety of women
portrayed in the *Odyssey*. In a sense, his reading is only the most extreme
form of the typical modern reaction to the *Odyssey*, which has regularly seen
its female characters as strangely important, albeit in a puzzling and even
contradictory way. Leaving aside older treatments by Decker and Perry,
which are now hardly readable, we find one mainstream modern critic,
commenting on Agamemnon's praise of Penelope in the Underworld ("the
fame of her excellence will never perish, the gods will fashion a beautiful
epic about the shrewd Penelope," 24.196–8), suggesting that those lines

come "near making our *Odysseia* a *Penelopeia*" (J. Finley 3). What I offer here is another interpretation of the *Odyssey* that highlights the fascinating and puzzling centrality of the women in it, especially Penelope, but an interpretation based on a culturally specific appreciation of ancient Mediterranean society. Such an appreciation, I believe, can be gleaned from the *Odyssey* itself, and it should extend to Homer's own activity, not as a novelist but as a performer. Because Butler accepted without question a British-capitalist view of women's—and men's—social character, he missed what I think is the real center of the *Odyssey*'s plot, which is the way in which Penelope, constrained as she is by the competing and irreconcilable demands of social propriety, exerts some degree of real control over events and makes possible the homecoming of her husband, outwitting many deadly enemies and a few friends in the process.

The Anthropology of Cunning (Mêtis)

This reading depends on changing Butler's premises. Of his two assumptions, concerning the way in which the *Odyssey* was produced and the type of society it reflected, the latter is much more important for our purposes. As to the former, we know now that the long tradition of early Greek epic poetry was not produced by writers at all, that the men (and conceivably in some places women?) whose profession was to sing heroic songs composed them afresh for each occasion, but did so from a repertoire of formulas and plots and type-scenes which served the same function as the material a jazz musician or an extempore speaker draws on in the course of improvising a performance on a familiar theme: he has done it all before but not in exactly this way (Kirk 1964, 1976). (The relation of Homer, at the end of that tradition, to writing remains controversial.) But what really led Butler astray was the assumption that well-bred men and women on the Greek island of Ithaka in the time of the Trojan War or during the Greek dark age would have behaved like ladies and gentlemen of his own time and class.

We may be quite sure that Odysseus and Penelope did not conduct themselves like Victoria and Albert. But how did they act? What was the appropriate cultural code followed or violated by Homer's characters? In the main we have to reconstruct this from the opinions and actions of the characters, allowing that what we read in the *Odyssey* is not a real society but a fictional case-study, one which presumably made sense to the real women and men who were its audience and who could appreciate both its verisimilitude in matters of human motivation and its archaizing idealization in matters of material culture (chariots, palaces, and the like).[5] But there is one external source which can be used to fill in the outlines of the cultural picture found

in the *Odyssey* itself, and that is descriptions of life in rural Greece today.*
Such descriptions emphasize the honor of families, the competition between
them for the limited resources of material goods and spiritual honor, and
the strategies of violence and deception that must (alas) be practiced to
preserve honor and avoid shame in this wretched world of ours. Of course
these twentieth-century reports should not be used to read anything into the
Odyssey that is not there. The usefulness of reading them is that they open
our urban eyes, accustomed to television and rear-view mirrors, to the clean
dirt streets of pre-industrial societies, where the gossip of neighbors and the
smell of goats are equally rank. If nothing else such accounts can jolt us out
of some of our unexamined assumptions about Odysseus and Penelope,
assumptions generated by idealizing, whitewashed pictures of ancient
Greece.

One theme that stands out in these accounts, and is fundamental to the
Odyssey, is the prevalence of secrecy and lying, which the natives see as
unfortunate necessities but which they nonetheless practice diligently, constantly, and craftily. In the *Odyssey*, too, people try to guard their secrets,
but privacy is hard to come by, particularly in Odysseus' house, riven as it is
with hostility and distrust, a sort of case-study in the tensions and behaviors
usually found between families rather than inside a household. The suitors
suspect that Telemakhos may try to poison them (2.328–30), while they are
in fact plotting his death by ambush. Antinoos warned the others to keep
quiet "lest someone take the news inside" to Penelope (4.775), and in fact
the herald Medôn was at that very moment on the other side of the courtyard
wall and heard all their plans as they "were weaving a plot (*mêtis*) within"
(4.678).[†] Helios similarly reveals a secret plot to Hephaistos, when he
sees Aphrodite and Ares in bed (8.270). That situation illustrates the social
necessity of cunning: Hephaistos' trickiness enables him to even the odds
against the stronger and swifter Ares (8.329–32).

Surrounded by enemies and threatened with death, Telemakhos advises
Eumaios not to visit old Laertes but to let Penelope *secretly* (*krubdên*) send a
trusted maid with the news of his return. Eumaios in the palace speaks to
Telemakhos "holding his head near, so that the others would not hear"
(17.592).[‡] Telemakhos in Book 1 speaks privately to Mentes, deliberately

---

*Finley 1978 was extraordinarily successful in promoting an anthropological analysis of
homeric society: "The social institutions and values make up a coherent system, and, from our
present outlook, a very alien one, but neither an improbable nor an unfamiliar one in the
experience of modern anthropology" (p. 9), though he wrote his original text in 1954 before
the flowering of Mediterranean anthropological studies.

†Twice in *Daphnis and Chloe* someone overhears important information and uses it (4.18,
29). Inquisitive bystanders may be a stock device of fiction, but they are apparently true to the
experiences, expectations, and habits of the audience.

‡The gesture and the formula for it are repeated in Sparta, but in that case Menelaos does
overhear (4.70).

sitting far away from the crowd (1.132–5) and waiting until the bard had begun to sing (1.155–7), to cover their conversation. Sound travels in this house: in the hall Odysseus can hear Penelope weeping in her room (20.92), and she can hear what each suitor in the hall is saying (20.389). The walls, as we say, have ears—unfriendly ears.

Peter Walcot (1977) has used modern reports of prevalent and normal Greek mendacity to situate culturally and socially the autobiographical lies told by Odysseus to everyone he meets. But lying, as described by du Boulay and J. Campbell and others, does not just mean telling a false story; it refers to a policy of systematic and deliberate misdirection, in matters great and small, in order to protect oneself in a social environment full of enemies and charged with unremitting suspicion. In particular, du Boulay describes how people not only lie to conceal their faults, since enemies will spread news of those faults and damage a family's honor, but also to conceal even trivial facts, since any information that gets out might turn out to be useful in another context. So, for instance, she reports that to prevent the possible shame of a failed marriage negotiation, the village priest (who was the match-maker) met in a cafe with a prospective groom, who was a mason from a nearby village, and discussed with him plans to recondition the church, talking of materials and prices. They then adjourned to his house and discussed the dowry, having covered their trail with the false talk of building, to mislead any people who might have been listening to them or observing them together (du Boulay 1976: 399; Gilsenan). Children are trained to be constantly vigilant against probing, innocent-sounding questions from neighbors and to tell plausible lies (du Boulay 1974: 188–9). Even friends and relatives outside the immediate family are not to be trusted, because those relationships often go sour and former friends will certainly use their knowledge of your weaknesses against you.

In addition to defensive lying, there is aggressive lying, as when Odysseus, newly landed with a pile of treasures on Ithaka, tells a young shepherd that he had to flee Krete for murdering a man who tried to take from him his Trojan booty (13.259–68). The threat is barely veiled and the implication would not be lost on a young Greek shepherd, though this one turns out to be Athena in disguise. Another facet of this continuously shrewd style of discourse turns up shortly thereafter when Odysseus, having learned the truth of Athena's identity, still thinks that she is lying to him about where they are: "I don't think I have actually reached Ithaka . . . ; I think you said this to tease me and to throw my wits off balance" (13.324–8). This resembles the parental teasing of children, observed by Friedl as a regular feature of childrearing practices designed to train the child to be wary of all people and all utterances.* As Mahaffy, one of the earliest to use observations

---

* "Lying to children is one aspect of the general attitude toward truth and falsity characteristic of the village's adults. In the village the word for lies, *psemata,* is used much more freely, with

of modern Greek behavior to interpret ancient texts, puts it, "to deceive an enemy is meritorious, to deceive a stranger innocent, to deceive even a friend perfectly unobjectionable, if any object is to be gained" (Mahaffy 1890: 27, cited by Walcot 1977: 4). The case in the *Odyssey* which has occasioned the most discomfort with modern readers is Odysseus' testing of his father Laertes, which serves no strategic purpose whatsoever. He approaches him to "test . . . whether he will recognize me" (24.215–6; cf. 221, 239). The gratuitousness of the game is clear from Odysseus' momentary hesitation to carry out his plan: "He hesitated whether to kiss and embrace his father . . . ; but he decided it would be craftier (*kerdion,* "better," "more profitable") first to test him with heart-cutting words" (24.235–40). Even close family relations, as Friedl has observed, are not exempt from painful teasing, indeed they may be a privileged site for learning to cope with the world's jabs, and Odysseus may simply be falling into an old family habit when he temporarily breaks the heart of his father.

The willingness to deceive, not only for defensive and aggressive purposes but simply as a habit of life—to keep in practice, as it were— should be taken together with the style of speaking and the comportment described in the previous chapter: cautious, guarded, and sensitive to the unspoken. That quality is summed up in the notion of a "reined-in mind." When Odysseus shares with Telemakhos his plans to remove the armor from the hall and to test the various members of his household, he says forcefully, "If you are truly my son and of my blood, let no one hear that Odysseus is inside," and Telemakhos replies, "Father, you will soon know what kind of spirit I have—slackminded never!" (16.300–1, 309–10). "Slackmindedness" (*khaliphrosunê*)* is a trait of children who have not yet learned to control their public personalities with constant vigilance by erecting a wall of discretion (*pais . . . nêpios êde khaliphrôn,* 19.530; 4.371). The opposite of the man with a reined-in mind is the babbler who guilelessly reveals to others information that may be used against himself or his friends. Athena praises Odysseus for being "close-minded" (*ankhinoos*) and "mentally restrained" (*ekhephrôn,* 13.332), that is, he always has his wits about him, reveals nothing to anyone without cause, and suspects in others a deviousness that might be equal to his own. The interpretation of *ekhe-* as not just "having" a good mind but as "restraining" one's speech and thoughts, playing close to the vest, is

---

less emotional intensity, and with a milder pejorative connotation than Americans use the English word. . . . Each man and woman expects to develop skills both in the art of guilefulness and in the art of detecting guilefulness in others. Vasilika's villagers are not humiliated because someone tries to deceive them; they become angry only if the deception succeeds. . . . Older children who have learned to turn the tables on their parents and try to deceive them are admired even as they are scolded" (Friedl 1962: 80).

*Not derived from *khalis,* "neat wine" (Hipponax), as opined by Liddell-Scott-Jones, but from *khalân,* "loosen, relax" (Chantraine).

supported by the similar formation *ekhethumos,* used by Hephaistos of his unfaithful wife Aphrodite: "she is beautiful but does not hold in her feelings" (8.320; Thornton 84). *Ekhephrôn,* of course, is a frequent epithet for Penelope too, whose strategic caution and self-control we will look at more closely below.

The image which sums up these traits for me is that moment at the end of Book 16 when Odysseus, once again disguised as an old beggar, and Telemakhos welcome Eumaios back to his hut, who brings with him the news that the heavily armed suitors have sailed back into the harbor after their failure to ambush Telemakhos. Odysseus and Telemakhos have just been plotting how they might remove the suitors' arms from the hall and so have a chance of overcoming them. When Eumaios, who is not privy to their secrets, inadvertently reminds them of the suitors' hostility and weaponry, "Telemakhos smiled, glancing across to his father, but he avoided the swineherd's eye" (16.476–7). That concealed smile and wordless glance are signs that Telemakhos knows and appreciates the deadly game he is involved in and that he has learned to keep his knowledge and intentions strictly to himself. He is no *khaliphrôn,* and behind his fixed, wordless look there lies a ceaseless activity of calculation, suspicion, and anticipation of the duplicities around him.

Multiple Perspectives, Gender Irony, and Victimage Theories

To round out this sketch of the strategies of deception and covert communication in Homer, let us turn to the habit of making confident assertions in the face of ambiguity. Uncertainty typifies the mental states of characters in the early books—is Odysseus alive or dead, should Penelope remarry and if so by what procedure, are the suitors paying appropriate court to Penelope? The questions are interdependent and insoluble, but this does not prevent characters from articulating positions which sound like statements of fact but whose actual meaning in context is somewhat less dogmatic. For instance, at various points in the narrative Penelope, Laertes, and Telemakhos state in unambiguous terms that Odysseus is dead, even though what they mean is something slightly less categorical, along the lines of "I'm not such a fool as to cherish a remote hope for his return, however much I fondly desire it." Telemakhos thus expresses himself both to friends (1.219–20) and to enemies (1.413–6), so it is not a simple matter of lying but a related habit of overstatement, frequently flavored with pessimism. One might recall here the self-dramatization found in the erotic magical papyri (Chapter Three).

What we must learn to appreciate about the firm assertions of Odyssean characters is that when they make such assertions they are often jostling for position, extending their area of confidence a bit farther than the facts warrant, and that they are perfectly aware of unstated qualifications, alternate possibilities, and opposing views. [*] This habit of vaunting is displayed by men and women alike, such as when Penelope despairs of her own situation, as she is frequently portrayed as doing. [†] One of the unwritten rules of this discourse is that, in any situation which admits of the slightest uncertainty of interpretation, exaggerations multiply within a framework of contest. We must always posit a polyphony of opinions firmly held, even when others keep their counsel.

Of chief interest to us in this connection are the utterances of men concerning women as a class. Misogyny, or better, distrust of women, is a common trope of male discourse in Mediterranean cultures (Brandes), but what is perhaps distinctive to the *Odyssey* is the very restricted conditions under which such suspicion finds expression. Alongside the extravagant praise of exemplary women such as Penelope and some of the heroines in Hades, Homer shows us just one character who, on two different occasions, both praises Penelope and yet slides into a condemnation of all women. When Agamemnon, whose experience with his wife is perhaps not to be taken as typical, meets Odysseus in the Underworld, he recounts his death at the hands of Aigisthos and Kassandra's at the hands of Klytemnestra: "so there is nothing more dreadful or shameless than a wife / [who plans such a deed]" (11.427–8). The omission of the second line in a large number of older manuscripts makes his statement a much wider generalization about all *gunaikes,* "wives" or "women." Similarly, in his next speech, there is textual doubt about the antiquity of Agamemnon's advice to return home secretly "since wives can no longer be trusted" (11.456). At whatever stage these lines entered or fell out of the tradition, the "no longer" shows that he is still centering his views on the example of Klytemnestra. It is perhaps not surprising that the tradition is unstable on this issue, in the former case attenuating its force, in the latter augmenting it. As we will see below, a certain deviousness or *mêtis* on Homer's part has set in play profound and temptingly misreadable ambiguities, particularly around the figure of Penelope.

Agamemnon seems to exempt Penelope from his strictures when he tells Odysseus that he at least has nothing to worry about from his discreet and crafty wife (11.444–6), but the force-field of Klytemnestra's example creates a shadow, in Agamemnon's view at least, even on Penelope: "Klytemnestra

---

[*] "'Outside the house everyone tries to make himself out a bit larger than he really is.' . . . Self-assertion [*egôismos*] is a type of *persona,* worn in public and discarded in private, which has as its conscious aim the achievement of a relative prestige for the wearer, and the vindication of himself or his family from the accusations and criticisms of the community" (du Boulay 1974: 75).

[†] It is common for critics to misread those expressions of despair as simple statements of fact. The disharmony between her despair and her efforts at strategic planning then gets read as a split in her consciousness.

cast shame on herself and on all women who will come hereafter, even she who is a woman of good works" (11.433–4). The same sentiments are attributed to Agamemnon in the final book, where he praises Penelope's excellence (*aretê*) as a subject for undying song and then condemns Klytemnestra to be the subject of a hateful song: "she gives a bad name to womankind, even to one who is good" (24.200–1).

I referred above to "the utterances of men concerning women as a class," but in the *Odyssey* that fear or suspicion of wives, so well attested in Mediterranean contexts, appears to be limited to this one character and to be based on his particular experiences with a notoriously unfaithful wife. Odysseus does not endorse his pessimistic extension of Klytemnestra's infamy to all wives, but merely comments that Zeus has singled out the house of Atreus for trouble "through the plots of wives" (*gunaikeias dia boulas*), namely, Helen and Klytemnestra. No other character in the epic delivers any similarly misogynistic lines. If we read Agamemnon's utterances as an individual reaction, formed under the cultural and rhetorical rule of defensive exaggeration, rather than as the quintessence of what all men actually believe about all women, then we can begin to appreciate the parallel and contrary instances of the *Odyssey*'s gender irony. I do not want to underestimate the *temptation* to read Agamemnon's universal suspicion of women as a controlling factor in the plot, but I would insist that a closer look at its location and articulation allows us to limit his generalized suspicion as a rhetorical exaggeration serving to characterize him individually. Agamemnon's is but one perspective among many—crucial, and pertinent to the thematics of the plot, but in no way determinant.

It is balanced by the opinions of one goddess, who likewise casts aspersions on the entire male (divine) sex. Kalypso is ordered by the council of the gods through Hermes to send Odysseus home. Since the passage contains material that will recur in Chapter Seven (p. 202), I will quote it here in full:

> You male gods are vile and exceedingly jealous,
> begrudging goddesses who sleep openly with mortal men,
> when one of us takes a loving husband.
> So it was when rose-fingered Dawn took Orion—
> you male gods who live so lightly were envious
> until holy Artemis of the golden throne killed him
> in Ortygia, visiting on him her gentle arrows;
> and so it was when fair-haired Demeter yielded to her
>   desire
> and slept in the loving arms of Iasion
> in a thrice-plowed furrow; Zeus soon learned of this
> and killed him by the cast of a bright thunderbolt.
> So now too you male gods resent that a mortal man
>   sleeps beside me . . .

The inclusion of Artemis along with the male gods rather than on the side of the goddesses shows the importance of sex in determining issues of gender. Because Artemis has no sexual relationship with a male, she can be treated not as a problematic or willful female but as a reliable collaborator with the interests of the male gods. Kalypso's protest, based on more cases than Agamemnon's, also has qualities of exaggeration—she generalizes from her current disappointment. Since most of the *Odyssey* is presented from the point of view of male actors and their goals, there is less temptation to single out Kalypso's perspective as somehow expressing the gender ideology of the epic—but it would be a mistake to ignore it.

I would view both Agamemnon's and Kalypso's strictures on the opposite sex as local expressions of the *Odyssey*'s sense of gender irony. Both take to an extreme the separation and distrust between the sexes, more particularly between spouses—a problem that is usually presented in a one-sided fashion as men's distrust of women—and both serve as background to what eventually emerges as the poem's major issue, the profound likemindedness of Odysseus and Penelope.

A charming illustration of an unlikeminded couple is Menelaos and Helen. On the evening when Telemakhos visits them in Sparta, husband and wife each tell a story of Odysseus at Troy. Helen recounts a daring adventure in which Odysseus, disguised by bruises and rags as a slave, entered the enemy city. She alone recognized him, washed and dressed him, and kept his identity secret while he killed many Trojans and escaped back to the Greek ships (4.238–64). Menelaos compliments her and then tells a story which counters hers. So far from being the one woman in Troy whom a Greek spy could trust, Helen almost succeeded in blocking the ruse of the Wooden Horse by walking around it and calling the men inside by name, imitating the voice of each one's wife. Only Odysseus' guile and fast-thinking saved them (4.266–89).

Menelaos' Helen and Helen's Helen are, on the immediate surface, two quite different characters. The one can be counted on for help when Odysseus is in a desperate situation surrounded by enemies, the other actively tries to destroy him and his men. The two versions have contradictory implications, but stand side by side without forcing an acknowledgment of the contradiction. Instead, both versions are presented politely and firmly, as if the audience would readily understand that multiple and irreconcilable versions are the norm in human affairs, and that husbands and wives (and neighbors) can agree to disagree (K. Baldwin). But on a deeper level these two Helens are also very similar, since both are cunning and insightful. She alone instantly recognizes Odysseus in disguise (as she instantly recognized Telemakhos earlier in the book, 4.138–46) and her power to masquerade almost defeats the strategem of the Horse.

The cunning of the two Helens, however, takes somewhat different forms, both of which anticipate or mirror Penelope's *mêtis* (Zeitlin 1981: 204–6). Helen's Helen, like Penelope, interviews the stranger and questions him, "but he craftily avoided her" (4.250). This Helen's activity is essentially domestic: she washes, anoints, and dresses Odysseus (an otherwise odd detail, since his dirt and rags are an essential part of his ruse). Menelaos' Helen is more active, not confined to her home, devising a plan to foil a whole platoon of enemies, and taking on different roles in order to do so. Though Penelope never leaves her house, her much-praised shrewdness is exhibited in two forms, similar to the Helens'. As hostess she entertains and interviews the disguised Odysseus, asking him questions, offering him clothing and a bath (how far she recognizes his identity is a more difficult question). As a more active agent defending her household from the on-slaught of a platoon of enemies, she devises the excellent trick of Laertes' shroud, unwoven each night, and (even more pertinent to the comparison) she sends deceptive messages to each suitor: "she raises everyone's hopes, and makes promises to each man, sending messages; but her mind intends other things" (2.91–2 = 13.380–1). Like Helen, Penelope imitates different women in order to deceive different men, as she takes on the feigned role of "your future bride" to each suitor in turn. She also *imitates* the stereotypi-cally good and simple housewife, as she weaves her shroud each day.

Penelope thus exercises her duplicity in the two Helenic ways, one re-stricted to her domestic role, the other involving imitation and false mes-sages. The two Helens, of course, have different allegiances (though a god is assigned responsibility for her actions in both instances, 4.261–2, 274–5), whereas Penelope, we are repeatedly assured, has but one. Even Agamem-non has no doubts on that score, and Odysseus receives assurances from others who should know—from his mother in the Underworld (11.181–3, in answer to Odysseus' direct question about his wife's faithfulness, 11.177–9) and from Athena (13.379–81).

Though many characters testify to the fame of Penelope for cunning, the poet also shows us the grave constraints under which she must operate and her feelings of despair at ever coming out of this long ordeal. For many readers it is the latter image of a helpless and lamenting Penelope which predominates, * but I propose that by emphasizing her victimage we do less

---

* "I think all critics put too much emphasis on Penelope's constant weeping. Odysseus, Menelaus and Telemachus weep frequently also, but weeping prevents none of them, or Penelope, from acting wherever possible" (Foley 1978: 23 n. 9).

We should also question the cultural meaning of her weeping. In a study of the anxieties of fishermen's wives, D. L. Davis writes, "It was only through long talks with informants about what it was like to be a fisherman's wife that I began to understand that worry was not to say 'I'm not healthy; life is too much for me; I can't handle it; nothing I do is ever considered important'; rather it said 'I'm a good wife; I'm concerned about my husband and I, like him, am deeply tied into the fishing complex and am indispensible to his ability to fish successfully.'

than justice to the shrewdness of the narrative. Murnaghan has recently argued that Penelope, though faithful, is the victim of the generalized suspicion of wives (1987a: 106; 1987b: 121) and further that the narrative itself imposes restraints on her consciousness:

> On the one hand, Penelope must not know that Odysseus is back until the end of her gradual recovery because her recognition of him actually signals its completion; on the other hand, she must know that Odysseus is back from the beginning because she cannot begin to recover until she does know. Only as she recovers does she become capable of helping Odysseus in his operations against the suitors, and thereby of bringing about the circumstances under which her actual recognition of Odysseus can take place. This means that, for most of the narrative, she must somehow know and acknowledge that Odysseus is back but still not recognize him. . . . Penelope acts out a kind of recognition of Odysseus but does not actually recognize him (1987b: 47, cf. 52)

Notice the frequent use of "must" in this analysis. Penelope is taken to be a victim not only of social pressures unwarranted in her case (1987a: 112) but also of the demands of a plot which puts her in a psychologically untenable position. But another reading is possible, one which avoids the assumptions of victimage. In favor of trying the experiment, one might note that this is the direction of much feminist anthropology. Speaking of the essays they edited on women's work and international migration, Sacks and Scheper-Hughes remark: "They continue the feminist tradition of seeing women not only as passive victims of their fate, but also as protagonists, as active shapers of their lives, even as they do so under conditions and circumstances not of their own making" (177).

Our major focus will be on the three encounters between Penelope and the beggar—her soliciting of gifts from the suitors while the beggar watches, her interview with the beggar, and her final recognition of Odysseus. Instead of viewing her as a pawn in the games of male characters and of the poet, I will show how active she is in coping with the forces arrayed against her. * Though it is quite clear from their reunion in Book 23 that Penelope still entertained doubts about the beggar's identity as Odysseus, there are good

---

A woman's worry over her absent husband was a kind of deeply felt spiritual empathy. It was one of the jobs of fishing that a man left to his wife" (D. L. Davis 141).

* "[Penelope] alone engages in an active struggle to maintain the cultural norm. She, not Odysseus' *dêmos*, dares to reprove the suitors' violation of the social order. . . . Penelope receives and cross-examines visitors, and tries to maintain standards of hospitality and a network of communication in Odysseus' disrupted family. . . . At 4.791–3 Penelope is compared to a beleaguered lion. Lion images are typically reserved for heroic men. In the disrupted Ithaca of the early Books of the *Odyssey* Penelope, far from being the passive figure of most Homeric criticism, has come remarkably close to enacting the role of a besieged warrior" (Foley 1978: 9–10).

reasons to think that everything she says and does in Book 19 is guided by her thought that the beggar might be, indeed, stands a very good chance of being, Odysseus. I will not argue that she recognizes her husband in that interview, but rather that she very actively tests him and reaches a point where his answers are sufficiently Odyssean to justify her gamble in setting up the contest of the bow.

The methodological point of this reading is to avoid being misled by Penelope's expressions of helplessness. Questioning the assumption that she is utterly and only a victim of circumstances, I will instead try to assess what kinds of power and intelligence are hers even under duress. In the parabola of these chapters, Penelope is our first token of the shrewd and effective activity of Greek women, laboring (to be sure) under great constraints— activity which is deliberately and programmatically underrated in most statements and portrayals by ancient men and consequently by modern scholarship.

Homer's Cunning

Before going over Penelope's scenes in the economy of Odysseus' return, we must also note something further about the other Butlerian premise, concerning the style of production and the goal of simply depicting personalities and scenes. It would also be methodologically constricted to assume that Homer is an utterly transparent narrator, always telling us all that can be known. As the characters he describes are normally devious and cautious about their words, so we should not deny to Homer too the possibility that he will avail himself of a certain cunning in setting out the cross-purposes of his plot. This is in keeping with the drift of homeric studies recently which sees the monumental poet as capable of subtle effects within the inherited tradition of type-scenes and formulae (Hainsworth, A. Edwards, Fenik, M. W. Edwards).

We can approach this feature of homeric narrative, namely, the craftiness not of the characters but of the author by way of the detour I mentioned through a scholarly satire from the second century C.E. The author was Ptolemy Chennos and we know of three works he wrote, each fascinating in a different way: an epic in twenty-four books entitled *Anti-homer,* a novel entitled *The Sphinx,* and (the work that is of interest here) a seven book parody of classical scholarship called the *Novel History* (Hercher, Chatzis, Dihle). We know its contents from an extended summary given by Photios (*Bibliothêkê* codex 190). Ptolemy's specialty is providing quite startling information that no one else has ever heard of, such as the fact that there were several famous women named Helen who lived during the time of the Trojan war—twenty-three in fact, one of whom, the daughter of Musaios, wrote an account of the Trojan war which Homer stole (149.^{b}22–5). That *is* news.

Later he informs us that an Egyptian woman named Phantasia composed versions of both the *Iliad* and the *Odyssey* before Homer; she deposited the books in a temple in Memphis and Homer came along, made copies, and followed them closely in putting together his own work (151ᵃ37-ᵇ5). I must say that Ptolemy is a man after my own heart, not so much because he believes in the authoress of the *Odyssey* but because he was obviously familiar with a vast range of scholarship and has no compunctions about sending it up. He is a liar on a grand, academic scale. It is unfortunate that this amusing purveyor of little-known facts has himself become so little known.

There is a real brilliance in some of his creations, such as his report (and this gets to the point of my digression) that Odysseus' real name was Outis and that he was given this name because he had such large *ôta*, ears (147ᵃ10– 1; as Prof. Mark Edwards remarks to me, the pun works even better with the homeric form, *ouata,* which is presumably what Ptolemy either used or expected his readers to note). That is truly outrageous. Odysseus, of course, employed the name Outis, meaning No-one, when he met the Kyklops. After Polyphemos' eye was put out with a burning stake, he cried out in pain and the other Kyklopes on the island came running to see what was the matter. He told them "My friends, Outis is killing me by a trick, not by straightforward violence" (9.408). They understand him to mean "No one is killing me by a trick nor by violence." So they reply, "Well, if no one is doing you violence, go say your prayers."

Now at this very moment when Odysseus' trap snaps shut and his verbal trick gets the better of Polyphemos, another trap is sprung—a verbal trick played by the author on the listening audience. There are two Greek words for "no"—*ou* and *mê. Ou* is used in regular declarative sentences, *mê* is used with some types of commands and conditional sentences. There is no difference of meaning between them: the shift from *ou* to *mê* occurs automatically as part of the grammatical system. The other Kyklopes reply to Polyphemos with a conditional sentence, "If no one is doing you vio- lence," so that the word *outis* from Polyphemos' sentence legitimately (though not necessarily) becomes *mêtis* in theirs. The trick—and it is only for our benefit—is that the Kyklopes' sentence, since the subject is now *mêtis,* also means (with a slightly different intonation) "If craftiness is doing you violence."[6] In case we might not appreciate the trick inside the trick, Odysseus immediately goes on to say "And so they left while I laughed in my heart, thinking how my name had deceived him, and my splendid *mêtis"* (9.413–14). The effect is simply dazzling: so elegant, so obviously planned, and yet so unforeseen (". . . possibly the cleverest use in all Greek," Stanford 105).

Since we suddenly realize the extent of the poet's cleverness at the very moment when Polyphemos is outwitted by Odysseus' cleverness, there is some point in saying that the poet has outwitted us. At least, we had been informed that a crafty game was being played between Odysseus and Polyphemos, but we had not been told that there was a second, unguessed game being played against us at the same time. The relation of the bard to the audience has at times a teasing, quasi-competitive aspect. He (one still presumes it was a he) does not tell us everything that is going on, the effect of which in the case of Polyphemos (and later Penelope) is to surprise us with a revelation of hidden cleverness, the poet's own *mêtis*.

Penelope and the Beggar

The groundwork has now been laid for reading Penelope's plot, using two frameworks that are comfortable and appropriate to the *Odyssey*—the anthropological, which looks at the systematic differences of behavior in cultures whose economy, values, and social organization are different from our own, and the narratological, which emphasizes the author's control of information so as to create certain effects of surprise and suspense in the audience. They come together under the single heading *mêtis*, that shrewdness in personal management which is an important feature of archaic Greek (as it is of some modern Greek) culture and, *a fortiori*, of Homer's own performance. This is, of course, an experiment. We cannot know with any first-hand certainty the degree and quality of a Penelope's or a Homer's maneuverability within their inherited constraints. But let us try out the possibility that both author and heroine are not simply victims of the performance rules within which they operate, and that both are capable of a strategically concealed cunning—Penelope to outwit her audience of suitors, Homer to outwit his listening audience.

Let us return for a moment to the anthropology of cunning, as outlined above. The secrecy of Odysseus' return, first adumbrated by Teiresias ("once you have killed the suitors in your hall, either by a trick or openly with sharp bronze," 11.119–20) and then by Agamemnon ("return secretly, not openly," 11.455), becomes a dominant concern when Athena appears to Odysseus in Book 13. She throws a misty veil over the landscape, transforming its appearance, so that Odysseus will from the beginning act cautiously, treating familiar people and places as strange ("lest his wife, his townsmen and his friends recognize him before he took revenge on the suitors' insolence" 13.192–3). Athena's point is the need, in these exceptional circumstances, for a hyper-cautious attitude: "Do not reveal yourself to anyone, man or woman" (13.308); "any other wanderer returned home would gladly run to his house to see his children and wife" (13.333–4). As is not infrequently the case with divine interventions, Athena is simply duplicating and manifesting Odysseus' own state of mind as the unremittingly suspicious man. For the next twelve books, Odysseus repeatedly confronts familiar and long-desired people as if they were perfect strangers.

Athena wants him to be, and he is, the model of perfect cunning, who will conceal himself even from friends whose faithfulness he has no reason to doubt. Principal among these are Penelope and Eumaios, both of whom Athena guarantees are reliable ("her heart always grieves, looking to the day of your return," 13.379; "the swineherd who is faithful to you, and cherishes your child and cunning Penelope," 13.405–6). The pairing of Penelope and Eumaios continues in Book 16, when Odysseus imparts to Telemakhos Athena's advice: "Let no one hear that Odysseus is inside, not Laertes nor the swineherd nor any of the house servants, and not even Penelope, but you and I alone will learn the women's bent and test the allegiance of each of the male servants" (16.301–5). Odysseus' interviews with Penelope and Eumaios are formally similar in that both are interrupted by a recognition by another person (Telemakhos, Eurykleia). Because Odysseus' relationship with his wife and retainers is seen as a conventional one, resting on the agreement of the parties, rather than a "natural" one, like that of father and son, the reestablishment of Odysseus' intimacy with either of them is a slow process (Foley 1978: 15). That pairing of Penelope and Eumaios will significantly recur in Books 21 and 23, but with a twist of homeric gender irony.

The guarantee of Penelope's reliability underlies the first scene in which she and Odysseus appear together. She descends the stairs, accompanied by maids and holding a veil before her face, intending to soften up* the suitors, to enhance her own domestic honor as wife and mother,† and in particular to deflect the murderous designs of the suitors on Telemakhos (18.158–68). The poet combines various signs in this scene to indicate both that Penelope is seducing the suitors, as she successfully elicits from them more bridal gifts, and that she is utterly innocent of any intentions to remarry (Levine, Byre). On the one hand, the suitors are enchanted (*ethelkhthen*) by her beauty, their knees weaken, and they all desire to sleep beside her (18.212–3); they send out to their estates for more bridal presents at her request (18.274–80). On the other hand, her impulse to appear before the suitors is attributed to Athena, who also undertakes her beautification while Penelope is napping (18.158, 187–96). At the cost of a certain awkwardness in the flow of the action, Penelope is thus protected from any imputation of wanting to appear

---

*Literally, "to open up (or spread out) their spirit," weakening their guard (Büchner 143). Their state will then be the opposite, as Thornton 146 n. 30 observes, of mental "tight-togetherness, with no gaps or interstices."

†It has been doubted whether the second of these intentions can be attributed to Penelope, on the grounds that in order for her to gain honor "in the eyes of her husband" (*pros posios,* 18.162) she would have to know that Odysseus was watching her (Büchner 143). But in a society where vigilance, curiosity, and gossip are paramount whatever she does in any circumstances will be observed and reported and will become part of her public reputation.

desirable in the eyes of strange men. Homer arranges both that she seduces and that she not be blamable for any seduction, since she is acting strictly in the interests of her household, her son, and her husband.

The protection of Telemakhos is her first goal, and she tries to do so by criticizing him as a child, implying to the suitors that he is not a threat to them as men. The very fact that she rebukes him in public is a humiliation which serves her aim of shielding him from their violence. But he foils her attempt to cast him as a child by asserting his grown-up tact and prudence, so she is compelled to try another strategy. *Since* he has reached manhood and his beard is growing, she says, it is time for her to remarry—an announcement which turns the suitors' heads and distracts them from their simmering plot to murder Telemakhos. To make her decision plausible she declares that Odysseus himself had told her in parting that when Telemakhos' beard began to grow she should marry whomever she chose (18.257–73).

At the end of her speech, Odysseus listening "rejoiced, because she elicited gifts from them, and she enchanted their spirits with honeyed words, while her mind intended other things" (18.282–3). Clearly he has no doubt about her allegiance to his estate and appreciates what we might call her faithful duplicity. We might well suppose that Penelope's account of Odysseus' parting words about Telemakhos' beard is her own invention, on the spur of the moment, and that this is an added reason why Odysseus is perfectly sure of her fidelity even as she acts out the opposite (Büchner 137–46; Allione 76). His unhesitating appreciation of her cleverness may also resonate with his own experience among the Phaiakians, where he enchanted (*kêlêthmôi*, 11.334) his listening audience, who admire his "beauty and his size" (11.337)—though they do not express a desire to sleep beside him—and from whom he solicited gifts to continue his tales (11.357–9). * Both Odysseus and Penelope are busy enriching the household and replenishing the store of goods devoured by the suitors, and both do so by similar means. This is an important case of that mental similarity or *homophrosunê* which characterizes their marriage.

The second encounter of Penelope and Odysseus is the famous interview in Book 19, which culminates in her decision to set up the contest of the bow and axe-heads on the following day. The scene is beautifully intimate and dramatic. The time is night, the suitors have left, and Penelope comes into the main room with some maids and sits by the fire where the beggar,

---

* Odysseus' first words to Penelope in the interview scene of Book 19 compare her to a king who receives gifts in abundance—from nature, not from suitors (Foley 1978: 11). Some of his words there are pregnant with meaning: "his trees are heavy (*brithêisi*) with fruit, his sheepflocks continue to bear (*tiktêi*) young." Her successful solicitation of gifts from the suitors puts her in a role of masculine control, them in the role of productive mothers.

Odysseus in disguise, is tending the flame. Let us back up a bit to assess what we might be led to expect from this interview. Penelope has good reason to be interested in this man, for a profusion of signs and messages had recently been given to her saying that her husband is at hand. The prophet Theoklymenos had announced to her that Odysseus is already on Ithaka (17.157). Of course, Penelope like any sensible Greek would not believe what a wandering prophet says, but she does listen and express a wish that it would turn out to be true. The appropriate attitude in modern Mediterranean towns is to be suspicious and skeptical, to appear indifferent, disbelieving, but always to keep one's ears open for more information to evaluate. Then Eumaios the swineherd had told her that this beggar has news of Odysseus from a neighboring island and that he is a compelling speaker (17.513–27). Eumaios is wholly faithful to Penelope and she knows that he is not a gullible man. His recommendation makes her very eager to hear what this vagrant has to say. She tells Eumaios to bring him in and then wishes aloud that Odysseus would return and kill the suitors. At that moment her son Telemakhos sneezed so hard that the house shook (*smerdaleon konabêse*)—a good sign! (17.539–47).

She prays that the sign will come true and then says to Eumaios about the beggar, "If I recognize him, that he is telling the whole truth, I will give him fine clothes." Let us pause a moment to detect a very fine and fleeting impression that brushes across the audience's mind, like the touch of an invisible nymph's hand. The first words of that utterance, by themselves, suggest that she might realize who the beggar really is (*ai k' auton gnôô*, 17.549), but the completion of the utterance requires us to reject that first, transient meaning in favor of one a little less premonitory: "If I recognize him as a truth-teller." The effect might be viewed as simply a by-product of using set phrases and formulas, but origin should not be confused with effect. Whatever its source, the poet has momentarily set in our minds— and then erased— the thought that Penelope might recognize Odysseus.

But the interview she asked for did not take place when she asked for it since Odysseus had refused, saying he was afraid of the crowd of violent suitors (17.564). What he feared, of course, was that they might be put on their guard if they saw Penelope conversing with him or, worse, overheard him say that Odysseus was nearby.* Among the important ears to beware of are the maids' (Harsh 10). Modern readings of Book 19 regularly ignore their presence altogether and read the scene as a simple two-person transac-

---

*His caution is not, and is not said to be, motivated by Agamemnon's warning against trusting one's wife. Yet the general male distrust of women and wives plays a very important role in Homer's communication with his audience. Rather than say that "Odysseus' action is influenced by the perspective of Agamemnon" (Murnaghan 1987a: 108), I would say that our interpretation of Odysseus' action is influenced by Homer's deployment of Agamemnon.

tion between Penelope and Odysseus (e.g., Vester 419). There are fifty serving women in Penelope's household, twelve of whom regularly sneak off at night to sleep with the suitors. In the politics of this house they are traitors, fifth-columnists.

One of the maids was responsible for betraying Penelope's earlier delaying tactic: Penelope had put off the suitors by weaving a large shroud for Odysseus' father Laertes, saying that she had to fulfill this duty before she could think of considering their offers. That episode is a good illustration of the competitive social system which demands that personal reputation be jealously defended because any default or even apparent default will be used as a weapon to lower one's value, one's honor. "If my father-in-law," she says, "with all his social status, were not to lie in a shroud woven by me, some of the village wives would use this resentfully against me" (19.146–7 = 24.136–7). The appeal to what the neighbors will say is one of the most powerful that can be invoked, and Penelope using that argument succeeded in putting off the suitors for three years. Her trick was that she got up at night and by lamplight unwove what she had woven during the day. The maid who betrayed her secret was probably the sassy Melantho, who twice insults the beggar in gratuitously nasty terms. At least I think this is what Penelope refers to when she says to Melantho "You shameless dog, don't think I don't know what you did—and you will pay for it!" (19.91–2).

Now when night falls the suitors depart to their respective lodgings. Odysseus had already encouraged some of the serving maids to leave the room, volunteering to tend the fire all night (18.313–9), and had cleared the hall of the rest when he and Telemakhos emptied the weapon racks and stored the arms in a locked room. But when Penelope comes into the main hall to interview him, she is of course accompanied by her personal maids and indeed by a large number whose job is to clear off the banquet tables and wash the dishes and sweep the floor. After Penelope sits down the first words spoken are not hers and not Odysseus' but Melantho's. She sasses the stranger in a most ungracious and unbecoming way, and she is answered both by Odysseus and by Penelope.

I take Melantho and maids like her to be very important actors, or presences, in this scene. They represent the fact that if any hint of collusion between Penelope and Odysseus were to be visible or audible, some observer (such as one of the maids) would use that to harm Penelope and to destroy Odysseus. The word for this suspicious and resentful attitude is *nemesaô:* it is the word used in the sentence I quoted above about village wives using information resentfully against Penelope, * and the same word occurs in the

---

*Nausikaa tells Odysseus that she is afraid of critical gossip if she should be seen in his company and also that she herself would *nemesô* any maiden who "mingled with men" before marriage (6.286–7).

first interchange between Odysseus and Penelope. She asks his identity—
which is of course the critical question—and he does not answer her question
but instead tells her how famous she has become like a wise and just king
ruling a fruitful land and begs not to be asked his identity, since telling his
story would just make him grieve and "I'm afraid one of the maids will feel
resentful, or even you yourself, and say that I'm just a maudlin drunk."
That concluding sentence of his first speech to Penelope can be heard as a
warning: *mê tis moi dmôôn nemesêsetai,* I fear that one of the *maids* will nurture
a resentment. We have been quite carefully told which maid will nurture a
resentment, and Melantho is just one of the dozen actively treacherous
servants. Of course, even when alone or before apparently faithful servants
one should not speak unguardedly.

Note how carefully Odysseus' warning is phrased, tucked inside a misleading context, because the maids are listening to this warning too: "I'm
afraid one of the maids will feel resentful, or even you yourself, and say that
I'm just a maudlin drunk." To a discreet and crafty weaver of wiles like
Penelope this is a sort of raised eyebrow or tilt of the head, saying "Be
careful what you say in front of these untrustworthy women." Penelope
seems to get the message: she manages in her next speech to tell the beggar
how faithful she is to Odysseus, how she longs for him, how she has been
clever in the trick of the weaving but was caught by the suitors through the
maids, and now she is at a loss: "I can not escape marriage and I have not
found another *mêtis*" (19.157–8) That sets up the problem between these two
sympathetic, but still guarded, interlocutors.

When I say that they speak guardedly in front of the maids I do not mean
to imply that if they were in private they would fall into each other's arms:
each remains self-controlled and defensive in relation to the other. Indeed,
even without the presence of the maids, their conversation would presumably remain just as guarded, since that is their habit. Each is testing the
other. Penelope says so explicitly: "Now, stranger, I propose to test you—
to see whether you truly entertained my husband, as you claim" (19.215–
7). Odysseus' plan to test everyone in his household, including Penelope,
had been alluded to by Athena ("Any other man would run home to his
children and wife, but it is not your way to hear their story before you test
your wife," 13.335–6) and confirmed by Odysseus to Telemakhos (16.301–
7).

The maids, we might say, are merely an external reinforcement of the
necessary caution that Penelope and the beggar display to each other, reminding the audience of the atmosphere of hostility and betrayal within
which all speech should be monitored. (The maids seem to be ignored in
the rest of the scene until they leave at 20.6.) Penelope does not know for
a certainty that this man is Odysseus: but she has reason to suspect it and
she tests her suspicions by the way she interviews him. Even though he

turns out, under her testing, to be very Odysseus-like, she withholds final assent as to his identity, since gods have been known to adopt human identities precisely to fool mortal women (M. Edwards 55).

Penelope's extra degree of caution puts her at the head of the line of heroines with whom she had earlier been compared by Antinoos—Tyro, Alkmene, and Mykene (2.120). Mykene is poorly attested, though she occurred in the Hesiodic *Great Ehoiai* (Pausanias 2.16.4), but the stories of Tyro and Alkmene are told in the *Odyssey*'s first Underworld scene. Each was deceived by a god who appeared to her in the form of her mortal husband or lover. Tyro, before she was married to Kretheus, was enamored of the river Enipeus and often swam in its beautiful streams. Poseidon assumed the river's likeness and in a cave-like bower formed by the waters he deflowered Tyro (11.235–45). Alkmene's story is told much more briefly, but was clearly very well known: while her husband Amphitryon was away, Zeus appeared to her in his shape and begot Herakles (11.266–8). These women are famous as the mothers of great heroes, but Penelope outdoes them in cleverness (*kerdea*) and insight (*noêmata*), "such as we have never heard of, not even among the women of ancient days," said Antinoos (2.117–22). Her superiority lies precisely in her unwillingness to be taken in by what might be merely a convincing replica, whether mortal or immortal, of her husband. *

The sympathy between them establishes a kind of emotional alliance, illustrating once again the deep similarity between them. Penelope weeps openly when the beggar tells of meeting Odysseus, and Odysseus weeps inside himself but shows no sign on his face.

> As she listened to him her tears flowed, her skin grew moist
> — as snow turns to wetness on the mountain peaks
> when the east wind thaws it after the west wind blows,
> and as it melts the streams run full;
> — so her beautiful cheeks were wet as she let her tears fall,
> crying for her husband, who was sitting beside her. But Odysseus,
> though he felt sorry for his wife as she grieved in her heart,
> hardened his eyes like horn or iron,
> unmoving in their sockets; by this trick he concealed his tears.
> (19.204–12, trans. Fitzgerald)

The one who controls the course of the dialogue is Penelope. After putting the first question about identity, she says she will test him and asks him to identify Odysseus' clothes, his appearance, and his companions (19.215–9).

---

*Odysseus shows a similar suspicion of goddesses, not immediately accepting Ino's veil, which might be "a trick woven by one of the immortals" (5.356–7), and making Kalypso swear an oath that she is not "planning any wicked injury" to him (5.179): Newton 15.

When he describes correctly the clothes that she had made herself, she recognizes these signs (*sêmat' anagnousêi*, 19.250) as proof that the beggar is no liar, or rather that the beggar can skillfully manage the truth he knows, for he may know more than he says. Homer's description of this is that Odysseus' story of being a Kretan prince who once met Odysseus is "a multiple lie that was like the truth" (19.203). The beggar continues by saying that Odysseus is on a nearby island begging goods (19.284) and that he is deciding whether to return openly or in secret (19.299), but that in any case he will come very soon (19.300–1). For the beggar to say that Odysseus is at this moment a beggar (*agurtazein*, not a poor vagrant but someone who is collecting goods) and that he is nearby and will return very soon, possibly in secret, is offering Penelope the possibility of seeing through his disguise, or at least of acting in such a way that, *if* he is Odysseus, he will be able to kill the suitors.

However, that thought cannot be expressed openly in the presence of enemies, and even without the maids Penelope must remain a bit puzzled and uncertain about this stranger's eloquent reticence. Penelope throws them off the scent in a way that tells the beggar she is following his drift.

> Ah, stranger,
> if what you say could ever happen!
> You would soon know our love! Our bounty, too:
> men would turn after you to call you blessed.
> But my heart tells me what must be.
> Odysseus will not come to me; no ship
> will be prepared for you. We have no master
> quick to receive and furnish out a guest
> as Lord Odysseus was.
> Or did I dream him?
> Maids, maids: come wash him.
>   (19.309–15, trans. Fitzgerald)

There is only one word here that Fitzgerald does not capture fully. What he translates as "master" is in Greek *sêmantores*, the plural for leaders, literally "sign-givers." Penelope says we do not have in this household "sign-givers" like Odysseus. Their conversation is an exchange of tentative and possible meanings, signs of truth that cannot be fully and openly spoken, both because of the listening maids and because of their own exemplary caution. After designating Odysseus as a sign-giver, she goes on to speak of her own powers of perception, of reading signs. She says that the beggar must be given a bath and treated well and that any suitor who dares to mistreat him the next day will be out of the running for her hand in marriage. "For how will you ever learn, stranger, that I do surpass all other women in intelligence and subtle *mêtis*, if you are kept in rags and filthy at our feast?" (19.324–8).

The guarded display and exercise of her *mêtis* is most effective when at the close of the interview she asks the beggar to interpret a dream she has had. Critical discussion of this passage has, without exception, assumed that Penelope is here a translucent speaker—simply, fully, and accurately conveying all that she saw and felt, as if she were the homeric narrator of facts and not a character with designs of her own. In fact, several recent readers have even "seen through" Penelope at this point, finding in her dream-affect of sorrow at the geese's death a revelation of her unconscious desire to keep the suitors with her and to marry one of them. "Penelope is secretly favorably inclined to the idea of marriage with one of the suitors."[*] Though Penelope does have dreams in the *Odyssey*, I see no reason to believe that she actually had this dream. It can be better seen in its context of covert and guarded negotiation as her attempt to convey a message to the beggar, whom she now has good reason to think may very well be Odysseus himself. Her talking about a dream is not a straightforward report but a stratagem, another way of addressing this possible-Odysseus without either committing herself to his identity or revealing to the maids her suspicions and her plotting.

In her dream an eagle swoops down from the mountains and kills all twenty of the geese in her courtyard; while she is mourning their loss *en per oneirôi*, "in the dream, that is," the eagle alights on the roof and speaks in a human voice, telling her that it is not a dream but a vision that will come true: the geese are your suitors and I am your husband who have now come home.

Note how odd this is. She has asked for an interpretation; but the dream itself contains its own interpretation, a unique event in the annals of oneirokrisy. She has in effect given the beggar both an allegory and its interpretation and is asking him whether she is right.[†] Just as Odysseus made up a dream

---

[*] Rankin 622: ". . . beneath the conventional expressions of longing, and the genuine grief, a part of her prefers one of the suitors, perhaps Amphinomus, who most resembles her husband of twenty years ago, to an aged stranger" (623). See also Devereux, Russo 1982: 9 n.12. If it is not a factual report at all, but rather Penelope's fiction—her way of communicating with this possible-Odysseus without letting the maids know what is on her mind, then her sorrow too is a deliberate misdirection. She pretends to be, even in her dream (*en per oneirôi*), naive and helpless (Marquardt 43–4).

[†] Amory 105–6 sees Penelope's telling of her dream and proposal of a contest as her way of testing her intuition that the stranger is Odysseus. "[His] assurance is so peculiarly explicit that Penelope must realize that Odysseus himself is speaking. This leaves the poet, who has decided to postpone his recognition scene until after the contest, with the problem of preventing an immediate acknowledgement of Penelope's recognition, and this he does very adroitly and in complete consonance with Penelope's character as he has portrayed it. She makes no reply to the stranger's remarkable statement. . . . That is, Penelope is not yet ready emotionally to accept Odysseus' return, so she does not admit her recognition of him, but just gives up the whole problem for the moment."

(in one of his false autobiographies, so it is doubly fictional, 14.495), so Penelope is here inventing a dream as a way of further safe communication with the fascinating stranger (Büchner 149 n. 1). The beggar replies that the interpretation of the dream in the dream is the correct one, since Odysseus himself (in the dream) has announced what will really happen: the suitors will die to a man.

Her response to this assurance is cautious, for two reasons: beyond the considerations of habitually cautious speech, the task of killing so many suitors, even with the advantage of surprise, is still overwhelming. "(Dreams) are not always fulfilled" (19.561). Her characterization of dreams as either cheating or real is posed strictly in terms of fulfillment: there is no uncertainty about the *meaning* of the dream, only about its validity. Dreams emerging "from the ivory (*elephantos*) gate mislead (*elephairontai*), since they bring words that are not fulfilled (*akraanta*); but those that come through polished horn (*keraôn*) accomplish (*krainousi*) real things" (19.565–7).[7] Penelope's acute sense of deception and of truths that might just miss coming true is like that attributed to Odysseus earlier in this scene: "He knew how to speak many lies that were like reality" (19.203). But at this point her language directs attention not so much to the detection of beguiling falsehood but to the issue of coming true. She seems to be saying that even if the beggar were to be Odysseus their joint "dream" of killing the suitors is simply too difficult to accomplish.

But she leaves the beggar in no doubt that she would view such a slaughter with heartfelt welcome (*aspaston*, 569) and that the day of her departure from Odysseus' house will be a "baneful dawn" (*êôs dus-ô-numos*, neatly echoed at the end of the line in the name of Odysseus, *O-dus-êos*, 571). Thus announcing her feelings about a forthcoming massacre, she also announces that she will set up a contest: whoever can string Odysseus' bow and shoot through a row of twelve axe-heads will be her husband.[*] The beggar replies that she should not delay the contest, for cunning Odysseus will arrive before the bow is strung (19.584–7). So it is that the means and opportunity to slaughter the suitors are provided by Penelope. Her plan, offered to the

---

[*]Combellack 39, who does not accept the notion that Penelope suspects the beggar's identity, nevertheless makes a clever point about Penelope's contest. Since "there is every reason to believe that no one but Odysseus (and possibly his son) could string the bow and shoot through the axes," the contest will either reveal the identity of her husband or, more likely, all the suitors will fail and she will be committed to marrying none of them. "The story told in this form not only saves Penelope from any charge of illogical conduct, but also has a special appropriateness to the extremely intelligent woman we have been assured she is. In the story as we have it, Penelope, the model of cautious, shrewd intelligence, acts on this one occasion like a rash, precipitate fool" (40). But Combellack reads too much into the conditions of the test when he imagines Penelope demanding that, if all the suitors fail, they abandon their wooing altogether. Cf. Marquardt 41.

beggar and confirmed by him, enables their common goal to be realized. In this sense I claim that she is a very active author or contriver of the revenge plot, setting it up for Odysseus to execute. Indeed, the chief advantage of a reading like this which emphasizes Penelope's activity and shrewdness is that it explains her otherwise mysterious, abrupt, and unmotivated decision to set up the contest of the bow. The alternatives are to read it as "a desperate instinct" (M. Finley 1978: 3) or, with the Analysts, to look for traces of scissors and scotch tape where hypothetical revisers have altered an earlier, coherent text.[*] Both are victimage theories, minimizing the control and intelligence of Penelope and Homer respectively.

The extreme notion that Penelope actually recognizes the true identity of the beggar in Book 19 was seriously developed by Philip Whaley Harsh.[8] In its literal form this is certainly untenable since Penelope would then have no reason to test his identity in Book 23 after the slaughter of the suitors and would not react to his passing her test with such an emotional release (Vester 418 n.9). Since Harsh wrote most traditionalists have rejected his reading and his supporters have given it a psychological twist that dramatically alters its impact. Ann Amory developed Harsh's analysis but added to it that Penelope acts largely on intuition and does not allow herself consciously to realize that she recognizes him (Austin 1975: 200–38). Others have taken this line even further, emphasizing that Penelope seems to live in a psychically charged world, prone to invasion by dreams and apparitions (Van Nortwick). But to say that Penelope is a creature of intuitions which she cannot explain even to herself underrates her own cunning and deprives her of the very qualities of control, planning, and initiative which she seems to be exercising with appropriate caution and determination in Book 19.[9] Of course we ought not to read Penelope as a cool incarnation of reason and strategy. She is genuinely distraught and uncertain much of the time, a condition she has compensated for by cultivating an all too tough mind (*thumon, apênea per mal' eonta*), as she puts it to Odysseus at 23.230.

In a sense this plotting activity of hers is fundamental to the poetics of the *Odyssey*, for just as Odysseus is a master story-teller and is compared to a epic singer at the climactic moment when he comes into possession of the bow (21.406–9, cf. 411 *aeise*), so Penelope is a master-weaver, and weaving is an appropriate image for the work of the epic poet who specializes not in recitals of heroic battle but the plotting and counter-plotting of a household

---

[*]Time has not been kind to the Analysts, both because their arguments are premised on a writerly, textual model rather than on the practices and possibilities of oral composition, and because their tradition developed an ethos of microscopic detection of "inconsistencies," vouched for only by the analyst's "unerring feeling for style" (Merkelbach 1951: 6), and at the same time freely invented hypotheses about rearrangement and interpolation on a massive scale. Merkelbach 1951 is an example of the madness of this method.

in conflict. The weaving in question is not just any old dry goods but specifically tricky and clever designing of interdependent tensions, the warp and woof of crossed purposes and inimical motives.[10] Athena helps Odysseus "weave a *mêtis*," a cunning plan to restore himself to his house (13.386), and when he feels the events are closing around him he wonders whether some god is "weaving a deceit" to entrap him (5.356). Penelope, of course, literally weaves a deceit in the form of Laertes' shroud, but she also "winds up balls of tricks," *dolous tolupeuô* (19.137), using the word for winding yarn. If weaving is a good metaphor for plotting and the *Odyssey* is preeminent in such plotting, then it is all the easier to see not only Odysseus but Penelope too as a figure of the poet, quietly working behind the scenes.[11]

Penelope's Trick and Homer's

But Penelope's story is not over yet. There is one final trick she and Homer have in store.[*] Just as we were outwitted at the same moment that Polyphemos was, so too in Book 23, when their final reunion takes place, there is a double trick—this time played by Penelope on Odysseus and by Homer on us.

After the slaughter of the suitors and the faithless maids, Odysseus commands Eurykleia to bring him fire and pitch to purify the house, and to summon Penelope and all the other women. The maids come running to him, they embrace him and kiss his head, shoulders, and hands, "and a sweet desire came over him for weeping and groaning, and he recognized all of them" (22.500–1). This moment of emotion and mutual recognition is plain and unsurprising; its very conventionality sets us up for the different reaction of Penelope. Eurykleia runs up the stairs to Penelope's sleeping quarters and wakes her with the news that "Odysseus has come" (23.7). Her first reaction is to criticize Eurykleia for losing her mind, or rather her closeness of mind: "Dear nurse, the gods have made you mad. They can turn the most cautious (*epi-phrona*) person into a fool (*a-phrona*) and they can reorient a slack-minded (*khali-phroneonta*) person to having a sound mind (*sao-phrosunês*)" (23.11–3). Readers have been puzzled by the negativity of her response, but it embodies two themes operative in Penelope's situation—the need for cautious testing rather than impulsive letting go, and the inscrutable role of the gods in warping human judgment. The possibility remains that some god looking like Odysseus, or using a mortal made to look like Odysseus, has executed the slaughter.

Puzzling, too, at first glance, is the next response of Penelope. When

---

[*]"Does Odysseus think that once he has washed off his wretched aspect Penelope will recognize him immediately? If he thinks so, he is either too cocky and sure of himself or simple of mind" (Pucci 92).

Eurykleia repeats that Odysseus has come and adds that he was the stranger whom the suitors made sport of, Penelope "rejoiced, and jumping out of bed embraced the old woman, and let a tear fall from her eyes" (23.32–3). The cold and warm responses might be taken to express, perhaps, some of the ambiguity she still feels about her situation, as it makes us feel some ambiguity about her. But the emotional switch should not be overplayed, since Eurykleia's second message is significantly different from the first: she now specifically identifies Odysseus as the *beggar,* whom Penelope knows and has tested, not just any old claimant to the title of her husband. Even on just waking up, Penelope's immediate reaction to the news of an "Odysseus" is hyper-cautious, as is her habit, but as soon as Eurykleia completes the equation "beggar = Odysseus" she becomes enthusiastic, asks for more information.

Her next response is again restrained, cautioning Eurykleia not to shout so loud and speculating that it might be no mortal at all but a god who killed the suitors (63). Both Eurykleia and Telemakhos in this scene hold it against Penelope that she retains doubts when everyone else is satisfied: "Your heart is always untrusting" (23.72); "Mother, cruel mother, do you feel nothing, drawing yourself apart this way from Father? Will you not sit with him and talk and question him? What other woman could remain so cold? Who shuns her lord, and he come back to her from wars and wandering, after twenty years? Your heart is hard as flint and never changes!" (23.97–103, trans. Fitzgerald).

Odysseus is more gracious, humorously excusing her distance as repugnance to his dirty clothes and body. Penelope alludes to the signs "which we two know, hidden from everyone else" (23.110) and Odysseus invites her to test him. The bath which follows offers a little break, so that Penelope's test can be felt as something of a surprise. When Penelope still does not respond to his rejuvenated and splendid self, Odysseus becomes impatient, comments on the hardness of her heart, and tells the old nurse to make the bed so that he can sleep alone: "for her heart is like iron" (23.172). Then she repeats the command to Eurykleia to make their bed and to move it outside the master bedroom on the ground floor. Odysseus flares up angrily, because (as he says) he built the house around that bed and one of its posts was an olive trunk rooted in the earth. If it can be moved, that means that some man has been allowed to enter their bedroom and cut through the trunk with an axe. But Penelope was lying—to test this man ("thus she spoke, testing her husband" 23.181) to see if he was truly Odysseus, who was the only one who knew the secret of their bed.

The immobility of the bed, and by extension of the faithful wife, was foreshadowed in the Phaiakian bard's song of Ares and Aphrodite—another bed trick. In the song Hephaistos' trick (*dolos*) was to make "chains that were unbreakable, with links inseparable, so that they would stay firmly in place (*empedon*)" (8.275), and this is in response to the deception and faithlessness of Aphrodite, whom those constraints will bind in one place.[12] Penelope's bed trick balances and counters Hephaistos', since she uses the image of a movable bed to suggest that of an unfaithful wife (both bed and wife's guardianship are *empedon*, 11.178–9, 23.203). But she does so not to prove her fidelity, which is not in question, but rather, by conjuring up a misleading image of infidelity, to force Odysseus to reveal himself.

Thus Odysseus *polumêtis,* the master-trickster ("father, they say your *mêtis* is the best among mortals," 23.124–5), is tricked—not for the first time *— and so in a sense are we. For at that moment we realize that the entire telling has been one-sided, slanted in favor of Odysseus and his enterprises.[13] This limitation to the perspective of male actors is, of course, socially proper and respectful of Penelope's interior space, hence no one would find it problematic during the course of the earlier performance. But when she tricks him the full force and deep ambiguity of the social pressures surrounding Penelope—and accepted by the poet as an unquestioned convention—become apparent. It is easy in this society to express distrust of women and wives, as the passers-by do when they hear the sounds of a wedding feast coming from Odysseus' house (Murnaghan 1987a: 110). "Married at last, I see—the queen so many courted. Sly, cattish wife! She would not keep—not she!—the lord's estate until he came" (23.149–51). Such malicious perspectives, here actually quoted, are to be imagined as always present, as bystanders of both sexes automatically assume the worst of women. But that ease of enunciation should not be wholly equated with either the author's or the character's convictions. Just as the passers-by are *wrong* in their perception of Penelope, so a simple and uncunning misogyny shows an inadequate grasp of the domestic and interpersonal complexities that constrain Mediterranean men and women. †

Homer did not encourage us to ask whether this man really was Odysseus, though we were occasionally asked to entertain doubts about Penelope's faithfulness.[14] But from Penelope's point of view—to which we were not given equal access—this man's identity is a real question, one she has been asking and testing throughout Book 19. She reached a conclusion firm

---

*Elsewhere when Odysseus thinks he is being particularly clever, he is outsmarted: once by Athena (14.250–2) and once by circumstances, when he insists on a reliable old woman rather than one of the flighty and treacherous young maids to wash his feet (19.336–48).

†Another irony separating that system from ours is the different implications of spousal affection: "Men scrutinize all the available evidence to assure themselves that their wives have remained faithful, for it is said that if a woman is having an affair, she will do anything to prevent her husband from discovering it. Her best means of disguise, claim the men of San Blas, is to be overtly affectionate toward her husband, in order to dispel his possible doubts. The social consequences of this view, of course, is that husbands and wives display little open affection for one another" (Brandes 228–9; cf. Abu-Lughod 222).

enough to act on; but this man, shrewd and cognizant as he obviously was, might still have been an imposter—or even a god. I take the author's avoidance of that issue to be a deliberate strategy: the story is told one-sidedly from the point of view of male anxiety and only when Penelope tricks Odysseus do we realize how one-sided the telling had been.

There is an interesting issue here, concerning the reproduction of social values in cultural performances. I emphasized at the beginning that social values cannot, should not be read into a text from the wrong society. The nineteenth-century Britain of Samuel Butler is the wrong frame in which to place the discourse of the *Odyssey*. On the other hand, finding the right frame is not enough, for a cultural product does not simply reproduce or exemplify conventional behavior patterns. Often enough, an author will dramatize those patterns and values in situations where conflict and uncertainty are paramount. The poet of the *Odyssey* is playing in an arena where the rules (of remarriage, of public assembly, of passing from youth to manhood, etc.) are not entirely clear, since societies do not come with a set of instructions as board games do (Bourdieu 1977).

The society for which and on which the *Odyssey* is composed lives with certain lies or fictions. One of the principal social lies is that women and men, whose work does not overlap, are really as different as their separate spheres. But what we are learning to appreciate, thanks to the work of observers like M. Clark and Herzfeld (1986), is the degree to which that separation of roles is not a divine commandment (though it may be spoken of as such) but a rhetorical strategy in a more complicated and shifting game plan.[*] Social propriety is both a moral requirement and a manipulable facade.

Much of the *Odyssey*, while it uses the language of rigid separation between women and men, also calls it into question. One contrast, which I find quite striking, is between the reactions of Penelope and Eumaios to learning the identity of the stranger. As noted above, these two are paired in several

---

[*]Herzfeld 1986 describes the two self-images employed by modern Greeks, one the face of public pride and unquestioned male control, the other recognizing women's domestic power. The temptation to conceal the latter is very great since foreign ethnographers are automatically regarded as members of the elite, from whom the nitty-gritty and somewhat shameful realism of domestic behavior should be hidden. "When a Pefkiot woman slapped her drunkard husband during one of my visits to their home, she was effectively signaling my inclusion into their domestic circle. She was not behaving like the submissive woman of the ethnographic stereotype; rather, she was adopting a different female role, one that was more appropriate to the intimacy of 'inside'. A young married couple who did ethnographic research in Methana similarly discovered not only that household economy often was controlled by 'physically and socially strong women,' but also that sexual joking was acceptable in mixed company 'so long as everyone present was married' (M. Clark 122–3). Clearly, what is important here is the audience; the actors' social competence encompasses the ability to shift between intimacy and formality as the occasion demands" (p. 219).

ways, since both represent achieved rather than "natural" relationships. One might expect, according to a simple gender norm, that women will react very emotionally, men less so. But when Penelope announces to the suitors the contest of the bow, Eumaios weeps aloud and the cowherd wails (21.82–3). They leave the hall, and the beggar follows them through the courtyard and outside the main gate. There he asks them about their fidelity to Odysseus and their willingness to help in taking vengeance on the suitors, and then at last reveals his identity, confirmed by the famous scar on his thigh. Their reaction is to weep aloud as they embrace him, and Odysseus, though returning their embrace, must restrain their outburst: "Stop weeping and groaning, lest someone come out of the hall and see you and report it inside" (21.228–9). Penelope, by what I take to be a designed contrast, reacts stonily to other people's convictions that Odysseus has returned, and only yields to her own desire for emotional release after he has passed her own unique test.

The contrast between Penelope and Eumaios is based partly on class as well as gender, since he, though a prince by birth (15.403–14), has been raised as a field slave, living on the far reaches of Odysseus' estate. Nevertheless Penelope, *qua* woman, might well be expected to be less shrewd and tough than she shows herself to be. Her endurance and cunning are astounding, and their impact is all the greater for the veiled presentation of them by Homer up to Book 23.

To conclude, let us observe the framework within which Homer's sometimes gamey portrayal of the sexes takes place, for it is not that of contemporary feminism and modern economic agents constrained by the needs of industry and capital. Homer's gender irony is focused not so much on relations between the sexes as between spouses—*gunê* as "wife" rather than "woman." The poem exalts a certain, quite explicit ideal of marriage. Marriage in the *Odyssey* is said to be at its best a union of two likeminded people (6.180–5). As Odysseus says to Nausikaa: "And may the gods accomplish your desire: a home, a husband, and like-mindedness (*homo-phrosunê*) with him—the best thing in the world being a strong house held in serenity where husband and wife think alike (*homo-phroneonte*). Woe to their enemies, joy to their friends! But all this they know best" (6.180–5).

But it is difficult to portray the intimacy of likemindedness and still be faithful to the public conventions that women stay in the house, weaving, veiled, guarding the stores, while men roam outside, fighting, farming, and winning goods to store. What the *Odyssey* demonstrates, in its cunning way, is that *mêtis* is not sex-specific. It does so by half-accepting the quiet wife convention for most of its length, and only at the end surprising us with the suddenly unmistakable realization that Penelope had chosen to put the bow into this stranger's hands, thinking that there was every likelihood that he was really Odysseus, but remaining only 99% certain. Only at the end when she has tricked him does the poet make us see that we had probably been underestimating her, taking her somewhat for granted, as Odysseus did. She, of course, is not all wives; like Odysseus she is the extraordinary case, the best wife for the best husband. But the focus of the poet's demonstration is that the excellence of being a husband and being a wife are in some sense the same.

At their reunion, this amazing poet distorts a traditional literary device to capture that central and hard-won intimacy which is supposed to be the ideal of marriage. A remarkable simile marks their mutual recognition—hers that he is really Odysseus, his that she is as clever as he is and that he had not realized it:

> Now from his breast into his eyes the ache
> of longing mounted, and he wept at last,
> his dear wife, clear and faithful, in his arms,
> longed for
>   as the sunwarmed earth is longed for by swimmers
> spent in rough water where their ship went down
> under Poseidon's blows, gale winds and tons of sea.
> Few men can keep alive through a big surf
> to crawl, clotted with brine, on kindly beaches
> in joy, in joy, knowing the abyss behind:
> so she rejoiced, her gaze upon her husband,
> her white arms round him pressed as though forever.
>   (Fitzgerald, modified: 23.231–40)

The simile begins as a picture of his feelings and ends as a picture of hers (Murnaghan 1987b: 45–6). We go into the simile on his side and come out (we do not know how) on hers. At this moment they embrace and feel the same feelings, think the same thoughts, as if they were the same person: for a moment we cannot tell which is which.[15] It is not easy to say in the cultural language of that highly stratified society that men and women are in any sense equal. But the author of the *Odyssey* has succeeded in doing so.

6
Double Consciousness in Sappho's Lyrics

Monique Wittig and Sande Zeig in their *Lesbian Peoples: Material for a Dictionary*[1] devote a full page to Sappho. The page is blank. Their silence is one quite appropriate response to Sappho's lyrics, particularly refreshing in comparison to the relentless trivialization, the homophobic anxieties and the sheer misogyny that have infected so many ancient and modern responses to her work.[2] As Mary Barnard (34) puts it:

> I wanted to hear
> Sappho's laughter
> and the speech of
> her stringed shell.
>
> What I heard was
> whiskered mumble-
> ment of grammarians:
>
> Greek pterodactyls
> and Victorian dodos.

The very eminent classical scholars from F. G. Welcker to Denys Page who have assembled and sifted through so much of what can or might be known of Sappho, and whose work is indispensable to us, had their own matrices of understanding, their own concerns and commitments, which were, I should think, no more and no less time-bound and culture-specific than are ours.[3] But I doubt that those scholars would have understood our matrices (feminist, anthropological, pro-lesbian), given that their expertise was in such things as ancient metrics ("pterodactyls") rather than in ancient mores, whereas we are able in some good measure to understand theirs. This is an example of what I will refer to below as double consciousness, a kind of cultural bi-lingualism on our part, for we must be aware of and fluent in using two systems of understanding. Because Lobel and Page assumed the validity of Victorian no-no's, they were (it now seems to us) deaf to much of what Sappho was saying, tone-deaf to her deeper melodies. The forms of both worship and anxiety that have surrounded Sappho in the ancient and modern records require some analysis.[4] Part of the explanation is the fact that her poetry is continuously focused on women and sexuality, subjects which provoke many readers to excess.[5]

But the centering on women and sexuality is not quite enough to explain the mutilated and violent discourse which keeps cropping up around her. After all Anakreon speaks of the same subjects. A deeper explanation refers to the *subject* more than the object of her lyrics—the fact that it is a *woman* speaking about women and sexuality. To some audiences this would have been a double violation of the ancient rules which dictated that a proper woman was to be silent in the public world (defined as men's sphere) and that a proper woman accepted the administration and definition of her sexuality by her father and her husband.

I will set aside for the present the question of how women at various times and places actually conducted their lives in terms of private and public activity, appearance, and authority. If we were in a position to know more of the actual texture of ancient women's lives and not merely the maxims and rules uttered by men, we could fairly expect to find that many women abided by these social rules or were forced to, and that they sometimes enforced obedience on other women; but, since all social codes can be manipulated and subverted as well as obeyed, we would also expect to find that many women had effective strategies of resistance and false compliance by which they attained a working degree of freedom for their lives. * Leaving aside all these questions, however, I simply begin my analysis with the fact that there was available a common understanding that proper women ought to be publicly submissive to male definitions, and that a very great pressure of propriety could at any time be invoked to shame a woman who acted on her own sexuality.

This is at least the public ethic and the male norm. It cannot have been entirely absent from the society of Lesbos in Sappho's time. Unfortunately, our knowledge of that period and place is limited to a few general facts and rumors—a culture of some luxury, at least for the wealthy; aristocratic families fighting each other for power; the typical sixth-century emergence of tyrannies (Myrsilos) and mediating law-givers (Pittakos). Sappho's kin were clearly active in this elite feuding since she was banished with them

---

*There was also the category of heroic, exceptional woman, e.g. Herodotos' version of Artemisia, who is used to "prove the rule" every time he mentions her (7.99, 8.68, 8.87f., 8.101), and the stories collected by Plutarch *de virtutibus mulierum*. The stated purpose of this collection is to show that *aretê*, "virtue" or "excellence," is the same in men and women, but the stories actually show only that some women in times of crisis have stepped out of their regular anonymity and performed male roles when men were not available (Schaps 1982).

from Lesbos to Sicily around the turn of the century. Lacking a reasonably dense texture of social information, such as we had for Chapters One to Three, and given the fragmentary state of her literary remains (in contrast to *Daphnis and Chloe* and the *Odyssey*), the kinds of anthropological investigation employed elsewhere in this book become much more difficult.

What I want to recover in this chapter are the traces of Sappho's consciousness in the face of these masculine norms of behavior, her attitude to the public ethic and her allusions to private reality. This is becoming a familiar topic and problem in feminist anthropology: Do women see things in the same way as men? How can gender-specific differences of cultural attitude be discerned when one group is muted? Does their silence give consent? Or have we merely not found the right questions to ask and ways of asking them? My way of "reading what is there"[*] focuses on the politics of space—the role of women as excluded from public male domains and enclosed in private female areas—and on Sappho's consciousness[†] of this ideology. My analysis avowedly begins with an interest in sexual politics—the relations of power between women and men as two groups in the same society. In some sense the choice of a method will predetermine the kind and range of results which may emerge: a photo-camera will not record sounds, a non-political observer will not notice facts of political significance. Thus my readings of Sappho are in principle not meant to displace other readings but to add to the store of perceptions of "what is there."

There are various "publics and privates" which might be contrasted. What I have in mind here by "public" is quite specifically the recitation of Homer at civic festivals considered as an expression of common cultural traditions. Samuel Butler notwithstanding, Homer and the singers of his tradition were certainly men and the homeric epics as we have them cannot readily be conceived as women's songs. Women are integral to the social and poetic structure of both *Iliad* and *Odyssey*, and the *notion* of a woman's consciousness is particularly vital to the *Odyssey*, as the previous chapter has shown. But Nausikaa and Penelope live in a male-prominent world, coping with problems of honor and enclosure which were differentially assigned to

---

[*] "A feminist theory of poetry would begin to take into account the context in history of these poems and their political connections and implications. It would deal with the fact that women's poetry conveys . . . a special kind of consciousness. . . . Concentrating on consciousness and the politics of women's poetry, such a theory would evolve new ways of reading what is there" (Bernikow 10–1).

[†] Consciousness of course is not a solid object which can be discovered intact like an easter egg lying somewhere in the garden (as in the Sapphic fragment 166 Leda is said to have found an egg hidden under the hyacinths). Sappho's lyrics are many-layered constructions of melodic words, images, ideas, and arguments in a formulaic system of sharable points of view (personas). I take it for granted that the usual distinctions between "the real Sappho" as author and speaker(s) of the poems will apply when I speak here of Sappho's consciousness.

women, and their "subjectivity" in the epic must ultimately be analyzed as an expression of a male consciousness. Insofar as Homer presents a set of conventional social and literary formulas, he inescapably embodies and represents the definition of public culture as male territory.*

Archaic lyric, such as that composed by Sappho, was also not composed for private reading but for performance to an audience (Merkelbach 1957; Russo 1973–4). Sappho often seems to be searching her soul in a very intimate way but this intimacy is in some measure formulaic (Lanata) and is certainly shared with some group of listeners. And yet, maintaining this thesis of the public character of lyric, we can still propose three senses in which such song may be "private": first, composed in the person of a woman (whose consciousness was socially defined as outside the public world of men); second, shared only with women (that is, other "private" persons: "and now I shall sing this beautiful song to delight the women who are my companions," frag. 160 L-P,⁶); and third, sung on informal occasions, what we would simply call poetry readings, rather than on specific ceremonial occasions such as sacrifice, festival, leave-taking, or initiation.† The lyric tradition, as Nagy argues, may be older than the epic, and if older perhaps equally honored as an achievement of beauty in its own right.

The view of lyric as a subordinate element in celebrations and formal occasions is no more compelling than the view, which I prefer, of song as honored and celebrated at least sometimes in itself. Therefore I doubt that Sappho always needed a sacrifice or dance or wedding *for which* to compose a song; the institution of lyric composition was strong enough to occasion her songs *as songs*. Certainly Sappho speaks of goddesses and religious festivities, but it is by no means certain that her own poems are either for a cult-performance or that her circle of women friends (*hetairai*) is identical in extension with the celebrants in a festival she mentions.‡ It is possible

---

*In this territory and at these recitations women are present—Homer is not a forbidden text to women, not an arcane *arrhêton* of the male mysteries. In the *Odyssey* (1.325–9) Penelope hears and reacts to the epic poetry of a bard singing in her home, but her objections to his theme, the homecoming from Troy, are silenced by Telemakhos. Arete's decision to give more gifts to Odysseus (*Od.* 11.335–41) after he has sung of the women he saw in the Underworld may be an implicit sign of her approval of his poetry. Helen in *Iliad* 6 delights in the fact that she is a theme of epic poetry (357–8) and weaves the stories of the battles fought for her into her web (125–8).

†Homer seems to include this possibility in the range of performing *klea andrôn* ["deeds of men"] when he presents Achilles singing to his own *thumos* ["spirit"], while Patroklos sits in silence, not listening as an audience but waiting for Achilles to stop (*Il.* 9.186–91).

‡Sappho is only one individual, and may have been untypical in her power to achieve a literary life and renown. Claims that society in her time and place allowed greater scope for women in general to attain a measure of public esteem are based almost entirely on Sappho's poems (including probably Plutarch *Lykourgos* 18.4, *Theseus* 19.3, Philostratos *Life of Apollonios*

that neither of these latter two senses of "private" were historically valid for Sappho's performances. Yet her lyrics, as compositions which had some publicity, bear some quality of being in principle from another world than Homer's, not just from a different tradition, and they embody a consciousness both of her "private," woman-centered world and the other, "public" world. This chapter is an experiment in using these categories to unfold some aspects of Sappho's many-sided meaning.

Poem 1: Many-mindedness and Magic

One of the passages in Sappho which has been best illuminated in recent criticism is her first (and now only) complete poem, *poikilophron athanat' Aphrodita.* The reason for thinking that it stood first in a collection of her works is that Hephaistion, writing a treatise on meters in the second century C.E., took it as his paradigm of what was by then called the Sapphic stanza. The very notion, however, of a first poem in a first book hardly makes sense in Sappho's world, where the text seems to have circulated at first as a script and score for professional and amateur performers. Then we have to allow for some three to four hundred years in which single songs, groups of songs, various collections which interested performers made for their own use were in circulation before the scholar-librarians at Alexandria assembled, sorted, and compared the many variant versions to produce a canonical corpus of Sappho's lyrics in eight or nine books.

There were in fact at least two editions produced at the Alexandrian library, one by Aristophanes (who seems to have invented the convention that there were exactly nine great lyric poets of early Greece; Pfeiffer 205) and one by his pupil and successor Aristarchos.[7] Two of her fragments survive in written copies which may actually pre-date those standard editions: one scrawled on a shard and one on papyrus, both of the third century B.C.E. (fragments 2 and 98). The survival of poem 1 is due to the fact that Dionysios of Halikarnassos, writing a treatise on style, chose it for quotation as an example of perfect smoothness. This is sheer good luck for us; he might have quoted Simonides.

In the handing on of the text from one scribe or performer to another until it reaches our modern editors, who fiddle with it some more before handing it over to us, further uncertainties are introduced. The works of Dionysios and Hephaistion were themselves copied many times over before they reached us. The sort of problem which infects even canonical book texts is illustrated by the first word in Sappho's poem 1. Some manuscripts of Dionysios and some of Hephaistion write *poikilothron',* which all modern

---

1.30). The invention of early women poets is taken to extremes by Tatian in his *adversus Graecos* and by Ptolemy Chennos (Chapter Five, p. 143–4).

editors prefer, and other manuscripts have *poikilophron* (Neuberger-Do-nath), for which a strong and interesting argument may be made. *Poikilo-phron* means "having a mind (*-phron*) which is *poikilos*," a notion usually translated by words like "dappled," "variegated," "changeful," "complex." It designates the quality of having many internal contrasts, whether per-ceived by the eye or by the mind. An embroidered robe is *poikilos,* Odysseus' crafty mind is *poikilos.*

I call attention to this not only as a lesson in the almost immeasurable distance, with all its stages of loss and distortion, which separates Sappho and her whole world from us but also because poem 1 is an astonishing example of *many-mindedness* (for want of a more elegant term). Other Greek lyric poets sing marvelous poems of hate and sorrow and personal ecstacy which is somehow never very far from regret and chagrin, but they do so from a single perspective, elaborating the mind and feelings of a single persona in a fixed situation. Sappho's poem 1, however, contains several personal perspectives, whose multiple relations to each other set up a field of voices and evaluations. This field-effect makes the rest of Greek lyric appear, by contrast, relatively single-minded, or as we can now say, not-*poikilos*. The field in poem 1 includes at least three Sappho's, two Aphrod-ite's, an unnamed girlfriend (representative of many), and (in virtue of echoing and parody effects) several homeric characters as well.

Let us consider the last first. Several analyses have developed the idea that Sappho is speaking in an imagined scene which represents that of Diomedes on the battlefield in *Iliad* 5 (Cameron 1949; Page 1955: 7; Svenbro; Stanley; Rissman). Sappho uses a traditional prayer formula, of which Diomedes' appeal to Athena at *Iliad* 5.115–7 is an example ("Hear me, Atrytone, child of aegis-bearing Zeus; if ever you stood beside my father supporting his cause in bitter battle, now again support me, Athena"), and she models Aphrodite's descent to earth in a chariot on the descent of Athena and Hera (5.719–72), who are coming to help the wounded Diomedes (5.781). Sappho asks Aphrodite to be her ally, literally her companion in battle, *summachos.*

> Intricate, undying Aphrodite, snare-weaver, child of Zeus, I pray thee,
> do not tame my spirit, great lady, with pain and sorrow. But come to me
> now if ever before you heard my voice from afar and leaving your father's
> house, yoked golden chariot and came. Beautiful sparrows swiftly
>   brought you
> to the murky ground with a quick flutter of wings from the sky's height
> through clean air. They were quick in coming. You, blessed goddess,
> a smile on your divine face, asked what did I suffer, this time again,
> and why did I call, this time again, and what did I in my frenzied heart
> most want to happen. Whom am I to persuade, this time again. . .
> to lead to your affection? Who, O Sappho, does you wrong? For one who
>   flees will

> soon pursue, one who rejects gifts will soon be making offers, and one who
> does not love will soon be loving, even against her will. Come to me even now
> release me from these mean anxieties, and do what my heart wants done,
> you yourself be my ally. *

About the Greek text we should first note that even this one integral poem has a nick on its surface. At the beginning of its fifteenth line (line 19 in the quatrain arrangement adopted in many editions), the manuscripts of Dionysios give a garbled reading and the papyrus copy (P. Oxy. 2288), which is from the second century C.E., although it gives a slightly more intelligible run of letters is still not entirely clear. Second, about pronunciation we have, I think, to confess that the music of a pitch-accent language is not easily appreciated by speakers of a stress-accent language, and further that there are deep uncertainties not only about the placement of the pitch in Aeolic Greek but about fundamental principles concerning their vowels and consonants. The ancient Greek grammarians tell us that Aeolic Greek was psilotic (that is, it did not use initial h), that its accent was everywhere recessive (did not fall on the final syllable of a word), that is used -sd- for -ds- and br- for initial -r-. But as Hooker has emphasized, this information is very dubious, in some cases being contradicted by inscriptions found on Lesbos, in others applying at most to orthography rather than to actual pronunciation, and in any case of questionable relevance to the state of verbal performance and the art of singing many centuries before the grammarians.

Just as we can demonstrate that virtually all biographical information recorded by the Peripatetic and Alexandrian scholars is based on inferences from the poems themselves, and are frequently mistaken inferences, because they had nothing but the texts themselves to work with, so the grammarians' dogmas are not based on any privileged access to the seventh century B.C.E. and in certain respects we actually know more than they did.

But with that very skeptical prelude, I invite you now to read aloud what was one of the most beautiful compositions in all of archaic Greek verse:

> poikilophron âthanat' Aphroditâ
> pai Dios doloploke, lissomai se,
> mê m' asaisi mêd' oniaisi damna, potnia, thûmon.
>
> alla tuid' elth', ai pota kâterôta
> tâs emâs audâs aïoisa pêloi
> eklues, patros de domon lipoisa chrûsion êlthes,

---

*Translations of Sappho in this chapter are my own; ellipses indicate that the Greek is incomplete.

arm' upasdeuxaisa; kaloi de s' âgon
ôkees strouthoi peri gâs melainâs
pukna dinnentes pter' ap' ôranôitheros dia messô,

aipsa d' exîkonto; su d', ô makaira,
meidiaisais' âthanatôi prosôpôi
êre' otti dêute pepontha kôtti dêute kalêmmi

kôtti moi malista thelô genesthai
mainolai thûmôi. "Tina dêute peithô
aps s'agên es san philotâta? Tis s', ô Psapph', adikêei?

kai gar ai pheugei, tacheôs diôxei;
ai de dôra mê deket', alla dôsei;
ai de mê philei, tacheôs philêsei kouk etheloisa.

elthe moi kai nûn, chalepân de lûson
ek merimnân, ossa de moi telessai
thûmos îmerrei, teleson; su d' autâ summachos esso.

One way of interpreting the correspondences which have been noticed is to say that Sappho presents herself as a kind of Diomedes on the field of love, that she is articulating her own experience in traditional (male) terms and showing that women too have manly excellence (*aretê;* Bolling 1959, Marry). But this view that the poem is mainly about *erôs* and *aretê* and uses Diomedes merely as a background model, falls short.[8] Sappho's use of homeric passages is a way of allowing us, even encouraging us, to approach her consciousness as a woman and poet reading Homer. The homeric hero is not just a starting point for Sappho's discourse about her own love, rather Diomedes as he exists in the *Iliad* is central to what Sappho is saying about the *distance* between Homer's world and her own. A woman listening to the *Iliad* must cross over a gap which separates her experience from the subject of the poem, a gap which does not exist in quite the same way for male listeners. How can Sappho murmur along with the rhapsode the speeches of Diomedes, uttering and impersonating his appeal for help? Sappho's answer to this aesthetic problem is that she can only do so by substituting her concerns for those of the hero while maintaining the same structure of plight / prayer / intervention. Poem 1 says, among other things, "This is how I, a woman and poet, become able to appreciate a typical scene from the *Iliad*."

Though the Diomedeia is a typical passage, Sappho's choice of it is not random, for it is a kind of test case for the issue of women's consciousness of themselves as participants without a poetic voice of their own at the public recitations of traditional Greek heroism. In *Iliad* 5, between Diomedes' appeal to the goddess and the descent of Athena and Hera, Aphrodite herself is driven from the battlefield after Diomedes stabs her in the hand. Homer identifies

Aphrodite as a "feminine" goddess, weak, *analkis*, unsuited to take part in male warfare (331, 428). Her appropriate sphere, says Diomedes exulting in his victory over her, is to seduce weak women (*analkides*, 348–9). By implication, if "feminine" women (and all mortal women are "feminine" by definition and prescription) try to participate in men's affairs—warfare or war poetry—they will, like Aphrodite, be driven out at spear point.

Poem 1 employs not only a metaphorical use of the *Iliad* (transferring the language for the experience of soldiers to the experience of women in love) and a familiarization of the alien poem (so that it now makes better sense to women readers), but a *multiple identification* with its characters. Sappho is acting out the parts both of Diomedes and of Aphrodite as they are characterized in *Iliad* 5. Aphrodite, like Sappho, suffers pain (*odunêisi*, 354), and is consoled by a powerful goddess who asks "Who has done this to you?" (373). Aphrodite borrows Ares' chariot to escape from the battle and ride to heaven (358–67), the reverse of her action in Sappho's poem (Benedetto, who refers to the poem as "Aphrodite's revenge"). Sappho therefore is in a sense presenting herself both as a desperate Diomedes needing the help of a goddess (Athena/Aphrodite) and as a wounded and expelled female (Aphrodite/Sappho) seeking a goddess' consolation (Dione/Aphrodite).

This multiple identification with several actors in an Iliadic scene represents on another level an admired feature of Sappho's poetics—her adoption of multiple points of view in a single poem. This is especially noteworthy in poem 1 where she sketches a scene of encounter between a victim and a controlling deity. The intensification of both pathos and mastery in the encounter is due largely to the ironic *double consciousness* of the poet-Sappho speaking in turn the parts of suffering "Sappho" and impassive goddess. Consider the cast of characters in poem 1, each different and each regarding the others with a look of mingled admiration and distrust. There is first the speaker in need, whose name we learn in line 15 is Psappo.* She is praying for help to Aphrodite, who is therefore the implied fictional audience of the entire poem and is to be imagined listening to all its words. Part of what Aphrodite hears is a narrative account of how she herself on a previous occasion mounted her sparrow-drawn chariot and drove down the sky and answered Sappho's prayers with a series of questions. This past-Aphrodite is not at all the same as the present-Aphrodite: the past-Aphrodite is an active character in the praying-Sappho's narrative, while the present-Aphrodite says nothing, does nothing, only listens—and presumably smiles.

One might wonder at the lengthy elaboration of the chariot-narrative, full of circumstantial detail, but I think the point is to create a slow build-up from distance to nearness, the goddess coming gradually closer to the

---

*We may take it as another measure of our distance from her that the pep and bite of the consonants in "Psappo," with all the p's sounded, have evaporated into the tired fizz of "Saffo."

speaker, taking her time (poetically, in the movement of the verse, even though she twice says it was a quick journey). As Aphrodite comes physically closer, she also becomes more vivid. First, her words are reported in indirect speech, and then she breaks into direct speech, so that Sappho the singer, impersonating Sappho in needful prayer, now suddenly is speaking in the voice of Aphrodite herself, so that the word "you," which from the beginning has been directed to Aphrodite, in line 15 now refers to Sappho. Fictional speaker and fictional audience change places, or rather the present-Aphrodite now hears from the mouth of praying Sappho the words which the past-Aphrodite spoke to the past-Sappho. The slow approach to this direct speech, starting far away (*pêloi*) in heaven, makes Aphrodite's words a kind of epiphany, a reported epiphany in a prayer asking for a repetition of the same.

For Sappho is once again tied up in a state of anxious desire. The three times repeated word for this is *dêute,* which is a contraction of *aute,* "again," and *dê,* an intensifying particle, something like "indeed," which gives a flavor to "again" which we might read as quizzical or ironic or pretended disappointment. Since the past-Aphrodite says "once again" to the past-Sappho, we are led to think of yet another Sappho, the one who got into the same fix before. The doubling of Aphrodite (present and past) and the tripling of Sappho (present, past, and . . . pluperfect) leads like the mirrors in a fun house to receding vistas of endlessly repeated intercessions, promises, and love affairs.

The appearance of an infinite regress, however, is framed and bounded by another Sappho. The person who we must think of as designing the whole is functionally and indeed practically quite different from any of the Sappho's in the poem. The author-performer who impersonates a character-in-need is not at the moment, at least *qua* performer, in need. In fact my primary impression of poem 1 is one of exquisite control, which puts Sappho-the-poet in a role analogous to Aphrodite's as the smiling, tolerant, ever helpful ally of her own *thumos,* "spirit." The guileful weaver, the many-minded one who performs intricate shifts of perspective, is fictionally Aphrodite but poetically Sappho herself.

The sounds of the first line are worth a close inspection, for they contain a meaning which is quite untranslatable. With the reading *poikilophron,* "many-minded," aided by the compound *âthanat',* "not-mortal," it might be possible to hear in the very name of Aphrodite a playful etymology: the negative prefix *a-* plus the root *phro-* would yield "no-minded." Certainly the verbal field of the poem, with all its references to guile and to Sappho going out of her mind, encourages the possibility. Note too how the sounds of *poikilophron* and *doloploke* are recycled: *poikilo-* and *-ploke* have just the same consonants.

Such attention to micro-accuracies is typical of much Greek verse, and for Sappho we have at least one other case of etymologizing a divine name in a novel way. Fragment 104a reads "Hesperos, bringing together everything which shining Dawn scattered, you bring the sheep, you bring the goat, you bring the child to its mother" (or possibly, "you bring the child away from its mother"). The two syllables of the Greek root meaning Evening Star, *(H)es-per,* are echoed in the word "you bring," *pher-eis,* three times repeated. J. S. Clay, who pointed this out (a scholiast on Euripides' *Orestes* had noticed it too), takes it as a revaluation of Hesiod's characterization of Dawn as the one who scatters the family and sends people to work.[9] This is a good example of how closely textured and in-wrought Sappho's verse can be, and what a high standard of complexity and intention we are justified in applying.

But if such weaving and complexity give *poikilophron* a good claim to being the first word of Sappho's poem 1, there are also attractive reasons on the side of *poikilothron',* which is most often taken to mean "sitting on an elaborately wrought throne." Although there certainly were, as Page (1955: 5) catalogues, elaborately wrought thrones, the interesting side of this compound word is not *thronos* meaning "throne" but a much rarer root, *throna,* found once in Homer, once in Theokritos, and several times in the Alexandrian poets Nikandros and Lykophron (Lawler, Bolling 1958, Putnam; see also Bonner). In the later poets it refers to some kind of magic drugs. Theokritos' young woman in Idyll 2 is trying to perform a ceremony which will enchant her lover and bring him back to her. She tells her servant to smear the drugs, *throna,* on the threshold of Delphis' house and say "I am sprinkling the bones of Delphis." "Sprinkle" is the standard translation of the verb *passô,* but homeric physicians also "sprinkle" drugs *(pharmaka)* onto wounds, so possibly the verb can include the more general action of applying or putting on.[10]

The homeric occurrence of the word is highly suggestive. Andromache is sitting at her loom, soon to hear the news of her husband Hektor's death. "She was weaving loom-cloth in a corner of the high house, a red double cloak, and she was sprinkling variegated *throna* on it" (*Iliad* 22.440–1): *en de throna poikil' epasse.* The conjunction of *throna* and *poikila* here might well tempt us to wonder whether Sappho actually did sing *poikilothron',* and if so what would it mean. The usual interpretation of *throna* in *Iliad* 22 is "embroidered flowers." "Embroidered flowers" is surely too diminished a translation of the *throna* which Andromache is "sprinkling" onto her cloth. Instead I would sketch the semantic field of *throna* as somehow including both drugs and weaving.

I have already noted that "sprinkle" *(passô)* is what one does with *throna,* whether they are put on wounds or on loom-cloth. For further connections between drugs and weaving, I would cite the figure of Helen the weaver, who not only weaves (literally, "sprinkles") the story of the *Iliad* into her loom-cloth (3.125–8) but when she is home with Menelaos sits near him with a basket of wool and a spindle and when the war-tales they tell make everyone melancholy she puts drugs (*pharmaka*) into the wine-bowl and has it served around (*Odyssey* 4.120–35, 219–33).

Another locus for the conjunction of weaving and drugs is the *kestos,* the girdle, of Aphrodite, which too is described as *poikilos* and contains worked into it the powers to charm and enchant (*Iliad* 14.214–21). Helen's drugs and Aphrodite's charmed girdle are powerful magic, using the word loosely to designate many forms of alternate, unofficial therapy. Since women did sing while spending long hours at the loom (so Kirke at *Odyssey* 10.221–2), I can readily imagine that some of those chants would wish good things onto the cloth and even that filaments of lucky plants and patterns of luck-bringing design would be woven into the best fabric.

In 1979 a new papyrus fragment of a Greek magical handbook was published which is very important for the fragmentary and suppressed history of that subject (Brashear; Maltomini; Obbink; Janko). Since most of the surviving collections of spells exist in copies made in the second to fourth centuries C.E., it is easy enough for traditional historians to dismiss all that as a late and alien intrusion into the sanctuary of rational Greek culture. But the new papyrus belongs to the late first century B.C.E. and confirms what is likely enough on other grounds—that the writing down of magic has a history comparable to other kinds of writing. Magical spells to produce love or cure a headache (both contained in the new papyrus) are like collections of natural marvels and folktales, the sort of cultural product which has a long and detailed oral history but which no one thought to write down until the changed social conditions of the Alexandrian and Roman empires. Certainly in the one area of magic which does have a continuous textual history from the sixth century B.C.E. to the sixth century C.E.—viz., curses written on lead and buried, sometimes with tortured dolls, in graves of the untimely dead—we can assert with confidence that the practice itself is ancient and uninterrupted.

For students of Sappho the fascinating feature of the new magical papyrus is that its language has some resemblance to that of poem 1. It involves an enchanted apple which is to be thrown in the direction of the intended love-object. The throwing of apples as a token of erotic interest is a quite widespread custom in Greek communities.[11] The incantation is a hexameter prayer to Aphrodite, asking her to "perfect this perfect song," or "fulfill a song of fulfillment," using the same word which Sappho repeats in her last stanza, "accomplish what my heart desires to accomplish." This is fairly standard in the language of prayer and request (*Iliad* 14.195–6). Standard too is the address to a great goddess as *potnia thea,* "lady goddess," found both in poem 1 and in the magical papyrus, but in the fragmentary magical text it is found next to the word *apothanô,* "I may die," which is found several times in Sappho (fragment 94: "I wish without guile to die;" fragment 31: "I seem to be little short of dying"). Closer still are the words *katatrechô, autos de me pheugei,* "I am running after, but he is fleeing from me" (column 2, line 12). Other magical papyri contain calls for assistance in terms as immediate and direct as Sappho's to Aphrodite to come and stand beside her in battle as a fellow-fighter: e.g., "Come and stand beside me for this project and work with me" (PGM XII.95). All of this may mean no more than that the magical papyrus shows the influence of Sappho, but the magical associations of *throna* (if that is the right reading) might explain why the later enchanter would naturally be drawn to echoing Sappho poem 1.

Poised between two possibilities—the many-mindedness of *poikilophron,* the magic of *poikilothron'*—I can see no way to decide that one must be right and the other wrong. Better to allow both to be heard and to appreciate how Sappho in poem 1 may be alluding to a goddess' magic and certainly is demonstrating her many-mindedness. Such multiple self-mirroring in the face of another, along with the alternation of viewpoints so that we in turn sympathize with and stand apart from each of the poem's five characters, is an achievement which reaches out into a different dimension, compared with the other Greek poets of the seventh and sixth centuries B.C.E. This complexity of understanding, which generates a field of personal perspectives, each regarding the other as alike but different, shows how comparable lyrics by poets of her time are quite truly and profoundly solo performances.

Such many-mindedness is intrinsic to the situation of Greek women understanding men's culture, as it is to any silenced group within a culture which acknowledges its presence but not its authentic voice. This leads to an interesting reversal of the standard (and oppressive) stricture on women's literature that it represents only a small and limited area of the larger world.[12] Such a view portrays women's consciousness according to the *social* contrast of public/private, as if women's literature occupied but a small circle somewhere inside the larger circle of men's literature, just as women are restricted to a domestic enclosure. But insofar as men's public culture is truly public, displayed as the governing norm of social interaction "in the streets," it is accessible to women as well as to men. Because men define and exhibit their language and manners as *the* culture and segregate women's language and manners as a subculture, inaccessible to and protected from extra-familial men, women are in the position of knowing two cultures where men know only one.

From the point of view of *consciousness* (rather than physical space) we must diagram the circle of women's literature as a larger one which includes men's literature as one phase or compartment of women's cultural knowledge. Women in a male-prominent society are thus like a linguistic minority in a culture whose public actions are all conducted in the majority language. To participate even passively in the public arena the minority must be bilingual; the majority feels no such need to learn the minority's language. Sappho's consciousness therefore is necessarily a double consciousness, her participation in the public literary tradition always contains an inevitable alienation.

Poem 1 contains a statement of how important it is to have a double consciousness. Aphrodite reminds "Sappho" of the ebb and flow of conflicting emotions, of sorrow succeeded by joy, of apprehensiveness followed by relief, of loss turning into victory. The goddess' reminder not to be single-mindedly absorbed in one moment of experience can be related to the pattern of the *Iliad* in general, where the tides of battle flow back and forth, flight alternating with pursuit. This is well illustrated in *Iliad* 5, which is also the homeric locus for the specific form of alternation in fortunes which consists of wounding and miraculous healing. Two gods (Aphrodite and Ares) and one hero (Aineias) are injured and saved.

Recuperative alternation is the theme of poem 1, as it is of *Iliad* 5. But because of Sappho's "private" point of view and double consciousness it becomes not only the theme but the *process* of the poem, in the following sense: Sappho appropriates an alien text, the very one which states the exclusion of "weak" women from men's territory; she implicitly reveals the inadequacy of that denigration; and she restores the fullness of Homer's text by isolating and alienating its deliberate exclusion of the feminine and the erotic.

For when we have absorbed Sappho's complex re-impersonation of the homeric roles (male and female) and learned to see what was marginal as encompassing, we notice that there is a strain of anxious self-alienation in Diomedes' expulsion of Aphrodite. The overriding need of a battling warrior is to be strong and unyielding; hence the ever-present temptation (which is also a desire) is to be weak. This is most fully expressed at *Iliad* 22.111–30, where Hektor views laying down his weapons to parley with Achilles as effeminate and erotic. Diomedes' hostility to Aphrodite (= the effeminate and erotic) is a kind of scapegoating, his affirmation of an ideal of masculine strength against his *own* possible "weakness." For, in other contexts outside the press of battle, the homeric heroes have intense emotional lives and their vulnerability there is much like Sappho's: they are as deeply committed to friendship networks as Sappho ("He gave the horses to Deipylos, his dear comrade, whom he valued more than all his other age-mates," 325–6); they give and receive gifts as Sappho does; they wrong each other and re-establish friendships with as much feeling as Sappho and her beloved. In a "Sapphic" reading, the emotional isolation of the Iliadic heroes from their domestic happiness stands out more strongly ("no longer will his children run up to his lap and say 'Papa,'" 408). We can reverse the thesis that Sappho uses Homer to heroize her world and say that insofar as her poems are a reading of Homer (and so lead us back to read Homer again) they set up a feminine perspective on male activity which shows more clearly the inner structure and motivation of the exclusion of the feminine from male arenas.

I return to the image of the double circle—Sappho's consciousness is a larger circle enclosing the smaller one of Homer. Reading the *Iliad* is for her an experience of double consciousness. The movement thus created is threefold: by temporarily restricting herself to that smaller circle she can understand full well what Homer is saying; when she brings *her* total experience to bear she sees the limitation of his world; by offering her version of this experience in a poem she shows the strengths of her world, the apparent incompleteness of Homer's, and casts new illumination on some of the marginal and easily overlooked aspects of Homer. This threefold movement of appropriation from the "enemy," exposure of his weakness and recognition of his worth is like the actions of homeric heroes who vanquish, despoil and sometimes forgive. Underlying the relations of Sappho's persona to the characters of Diomedes and Aphrodite are the relations of Sappho the author to Homer, a struggle of reader and text (audience and tradition), of woman listening and man reciting.

Poem 16: What Men Desire

A sense of what we now call the sexual politics of literature seems nearly explicit in poem 16:

> Some assert that a troup of horsemen, some of foot-soldiers, some that a
> fleet of ships is the most beautiful thing on the dark earth; but I
> assert that it is whatever anyone desires. It is quite simple to make
> this intelligible to all, for she who was far and away preeminent in beauty
> of all humanity—Helen—abandoning her husband, the . . . ,
> went sailing to Troy and took no thought for child or dear parents, but
> beguiled . . . herself . . . , for . . . lightly . . . reminds me now of
>   Anaktoria
> absent: whose lovely step and shining glance of face I would prefer
> to see than Lydians' chariots and fighting men in arms . . . cannot be . . .
> human . . . to wish to share . . . unexpectedly.

[This is a poem of eight stanzas, of which the first, second, third and fifth are almost intact, the rest lost or very fragmentary.]

It is easy to read this as a comment on the system of values in heroic poetry. Against the panoply of men's opinions on beauty (all of which focus on military organizations, regimented masses of anonymous fighters), Sappho sets herself—"but I"—and a very abstract proposition about desire. The stanza first opposes one woman to a mass of men and then transcends that opposition when Sappho announces that "the most beautiful" is "whatever you or I or anyone may long for." This amounts to a re-interpretation of the kind of meaning the previous claims had, rather than a mere contest of claimants for supremacy in a category whose meaning is agreed upon (Wills, duBois 1978). According to Sappho, what men mean when they claim that a troup of cavalrymen is very beautiful is that they intensely desire such a troup. Sappho speaks as a woman opponent entering the lists with men, but her proposition is not that men value military forces whereas she values desire, but rather that all valuation is an act of desire. Men are perhaps unwilling to see their values as erotic in nature, their ambitions for victory and strength as a kind of choice. But it is clear enough to Sappho that men are in love with masculinity and that epic poets are in love with military prowess.

Continuing the experiment of reading this poem as about poetry, we might next try to identify Helen as the Iliadic character. But Homer's Helen cursed herself for abandoning her husband and coming to Troy; Sappho's Helen, on the contrary, is held up as proof that it is right to desire one thing above all others, and to follow the beauty perceived no matter where it leads. There is a charming parody of logical argumentation in these stanzas; the underlying, real argument I would re-construct as follows, speaking for the moment in Sappho's voice. "Male poets have talked of military beauty in positive terms, but of women's beauty (especially Helen's) as baneful and destructive. They will probably never see the lineaments of their own desires as I do, but let me try to use some of their testimony against them, at least to expose the paradoxes of their own system. I shall select the woman whom men both desire and despise in the highest degree. What they have damned her for was, in one light, an act of the highest courage and commitment, and *their own poetry* at one point makes grudging admission that she surpasses all the moral censures leveled against her—the Teichoskopia [Survey from the Wall, *Iliad* 3.121–244]. Helen's abandonment of her husband and child and parents is mentioned there (139, 174), and by a divine manipulation she feels a change of heart, now desiring her former husband and city and parents (139) and calling herself a bitch (180). But these are the poet's sentiments, not hers; he makes her a puppet of his feeling, not a woman with a mind of her own. The real Helen was powerful enough to leave a husband, parents and child whom she valued less than the one she fell in love with. (I needn't and won't mention her lover's name: the person—male or female—is not relevant to my argument.) Indeed she was so powerful that she *beguiled Troy itself* at that moment when, in the midst of its worst suffering, the senior counselors watched her walk along the city wall and said, in their chirpy old men's voices, 'There is no blame for Trojans or armored Achaians to suffer pains so long a time for such a woman' (156–7)."

So far I have been speaking Sappho's mind as I see it behind this poem. There is an interesting problem in lines 12ff., where most modern editors of Sappho's text have filled the gaps with anti-Helen sentiments, on the order of "but (Aphrodite) beguiled her . . . , for (women are easily manipulated,) light(-minded . . .)." We do not know what is missing, but it is more consistent with Sappho's perspective, as I read it, to keep the subject of *paragag'*, "beguiled," the same as in the preceding clause—Helen. "Helen beguiled . . . itself (or, herself)," some feminine noun, such as "city" (*polis*), "blame" (*nemesis*), or the like. What is easily manipulated and light-minded (*kouphôs*) are the senior staff of Troy, who astonishingly dismiss years of suffering as they breathe a romantic sigh when Helen passes.

Poem 31: Sappho Reading the Odyssey

Perhaps Sappho's most impressive fragment is poem 31:

> That one seems to me to be like the gods, the man whosoever sits facing you and listens nearby to your sweet speech and desirable laughter—which surely terrifies the heart in my chest; for as I look briefly at you, so can I no longer speak at all, my tongue is silent, broken, a silken fire suddenly has spread beneath my skin, with my eyes I see nothing, my hearing hums, a cold sweat grips me, a trembling seizes me entire, more pale than grass am I, I seem to myself to be little short of dead. But everything is to be endured, since even a pauper . . . .

The first stanza is a *makarismos*, a traditional formula of praise and well-wishing, "happy the man who . . . ," and is often used to celebrate the prospect of a happy marriage (Snell, Koniaris, Saake 17–38). For instance, "That man is far and away blessed beyond all others who plies you with dowry and leads you to his house; for I have never seen with my eyes a mortal person like you, neither man nor woman. A holy dread grips me as I gaze at you" (*Odyssey* 6.158–61). In fact this passage from Odysseus' speech to Nausikaa is so close in structure (*makarismos* followed by a statement of deep personal dread) to poem 31 that I should like to try the experiment of reading the beginning of Sappho's poem as a re-creation of that scene from the *Odyssey*.

If Sappho is speaking to a young woman ("you") as Nausikaa, with herself in the role of an Odysseus, then there are only two persons present in the imagined scene (Del Grande). This is certainly true to the emotional charge of the poem, in which the power and tension flow between Sappho and the woman she sees and speaks to, between "you" and "I." The essential statement of the poem is, like the speech of Odysseus to Nausikaa, a lauding of the addressee and an abasement of the speaker which together have the effect of establishing a working relationship between two people of real power. The rhetoric of praise and of submission are necessary because the poet and the shipwrecked man are in fact very threatening. Most readers feel the paradox of poem 31's eloquent statement of speechlessness, its powerful declaration of helplessness; as in poem 1, the poet is masterfully in control of herself as victim. The underlying relation of power then is the opposite of its superficial form: the addressee is of a delicacy and fragility which would be shattered by the powerful presence of the poet unless she makes elaborate obeisance, designed to disarm and, by a careful planting of hints, to seduce.

The anonymous "that man whosoever" (*kênos ônêr ottis* in Sappho, *keinos hos ke* in Homer) is a rhetorical cliché, not an actor in the imagined scene. Interpretations which *focus* on "that someone (male)" as a bridegroom (or suitor or friend) who is actually present and occupying the attention of the addressee miss the strategy of persuasion which informs the poem and in doing so reveal their own androcentric premises. In depicting "the man" as a concrete person central to the scene and god-like in power, such interpretations misread a figure of speech as a literal statement and thus add the weight of their own pro-male values to Sappho's woman-centered consciousness. "That man" in poem 31 is like the military armament in poem 16, an introductory set-up to be dismissed. We do not imagine that the speaker of poem 16 is actually watching a fleet or infantry; no more need we think that Sappho is watching a man sitting next to her beloved. To whom, in that case, would Sappho be addressing herself? Such a reading makes poem 31 a modern lyric of totally internal speech, rather than a rhetorically structured public utterance which imitates other well known occasions for public speaking (prayer, supplication, exhortation, congratulation).

My reading of poem 31 explains why "that man" has assumed a grotesque prominence in discussions of it. Androcentric habits of thought are part of the reason, but even more important is Sappho's intention to hint obliquely at the notion of a bridegroom just as Odysseus does to Nausikaa. Odysseus the stranger designs his speech to the princess around the roles which she and her family will find acceptable—helpless suppliant, valorous adventurer, and potential husband (Austin 1975: 191–200). The ordinary protocols of marital brokerage in ancient society are a system of discreet offers and counter-offers which must maintain at all times the possibility for saving face, for declining with honor and respect to all parties. Odysseus' speech to Nausikaa contains these delicate approaches to the offer of marriage which every reader would appreciate, just as Alkinoos understands Nausikaa's thoughts of marriage in her request to go wash her brothers' dancing clothes: "So she spoke, for she modestly avoided mentioning the word 'marriage' in the presence of her father; but he understood her perfectly" (*Odyssey* 6.66f.). Such skill at innuendo and respectful obliquity is one of the ordinary-language bases for the refined art of lyric speech. Sappho's hint that "someone" enjoys a certain happiness is, like Odysseus' identical statement, a polite self-reference and an invitation to take the next step. Sappho plays with the role of Odysseus as suitor extraordinary, an unheard of stranger who might fulfill Nausikaa's dreams of marriage contrary to all the ordinary expectations of her society. She plays too with the humble formalities of self-denigration and obeisance, all an expansion of *sebas m' echei eisoroôsa,* "holy dread grips me as I gaze on you" (*Odyssey* 161).

"That man is equal to the gods": this phrase has another meaning too. Sappho as reader of the *Odyssey* participates by turn in all the characters; this alternation of attention is the ordinary experience of every reader of the epic and is the basis for Sappho's multiple identification with both Aphrodite and Diomedes in *Iliad* 5. In reading *Odyssey* 6 Sappho takes on the roles of both Odysseus and Nausikaa, as well as standing outside them both. I suggest that "that man is equal to the gods," among its many meanings, is a reformulation of Homer's description of the sea-beaten Odysseus whom Athena transforms into a god-like man: *nun de theoisin eoike toi ouranon eurun echousin,* "but now he is like the gods who control the expanse of heaven" (6.243). This is Nausikaa's comment to her maids as she watches Odysseus sit on the shore after emerging from his bath, and she goes on to wish that her husband might be such.[13] The point of view from which Sappho speaks as one struck to the heart is that of a mortal visited by divine power and beauty, and this is located in the *Odyssey* in the personae of Odysseus (struck by Nausikaa, or so he says), of Nausikaa (impressed by Odysseus), and of the homeric audience, for Sappho speaks not only as the strange suitor and the beautiful princess but as the *Odyssey* reader who watches "that man" (Odysseus) face to face with the gently laughing girl.[14]

In performing this experiment of reading Sappho's poems as expressing, in part, her thoughts while reading Homer, her consciousness of men's public world, I think of her being naturally drawn to the character of Nausikaa, whose romantic anticipation (6.27) and delicate sensitivity to the unattainability of the powerful stranger (244f., 276–84) are among the most successful presentations of a woman's mind in male Greek literature.[15] Sappho sees herself both as Odysseus admiring the nymph-like maiden and as Nausikaa cherishing her own complex emotions. The moment of their separation has what is in hindsight, by the normal process of re-reading literature in the light of its own reformulations, a "Sapphic" touch: *mnêsêi emei',* "Farewell, guest, and when you are in your homeland remember me who saved you—you owe me this" (*Odyssey* 8.461–2). These are at home as Sappho's words in poem 94.6–8: "And I made this reply to her, 'Farewell on your journey, and remember me, for you know how I stood by you'" (Schadewaldt 1936: 367).

Gardens of Nymphs

The idyllic beauty of Phaiakia is luxuriously expressed in the rich garden of Alkinoos, whose continuously fertile fruits and blossoms are like the gardens which Sappho describes (esp. poems 2, 81b, 94, 96), and it reminds us of Demetrios' words, "Virtually the whole of Sappho's poetry deals with nymphs' gardens, wedding songs, eroticism." The other side of the public/ private contrast in Sappho is a design hidden in the lush foliage and flower cups of these gardens. There are two sides to double consciousness: Sappho both re-enacts scenes from public culture infused with her private perspective as the enclosed woman and she speaks publicly of the most private, woman-centered experiences from which men are strictly excluded. They are not equal projects, the latter is much more delicate and risky. The very formulation of women-only secrets, female *arrhêta*, runs the risk not only of impropriety (unveiling the bride) but of betrayal by misstatement. Hence the hesitation in Sappho's most explicit delineation of double consciousness: *ouk oid' otti theô, dicha moi ta noêmmata*, "I am not sure what to set down, my thoughts are double," could mean "I am not sure which things to set down and which to keep among ourselves, my mind is divided" (51).

Among the thoughts which Sappho has woven into her poetry, in a way which both conceals and reveals without betraying, are sexual images. These are in part private to women, whose awareness of their own bodies is not shared with men, and in part publicly shared, especially in wedding songs and rites, which are a rich store. of symbolic images bespeaking sexuality (Bourdieu 1979: 105; Abbott chap. 11). The ordinary ancient concern with fertility, health, and bodily function generated a large family of natural metaphors for human sexuality and, conversely, sexual metaphors for plants and body parts. A high degree of personal modesty and decorum is in no way compromised by a daily language which names the world according to genital analogies or by marriage customs whose function is to encourage fertility and harmony in a cooperative sexual relationship.

The three words which I will use to illustrate this are *numphê*, *pteruges*, and *mêlon*. The evidence for their usage will be drawn from various centuries and kinds of writing up to a thousand years after Sappho; but the terms in each case seem to be of a semi-technical and traditional nature rather than neologisms. They constitute the scattered fragments of a locally variegated, tenacious symbolic system which was operative in Sappho's time and which is still recognizable in modern Greece.

Numphê has many meanings: at the center of this extended family are "clitoris" and "bride." *Numphê* names a young woman at the moment of her transition from maiden (*parthenos*) to wife (or "woman," *gunê*); the underlying idea is that just as the house encloses the wife and as veil and carriage keep the bride apart from the wedding celebrants, so the woman herself encloses a sexual secret. * "The outer part of the female genital system

---

* "One of the men in Chios, apparently a prominent figure of some sort, was taking a wife and, as the bride was being conducted to his home in a chariot, Hippoklos the king, a close

which is visible has the name 'wings' (*pteruges*), which are, so to speak, the lips of the womb. They are thick and fleshy, stretching away on the lower side to either thigh, as it were parting from each other, and on the upper side terminating in what is called the *numphê*. This is the starting point (*archê*) of the wings (labia), by nature a little fleshy thing and somewhat muscular (or, mouse-like)" (Soranos *Gynaecology* 1.18).

The same technical use of *numphê* to mean clitoris is found in other medical writers[16] and lexicographers,[17] and by a natural extension is applied to many analogous phenomena: the hollow between lip and chin (Rufus *Onom.* 42, Pollux 2.90, Hesychios), a depression on the shoulder of horses (*Hippiatr.* 26), a mollusc (Speusippos ap. Athen. 3.105B), a niche (Kallixinos 2 = Müller *FHG* 3, p. 55), an opening rosebud,* the point of a plow (Pollux 1.25.2; Proklos *ad* Hesiod *Erga* 425)—this last an interesting reversal based on the image of the plowshare penetrating the earth.

The relation of *numphê*, clitoris, to *pteruges*, wings/labia, is shown by the name of a kind of bracken, the *numphaia pteris*, "nymph's-wing," also known as *thelupteris*, "female wing," by the name of the loose lapels on a seductively opening gown (Pollux 755, 62, 66 = Aristophanes frag. 325 OCT), and by the use of *numphê* as the name for bees in the larva stage just when they begin to open up and sprout wings (Aristotle *Hist. Anim.* 551.^{b}2–4; Photios *Lexikon s.v. numphai;* Pliny *Nat. Hist.* 11.48).

This family of images extends broadly across many levels of Greek culture and serves to reconstruct for us one important aspect of the meaning of "bride," *numphê* as the ancients felt it.[18] Hence the virtual identity of Demetrios' three terms for Sappho's poetry: nymphs' gardens, wedding songs, eroticism. Several of Sappho's surviving fragments and poems make sense as a woman-centered celebration and revision of this public but discreet vocabulary for women's sexuality.

---

friend of the bridegroom, mingling with the rest during the drinking and laughter, jumped up into the chariot, not intending any insult but merely being playful according to the common custom. The friends of the groom killed him" Plutarch *mul. virt.* 244E.

*Photios *Lexikon.* s.v. *numphai:* "And they call the middle part of the female genitals the *numphê;* also the barely opened buds of roses are *numphai;* and newly-wed maidens are *numphai.*" The equation of flowers and female genitals is ancient (Krinagoras *Anth.Pal.* 6.345, Achilles Tatius 2.1) and modern (art: Lippard, Dodson, Chicago 1975, 1979; poetry: Lorde, "Love Poem" in Bulkin and Larkin). Sappho appears to have made the equation of bride and roses explicit, according to Wirth.

I would not reject the suggestion that Sappho's feelings for Kleis, as imagined in fragment 132, were given a consciously lesbian coloring: "I have a beautiful child, her shape is like that of golden *flowers,* beloved Kleis; in her place I would not . . . all Lydia nor lovely . . . ." Indeed, taking it a step further, this "child" (*pais*) may be simply another metaphor for clitoris (*Kleis/ kleitoris*). The biographical tradition which regards Kleis as the name of Sappho's daughter and mother may be (as so often) based on nothing more than a fact-hungry reading of her poems. (The same name occurs at frag. 98b1.) On flowers and fruit see Stehle 1977.

The consciousness of these poems ranges over a wide field of attitudes. The first, in fragment 105a, can be seen as Sappho's version of male genital joking,[19] but when applied to the *numphê* Sappho's female ribaldry is pointedly different in tone:

> Like the sweet-apple [*glukumêlon*] ripening to red on the topmost branch,
> on the very tip of the topmost branch, and the apple-pickers have
>   overlooked it—
> no, they haven't overlooked it but they could not reach it.

Mêlon, conventionally translated "apple," is really a general word for fleshy fruit—apricots, peaches, apples, citron, quinces, pomegranates. In wedding customs it probably most often means quinces and pomegranates, but for convenience sake I will abide by the traditional translation "apple." Like *numphê* and *pteruges, mêlon* has a wider extension ef meanings, and from this we can rediscover why "apples" were a prominent symbol in courtship and marriage rites.[20] *Mêlon* signifies various "clitoral" objects: the seed vessel of the rose (Theophrastos *Hist. Plant.* 6.6.6), the tonsil or uvula,[*] a bulge or sty on the lower eyelid (Hesychios *s.v. kula*), and a swelling on the cornea (Alexander Tralles *peri ophthalmôn,* ed. Puschmann, p. 152). The sensitivity of these objects to pressure is one of the bases for the analogy; I will quote just the last one. "And what is called a *mêlon* is a form of fleshy bump (*staphulôma,* grape-like or uvular swelling), big enough to raise the eyelids, and when it is rubbed it bothers the entire lid-surface."

Fragment 105a, spoken of a bride in the course of a wedding song, is a sexual image. We can gather this sense not only from the general erotic meaning of "apples" but from the location of the solitary apple high up on the bare branches of a tree,[†] and from its sweetness and color. The verb *ereuthô,* "grow red," and its cognates are used of blood or other red liquid appearing on the surface of an object which is painted or stained or when the skin suffuses with blood (Hippokrates *Epid.* 2.3.1, *Morb. Sacr.* 15, *Morb.* 4.38 of a blush).

The vocabulary and phrasing of this fragment reveal much more than a sexual metaphor, however; they contain a delicate and reverential attitude to the elusive presence-and-absence of women in the world of men. Demetrios elsewhere (148) speaks of the graceful naivete of Sappho's self-correction,

---

[*] Rufus *Onom.* 64; Galen *de usu partium* 15.3: "The part called *numpha* gives the same sort of protection to the uteri that the uvula gives to the pharynx, for it covers the orifice of their neck by coming down into the female pudendum and keeps it from being chilled." Sappho's fragment 42, on the warmth afforded by enfolding wings (*ptera*), may be read of labia as well as of birds.

[†] "In other parts (of Macedonia) . . . , especially among the Wallachs, a pole with an apple on top and a white kerchief streaming from it . . . is carried by a kilted youth in front of the wedding procession" (Abbott 172).

as if it were no more than a charming touch of folk speech when twice in these lines she changes her mind, varying a statement she has already made. But self-correction is Sappho's playful format for saying much more than her simile would otherwise mean. The words are inadequate—how can I say?—not inadequate, but they encircle an area of meaning for which there have not been faithful words in the phallocentric tradition. The real secret of this simile is not the image of the bride's "private" parts but of women's sexuality and consciousness in general, which men do not know as women know. Sappho knows this secret in herself and in other women whom she loves, and she celebrates it in her poetry. Where men's paraphernalia are awkwardly flaunted (bumping into the lintel, frag. 111, inconveniently large like a rustic's feet, frag. 110), women's are protected and secure. The amazing feature of these lines is that the apple is not "ripe for plucking" but unattainable, as if even after marriage the *numphê* would remain secure from the husband's appropriation.[21]

Revision of myth is combined with a sexual image in fragment 166: *phaisi dê pota Lêdan uakinthôi pepukadmenon / eurên ôion,* "They do say that once upon a time Leda found an egg hidden in the hyacinth." As the traditional denigration of Helen was revised in poem 16, so the traditional story of Helen's mother is told anew. Leda was not the victim of Zeus' rape who afterwards laid Helen in an egg, rather she discovered a mysterious egg hidden inside the frilly blossoms of a hyacinth stem, or (better) in a bed of hyacinths when she parted the petals and looked under the leaves. The egg discovered there is

(1) a clitoris hidden under labia
(2) the supremely beautiful woman, a tiny Helen, and
(3) a story, object, and person hidden from male culture. *

The metaphor of feeling one's way through the undergrowth until one discovers a special object of desire is contained in the word *maiomai,* "I feel for," "I search out by feeling." It is used of Odysseus feeling the flesh of Polyphemos' stomach for a vital spot to thrust in his sword (*Od.* 9.302), of animals searching through dense thickets for warm hiding places (Hesiod *Erga* 529–33), of enemy soldiers searching through the luxurious thicket for the hidden Odysseus (*Od.* 14.356), of Demeter searching high and low for her daughter (*Hom. Hymn* 2.44), of people searching for Poseidon's lover Pelops (Pindar *Ol.* 1.46). The contexts of this verb are not just similar by accident: *maiomai* means more than "search for," it means "ferret out," especially in dense thickets where an animal or person might be lurking.

---

* The verb *pukazô* refers not to just any kind of "hiding" but to covering an object with clothes, flower garlands, or hair, either as an adornment or for protection. "Thick" flowers (*huakinthon / puknon kai malakon*) cover the earth to cushion the love-making of Zeus and Hera (*Iliad* 14.347–50).

In view of the consistency of connotations for this verb there is no reason to posit a shifted usage in Sappho 36, as the lexicon of Liddell-Scott-Jones does. As those lexicographers read it, Sappho's words *kai pothêô kai maomai* are redundant—"I desire you and I desire you." Rather they mean "I desire and I search out." I would like to include the physical sense of feeling carefully for hidden things or hiding places.[22] In the poetic verb *maiomai* there is a physical dimension to the expression of mutual passion and exploration. Desire and touching occur together as two aspects of the same experience: touching is touching-with-desire, desire is desire-with-touching.

The same dictionary which decrees a special meaning for *maiomai* when Sappho uses it invents an Aeolic word *matêmi* (B) = *pateô*, "I walk," to reduce the erotic meaning of a Lesbian fragment of uncertain authorship, Incert. 16: "The women of Krete once danced thus—rhythmically with soft feet around the desirable altar, exploring the tender, pliant flower of the lawn." *Matêmi* is a recognized Aeolic equivalent of *mateuô*, akin to *maiomai*. The meanings "ferret out," "search through undergrowth," "beat the thickets looking for game," "feel carefully" seem to me quite in place. Appealing to a long tradition, Sappho (whom I take to be the author) remarks that the sexual dancing of women, the sensuous circling of moving hands and feet around the erotic altar and combing through the tender valleys, is not only current practice but was known long ago in Krete.

I have been able to find no *simple* sexual imagery in Sappho's poems. For her the sexual is always something else as well. Her sacred landscape of the body is at the same time a statement about a more complete consciousness, whether of myth, poetry, ritual, or personal relationships. In the following fragment, 94, which contains a fairly explicit sexual statement in line 23 (West 322), we find Sappho correcting her friend's view of their relation.

> . . . Without guile I wish to die. She left me weeping copiously and said, "Alas, what fearful things we have undergone, Sappho; truly I leave you against my will." But I replied to her, "Farewell, be happy as you go and remember me, for you know how we have stood by you. Perhaps you don't—so I will remind you . . . and we have undergone beautiful things. With many garlands of violets and roses . . . together, and . . . you put around yourself, at my side, and flowers wreathed around your soft neck with rising fragrance, and . . . you stroked the oil distilled from royal cherry blossoms and on tender bedding you reached the end of longing . . . of soft . . . and there was no . . . nor sacred . . . from which we held back, nor grove . . . sound. . . .

As usual the full situation is unclear, but we can make out a contrast of Sappho's view with her friend's. The departing woman says *deina pepontha-men*, "fearful things we have suffered," and Sappho corrects her, *kal' epascho-men*, "beautiful things we continuously experienced." Her reminder of these beautiful experiences (which Page 1955: 83 calls a "list of girlish pleasures") is a loving progression of intimacy, moving in space—down along the body—and in time—to increasing sexual closeness: from flowers wreathed on the head to flowers wound around the neck to stroking the body with oil to soft bed-clothes and the full satisfaction of desire. I would like to read the meager fragments of the succeeding stanza as a further physical landscape: we explored every sacred place of the body. To paraphrase the argument, "When she said we had endured an awful experience, the ending of our love together, I corrected her and said it was a beautiful experience, an undying memory of sensual happiness that knew no limit, luxurious and fully sexual. Her focus on the termination was misplaced; I told her to think instead of our mutual pleasure which itself had no term, no stopping-point, no unexplored grove."

Poem 2 uses sacral language to describe a paradisal place (Turyn) which Aphrodite visits:

> Hither to me from Krete, unto this holy temple, a place where there is a lovely grove of apples and an altar where the incense burns, and here is water which ripples cold through apple branches, and all the place is shadowed with roses, and as the leaves quiver a profound quiet ensues. And here is a meadow where horses graze, spring flowers bloom, the honeyed whisper of winds. . . . This is the very place where you, Kypris . . . , drawing into golden cups the nectar gorgeously blended for our celebration, then pour it forth.

The grove, Page comments, is "lovely," a word used "elsewhere in the Lesbians only of *personal* charm" (1955: 36). But this place is, among other things, a personal place, an extended and multi-perspectived metaphor for women's sexuality. Virtually every word suggests a sensuous ecstasy in the service of Kyprian Aphrodite (apples, roses, quivering followed by repose, meadow for grazing, spring flowers, honey, nectar flowing). Inasmuch as the language is both religious and erotic, I would say that Sappho is not describing a public ceremony for its own sake but is providing a way to experience such ceremonies, to infuse the celebrants' participation with memories of lesbian sexuality. The twin beauties of burning incense on an altar and of burning sexual passion can be held together in the mind, so that the experience of either is the richer. The accumulation of topographic and sensuous detail leads us to think of the interconnection of all the parts of the body in a long and diffuse act of love, rather than the genital-centered and more relentlessly goal-oriented pattern of love-making which men have been known to employ.

I have tried to sketch two areas of Sappho's consciousness as she has registered it in her poetry: her reaction to Homer, emblematic of the male-centered world of public Greek culture, and her complex sexual relations with women in a world apart from men. Sappho seems always to speak in many voices—her friends', Homer's, Aphrodite's—conscious of more than a single perspective and ready to detect the fuller truth of many-sided desire. But she speaks as a woman to women: her eroticism is both subjectively and objectively woman-centered. Too often modern critics have tried to restrict Sappho's *erôs* to the strait-jacket of spiritual friendship.

A good deal of the sexual richness which I detect in Sappho's lyrics is compatible with interpretations such as those of Lasserre and Hallett 1979,[23] but what requires explanation is their insistent denial that the emotional lesbianism of Sappho's work has any physical component. We must distinguish between the physical component as a putative fact about Sappho in her own life and as a meaning central to her poems. Obviously Sappho as poet is not an historian documenting her own life but rather a creative participant in the erotic-lyric tradition.[*] My argument has been that this tradition includes pervasive allusions to physical *erôs* and that in Sappho's poems both subject and object of shared physical love are women. We now call this lesbian.[†] To admit that Sappho's discourse is lesbian but insist that she herself was not seems quixotic. Would anyone take such pains to insist that Anakreon in real life might not have felt any physical attraction to either youths or women?

It seems clear to me that Sappho's consciousness included a personal and subjective commitment to the holy, physical contemplation of the body of Woman, as metaphor and reality, in all parts of life. Reading her poems in this way is a challenge to think both in and out of our time, both in and out of a phallocentric framework, a reading which can enhance our own sense of this womanly beauty *as subject and as object* by helping us to un-learn our denials of it.

---

[*] Late Greek rhetoric maintains the tradition of praising a public official at a ceremonial event by a declaration of love. Himerios (48) and Themistios (13) tell their audiences that the honored official is their *erômenos,* boyfriend.

[†] "Women who love women, who choose women to nurture and support and create a living environment in which to work creatively and independently, are lesbians" (Cook 738).

7
The Laughter of the Oppressed:
Demeter and the Gardens of Adonis

One of the more provocative reports which have come down to us concerning ancient Greek women is that they gathered several times a year apart
from men and indulged in hilarious obscenity. At certain festivals of Demeter
and Aphrodite women's ribald laughter, mixed in some cases with lugubri-
ous mourning, rang out from the rooftops of Athens or the hilltop enclosure
just south of the Pnyx or the precinct at Eleusis. The texts, meager as they
are, which speak of women's rituals and gatherings (scraps of Aristophanes,
Menander, various scholiasts and lexicographers) must be used with the
customary caution, since their *attitude* to women's independent operations
is likely to be colored by anxiety, suspicion, or contempt. Above all, they
are likely to miss the consciousness of the women themselves about the
meaning of their ritual and festive acts. Both ancient and modern male
interpreters tend to feel a certain discomfort at the spectacle of women in
groups laughing uproariously as they handle genital-shaped cookies and
other objects of sexual significance. But if we can filter out the reporters'
masculinist attitudes and study the unarguable facts of the Stenia, Thesmophoria, Haloa, and Adonia, the possibility of an alternative consciousness,
a women's perspective on sex and gender, may appear.

In Sappho's case, we have seen evidence of an alternative point of view,
but her resisting consciousness about public, male norms might be due to
her exceptional talent and strong individual personality. She appears as a
unique beam of light in an otherwise dark period, and we should be wary
of automatically assuming that her perspectives were typical of Greek
women even in her own time, much less in the Athens of two and more
centuries later. Yet it would be intriguing (would it not?) to discover that
Sappho's critical stance was in some measure and fashion shared more widely
by Greek women, that she was in some ways less the exception and more
the rule.

The goal of this chapter is to sketch the possibility—no more than that—
of a different consciousness on the part of Greek women concerning the
meanings of sex and gender from those enunciated by their husbands and

fathers. The location for women's realization of this counter-ideology are the women's-only festivals. These are treated in a most original and stimlulating fashion by Detienne in his *Gardens of Adonis* (1977)—though his phallocratic bias will be criticized below. Detienne's method is structuralist: the meaning of a single ritual gesture or object is determined by its place within a larger set of contrasts, both within the bounds of a single festival and in comparison with similar festivals. Thus, the meaning of Demeter's caverns and serpents in the early autumn can be located by putting them in contrast with Aphrodite's rooftop gardens in the high summer.

To Detienne's calculus of contrasts I will add Stehle's (forthcoming) analysis of a set of important narratives about great goddesses and their young male lovers, stories generally known in Greek culture and particularly well attested in Sappho. These myths can be read in one way by men, but in quite another way by women. The congruence of that narrative pattern with the structure of women's ritual acts is striking enough to suggest at least the possibility that women saw in their religious actions involving grain and sprouts a celebration of their female power over life and sexuality within the peripheral and annoying constraints of male pretensions. What will appear, if this reading is right, is a different figuration of the phallos, a different evaluation of both sex and gender in Greek society, one which was expressed and shared by women when they were freed from the oversight and interpretive control of men.

The Gardens of Adonis

In late July, when the Dog Star Seirios rose, signaling the hottest time of the year, private groups of women held nocturnal festivities on the rooftops in honor of Adonis, Aphrodite's unfortunate young lover.[1] The celebrants, it seems, were not organized according to any city-wide rule but simply consisted of neighbors and friends who happened to decide to keep the traditional festivities together.[2] Indeed, the official religious calendar of the *polis* had nothing to say about the Adonia—the arrangements, materials, conduct, and finances were all in the hands of the informal groups of women who danced and chanted and played on the housetops for at least one and possibly more nights.

The late Greek lexicographers give very spare definitions of the Adonia and its most interesting feature, the *kêpoi Adônidos* (gardens of Adonis). Hesychios, in addition to recording that *adônêis* is the name of a swallow and a lettuce and that *adônis* is a fish and the Phoenician word for Lord and the name of a throw of the dice, has the following entry for *Adônidos kêpoi:* "at the Adonia they bring out images (*eidôla*) and gardens in terracotta vessels and they prepare for him [Adonis] gardens with all types of vegetation, such as fennel and lettuce; for they say that he was laid out by Aphrodite among the lettuce." The *Souda* repeats much of that and adds that the Adonis gardens are gardens up in the air, and that their proverbial meaning is to denote superficial and insubstantial things—untimely, short-lived, and not rooted. Photios adds that the Adonia festival is said by some to be in honor of Adonis, by others of Aphrodite, and that it is derived from the Phoenicians and Cyprians.[3]

Photios cites four poets of Old Comedy (Pherekrates, Kratinos, Plato, and Aristophanes), and it appears from other sources that Adonis and his cult were popular subjects on the Athenian comic stage in the fifth and fourth centuries.[4] The play titles *Adonis* and *Adoniazousai* are attested for seven different poets,[5] and fragments of other plays contain references to the feast, as in Pherekrates fragment 170 Kock: "we are celebrating the Adonia and weeping for Adonis," which may well be spoken not by a woman in a literal sense but by a man fancifully explaining his tears, as Dionysos and Xanthias try to explain away their yelps of pain at *Frogs* 649–61.

There are only three literary texts of any real substance that are informative about the Adonia in the classical period, and each is in its own way tendentious. Two are from comedy, which always is liable to put a contemptuous or ironic spin on its references to women, and one is from Plato. The earliest is from Aristophanes' *Lysistrata* (411 B.C.E.). After the women have successfully occupied the Akropolis, a feisty, spluttering little man comes on stage. He is the Proboulos or Commissioner of Public Safety, demanding to know what is going on.

What's this! An outbreak of female self-indulgence,
beating their drums and continually chanting "Sabazios, Sabazios"?
Is this more of that Adonisism on the roofs,
which once I heard during an Assembly meeting:
that wretched Demostratos was proposing
a naval expedition to Sicily, while his wife, dancing,
shouted "Woe for Adonis!" Then Demostratos proposed
that we draft Zakynthian hoplites;
while his wife, a teensy bit drunk on the roof,
exclaimed "Beat your breasts for Adonis!" (387–96)

In the play this pompous character gets his comeuppance, as the women defend their closing of the city treasury in Athena's temple to stop the interminable Peloponnesian War. At the end of his scene the Commissioner is wrapped up in women's veils and hustled off the stage like a corpse in winding cloths. He is what we might call a "harumph!" character, a scowling disapprover who exaggerates the suspicion that many men may have felt about the keening and dancing and "self-indulgence" of women on the housetops. Note that the display seems to involve only women but that the goings on are not secret. They are visible and audible, though segregated from ordinary terrestrial life by elevation to the roofs. About a hundred years later Menander opened his *Samia* with the confession of a young man named Moschion who got his girlfriend pregnant one night during the Adonia (Weill 1970). She is the daughter of a poor man who lives next door to Moschion's wealthy father, who is keeping a Samian *hetaira* (courtesan) as his mistress. The women of the two households have become friends and naturally celebrate the Adonia together.

> The girl's mother took kindly to my father's Samian
> mistress, and she frequently visited them and they
> were often at our house. Once I was returning
> from the country and I happened to find them gathered
> here at our house to celebrate the Adonia
> with some other women. As one would expect, the feast
> featured much joking, and I was there, you might say,
> as a spectator; for their noise made it impossible
> for me to sleep. They were carrying some gardens
> onto the roof, dancing, celebrating the whole night long,
> scattered here and there. I hesitate to tell the rest.
> Perhaps I am ashamed when I needn't be—
> but I *am* ashamed. The maiden became pregnant:
> from this you can infer what I did. (35–50)

Because the female participants from several households are caught up in their various forms of riotous behavior and are spread out over the roof, Moschion and his girlfriend are evidently able to take advantage of the confusion to tryst in a corner somewhere.[*] When she gets pregnant, he admits his responsibility to her mother and undertakes to marry her. As in *Lysistrata,* the women's partying and its rituals appear to be informally organized and perfectly open to view. Though men do not participate they can see what is going on and, in Moschion's fictional case, take advantage of the unusual availability of a normally chaperoned maiden.

These descriptions, each with a comic slant, of the women's festivities are illustrated by a series of fifth- and fourth-century vases (Metzger, Weill 1966), showing women ascending by ladders to the rooftop, carrying baskets and pots with sprouts in them and platters of raisins. No men figure in this type of scene, if one discounts the occasional hovering Eros. The women are finely dressed but in no way lasciviously inclined. The circulation of such vases again shows that the Adonia was no secret orgy but an acceptable, if loud and riotous, women's rite.

---

[*] Very little is said about the nameless girlfriend, but she seems to be a willing partner, not a rape victim as in other plays.

The meaning of the gardens themselves is best approached through Plato, who refers to them at *Phaidros* 276B:

> Tell me this: will the sensible farmer, who cares about his seed and wants it to reach fruition, sow it in summertime in gardens of Adonis and gladly watch it growing for eight days, or would he only do such a thing for a joke and for the sake of a festival, when and if he were to do it? But the seed he takes seriously he will sow in a proper location, using his agricultural knowledge, and he would rejoice to see his seeds reaching their fruitful goal in the eighth month.

Where the representations in comedy describe the women's behavior, Sokrates does not even mention that the gardens are part of a women's rite but focuses on the fact that the seedlings in the gardens of Adonis do not reach fruition. The paroemiographers bring this out too, since the proverb "You are more fruitless than the gardens of Adonis" was derived from the controlled growth and withering of the sprouts. "The proverb applies to those who are unable to produce anything worthwhile; it is mentioned by Plato in the *Phaidros*. These gardens of Adonis are sown in ceramic vessels and grow only to the point of becoming green. They are borne away along with the dying god and are thrown into springs" (Zenobios 1.49).[6] "Gardens of Adonis—applies to things untimely and not rooted. Adonis, the beloved of Aphrodite, as the story goes, died before his maturity (*prohêbês*). Those who celebrate this feast sow gardens in vessels; the plants quickly wither since they have not taken root; these are called Adonis'" (Diogenianos 1.14).[7] And the Emperor Julian: ". . . the gardens which women sow in pots for Aphrodite's husband, piling up some composted earth; they turn green for a short while and suddenly wither away" (*Symposium* 329 C-D).

This group of references enables us to establish the essential procedure around which the dancing and singing took place, namely, that seeds of various sorts (lettuce and fennel are mentioned specifically[*]) were planted in enriched, composted[8] earth in portable vessels, watered thoroughly and placed in the bright summer sun until the sprouts appeared. They were then deprived of water and allowed to turn brown and to shrivel up. Then in a mock funeral, imitating that of Adonis, the earth and dessicated vegetation were carried to a spring or to the sea and dumped. The sprouting must have taken some days[†]—Plato speaks of eight—but it is not clear how many of those days were devoted to keeping the holiday in the raucous manner described. It may have been as little as one, since no source mentions a

---

[*]Wheat and barley are mentioned by the scholiast on Theokritos 15.112.

[†]Lettuce takes four or five days to germinate (Theophrastos *History of Plants* 7.1.3). The winter crop of herbs and vegetables, including lettuce, was regularly planted after the summer solstice (Theophrastos *HP* 7.1.2).

number of days and Menander's character implies that carrying the vessels to the roof took place at the same time as the festive funeral. Perhaps the shoots were grown and allowed to wither during the week or so before the celebration itself. But we would probably be wrong to impose too much system on a practice that was informally organized rather than controlled by the *polis*. We should rather imagine that a gathering of women friends for the Adonia had as much a regular format as, say, a modern birthday party or a Christmas tree-trimming, at which the general course of events is known in advance but many variations of detail in conduct and style are allowable.

Demeter's Rites

Plato's reference to eight days may be not an exact figure but an estimate, based on the contrast he sees with the eight months necessary for the germination and slow growth of cereal crops—principally, wheat and barley. * In any case, it is the implied contrast of rooted with unrooted, of fruitful with fruitless growth which gives us a structural contrast and a possible handle on the significance of the gardens. Detienne (1977) has developed this by systematically contrasting another women's rite, the Thesmophoria, also devoted to the cultivation and care of seeds.

The Thesmophoria is one of the oldest Greek festivals, observed throughout the Greek world in autumn just before the rains come and the cereal crops are sown. In Athens it was conducted over a three-day period on the eleventh, twelfth, and thirteenth days of the month Pyanopsion. Since the tenth was also a local Demeter festival at Halimous on the coast and the ninth was another Demetrian festival called the Stenia, there was in effect a five-day period of women's religious activities.

As regards the participation of men, there are two significant contrasts between the Adonia and the Demeter festivals. On the one hand men were rigorously excluded from participation in the Athenian Demeter festivals, which were referred to as women's mysteries. Even if (as we will see) these mysteries were not a perfectly kept secret, men were still not granted access to the ceremonies, as is particularly clear from the plot of Aristophanes' *Thesmophoriazousai,* in which an old relative of Euripides is depilated and dressed in drag to infiltrate the women's festival. Kleisthenes in that play, who reveals to the women the secret identity of the infiltrator, does not count as a man since he is a *kinaidos* and therefore an honorary woman (574–

---

* Wheat and barley take a week to germinate (Theophrastos *HP* 8.1.5) and are harvested in seven to eight months, more for wheat (Theophrastos *HP* 8.2.7).

6). * Though the Adonia was an affair for women, we find no particular emphasis on secrecy or male exclusion.

On the other hand men had a compelling interest in the successful conduct of Demeter's rites and bore the responsibility for financing them.[9] The *polis*, considered as a corporation of households (*oikoi*) occupying an agricultural territory, depended on the fertility of its region for its basic food supply of wheat and barley. The Thesmophoria was a gathering of citizen-wives to ensure this fertility by certain traditional procedures, involving piglets and phallic cookies whose remains were mixed with the seed which would shortly be sown. In a sense, the Demetrian feasts were official business of the *polis*, but carried out with a good deal of practical autonomy by women. Since the site of the Thesmophorion is adjacent to the men's place of assembly (the Pnyx: Thompson), the parallelism between women's meetings and men's was obvious. During the days of the Thesmophoria if an Assembly was to be held, it was held not in the Pnyx but in the theater;[†] the men's political business was displaced by the women's higher duties to Demeter and her grain.

The sources for the Stenia, Thesmophoria, and Haloa tell us that ribald laughter was a notorious element in these rites. "The Stenia is an Attic festival; . . . they scoff and say outrageous things" (Hesychios); "women celebrating the Stenia blaspheme and speak outrageously" (Hesychios); "the Stenia is an Attic festival on the day when Demeter rose up from the earth; during it the women sass each other at night. So writes Euboulos" (Photios). The fact that it was the comedian Euboulos who refers to this festival sass or outrageous talk (*loidoria*) does not compromise the evidentiary value of the picture which emerges.

More detail about this Demetrian mockery is given in a very informative scholion to Lucian describing the Haloa, held on the twenty-sixth day of the winter month Poseideon.

> The Haloa is an Attic festival comprising mysteries of Demeter and Korê and Dionysos for the cutting of the vine and the tasting of the wine that has already been set aside. Shameful images of male genitals are prominently featured, about which they say that they are a token of human generation, since Dionysos gave us wine as a tonic drug that would promote intercourse. He had given it to Ikarios, whom some shepherds actually killed because they did not realize how the drinking of wine would affect them. Then they went mad because they moved insolently

---

*Aelian fragment 44 tells the story of Battos, founder of Kyrene, who tried to observe the mysteries of the Thesmophoria: the women, their faces and hands smeared with sacrificial blood, set upon him with swords and castrated him. Pausanias 4.17.1 relates a similar episode from the early history of Sparta.

†IG II² 1006.50–1. So too in Thebes: "The Council·was meeting in the agora porch since the women were celebrating the Thesmophoria in the Kadmeia" (Xenophon *Hellenika* 5.2.29).

against Dionysos himself. Driven thoroughly mad in connection with the very image of their shame, they received an oracle saying that they would recover their sanity when they made and erected clay genitals. Once this had been done, they were freed of their problem. This festival is a memorial of their experience.

On this day there is also a women's ceremony conducted at Eleusis, at which much joking and scoffing takes place. Women process there alone and are at liberty to say whatever they want to: and in fact they say the most shameful things to each other. The priestesses covertly sidle up to the women and whisper into their ear—as if it were a secret—recommendations for adultery. All the women utter shameful and irreverent things to each other. They carry indecent images of male and female genitals. Wine is provided in abundance and the tables are loaded with all the foods of earth and sea except those which are forbidden in the mystical account, that is, pomegranate, apple, domestic birds, eggs, and of sea creatures red mullet, *eruthinos* [a hermaphrodite fish], blacktail, crayfish, and dog-fish. The archons set up the tables and leave them inside for the women while they themselves depart and wait outside, showing to all inhabitants that the types of domestic nourishment were discovered by them [the Eleusinians] and were shared by them with all humanity. On the tables there are also genitals of both sexes made of dough. It is called the Haloa because of Dionysos' fruit, since *alôai* are vine shoots (Rabe 279–81)

There has been much disagreement with this unknown scholar on the reason for the name Haloa, most moderns preferring a more Demetrian explanation in terms of *halôs* (threshing floor or circular assembly place), even though no threshing actually occurs in mid-winter—nor for that matter, any cutting of grapes either. But the scholiast's slide from the Haloa, a women's-only Demeter feast, to Dionysos is very suggestive, for he seems to be talking about the Rural Dionysia, with its phallic processions, which occurred in the same month Poseideon.[10]

It looks as if in the depths of rainy winter men and women separated from each other, each to conduct a memorial rite representing some themes of sex and gender. Men celebrated wine and its powers of arousal, telling the story of how surprised they first were to discover that it gave them erections. The thought that they might be permanently locked into that shameful position drove them to kill Ikarios and to assault, probably rape, Dionysos himself. The significance of the phalloi carried in the local parades of the Rural Dionysia, according to this story, is gratitude for deliverance from a state of permanent satyriasis. One imagines that there were mixed feelings about this: wine is cherished as a sexual tonic but not without a reminder of the rhythms of life and the care men should exercise not to be dominated by their own lower members. The combination of hilarity and repentance is not dissimilar to the Adonia's mixture of mourning and revelry.

For the women at Eleusis we are not given an explanation of why they carried images of male and female genitals. But the phenomenology of the feast as a time of playful sexual liberation is clear enough. As the priestesses circulated through the crowd and gave whispered advice about adultery, the strictest constraint on women—the root of all Mediterranean male anxiety about wives—was breached. Their toying with the notion of adultery is still somewhat circumspect, not shouted from the housetops. One imagines knowing smiles, bright eyes, and perhaps a blush or two. More intriguing are the bakery genitals on the table. Presumably they were eaten, and if so, we may wonder with what licking of lips, what nips and bites, what gestures with the food and offers to share. Some such behavior, in addition to the verbal indecency, has shocked the scholiast, who regards the whole business as "shameless."

The sexual objects at the Thesmophoria were both literal and symbolic. At some time before the festival sacrificed piglets and phallic cookies were placed in underground pits in the Thesmophorion. Such pits, with pig bones and votive pigs, have been found at other Demeter sanctuaries, though no trace remains of them at Athens (Burkert 1985: 243). It is unclear how far in advance these deposits (*thesmoi*) were made. Guesses have ranged from the women's Skira festival (four months earlier) to the Stenia, just two days before the Thesmophoria. * The most detailed account is once again a scholiast on Lucian:

> The Thesmophoria are a Greek festival containing mysteries. The same [mysteries?] also go under the name of Skirophoria. They are celebrated, according to the more mythical account, because when Korê was seized by Plouto while picking flowers, there was a swineherd named Eubouleus tending his pigs in that place and they were all swallowed up in the chasm along with Korê. Women known as Bailers (*Antlêtriai*), who have stayed pure for three days, bring up the rotten remains of the objects that had been thrown down into the pits. Descending into the secret chambers, they bring the material back and place it on the altars. They believe that whoever takes some of it and scatters it along with his seed will have a good crop. They also say that there are serpents down in the chasms, who eat most of what is thrown in; therefore the celebrants clap and shout when the women are bailing and when they replace those figures—to make the serpents go away, whom they consider to be the guardians of the secret chambers.
>
> The same [mysteries] also go under the name of Arretophoria. They are celebrated with the same rationale concerning the growth of fruits and human generation. Here too unspeakable (*arrhêta*) sacred things are carried up; they are replicas of serpents and male genitals, made of dough from wheat flour. They pluck pine

---

*Deubner opted for the Skira, but with Simon we may wonder whether after four months of a hot Greek summer (even in a cavern) there would have been enough left of bones and crumbs so that each family could have some. She suggests, and I find it very plausible, that the offerings were laid down shortly before the festival and gathered up at the end of the day of Fasting. One might see a coordination between the three-day chastity period for the Bailers (see next quoted text) and the period when the sacred goop was rotting underground.

cones because of that tree's prolific seeding. They are thrown into the pits, the so-called secret chambers, along with the piglets, as we said earlier, whose proliferation of progeny is a symbol of the generation of fruits and of humans; it is a sort of thank offering to Demeter, since her gift of the Demetrian fruits tamed the human race. The previous explanation of the festival is the more mythical, this one is more in terms of nature. It is called the Thesmophoria because Demeter is named *thesmophoros,* since she laid down the customs or ordinances (*thesmous*) by which human beings must work and produce food (Rabe 275–6).

The three days of the festival are known as the Ascent (*anhodos*), Fasting (*nêsteia*), and Fine Birth (*kalligeneia*). The Ascent is probably named from the spectacle of women gathering from all over Attika, climbing up the hill in a heavily laden procession. * They had to bring food, sacrificial animals, tents, deme offerings for the priestesses, and fronds to sleep on. Two women were elected by the women of each deme to be magistrates (*archousai*), evidently a signal honor (Isaios 8.19). The day of Fasting involved not only abstention from food but sitting on the ground. The gloom and sadness of this day dominates our sources, who refer somewhat less to the obscenity and hilarity of the Thesmophoria and more to its middle day of restraint.[11] But brief and undoubted allusions are also made to the scoffing and obscene hilarity which characterized other Demetrian festivals. "At the Thesmophoria they say that the women jeer" (Apollodoros 1.30). Kleomedes, a Stoic astronomer, criticized Epicurus' language as indecent: "some of his expressions one would say came from brothels, others are like the things said at Demetrian festivals by women celebrating the Thesmophoria" (*de motu circul. corp. cael.* 2.1). It seems natural to attach this behavior to the first and third days rather than to the second. †

---

* So the scholiast on Aristophanes *Thesmophoriazousai* 585, who notes that "some also refer to that day as the Descent (*kathodos*) after the deposit of the Thesmophoria" (Deubner 54). The flowery meadow of Enna, just outside Syracuse, where the original rape of Korê took place, is also a high region, smooth on top but cut off by sheer cliffs (Diodoros 5.3.2).

† Diodoros too notes the *aischrologia* (obscene speech) at the Thesmophoria, with both Sicily and Athens in view (5.4.7). Two other obscure practices might be interpreted in a playful way: Hesychios defines the *morotton* as "an object woven from bark, with which they strike each other at the Demetrian festivals." Leaving thoughts of primitive fertility whipping to one side, one might imagine such an event to have been conducted like a pillow fight in a girls' dormitory. The "Pursuit" or "Chalkidian Pursuit" is said to be either a sacrifice (Hesychios) or "a custom derived from the women's prayer in a certain war that the enemy would be pursued, and it happened that they fled all the way to Chalkis; this is Semos' explanation." Depending on how vigorous and hilarious we imagine Athenian wives to be on this occasion, we might also conjecture that an actual chase of some sort took place. When Euripides' relative in drag is unmasked, there is a kind of pursuit of his penis as it slips back and forth between his legs (Aristophanes *Thesmophoriazousai* 643–8). Is his long squat to pee at lines 611–6 an iconic parody of the women sitting on the ground on the Fasting Day? Demetrian laughter at Eleusis is associated with the figure of Baubo or Iambe, who exposed herself to the mourning mother: Olender.

The symbolism of the Thesmophoria is easier to interpret than that of the Haloa, Stenia, or Adonia. Under the obvious concern with promoting fertility there is a structured opposition of the sexes. * Women alone conduct the rites; the principal agents must avoid sexual intercourse for three days before their descent. The sacred items are familiar male and female symbols: piglets are a well known stand-in for female genitals (Golden 1988) and they are thrown into the pits along with phallic cookies. † The two items are further contrasted as raw and cooked, as natural and cultural, so that the blending of their decayed remains in the pits is an even more powerful amalgamation of opposites. The procedures for handling them too are structured by sexual opposition, if we accept the equation of serpents with maleness. The women are above, the serpents below; when the Bailers descend to collect the flesh and dough fragments, the women above shout and clap to drive away the serpents temporarily, thus keeping the boundary between female and male secure and welldefined.

In a striking display of structuralist method, Marcel Detienne in his *Gardens of Adonis* has combined exotic and popular lore about plants and spices, rites and myths, into a framework for interpreting, among other things, the Thesmophoria.[12] He identifies or constructs an opposition between the Adonia and Thesmophoria, such that (like the passage from Plato's *Phaidros*) the basic significance of the pair is the difference between short-lived pleasure and long-term, fruitful work. The eight-day sprouts are identified with non-productive sex and with a life of soft luxury, the eight-month crops with nature's unperverted laws and the cycle of hard work necessary to grow wheat and barley, the basic crops of human sustenance. His interpretations gain a good deal of richness from his use of overlooked lore about plants, culled from medical writers like Dioskorides. Adonis' connection with lettuce, for instance, is related to the belief that it was an antaphrodisiac.

In two diagrams (82, 107) he sets out the contrasts between the Adonia and Thesmophoria. (His focus on the Thesmophoria alone, to the exclusion of the other Demeter festivals, is one reason for the distortion that shows

---

*Pausanias 7.27.9–10 describes a festival of Demeter Mysia outside of Pellene, without specifying the time of year. It occupies seven days: on the third day men (and male dogs) are excluded from the sanctuary, but on the next day the men return and both sexes indulge in scurrilous banter about the other. Compare the semi-choruses of old men and old women in *Lysistrata*. Robertson 11 dissociates this festival from the Thesmophorian type, but it certainly has the general Demetrian features—obscenity and structured (though only partial) sexual segregation.

† Varro notes how primitive was pig sacrifice, being used in Demetrian rites, treaties between enemies, and at marriages in Etruria. "The ancient Latins too, and also the Greeks in Italy, seem to have done the same; for our women, particularly nurses, give the name *porcus* (pig) to the nature which makes maidens female, and Greek women call it *choiros* (pig), signifying that it is ready for marriage" (*Res Rustica* 2.4.9–10).

up in his interpretation.) He characterizes the Adonia as a time of amusement and distraction, the Thesmophoria as devoted to serious farming. The Adonia planting is an eight-day period of growth in pots at an inopportune time, the Thesmophoria's seed enhancement inaugurates the proper eight-month growth of fruitful grain in Mother Earth. So far so good, but other contrasts he draws are not so apposite, such as that between feasting and fasting. The sources do not emphasize food consumption at the Adonia, and the Thesmophoria certainly contained feasting after its middle day of fasting. This is just the smallest instance of Detienne's trimming the evidence. He further identifies the Adonia as a festival of courtesans, in contrast to the Thesmophoria's celebrants, who are lawful wives, and he portrays the Adonia as a regular occasion for seduction, to which men were invited by their mistresses, while men were rigorously excluded from the Thesmophoria and continence was emphasized.

A more careful look at the evidence for these assertions will show that they are not well-founded, but the ultimate sticking point of Detienne's interpretation comes when he identifies the Thesmophoria with men, who are taken to be the managers of legitimate agriculture, and the Adonia with women, who in the male tradition were thought to be unusually lascivious at high summer. Something is wrong here. The notion that women gathered for both festivals in order to express the excellence of male farmers and the tawdriness of pleasure-bent females seems counter-intuitive. It would imply a complete assimilation of women's consciousness, even on occasions of relative autonomy, to the ruling categories of male discourse. We have seen in Part One that those categories are part bluff and part fantasy, and Part Two has so far suggested that women's lives and thoughts, though usually hidden, could be crafty and independent. To interpret ancient female rites of fertility in terms of good male agriculture as opposed to bad female sexiness is surely a patriarchal appropriation. There is a blind spot in Detienne's masculinist vision, which has caused him to overlook some evidence and misread crucial texts.

As Burkert says (242), it is not entirely clear who attended the Thesmophoria. Legitimate wives with property-owning husbands were obviously central. Stray pieces of information suggest that slaves were excluded but that unmarried maidens and mistresses might not have been.[13] Still, one may concede that the rites of the Thesmophoria were principally, perhaps exclusively, in the hands of citizen-wives. But was the Adonia a festival principally or exclusively of courtesans? The two passages cited above, from Aristophanes and Menander, prove the opposite. In *Lysistrata* the woman on the roof shouting while Demostratos speaks in Assembly is *hê gunê*, "his wife."* So the only female Adonia celebrant attested for the fifth century is

---

*Not, as the scholiast misinterprets it, *tis gunê*, "a woman."

a citizen-wife.[*] In Menander's *Samia* the women of several households come together on Moschion's roof: one is the Samian courtesan whom his father is keeping, but the neighbors are a citizen-wife and her daughter. The other women are unspecified.

Where does Detienne pick up his notion that the Adonia was a courtesans' special feast? Many of the texts which mention the Adonia are from Athenian comedy, such as one from Diphilos' *Painter* (frag. 42 Kassel-Austin) in which a cook explains how he chooses only wealthy and liberal-spending clients to work for: "the place I'm taking you now is a brothel, where a courtesan and other prostitutes are celebrating the Adonia richly; you will stuff yourself freely and go away with a full pocket of food." In Diphilos' *Theseus* (fragment 49 Kassell-Austin) three Samian maidens, their status not specified, are drinking and telling riddles at the Adonia. One asks what is the strongest thing in the world, and receives the answers "iron," which can cut everything else; "a blacksmith," who can bend iron; and "a penis," since it can dominate the blacksmith and make him groan. But one cannot infer that, because some comic courtesans kept the Adonia, only (or even mainly) courtesans were involved with the feast. Attic comedy in the fourth century contained a large number of roles for courtesans, some of them powerful and witty Mae West figures, so it is only natural that they should be shown doing various women's things, including partying.

Alkiphron's *Letters of Courtesans* is largely based on fourth century comedy, and the collection contains one letter mentioning the Adonia (4.14). But here too the circle of women includes at least one apparently legitimate wife: "we were all there—even Philoumena, recently married and jealously guarded, managed to put her husband into a fine sleep and showed up—late, but she came" (2). The circle of named women seems to be mainly courtesans, as is fitting both for comedy and for Alkiphron's design. The fictional author of the letter is Megara, rebuking Bacchis for not coming to a women's sacrifice of some sort, to which she had been invited a long time in advance. The party in question is not the Adonia but one of the many observances which women could hold for social-cum-religious reasons.[†] At one point the writer seems to characterize all the women as courtesans, but she is ironically referring to the hoity-toity attitude adopted by Bacchis:

---

[*] "And yet, as Aristophanes tells us (*Lys.* 391–7), wives took part, and not just courtesans as Detienne repeatedly seems to imply" (Eichholz 235).

[†] Note the opening lines of *Lysistrata,* which refer to privately organized festivities for Bacchos, Pan, Aphrodite, and an otherwise unknown Birth-goddess, all evidently outside the state's calendar and superintendance. At line 700 in the same play, the women sing, "Just yesterday I was holding a picnic for Hekate." This plethora of informal gatherings is largely undocumented. A graffito list of women's names on a tile, found at the Spartan temple of Apollo, must have some ritual or other religious significance: Edmundsen.

"So you have become a virtuous lady now, and you cherish your lover—well, lucky you and your good reputation: the rest of us are just prostitutes and sluts! Hmph!" (2). The sacrifice to which Bacchis was invited is described as a picnic, lasting through the night, with many drunken frolics and no men present. One of the gamey events they indulge in is an elaborately described contest between two women to see who has the lovelier buttocks (4–6). The letter closes with an invitation to the coming Adonia at the house of Thettale's lover. Since Bacchis avoided the last party because of her devotion to her lover, Megara invites her to bring not only a garden and an Adonis image but her live Adonis-lover as well: "we will carouse with our lovers" (8). This is clearly not a description of regular practice, even on the part of courtesans, but is a concession to include a reluctant friend. Yet Detienne has used it to generate an image of the Adonia as a festival to which men were invited by lascivious women of low status (82). Detienne is sometimes excellent at diagnosing what he calls "ideologies in hermeneutic disguise" (Detienne 1979: 69), but when it comes to his own perceptions of gender meanings and their realization in practice, he can be seen to have imposed a masculinist grid which not only misrepresents the factual events but makes it impossible to know what women might have thought they were doing.

One important facet of Detienne's patriarchalism is his insistence on the distinction between courtesans and legitimate wives.* It may be doubted that Athenian women always felt as strongly about this social differentiation as their husbands and Detienne do. The women of the *Samia,* for instance, are next-door neighbors and friends, though one is a mistress and courtesan, the other a proper Athenian wife. For comparison one may cite the observations of Wikan, who lived in a town of Oman, where the social ideology dictates the usual sharp Mediterranean distinction between adulterous women and chaste wives. In one circle of neighborhood friends were seven impeccably virtuous married women and one flagrantly adulterous woman, twenty-five years old, married and the mother of two children. "She let herself be fetched and dropped by car at the gate of her house for everyone, save her husband, to see" (639). "Sheikha, despite her flagrant violation of the community's most cherished ideals, remained an intimate member of the same little neighbourhood group. . . . I asked Sheikha's neighbours about the reasons for their apparent lack of indignation with her, when they

---

* "And even if the message elicited by Detienne is the right one, we have to ask, why was it transmitted? For according to Lévi-Strauss' doctrine, such a question is not merely legitimate but vital. If I understand Detienne correctly, the answer is that the contrast between the Thesmophoria and the Adonia serves to make the distinction between marriage and concubinage clearer than it was in contemporary Greek society (pp. 238–9). This is unconvincing if only because the message, so far from resolving a contradiction in society as Lévi-Strauss' prescription demands, would seem to accentuate it" (Eichholz 235).

had so clearly stated that prostitution was shameful and sinful. They would answer, 'Yes, it is very shameful. But it is her husband alone who has the right to complain about it and punish her. What reason should we have to be angry? She has done no wrong towards us—on the contrary. She is always kind and helpful and hospitable'" (640). Sheikha may be a sexpot but she has a heart of gold, not unlike courtesans in New Comedy, and her women neighbors value her daily courtesy and generosity. Her adultery is an offense only against her husband, and her neighbors do not feel responsible to chastise her, which is strictly his prerogative.

If Detienne has appropriated women's rites in one fashion, Baudy has gone even farther. According to Baudy, the meaning of the Adonis gardens is male paederastic rites of initiation. If we had some trouble comprehending why women would be celebrating their own inferiority in Detienne's interpretation, Baudy's reading must defeat all understanding. The style of argumentation is a blend of mistakes and non-sequiturs. For instance, he first sets up the paederastic theme through a Hellenistic poem, *To the Dead Adonis*, found in Gow 166–7. In this rather refined and pretty account Aphrodite summons the boar who killed Adonis, and he confesses to her that he had seen the sleeping Adonis and found him so beautiful that he tried to kiss him. But, forgetting that he had tusks, he accidentally gored the boy to death. Baudy combines this with a wholly different version, according to which the boar was the jealous Ares in disguise, to suggest that the core of the Adonis story is a sexual-competitive-initiatory relation between older warriors and ephebes. He then summons into play all the familiar material about hunting and male initiation. Once again, the celebrant women have been entirely erased from the picture.

The Enclosing Goddess

To launch our own attempt to read women's meanings for the Thesmophoria and Adonia, let us turn to the work of Eva Stehle (forthcoming). In a very elegant and insightful talk to the Berkshire Conference on Women's History, Stehle noted a certain preference in Sappho for the tales of great goddesses carrying off young mortal lovers. These stories are not the exclusive property of Sappho but their occurrence in her work is suggestive.

The best documented is Dawn (Eôs), who was much given to snatching up and carrying off beautiful young men. Homer and Hesiod mention in passing that at one time or another she carried off Orion (*Od.* 5.121), Kleitos (*Od.* 15.250), Kephalos (*Theog.* 986), and Tithonos (*Theog.* 984). The story of Tithonos is told at some length in the Homeric Hymn to Aphrodite (218–38): after seizing Tithonos for his beauty, Dawn asked Zeus to make him immortal, which he did, but she forgot to ask for eternal youth as well. For a while she enjoyed his company but when the first grey hairs appeared she stopped sleeping with him; she kept him fed and clothed in her quarters, but as he got older and older and finally could not move at all she put him away in a room and closed the door. Only his voice lived on. Sappho fragment 58 is very broken but it contains the lines "rosy-armed Dawn . . . carrying off to the ends of the earth" along with references immediately before that to old age visible on one's skin and black hair turned [white] and weak knees. The conclusion seems inevitable that in some fashion or other Sappho dealt with Dawn's seizure of Tithonos and with his eventual fate.*

What Sappho sang about Selene (Moon) and the young hunter Endymion is not as clear. We simply know (from a scholiast on Apollonios of Rhodes 4.57) that she told the story. From other sources we know that Endymion was a young hunter associated with a cave on Mount Latmion in Karia: he is usually said to have been cast into an eternal sleep. Stehle perceives a pattern here. The ever-aging Tithonos and the never-aging Endymion have this in common—after the goddess has enjoyed them, both are put away in an enclosed space and are forever powerless, quiescent either in perfect sleep or in perfect senescence. If it is fair to put these two side by side we have an underlying story-pattern in which the male figure, after the goddess has loved him, is either eternally young and helpless or eternally old and helpless. In either case he has been placed outside the rhythms of ordinary human time as he has been placed outside ordinary social space. That the goddess carries the man away to her own house is a reversal of the patrilocal or virilocal pattern prevalent (though not universal) in Greek towns. The implied permanence of the union makes it a quasi-marriage. This is quite different from what gods do when they desire mortal women. Male deities come down and consummate their desire on the spot, then leave the maiden behind to become the founding mother of an important race or noble family line, usually after much suffering and disgrace.

The third Sapphic story of this type joins youth and age together. An old man named Phaon ran a ferry across one of the straits of Lesbos. Aphrodite took on the appearance of an old woman and after he had ferried her across he asked for no payment, so she rewarded him by transforming him into a young and exceedingly handsome man. According to Pliny (*nat. hist.* 22.20), the folklore of plants entered the story. The *erynge* or sea-holly has a root which takes the form of either male or female genitals; if a man finds one with the male-shaped root he becomes sexually attractive. Pliny connects this bit of lore with Sappho and Phaon. But if nature has powers to turn a withered old man into an attractive young man, she also has powers to reverse the effect. Aelian (*var. hist.* 12.18) records that Aphrodite hid Phaon among the lettuces. The comparison with Tithonos and Endymion leads us

---

*Ibykos (frag. 8 Page) mentioned Dawn's rape of Tithonos in tandem with Zeus' of Ganymede.

to expect that the goddess will put her mortal lover away in a space removed from ordinary civilization, but why in a lettuce patch? The answer depends on herbal knowledge which few of us have occasion to use, but in Greek culture the antaphrodisiac properties of lettuce were well known and frequently referred to (Detienne 1977:67–8).

Moreover the lover hidden in the lettuce bed is not Phaon but Adonis, who is our fourth example. Sappho records that the dead Adonis was laid out by Aphrodite in a lettuce bed (frag. 211 b iii) and the same association is reported by Kallimakhos and by two Attic comedians, Kratinos and Euboulos, the latter in a play called *The Impotent Men* (*Astutoi*), literally "Those who are not erect." On the level of surface narrative the details vary: Kallimakhos and Kratinos say that Aphrodite *hid* Adonis in a lettuce bed, which might suggest that she was trying to save him from the wild pig which killed him. Sappho and Euboulos say rather that Aphrodite laid out the dead Adonis in a lettuce bed after the boar gored his thigh. The variation of details serves to show us what features of the myth are not important. In contrast to Frazer and all those who saw in Adonis a vegetation spirit, it does not matter whether Adonis is dead or not. Like Tithonos, Endymion, and Phaon, Adonis' essential fate is to be no longer erect, decisively and permanently so. Tithonos' permanent aging, Endymion's permanent sleep, Phaon and Adonis tucked away in the lettuce patch are four versions of the same exemplary tale. He whom a goddess loves ceases to be a phallic man, enters instead a state of permanent detumescence. The goddess still cares for him but puts him away in a cradle or cupboard somewhere in her house or in that part of nature which is her territory—a mountain cave or a garden.

It is not clear how this whole set of stories was taken. The same narrative can always be told with very different emphases and to support quite different points of view. Greek men undoubtedly told such tales as warnings about what dangerous female powers could do to them. Fears of impotence and castration ran high in the phallocentric half of Greek society. Even to peek at a powerful woman in the privacy of her own territory brought blindness to Teiresias and sudden death to Aktaion, both of whom were young hunters like Endymion (Kallimakhos *Hymn* 5.75, 109). For men, such stories may serve as fearful images which justify their keeping away from women's spaces.

But a more interesting question is, How did Sappho and the community of women understand such tales? For Sappho herself there is not much left to say. In fragment 58 she may have presented an analogy between herself and Tithonos. Though his physical strength dwindled away to nothing, his voice endured, babbling endlessly (*Homeric Hymn* 5.237). A fifth-century mythographer and historian of Lesbos, Hellanikos, records that Dawn changed Tithonos into a cicada, so that his beautiful voice might continue to be heard. Sappho's fragmentary lines about someone's old age are immediately preceded by a reference to a sweet, song-loving tortoise-shell, that is, a lyre. It is just possible that Sappho compared the immortality of her lyrics with the eternal voice of the chirping Tithonos. It is a familiar lyric theme: though I will die, my songs will live on forever. I like the image of Sappho saying that she, like Tithonos, has been carried off by the loving arms of the Dawn. As to the other ephebes in our set, the fairly frequent reports that Sappho herself was in love with Phaon must be a garbled version of something else. Perhaps she spoke in the person of Aphrodite, as she does in Poem 1. Other versions of Endymion's story say that he tried to rape Hera and was punished by Zeus—cast down into Hades (Hesiod) or into eternal sleep (Epimenides). Stehle conjectures that Sappho may have conflated the traditional sleeping Endymion with a goddess-lover. About Adonis in Sappho we merely know that she incorporated two ritual refrains: "O woe for Adonis" (frag. 168) and "Delicate Adonis is dying, Aphrodite; what should we do? Beat your breasts, maidens, and tear your garments" (frag. 140a).

But though we cannot go very far in establishing the sense and tenor which Sappho gave to these four myths, we can ask a slightly different question: How do these myths connect with what we know of women's rites? Adonis gives us the direct connection. Stehle provides the intepretive context. If we cut out the intrusive phallic elements from Detienne's account, we may yet be able to see the Adonia as Greek women saw it. There *is* a real contrast drawn between the eight-month agricultural labor needed to produce Demeter's grain and the eight-day sprout-and-fizzle of Adonis' gardens. The Demeter festival, as our sources say, promotes the generation both of crops and of humans. Men's role in both cases is to plow and to plant the the seed. It is Mother Earth who does the eight months' labor, as it is human mothers who carry the long burden of human generation. It is women who civilize Demeter's wheat, turning it first into flour, then into bread; it is women who nurture and train children. If any contrast is to be drawn between the respective roles of the sexes in cultivating these natural processes, men must be placed squarely on the side of Adonis, Aphrodite's eager but not long enduring lover. What the gardens with their quickly rising and quickly wilting sprouts symbolize is the marginal or subordinate role that men play in both agriculture (vis-à-vis the earth) and human generation (vis-à-vis wives and mothers).*

So I would suggest that in the growing and wilting of the sprouts we can see, among many other meanings, a sexual joke of the sort for which other women's festivals were a primary location. One may detect a small gleam of misandric humor about men's sexuality as a thing which disappears so

---

*"Male symbolism is not absent in the [Thesmophoria], but is merely an adjunct, reduced to instrumental terms, objects which the women handle and use to enhance their own dominant role in procreation" (Zeitlin 1982: 146).

suddenly: "O woe for Adonis!" Poor little thing, he just had no staying power. There is a vase which illustrates such an interpretation, a red-figure pelike in the British Museum (see frontispiece). A woman with an extraordinarily sweet and knowing smile on her face is tending a crop of phalloi, growing like asparagus in front of her. The lines of white paint from her right hand seem to indicate that she is sprinkling water on them. Deubner associated it with the Haloa, seeing the phalloi as real objects that have been placed in the ground, but this is to overestimate the documentary value of the picture. I suggest rather that the scene is humorous fantasy, not necessarily associated directly with the Adonia (since the plants are not in pots) but illustrating the same cultural equation.

On the surface the myths of Dawn and Aphrodite might look as if they were simply about women's *erôs,* their desire sometimes for handsome young men. But in each case the narrative brings the lover quickly to a dormant state which can be read not only as a genital but also as a social allegory, a statement that women and goddesses have primary control of the processes of production and reproduction, that women enjoy relative independence from male performance in the basic life processes. And it is incidentally a joke on men's *erôs.* In the communities of women such knowledge is shared, passed around, and passed on. The many religious-social gatherings of ancient Greek women, so few of which were noted by men, are the obvious location for sharing knowledge about male adequacy—or inadequacy.

The limitations constraining this essay should be obvious enough, but perhaps it is worth spelling them out. The limited question "What were women laughing at?" is just a small facet of the ensemble of meanings that must have been involved in the Demetrian festivals. I have made no attempt to give a general theory of Demeter and Korê and their separation, of the Eleusinian initiations shared by men and women alike, or of the antique agricultural significance of the rites and their incorporation into the political life of Athens. Further, the sources are evidently male authors, whose sense of shock at ritual obscenity may have exaggerated its role beyond what it would have seemed to women participants. And finally I am limited by my own partial perspective and set of interests as a American male Classicist, groping to recover by means of ancient and modern texts a more lively and authentic sense of Mediterranean sex/gender relations. The resulting account may, I fear, still be overly preoccupied with phallic issues of interest to men: instead of claiming that "phallic men are central," as Detienne's account does, mine claims that "phallic men are peripheral and their pretensions amusing." In both cases the focus is on men. And, in a sense, the energy of this essay has been directed as much or more towards Detienne as towards Demeter, and it may appear to some to be an undignified male squabble rather than the feminist exploration we would really like. But each scholar must contribute what he or she can to the corporate enterprise.

The question of how women in male-dominant cultures define and interpret reality, particularly the social and erotic aspects of their own sexuality, is extremely hard to answer for ancient societies, easier but still very difficult for contemporary societies. Safa-Isfahani, for instance, reports on the musical mimes and skits at women's parties in Iran. Though not entirely unknown to men, who occasionally parody womens' skits in bawdy songs, these little plays are almost exclusively performed by and for women.* Sex and the problems of gender feature prominently in them: a woman giving birth to a child without the support of her husband or family, a woman seducing a vegetable seller (played by a woman in drag) in the marketplace with suggestive and aggressive language, a striptease game ("I have ants" "Where do you have them?" "Here, and here, and here; what am I to do?" "Take it off! Take it off!"), and the selection of a husband. A young female character explains why each of her suitors is unacceptable in terms of his work, punning on the double meaning of "work" as making love: the grocer works with short weights, the butcher minces his meat, the mullah works bent over, the army colonel works with guns and cannons.

In this collection of texts women's consciousness about their sexuality is framed within the terms and problems created for them by normative conventions, but the women are not passive participants in their own domination, rather they are "vital protagonists interacting with the structures of their domination, necessarily exercising some degree of autonomy, not only in defining and interpreting but in redefining and reinterpreting how the dominant structures define and interpret them" (Safa-Isfahani 34). Women in these skits are active sexual and social subjects, often defying or thumbing their noses at the public conventions which supposedly determine the limits of their behavior.†

Women's alternate and subordinate discourses take many forms in different cultures, with various relations of resistance and accommodation to patriarchal standards (Warren and Bourque). On the basis of such fragile evidence as we have, it would be temerarious to insist that we have now recovered the sense of ancient Greek women's laughter, but the picture here drawn is at least more consistent with the reported facts and with comparative studies of women in other male-dominant societies. It also pushes the analysis in a more positive direction, asking us to imagine more fully the subjective world of ancient Greek women apart from the male discourse of bluff and prescription. Instead of assuming that women "accept the [patriarchal] notions of how they are supposed to feel, think, and act, because

---

*Pictures of these parties will appear in Bauer (forthcoming).

† When a woman asks about her ailing lover and promises to tend him, some of the therapies she will provide assume that the lover is a woman—applying eye shadow and rouge, rubbing breasts. Safa-Isfahani (43) merely comments that the woman both is the subject of the song and projects herself as the object of it.

they are influenced by the weight of moral or mechanical sanctions or because they internalize these structures through socialization and enculturation processes" (Safa-Isfahani 33), ancient scholiasts and modern classicists would have done better to ask "Why are the women laughing?" It may seem a paradox that the one thing Detienne's phallocentric analysis could not see was the phalloi, but that is not strange at all. What a masculinist vision cannot see is that men do not constitute the world and are not in fact its ruling norm but are rather a distinct sub-category of the world. Masculinist theory, unlike feminist theory, cannot recognize itself as such and can certainly never see how funny it sometimes looks.

To close this chapter and this book, let me reiterate the shift in perspective that occurs when we we try to imagine women's outlook on shared cultural meanings. The dominant discourse presents them as enclosed, passive, and ideally subservient, but women's consciousness of (and cooperation with) that ideology is balanced by a set of practices that beget a different understanding. Women's double consciousness about their own existence and about men's representations of it is connected with their encompassing activities—birth, nurturance, and care of the dead—activities in which they manage and control the fundamental course of life.

North African women spend a great deal of time and energy weaving large pieces of cloth. The rituals which surround the loom are parallel to those of birth, child-rearing, and death (Messick). A woman straddles the warp and beams just before they are set up, as if giving birth; when the two sets of warps begin to cross, the fabric acquires a "soul," and men are required to leave the room, as is the case in childbirth; neighbors are expected to utter a blessing on the work, as they would for a child; the stretched warps are beaten to insure even tension and to give the future cloth more "fear," just as a child is disciplined; and when the finished cloth is cut from the loom, the weaver daubs water across across the warps and utters the testimony of the faith, both actions that are done for a dying Muslim. The consciousness expressed in these work-rituals is clear: women, in their ordinary role as providers of household products, encompass the lives of men, bring them into being and ultimately send them into the next world. *

The cloth being woven is specifically compared to a son, whose life falls into two stages: when the warp is being set up, it is like a boy; when the weft threads are added, the cloth begins to show signs of resistance, like an adolescent boy growing into a man and assuming a new social dominance over his mother. The process of weaving thus represents in miniature and

---

*Froma I. Zeitlin points out to me that Artemidoros 3.36 implies the same equation: "Weaving on a loom is like life: he who dreams he is just beginning to weave is predicting a long life; he who is at moment of cutting off will have a short one; and the cut-off cloth signifies death."

symbolic form women's relations to the life cycle and particularly to men—as infants, boys, adults, and finally as deceased. Women, in a sense, enclose men's lives, watching and guiding the process of their development. Women's cultural discourse "typically offers a commentary upon the male-perspective world. While the discourse is outwardly built of much that is 'shared' with males, all such material is recast, augmented, and encapsulated in a world-frame constituted by women" (Messick 217).

We may have extremely restricted access now to that world-frame constituted by ancient Greek women but we have every good reason to suppose that it could be characterized as an enclosing vision rather than an imprisoned one. As this book has tried to show, the constraints of desire are socially constructed norms originating in a public, patriarchally organized order. Though women are a central topic in the articulation of those norms, the point of such behavioral standards has more to do with the social relations between men than with the control of actual women. Behind the facade of public docility women had lives of their own and, arguably, a more comprehensive understanding of men than men had of women.

Appendix One
Artemidoros of Daldis:
Dream Analysis
Book One, chapters 78–80

78. The best set of categories for the analysis of intercourse [*sunousia*] is, first, intercourse according to nature [*kata phusin*] and convention [*nomos*] and customary usage [*ethos*], then intercourse against convention [*para nomon*], and third, intercourse against nature [*para phusin*].

First, this is the way it is with conventional intercourse. To have sex [*migênai*] with one's own wife [*gynê*] when she is willing and desirous and non resistant to it is good, equally for all who dream it. For the woman is either the dreamer's professional skill or the business whereby he provides himself with pleasures, or it is that which he manages and controls as he would a wife. This dream signifies the profit he makes on such resources, for as people take pleasure in sex [*aphrodisia*] so they take pleasure in profits. If the woman resists or does not offer herself, it signifies the opposite. And let the same analysis apply to a mistress.

To have sex with women who are prostitutes and who take their stand in front of brothels signifies a minor embarrassment and a small outlay; for people who consort with these women incur shame and expense. But they are good for every project of work you may undertake, for some people call them "working girls" and they offer themselves with nary a refusal.

It would be good to dream of entering whore houses and being able to leave, since being unable to leave is certainly bad. I know someone who saw himself enter a whore house and be unable to come out, and he died not many days later, as the logic of the dream demanded; for this kind of place is referred to as a common bawdy house just as a cemetery is called a common resting place and much human seed there perishes. There is a reasonable similarity therefore between a whore house and death. But the women have nothing in common with the place: they signify good things, only the place itself is not good. Therefore prostitutes who walk the street are a more profitable dream to see. The women who mind workshops and stalls, vending merchandise and receiving payment, are good to see and have sex with in dreams.

If in a dream one appears to penetrate an unfamiliar woman and if she is beautiful and gracious and decked out in rich, soft clothes and golden jewelry and offers herself—it is good for the dreamer and shows that he will accomplish something or other fairly major. But if she is old, ugly, repulsive, sloppy, an eyesore in every way and if she does not offer herself, it means the opposite; for one must think of unknown women as images of how projects will turn out for the dreamer. The looks and bearing of the woman correspond to the outcome of the dreamer's business.

To have sex with one's own female slave or male slave is good, for slaves are the dreamer's possessions, therefore taking pleasure in them signifies the dreamer's being pleased with his own possessions, most likely because of their increase in number or value.

To be penetrated by one's house slave is not good. This signifies being despised or injured by the slave. The same applies to being penetrated by one's brother, whether older or younger, or *a fortiori* by one's enemy.

Having sex with a known and familiar woman when one is feeling sexy and desires her in the dream predicts nothing, because of the overriding intensity of the desire. But if he does not desire her, it is good, provided the woman is well-favored, for he will undoubtedly achieve something profitable from the woman he sees or with her help. For she who offers her body to someone would in all likelihood offer things that pertain to the body. Often such a dream is beneficial if it occurs to a man who is privy to a woman's secrets, for such a woman allows one to touch her private parts.

To penetrate a woman who is conventionally [*kata nomous*] married and subject to a man is not good, because of the convention. For the punishments which convention applies to a man caught in adultery are what the dream signifies.

To be penetrated by an acquaintance is profitable for a woman, depending on what sort of man is entering her. For a man to be penetrated by a richer, older man is good, for the custom is to receive things from such men. To be penetrated by a younger, poorer man is bad, for it is the custom to give to such. The same meaning applies if the penetrator is older but poorer.

If a man dreams of manipulating his penis he will penetrate his male slave or female slave, because the hands applied to his penis are serving him. If he has no servants, he will undergo some penalty because of the useless ejaculation of semen. I know a slave who dreamed he was masturbating his master and he became the chaperon and overseer of his children, for he held in his hands the master's penis, which signifies his children. Again, I know someone who dreamed he was masturbated by his master: he was tied to a pillar and received many blows, thus being beaten off by his master.

II. Concerning intercourse contrary to convention, one must analyze as follows. To penetrate a son under five years of age signifies the child will die, a result which I have often observed. Probably the significant connection is the infant's corruption, for we call death a corruption. If the child is over five but under ten, he will be sick and the dreamer will be foolishly involved in some business and will take a loss. The sickness is signified by the pain of a child being penetrated before the right age and season, the dreamer's loss is through his folly, for it is not the act of a man of sound mind to penetrate his own son or any other boy of that age. If the son is a young adolescent and the father is poor, he will send his son to a teacher and the tuition he pays for his son will be a kind of expenditure into him. If a rich man has this dream, he will give his son many gifts and transfer property to his name, undergoing a loss of substance.

To have sex with a son already grown is good for a man who is out of the country, for the dream signifies coming together and abiding together, by the name "sexual union" [*sunousia*]. But for one who is already with his son and living at home it is bad; they will necessarily experience a separation from each other, because the intercourse of men for the most part takes place by one turning his back on the other.

To be penetrated by one's son signifies violent injury from the son, an injury which the son too will regret.

If a man dreams of penetrating his own father, he will become a fugitive from his fatherland or will develop an enmity with his father. For either the father himself will turn away from him or the whole *pop*ulation, which has the same signification in dreams as one's "pop."

A daughter who is quite small, not yet five years old, and one who is under ten, signify the same as the son. When the daughter is of a marriageable age, she will move to her husband's house, and the man who has the dream will provide her with a dowry, thus incurring a kind of loss of substance. I know one man who had this dream and then lost his wife; this makes sense in dream logic, because then the surviving daughter began managing the house and exercised the roles of wife and daughter alike.

If a man dreams he lies with his married daughter, the daughter will separate from her husband and return home so as to be with him and live with him. It is good for a poor man with a wealthy daughter to have sex with her; for it is by receiving many benefits from her that he will take his pleasure. Oftentimes wealthy men who see this dream have, even against their will, given something to their daughters, and sick men have died, being survived by daughters who are heiresses.

Discussion of sisters is superfluous, as they signify the same things as a daughter.

To penetrate one's brother, whether older or younger, is good for the dreamer; for he will be above his brother and will look down on him.

He who penetrates a friend will develop an enmity with him after inflicting some prior injury.

79. The analysis of the mother is intricate, elaborate, and susceptible of many discriminations. It has eluded many dream analysts. It goes as follows:

The intercourse [*mixis*] in itself is not sufficient to show the intended significance of the dream, but the postures and positions of the bodies, being different, make the outcome different. First we should speak of frontal [*sunchrôta*, "flesh to flesh"] penetration with a living mother—for it also makes a difference in the meaning whether she is alive or dead (in the dream). So if one penetrates his own mother frontally—which some say is according to nature [*kata phusin*]—and she is alive, if his father is in good health, he will have a falling out with him, because of the element of jealousy which would occur no matter who was involved. If his father happens to be sick, he will die, for the man who has the dream will assume authority over his mother as both son and husband. It is a good dream for all craftsmen and laborers, for it is usual to refer to one's craft as "mother" and what else could sexual intimacy [*plêsiazein*] with one's craft signify except having no leisure and being productive from it? It is good too for all office-holders and politicians, for the mother signifies the fatherland. So just as he who has sex [*mignumenos*] according to the conventions of Aphrodite [*kata nomon Aphroditês*] controls the entire body of the woman who is obedient and willing, so too the dreamer will have authority over all the business of the city.

And he who is on bad terms with his mother will resume friendly relations with her, because of the intercourse, for it is called "friendship" [*philotês*]. And often this dream has brought together to the same place those who were dwelling apart and has made them be together [*suneinai*]. Therefore it brings the traveler too back to his native land, provided his mother happens to be living in the fatherland; otherwise, wherever the mother is living, that is where the dream is telling the traveler to proceed.

And if a poor man who lacks the essentials has a rich mother he will receive what he wants from her, or else he will inherit it from her when she dies not long after, and thus he will take pleasure in his mother. Many too have undertaken to care and provide for their mothers, who in turn take pleasure in their sons.

The dream sets right the sick man, signifying that he will return to the natural state [*kata phusin*], for the common mother of all is nature, and we say that healthy people are in a natural state and sick people are not. Apollodoros of Telmessos, a learned man, also remarks on this. The significance is not the same for sick people if the mother (in the dream) is dead, for the dreamer will die very shortly. For the constitution of the dream woman dissolves into the matter of which it is composed and constituted, and most of it being earth-like reverts to its proper material. And "mother" is no less a name for the earth. What else could having sex with a dead mother signify for the sick man but having sex with the earth?

For one who is involved in a suit over land or who wants to buy some land or who desires to farm, it is good to have sex with a dead mother. Some say that it is bad for the farmer alone, saying that he will scatter his seeds on dead land, that is, he will have no yield. But in my opinion this is not at all correct, unless however one repents of the intercourse or feels upset.

Further, he who is in a dispute over his mother's property will win his case after this dream, rejoicing not in his mother's body but in her property.

If one sees this dream in one's native country he will leave the country, for it is not possible after so great a crime [hamartêma] to remain at the maternal hearths. If he is upset or repents the intercourse he will be exiled from the fatherland, otherwise he will leave voluntarily.

To penetrate one's mother from the rear [apestrammenên] is not good. For either the mother herself will turn her back on the dreamer or his fatherland or his craft or whatever might be his immediate business. It is also bad if both are standing upright during intercourse, for people adopt such a posture through lack of a bed or blankets. Therefore it signifies pressures and desperate straits. To have sex with one's mother on her knees is bad: it signifies a great lack because of the mother's immobility.

If the mother is on top and "riding cavalry," some say this means death for the dreamer, since the mother is like earth, earth being the nurturer and progenetrix of all, and it lies on top of corpses and not on top of the living. But I have observed that sick men who have this dream always die, but healthy men live out the remainder of their lives in great ease and just as they choose—a correct and logical outcome, for in the other positions the hard work and heavy breathing are for the most part the male's share and the female role is relatively effortless; but in this posture it is just the opposite—the man takes pleasure without laboring. But it also allows him who is not in the light to be hidden from his neighbors, because most of the telltale heavy breathing is absent.

It is not advantageous to employ many and various positions on one's mother, for it is not right to be insolent [enhubrizein] with her. That the other positions are human inventions prompted by insolence, dissipation, and debauchery and that the frontal position alone is taught by nature is clear from the other animals. For all species employ some regular position and do not alter it, because they follow the rationale [logos] of nature. for instance, some mount from behind (horse, ass, goat, cow, deer, and other four-footed animals), some first bring their mouths together (vipers, doves, weasels), some are very quick (sparrows), some by the weight of their mounting force the females into a sitting position (all birds), some do not even approach each other but rather the females gather up the seeds emitted by the males (fish). Thus it is reasonable to think that humans have the frontal position [proschrôta] as their proper one [oikeion], and have devised the others when they gave in to insolence and dissipation.

The most awful dream of all, I have observed, is to be fellated [*arrêtopoieis-thai*, "do the unmentionable"] by one's mother. For it signifies the death of children and loss of property and serious illness for the dreamer. I know someone who had this dream and lost his penis; it makes sense that he should be punished in the part of his body which erred. If one dreams of being fellated by his own wife or mistress, there will be bad feeling or a divorce in the marriage or the relationship—for it is not possible [*enesti*] to share food or kisses with such a woman—unless the woman in question is pregnant, in which case she will lose the foetus, because of the unnatural [*para phusin*] reception of the seed. Further, the wife who is wealthier than her husband will repay many loans for him, and a woman who lives with a slave will use her own money to free the man, and thus it will come about that the man's "necessity"—which is a name for the penis—that is, his constraint, will be absolved.

He who is fellated by a friend or a relative or a child who is no longer an infant will develop an enmity with the fellator; he who is fellated by an infant will bury the infant, for it is no longer possible to kiss such a one. He who is fellated by an unknown person will suffer some penalty or other, because of the useless ejaculation of seed.

If one dreams of performing oral sex [*arrêtopoiêsai*] on someone else and that person is an acquaintance, whether man or woman, he will develop an enmity with that person, because it is no longer possible [*dunasthai*] to share mouths. If it is an unknown person, the dream is a bad one for all except for those who earn their living by their mouths, I mean flutists, trumpet-players, rhetors, sophists, and others like them.

80. As to intercourse against nature one would say as follows: to dream of having sex with oneself prophesies, for a rich man, loss of substance and great need and hunger, because of the absence of another body; for a poor man, serious illness or incredible torture, for a man could not have sex with himself without great torture.

If a person dreams of kissing his own penis, if he is childless, he will have children; if his children are in another city he will see them return and will kiss them. Many after this dream, who did not have wives already, got married.

If a person dreams of fellating himself, it is good for a poor man or a slave or a debtor, for they will circumvent their own necessity. But it is evil for a man who has or wants children, for he will lose his children or never have them. For the penis is like children and the mouth is like a grave; whatever the mouth takes in it destroys and does not preserve. This dream also deprives one of a wife or mistress, for he who can provide himself with sex has no need of a wife. For all others, it prophesies either deep poverty or illness, so that they rely on their essential possessions for nourishment, that is, they will sell what they would rather not, or so that they become thin and emaciated from illness to such an extent that they can bend their mouth down to their penis.

If a woman penetrates a woman she will share her secrets [mustêria] with her. If she does not know the woman she penetrates, she will undertake useless projects. If a woman is penetrated by a woman, she will be separated from her husband or will be widowed; however she will nonetheless learn the secrets of the other woman.

To have sex with a god or goddess or to be penetrated by a god signifies, for a sick person, death, for the soul prophesies meetings and minglings [mixeis] with the gods when it is near to leaving the body in which it dwells. For others, if they enjoy the intercourse, it signifies profits from their betters; if they do not enjoy it, fears and anxieties. Sex with Artemis, Athena, Hestia, Rhea, Hera, or Hekate alone is not favorable even if one enjoys it; the dream prophesies the dreamer's death not far off, for the goddesses are awesome and we suppose that people who make a pass at them will come to no good pass. To have sex with the moon is very favorable for sea-captains and navigators and importers and astronomers and men who love to travel abroad and vagrants, for the rest it signifies dropsy; the former are aided by the lunar movement and its fundamental necessity for their studies, the latter are destroyed by its aqueous nature.

Sex with a corpse, whether man or woman, except for one's mother, sister, wife, or mistress, and being penetrated by a corpse is very unsettling; they change into earth, and to penetrate them is nothing else than to be thrust into the earth, while to be so penetrated is to receive earth into one's body. Both of these signify death, except for people living in some foreign place and not where the corpses in question have been buried; for them it prophesies return to that land. And it restrains those who want to leave their own land.

In dreams of having sex with any kind of animal, if the person dreams that he mounts the animal, he will receive a benefit from an animal of that particular species, whatever it is. We will explain this in the section on hunting and animals. If he is mounted, he will have some violent and awful experience. Many, after these dreams, have died. So much for sex.

Appendix Two
Phusis and *Natura* Meaning "Genitals"

One of the most significant facts about the words *phusis* and *natura* is that in ordinary everyday language they meant genitals.[1] This is a massive fact, about which the lexicons have little to say because they share the interests of the more talkative and "legislative" members of ancient society.[*] *Phusis* meaning genitals is a linguistic usage that takes us out of the ideological smokers and into the kitchens, the marketplace, the farmyards; it turns up principally in the quasi-technical writers: physicians, pharmacists, veterinarians, farmers, omen-readers, dream-interpreters and the like.

The earliest instances may be those in the Hippokratic *Gynaecology* (2.37 = 569 Kühn) and *Aphorisms* (27 = 643 Kühn), both discussing the prolapsed womb: "If the womb descends outside the *phusis*. . . ." The usage is found also in fifth- and fourth-century comedy,[2] and in other distinctly popular rather than elite contexts, such as in a recipe for a contraceptive that requires the soaking of chickpeas in menstrual blood and placing them in one's *phusis* (*Papyri Graecae Magicae* XXXVI.323). The aphrodisiac plant *saturion,* applied in an ointment to a man's penis in the hour before intercourse, promotes conception because it has a drying effect on the woman's *phusis.*[†] One handbook of magic contains a poem in catalectic iambic tetrameters designed to make Hekate angry against someone by repeating the awful things which

---

[*] An extreme case is the Appendix to Lovejoy and Boas, which lists 66 finely discriminated senses of the words *phusis* and *natura,* but does not include "genitals." The venerable traditions of classical philology are unsurpassed in amassing information within certain parameters, but it is equally true that they have not been critical in examining those parameters. Compared with the sophistication of modern social studies, we classicists stand on the shoulders of pygmies.

[†] Kyranides 1.18.15 and 23 (cited by book, chapter and line-numbers in the edition of Kaimakis). This is powerful medicine: "But before anointing your penis, you should smear it with honey; if you don't it will swell incredibly from the drying agent and overextend itself to a size incommensurate with the woman on account of unspeakable pleasure. Similarly if a woman anoints a little piece of wool with it and puts it on her genitals, she will readily conceive and will experience great arousal and pleasure."

217

the person in question said about Hekate: "He said that you performed the following deeds—you killed a man, drank his blood, ate his flesh, used his intestines as your girdle, stripped off his skin and put it into your *phusis*. . . ." (*PGM* IV.2597).[3] An Attic curse tablet mentions various extremities (*akrôtêria*) of an enemy—feet, hands, head, *phusis* (IG III. Pars III. 89). A love spell demands that the victim's name is to be written with ass' blood and Typhon must be invoked to set her heart and soul on fire so that "she will come and join her female *phusis* to my male *phusis,* now, now, quickly, quickly" (*PGM* XXXVI.83, also lines 113, 150). A more sadistic sex charm (*PGM* IV.296ff.) involves a wax image of a woman crouching, with a formula inscribed on each specific body part. In this list *phusis* comes after *hupogastrion* (stomach) and before *pugê* (butt) (line 318). In the second phase of the ritual, thirteen nails are to be placed in the image—two into the *phuseis,* that is, vagina and anus. There is, by the way, just such an image, a terracotta in the Egyptian antiquities collection of the Louvre, accompanied by a small lead scroll praying that the woman's love be bound exclusively to one man.[4]

On about the same level of popular technology there is a veterinary remedy for a mare's *phusis* (*Hippiatrika* 15.8 = I.88.4 [Teubner]) and an equine aphrodisiac to be smeared on a mare's *natura* to attract a fastidious stallion (Varro *res rusticae* 2.7.8). When ewes are pregnant it is a nuisance to have the rams still mounting them, so Varro advises tying wicker baskets *ad naturam* (2.2.14). Sows in heat are ferocious, says Pliny, but their rabidness can be mitigated by sprinkling vinegar on their *natura* (*n.h.* 10.181; cf. 28.176 for an ear-ache remedy prepared from the "natural" secretions of calves).[*] Still in the animal realm but moving from the practical to the fantastic Horapollo, explaining the hieroglyph for a vulture, informs us that when the vulture wants to conceive she opens her *phusis* to the North Wind (1.11).[†] Lucius, turning into an ass in Apuleius' *Golden Ass* 3.24, describes the lengthening of his ears and his nose, the sprouting of a hairy tail, and finally (small consolation) his *natura crescebat* ("increased") so that not even the lusty maid Photis could any longer accommodate him. Later in the same novel, farmers plan to castrate him, to cut off his *natura* (7.26). Castration is also the subject in pseudo-Phokylides 187 ("Do not cut off a youth's child-begetting male *phusis*") and—after the fact—in Petronius *Satyrica* 119.24 (*quaerit se natura nec inuenit*).[‡]

---

[*] The veterinarian discourse in which *natura/phusis* seems at home may have influenced the choice of words in an Atellan farce to describe Tiberius as "an old billy-goat licking the *natura* of does" (Suet. *Tib.* 45).

[†] In hieroglyphics, "the vulture stands for the word 'nature,' since that species of bird contains no males" (Ammianus Marcellinus 17.4.11).

[‡] Theophanes *Chronographia* I. p. 296 de Boor: "They butchered Anastasios, the great patriarch of Antioch, and put his *phusis* in his mouth."

Artemidoros recorded a dream in which a woman saw wheat stalks grow from her breasts and then curve down and enter her *phusis* (5.63). He identifies this as an incest dream, the wheat stalks signifying her son and their entry into her *phusis* the intercourse. *Natura* means vagina in Cicero's description of a woman's sexual dream (*de div.* 2.145; the same story and word repeated in Tertullian *de anima* 46.5). Augustine refers to this text explicitly when he is explaining "natural" sex as procreative intercourse: "for this reason that part of the body is properly and regularly called *natura*" (*Op. imperf. c. Julian.* 5.17 = *Patrologia Latina* 45.1450). Cicero also uses *natura* to designate the distinctive feature of herms (*nat. deor.* 3.56), as Minucius Felix does of bishopricks.* Julius Obsequens' chronicle of prodigies includes a baby girl born in the year 94 B.C.E. who had two heads, four legs, four arms, and *gemina feminea natura* (51; cf. 53, *mulier duplici natura inventa*). When the midwife attending Jesus' mother tells Salome that she has just witnessed a virgin birth, Salome—a doubting Thomas, she—says "Unless I put my finger in and explore her *phusis,* I shall not believe that a virgin has given birth" (*Protoevangelium Jacobi* 20–21 Tischendorf). Diodoros describes the medical analysis of an apparently spontaneous sex-change in the case of a young married woman who developed a penis: "the doctors decided that the *phusis* of a male had been hidden in an egg-shaped area of her female *phusis*" (Diodoros of Sicily 32.10.7; cf. 32.11.1, 12.3). The young woman then changed her clothes and her name and joined the royal cavalry. Hesychios glosses the word for hearth-fires (*escharai*) as meaning "among other things the *phuseis* of women." One of the Latin-Greek glossaries contains the entry *rima—gunaikeia phusis* (i.e., "crack—female *phusis*").[5]

All of these seem to be ordinary and unselfconscious usages of the sort that we may call popular-technical. There is a certain medical aspect also to the passage in the *Metamorphoses* of Antoninus Liberalis (41), in which the difficulty of King Minos—he ejaculated serpents and scorpions—is solved by Prokris. She shapes a piece of goatskin so that it fits into a woman's *phusis* and after Minos has ejaculated into it he has sex safely with his wife Pasiphae. In one late Latin text,[6] a mixture of ingredients is to be placed on a young woman's *fisis* so that when the midwife (*obsetrix*) examines her she will find her still a virgin. The crossover of a Greek word is interesting and there is a slim chance that *natura* in this sense may be influenced by Greek habits of speech. Varro uses it four times of women and female animals, but never in such a way that it is unambiguously a native Latin colloquialism rather than a turn of phrase picked up from his Greek sources (2.2.14, 2.4.10, 2.7.8,

---

* "Christians worship the head of an ass and some even adore their bishop's genitalia, *quasi parentis sui adorare naturam*" (9.4). The pun is from Herman Melville, *Moby Dick,* chapter 95, "The Cassock."

3.12.4). Sometimes *phusis* refers to the anus (of men, women, or animals), *
but far and away the predominant sense is genitals, and almost always female
genitals.

A few instances of *phusis* and *natura* as genitals occur in the higher realms
of literature, and they seem to betray the popularity of the expression by
their coyness: one epigram, for instance, reads: "A maiden increased her
worldly wealth not by her *technê* but by her *phusis*."[7] The cleverness is not
merely in the juxtaposition here of a primary, decent meaning (nature as
opposed to art) with a secondary, indecent meaning (vagina) but also in the
unexpected use of a folk word in fine writing. The medical-popular texts,
however, never joke about a double meaning and show no hesitation simply
to call a *phusis* a *phusis*.

---

*Julius Obsequens 40 (*posteriore natura*); *PGM* IV.326; when Lysistrata admires the "chasms
front and back" of the Korinthian delegate, the scholiast gives a stage direction: "She says this
while touching her two *phuseis*" (Aristophanes *Lys.* 92).

Notes

Introduction

1 "It is popularly believed in modern times that legal restrictions upon sexual conduct are a creation of Christianity and that ancient sexuality was free from legal curbs on sexual expression" (Brundage 15).

2 [Dem.] 25.57: Zobia is not even called by the more honorific term *gunê* ("wife"/"woman") but is rather referred to as *hê anthrôpos* ("female human being") and *gunaion* (diminutive of *gunê*).

3 *Eth. Nikom.* 1160^{b}33–34. Lacey 159–61, 167–9; Aiskhines refers to widows controlling their property as a regular, though not praiseworthy, state of affairs (1.170–1). Schaps 1979, de Ste. Croix.

4 Sweet, Cronin, Dubisch 1986a, Herzfeld 1985a.

5 As passive to active—*Gen. Anim* 2.4: 738^{b}20–23. For bibliography see Halperin 1989: 193, n.23.

6 On Amazons, see duBois 1982, Tyrrell; *Amazons* was the title of at least two comedies, by Kephisodoros and Epikrates; on rebellious wives in drama, Foley 1981, 1982. Two stories express male fears of house-work as feminizing: Herakles acting as Omphale's serving-maid and Sardanapallos (Arist. *Pol.* 5.10: 1312^{a}1–4).

7 *k' ha duskolainei pros eme kai brenthuetai / taut' auta dê 'sth' ha ka'm' epitribei tôi pothôi.*

8 Other important works are Blum and Blum 1965, 1970, Walcot 1970, Bailey, Dimen [Schein], du Boulay 1974, 1976, Loizos, Dionisopoulos-Maas, Danforth and Tsiaras, M. Clark, Doumanis, Handman, Danforth 1983, Piault, Dubisch 1986a, and Friedl 1986.
   The principal systematic work on the Mediterranean area is J. Davis, though he pays scant attention to questions of gender. His bibliography is supplemented by Gilmore 1982.

1 Unnatural Acts: Erotic Protocols in Artemidoros' Dream Analysis

1 "In any approach that takes as predetermined and universal the categories of sexuality, real history disappears" (Padgug 5).

2 Sorof, Ehrenberg, Heinimann, Pohlenz, Adkins, Guthrie 1971a, De Romilly, Köster.

3 ". . . 'nature' and 'culture,' as culturally defined rather than natural concepts, are unstable,

historically relative assumptions," Foley 1981a: 147; Kelly-Gadol, Mathieu, MacCormack and Strathern.

4 An example of the tendency to construct a specious genealogy for cherished modern values is the thesis that the Stoics developed the marital ideal expressed in Plutarch's *Erôtikos*, namely that husbands and wives should not only cooperate but even desire one another. For an analysis and refutation see Babut 108–13. A good general treatment of Plutarch's uniqueness on these issues is Goessler.

5 Lykourgos *Against Leokrates* 82–110, Aiskhines *Against Timarchos* 141–53, and Demosthenes 19.243–56 are good examples.

6 Aristophanes prided himself on being an exceptionally witty and intelligent Athenian, but he does not see philosophers as his rivals on this score. Philosophers as buffoons: Ameipsias' *Konnos* had a chorus of 'thinkers'/'worriers' (*phrontistai*); Eupolis' *Flatterers* represented the wealthy Kallias and his household of philosophers; Aristophanes *Clouds*; Epikrates frag. 10 *PCG* (frag. 11 Kock). Carrière 62–66; Gailly; Frischer 55–60.

7 E. g., Guthrie 1971a, who operates on two false premises, that the *nomos/phusis* contrast was taken seriously by the general public and that philosophers were important to society at large.

8 Actually born at Ephesos, but he styled himself a Daldian to honor the little Lydian town where his mother was born (3.66: 235.13–22).

   References are to book and section of *Artemidori Daldiani Onirocriticon Libri V*, ed. Roger A. Pack (Leipzig 1963). Longer sections are also referenced, after a colon, by page and line number of Pack's edition, unless the citation occurs at the very opening of the section. Translations in this essay are my own. There is an English translation by White, a German translation by Kaiser, a French translation by Festugière, and an Italian translation by Corno. The three chapters on sexual dreams were translated by Paul Brandt [Hans Licht] in *Anthropophyteia* 9 (1912) 316–28, rectifying their omission from Krauss's 1881 version. De Becker has a fairly sensitive appreciation of Artemidoros.

9 Cf. 5.proem: 301.10. "When I was in Kyllênê . . . ." (1.45). Artemidoros refers to some dreamers in particular cities, presumably having been there himself: "I knew a lyre-player in Smyrna" (1.64: 70.4), "an artist in Korinth" (4.proem: 240.17), "a carpenter in Kyzikos" (4.proem: 242.13), "a man in Miletos" (4.24: 260.19), Magnesia (4.36), Olympia (5.55), Nemea (4.7), Pergamos (4.33: 267.19), Rome (5.69). Artemidoros is, by the standards of the Second Sophistic, a relatively naive author who gives every indication of being dedicated to the truth of his profession and not to a pretense of learning. It is wholly credible that, as he claims (1 proem: 2.10), he searched out even the rare books on his subject and that he had read everything pertinent to onirocritics; but far from being boastful about his extensive reading, he ranks all manuals a poor second to actual experience in listening to dreams and following their outcomes (1.12; 4.4).

10 The controversies are reviewed by Cicero *de divinatione*, the practices themselves in Bouché-Leclercq.

11 It may be out of respect for some readers' piety that Artemidoros says so little about the cause of dreams. He does not deny that there is a divine realm of some sort that oversees the universe, including the soul's sending of dreams ("who- or whatever it is that guides us," 1.2: 6.2), but he studiously avoids committing himself on the question of the gods' role in dream communication: "I am not going to discuss Aristotle's question about whether the cause of dreaming lies outside us and is from a god or is something inside us which conditions our soul and acts as a natural concomitant to it" (1.6). The reference to Aristotle's *On Prophecy in Sleep*, a vigorous refutation of the divine origin of dreams, at least hints at the acceptability of a wholly naturalistic understanding of dream causation.

(In what Dodds 120 calls his "romantic youth," Aristotle had written about the soul's innate powers of divination: "when in sleep the soul is by itself, then it recovers its proper nature and prophesies and announces things to come," *On Philosophy* frag. 10 Rose.) For the strength of Artemidoros' feelings about claims that the gods sent dreams to invalids sleeping in temples, see Winkler 1982b. The issues of skepticism and piety in the *Oneirokritika* deserve a lengthier treatment, which I hope to give elsewhere.

12 Called "theorematic" dreams, because they contain a direct vision or picture (*theôrêma*) of what will occur (*theôroumena*, 1.2: 6.12; *hôs theôrountai*, 4.1).

13 Called "allegorical" dreams. "Allegorical dreams are those which signify things through other things: in them the soul engages in a natural process of riddling" (1.2: 5.9).

14 Since people whose individual customs are different from the common ones also know the prevalent norm, their dreams may avail themselves of either the private or the common meaning. At one point Artemidoros lays down the principle that in cases of conflict the common meaning should prevail (4.2: 245.13).

15 "The very ancient writers distinguished, saying that it was a good dream for poor men but a bad dream for rich men," 2.9: 110.14.

16 Discussions of this identification are cited in Pack xxv–xxvi. Behr 182 n.23 argues that Maximus is too late to be the dedicatee of Artemidoros. Artemidoros is certainly older than Maximus, for he began composing the *Oneirokritika* after 140 C.E. (1.26: 33.10), at which time he was probably at least fifty years old (4.24: 259.20). Eusebios places Maximus' floruit in 152 and the *Souda* declares that he was in Rome under Commodus. Behr stresses the *Souda* testimony, but Maximus' presence in Rome after 177 is not a compelling ground on which to deny that he might have been prestigious enough already in the 140s to be the dedicatee of the *Oneirokritika*.

17 *scribit amatori meretrix, dat adultera munus.* Petronius *Satyrika* frag. 30.14 Müller. Daphnis and Chloe dream *oneirata erôtika* before they know exactly what to do (Longus 2.10.1).

18 *Republic* 9.571B–572B. The analogy with satyrs is implied in the verb "prance," *skirtâi.*

19 *hêdontai men [gar] hoi anthrôpoi tois aphrodisiois, hêdontai de kai tais ôpheleiais,* 1.78: 86.27.

20 Henderson 1975: 22, 25, 183–6; Shipp; Jocelyn; ancient texts are extensively cited by Krenkel. *Tesserae lusoriae* (ivory tablets for games) are inscribed with pejorative epithets such as *cun(n)ilinge, cinaede,* and *patice:* Hülsen; Hallett 1977, esp. 156. Galen casually refers to fellatio as unnatural (in a context implying that it can be quite difficult to resist that temptation to pleasure: —vol.5, p. 30 Kühn), though he elsewhere recognizes that calling someone a fellator is simply a way of being abusive—on a par with saying that someone eats feces (*de simplic. medic.* 10.1, vol. 12, p. 249 Kühn). Galen notes in the same passage, however, that cunnilingus is more disgusting than fellatio.

21 *Hetairai* are identified as the proper partners for prolonging and varying erotic pleasure, among which anal intercourse is sometimes specified as the most special treat. It is therefore a pleasure the proper wife would refuse to grant: Aesop 109 Perry is the best statement; also Aristophanes *Ploutos* 149–55, *Peace* 876, *Anth. Pal.* 5.129 (*panta pathainetai*), Catullus 110 (*meretricis . . . quae sese toto corpore prostituit*), Martial 9.67, 10.81, Apuleius *AA* 3.20.
The other side of the coin is that wives are forbidden to luxuriate in erotic pleasure or even to initiate sex. Plutarch *Conjugalia Praecepta* is the classic formulation: for a wife to initiate sex is whore-like (140D); a man may enjoy drinking and sex-play with prostitutes and with his maidservants, but he must always respect the dignity of his wife by keeping her entirely separate from those activities (140B); cf. *Quest. conviv.* 613A. Wine is sometimes a metonym for the same restrictions: Plutarch frag. 157 on the opposition of Hera and Dionysos (all the more significant since wives could on occasion attend public dinners,

Quest. conviv. 7.8.4: 712E); Plato *Laws* 775B-D.

Luxurious sex with legitimate wives is also part of the anti-Spartan image: Aristophanes *Lysistratê* 1174, Athenaios 13.602D-E, Photios *Lexikon* s.v. *kusolakôn*. It is hard to find texts that lie outside these tendentious traditions, but *PGM* 14.351–53 and *CIL* 10.4483 come closest: both are addressed to mistresses, but with no emphasis on the wife/whore dichotomy.

2 Laying Down the Law: The Oversight of Men's Sexual Behavior in Classical Athens

1 McIntosh, Weeks, Epstein; fuller bibliography in Halperin 1989: 159, n.21, and 162, n.52.

2 Population figures are at best estimates of the reliability of ancient estimates, themselves contradictory. The citizen-body (ball park figures: 30,000–40,000 in the fifth century, 21,000 in the later fourth century) was roughly matched by their wives, outnumbered both by their children and by their other statutory subordinates (prostitutes, domestic and industrial slaves) and, when we can measure it in 316, was just double that of resident-aliens. Gomme 1927, 1933, 1959, A. Jones 161–80, Meiggs, Ruschenbusch 1981a, 1981b, Rhodes 1980, Duncan-Jones, Hansen 1981, 1986, Patterson 40–81.

3 Three cases are cited in Deinarchos 1.29, all of which may involve sexual aggression of citizens over slaves-who-are-really-free: a youth kept in a mill, a woman from Rhodes who played the lyre at the Eleusinia and was "disgraced" (*hubrisen* = raped), a girl from Olynthos put into a brothel.

4 See Aiskhines 1.43 and Dem. 25.57 (citizens bullying metics) and Aiskhines 1.195 (let Athenians who are boy-hunters turn their attention to foreigners and metics so that citizen-boys will not be injured by being declassed as prostitutes).

5 "This colourful speech [Dem. 54] . . . brings out the violence that is a neglected feature of Athenian life," Osborne 50.

6 IG II^2 1368, 1369; Raubitschek.

7 Lys. 3.20, 47; Dem. 54.44. For the significance of this criterion, see Davies.

8 *Prohistasthai* + genitive ("manage") was not a common locution for these concerns, though it is found in the classical period (Herodotos 2.173, Xen. *Mem.* 3.2). Plutarch happens to use it in a context appropriate to our subject: "Verres had an adolescent son who seemed not to be managing his youthful beauty in a manner befitting a free person. When Verres criticized Cicero for softness (*malakia*), he replied 'It is your sons at home who should be criticized,'" *Life of Cicero* 7. 864C.

9 Nature itself, it could be claimed, had segregated the sexes by physical and psychological toughness: *malakôteron gar to êthos esti to tôn thêleiôn*, "the female character (in all species, as a rule) is softer," Aristotle *Hist. Anim.* 9.1: 608ª25. Saïd.

The zero-sum logic here described seems to be a common denominator in the gender clichés of the entire family of Mediterranean cultures. It is attested just as vividly in Roman texts: a cook who has just been beaten in Plautus' *Aulularia* complains that he is "softer than a *cinaedus*" (422); the verb which expresses the transformation of Ovid's Hermaphroditus into a woman is *mollescere* (*Met.* 4.386).

That is why there is no word for (anatomical) sex in Greek. "The notion of sex never gets formalized as a functional identity of male and female but is expressed solely through the representation of asymmetry and of complementarity between male and female," female being merely the opposite to the male. Sex as an abstract, homogeneous, unified notion, something *common* to each of the two genders, has no place in this asymmetrical system. See Manuli 201 n.1.

10 Schauenberg; Dover 1978: 105; for another interpretation see Pinney.

11 Rhodes 1981: 617, 1982: 178. Instances of routine *dokimasia* not resulting in a trial: Dem. 40.34, 59.3 and 72, Aiskhines 3.31.

12 Lysias 16, 25, 26, 31; Kratinos *Cheiron* frag. 9 Kock, Xen. *Mem.* 2.2.13, Deinarchos 2.17.

13 Meidias' accusation against Demosthenes during his *dokimasia* for Council-membership was just one of a string of public attacks, Dem. 21.111.

14 Rhodes 1981: 510–1 takes Dein. 1.71 as referring to a real *nomos*, but that would amount to a property qualification for speaking in the Assembly. Deinarchos' wording may be deliberately misleading on this point.

15 *prohestanai tou dêmou*, Dein. 1.71.

16 Timarchos not only "wolfed down" his patrimony like food, he "gulped it down" like wine, 1.96. The mythic narrative that captures these fears is that of Erysichthon, who devoured his father's estate (Hellanikos, FGrHist 4 F 7; Kallimakhos *Hymn to Demeter* 31–117) and repeatedly sold his daughter (Nikandros = Ant. Lib. 17.5, Lykophron 1393–6).

17 As in Deinarchos 2.16–8, against Speakers who are "receivers of gifts," with a similar appeal to the qualifications for *dokimasia rhêtorôn*.

18 Alkibiades prostituted himself and committed incest with his sister (Lysias 14.26–8, 41). "If I had to give an individual account of his adulteries, wife-stealing, and all his other violent and lawless behavior, there would not be enough time to do so," Andokides *Against Alkibiades* 10. Another innuendo of incest: Isaios 5.39. Andokides charges Epichares not only with having prostituted himself at a low price to any comer, not only with having made a living wage at this occupation, but with being ugly to boot (*de myst.* 100—in reply to similar charges from Epichares). "What Nikomachos' father practiced when he was a young man . . . it would be very troublesome to relate," Lysias 30.2. Dem. 45.77–9; Dem. 24.126, 181.

19 "For how long has Timarchos been a leader of the people? A long time" Dem. 19.286. Timarchos authored more than a hundred pieces of legislation during his long and famous career (hypothesis to Aiskhines 1). He was also conspicuous from youth for his beauty, according to Aiskhines.

20 Perlman, Hansen 1983, 1987: 50–69. "If the subject were a new one, men of Athens, I would have waited until the majority of those who are accustomed to deliver their opinion had spoken and if I agreed with one of their opinions I would have held my peace," Dem. 4.1 (= *Prooim.* 1) Of course every citizen had in theory a right to speak: Dem. 25.29.

21 Aiskhines 1.2. "In the forensic speeches prosecutors usually justify their indictments by referring to personal enmity and an apparently disinterested prosecutor was almost invariably stamped as a sycophant" (in modern terms, an ambulance chaser), Hansen 1976: 121. Roberts 55–83.

22 *quid si tandem iudice {naturâ} hanc causam ageremus, quae ita divisit {virilem et} muliebrem personam ut suum cuique opus atque officium distribueret, {et} ego hunc ostenderem muliebri [codd. tui liberi] ritu esse suo corpore abusum [codd. adlusum]: nonne vehementissime admiraretur, si quisquam non gratissimum munus arbitraretur virum se natum sed depravato naturae beneficio in mulierem convertere properasset?* (Latin translation in Rutilius Lupus 2.6); Barabino.

23 Each species has a single *phusis* but we humans have as many *tropoi* as there are individual people: Philemon 1.89 Kock; "from my earliest childhood I have had a desire for a certain something, just as everyone else does for something or other—horses, dogs, money, public

office," Plato *Lysis* 211D; Aristophanes *Wasps* 67–88. From earlier Greek literature one can cite Homer *Odyssey* 14.228 *allos gar t' alloisin anêr epiterpetai ergois* and, using an earlier form of *phusis*, Arkhilokhos 25 West. Dover 1978: 62.

24   Dover 1974: 88–90; Holwerda 70–1, 112; Thimme. *Orgê* is an older (perhaps poetic?) term.

25   A young man defends his right to speak: "It is not the quantity of our years that differentiates us from each other in respect to good counsel but rather our nature and practices," Isokrates 6.4.

26   *hêgeito gar einai pros hetairian pollôi kreittô phusin nomou kai tropon genous kai prohairesin anangês.* Isok. 1.10.

27   *Kyr.* 1.1.6. On *phusis* meaning individual talent, see Shorey.

28   "He was the first to systematize this human science so as to learn each man's *phusis*," Porphyry *Vit. Pyth.* 13.

29   The sources on physiognomy, Cicero and ps.-Plutarch, tell tales of one Zôpyros who brought the science to Athens; a *Zôpyros* is listed as a work by Phaido in Diog. Laert. 2.105. The texts and testimonia are collected and analyzed by R. Förster, the medical and rhetorical precedents are discussed by Joly, cf. Lloyd 1983: 18–26.

30   Translation in Barnes 1984 vol. 1, pp. 1237–50.

31   Arkhippos frag. 45 Kock (= Plutarch *Alkibiades* 1); Com. adesp. 339 Kock; Clem. Alex. *Paid.* 3.69.

32   Ar. *Wasps* 686–8 describes the stride of a *katapugôn;* cf. Eupolis 163 Kock; Suet. *peri blasphêmiôn* s.v. *chalaibasis* (Taillardat 52).

33   Later descriptions of the effeminate male, called *androgynos*, in Adamantios *Physiognômonika* 1.19, 23; 2.21, 38, 39, 41, 42, 52, 59 Förster and anon. *de physiognomonia* 98 (Förster [1893] II.123); see Gleason.

34   Arist. *Physics* 230^{a}18-b10: "place" is the favored category for discriminating natural/unnatural.

35   *Gen. Anim.* 718^{a}2–4, 728^{a}10–7, 738^{b}28–^{a}6.

36   The theory was re-invented, or quite possibly lifted from Aristotle without attribution, by Paolo Mantegazza in his *Gli amori degli uomini* (1885), trans. Samuel Putnam *The Sexual Relations of Mankind,* ed. Victor Robinson (New York 1935) pp. 89–90: "Anatomicians are acquainted with the spinal nervous structure which has to do with lustful desire, and they know how intimate a relationship there is between those nerves distributed in the intestinal and rectal tract and those which run down to the genital organs. I personally believe, it is by an anatomic anomaly that the sensual nerve branches are deflected to the rectum; this explains how it is their excitation produces in the *patici* a venereal orgasm, which in ordinary cases may only come through the love organs."

3   The Constraints of Desire: Erotic Magical Spells

1   Polemo *de physiognomonia liber* chapter 69, in Förster.

2   *Papyri Graecae Magicae* (abbreviated PGM), ed. Karl Preisendanz. PGM contains Greek papyrus texts numbered I-LXXXI, "christian" papyrus spells numbered P1–24, ostraka numbered O1–5, and two wooden tablets numbered T1–2. In this chapter, roman numerals refer to the texts in PGM; numbers higher than LXXXI refer to the sequence used in the English translation of PGM: Betz, abbreviated *PGM-Translation,* which unfortunately does not contain Preisendanz's non-papyrus and "christian" material. As the editor makes clear on p. ix, *PGM-Translation* is conceived within a christian interpretive framework, which

explains its sectarian omission of Preisendanz's "christian" papyri. I suspect that the omission of the ostraka is similarly motivated, since two of them are "christian" magic (O3–4). For demotic spells I use the reference system in *PGM-Translation:* PDM + lower-case roman number.

A. Audollent *Defixionum Tabellae* (abbreviated DT) (Paris 1904).

3 Aune; an exciting treatment of the larger interpretive issues in Phillips esp. 2711–32 on "magic."

4 Maloney, especially the essays by Dionisopoulos-Mass and by Garrison and Arensberg; Herzfeld 1980; Galt. For ancient material, see O. Jahn, Moreau.

5 "While an understanding of stratified agrarian societies may provide a first-level explanation for 'virginity complexes,' any particular instance of the complex must be understood within its specific historical context. Women's chastity may be a primary idiom used by people in stratified agrarian societies for negotiating claims to unequal privileges, but it is not the only idiom" (Collier 1986: 102).

6 Dionisopoulos-Mass 58–60. For another modern account of love magic see Mrabet.

7 Sulla's success was summed up in the name granted to him by the Senate—Epaphroditos (Appian *Civil Wars* 1.97). Other *kharitêsia* (spells or amulets to acquire charm—*kharis*): VII 215 ("Stele of Aphrodite," a tin amulet), IV 2226–9 (a gold amulet for *philtra*), VII 186–90 (right leg of a living gecko caught in a graveyard and worn as an amulet; brings victory as well as charm), XII 182–9 (a prayer to the lord who is the *kharitêsion* of the kosmos to grant unfailing free speech "and let every tongue and every voice listen to me"). A Coptic shard contains the prayer: "Fill (this engraved shard) for me with every wish, every love which is sweet, every peace, every delight at once!" (*Enchoria* 5 [1975] 115–8, revised by G. Browne *ZPE* 22 [1976] 90–1).

8 "Give me praise and love (before So-and-So, son of) So-and-So today . . . (But as for my enemies) the sun shall impede their hearts and blind their eyes . . ." PDM xiv 309–34.

9 E. N. O'Neil in *PGM-Translation* 146.

10 *kharis/nikê* (charisma and victory, 36), *praxis/kharis* (successful business and charm, 62), *alkê/morphê* (power and beauty, 30), *prosôpou eidos/alkê hapantôn kai pasôn* (a handsome face and power over all men and women, 5–6). A similar juxtaposition of personal success, triumph over enemies, and erotic ambitions are promised for a ring at PGM XII 270–350: "Wearing it, whatever you may say to anyone, you will be believed, and you will be pleasing to everybody" (278–9).

11 Licht; Hopfner 273–305. The Latin for "drug," *venenum,* is apparently derived from *Venus* and thus fundamentally meant aphrodisiac. Cf. Afranius frag. 380–1 Ribbeck.

12 "A vessel inquiry which a physician in the district of Oxyrhynchos gave me," PDM xiv 528.

13 The original purpose of wine was to promote intercourse, according to the scholiast on Lucian (p. 280.3ff Rabe): . . . *hoti ho Dionysos dous ton oinon paroxuntikon pharmakon touto pros tên mixin pareschen.*

14 Kyran. 1.5.15–8; rocket seed ground with pine cones in wine was a widely known aphrodisiac—P. Lit. Lond 171, cf. Dioskorides *Mat. Med.* 2.140, P. Lond. 121ʳ182–84.

15 Pliny *nat. hist.* 26.95, 96, a knowledge attributed to Thessalian women by Dioskorides *Mat. Med.* 3.126.

16 Pliny *nat. hist.* 27.65, Diosk. *Mat. Med.* 3.126; cf. Dioskorides *Euporista* 2.96.

17 Plutarch *de tuend. san. praec.* 126A, *conj. praec.* 139A.

18 Kenney esp. 380–90; Lowes; Ciavolella.

19 Appian *Bell. Syr.* 59–61; Plutarch *Demetrios* 38; Lucian *de dea Syria* 17–8; Val. Max. 5.7.3. Rohde 55–9; P. M. Frazer; Amundsen. Asmus analyzes the physiognomonic tradition reflected in this widely known story. Plato *Lysis* 204C reflects the topos: commenting on a young man's blush, Sokrates says, "I have this god-given talent for instantly discerning who feels *erôs* and who is its object." In *Daphnis and Chloe* Dionysophanes, "seeing that Daphnis was pale and secretly crying, instantly detected (*ephôrase*) his passion" (4.31).

20 The pulse of Justus' ailing wife quickened when the name of the dancer Pylades was mentioned: *Prognosis* 6 (XIV 630–4 Kühn = CMG V.8.1, ed. V. Nutton, pp. 100–4); the same incident is referred to in his *Commentary on Hippokrates' Prognostics* I.8 (XVIIIB 40 Kühn = CMG V.9.2, ed. Diels, p. 206).

21 VII 285–9; 619–27; 643–51. VII 969–71 (partly in code) is a written equivalent which obviates the awkwardness of long mumbling while someone is waiting for their drink.

22 XIII 319–20 (wasps caught in a spider web!); PDM xiv 376–94, 428–50, 636–69, 772–804.

23 Pliny *nat. hist.* 27.57; Dioskorides *Mat. Med.* 4.131.

24 VII 973–80, CXIX. A related form of touch-magic at Plato *Meno* 80A, where Meno feels numb and helpless because of Sokrates' wizardry, as if he has been touched by an electric eel. CXXVII: a man whose loins have been touched with the brain of an electric eel will bend over and not be able to stand upright.

25 "Lead forth and bind fast Matrona, daughter of Tagenes, whose *ousia* you now have, the hairs of her head, that she may not have sex . . . with any other man except Theodoros, son of Techosis," Wortmann 1968: 60, lines 19–23. PDM xiv 1075, "put the hair of the woman in the leaf." Preisendanz 1918. In other *agôgai*, *ousia* is attached to the head or neck of a kneeling doll (IV 302–3) or wrapped with a papyrus incantation and placed in a box (XV) or put inside an inscription on ass' hide and placed with vetch in a dead dog's mouth (XXXVI 361–71).

26 Wortmann 1968: 69 cites also Pap. Harris (Danks Vid. Selsk. 14/2, 1927) and the Cairo tablet (*SEG* 8 [1937/8] 574).

27 XXXVI 68–101; 102–34; 295–310; in the lunar calendar at VII.295 the moon in Aries is a propitious time for *empura* and *agôgima*.

28 Looking at the moon: IV 2708; "late at night, in the fifth hour, facing Selene (the Moon) in a pure room . . . ; when you see the goddess turning ruddy, know that she is already attracting her," VII 874–5, 889–90; LXI 6; "before Isis in the evening when the moon has risen," lxi 118; "in the waning of the moon when the goddess is in her third day," XII 378–9; the same day is chosen for a necromantic ceremony in Heliodoros *Aithiopika* 6.14.2. If a rooftop is not available, one may make do with the ground, LXI 6.

29 Sleeplessness is a central aim too of erotic rituals which do not mention a time of performance, such as IV 2943–66, VII 374–6, 376–84. These could be plausibly grouped with our night scenes.

30 "Let her have only me in her mind (*kata noun*)," IV 1520, 2960–1; *solum me in mente habeat,* DT 266.19; Maltomini *Civiltà class. e cris.* 1 (1980) 376 supplements CCXXII along these lines. A rare trace of the lover's obsession at Wortmann 64, line 78: "Matrona . . . whom Theodoros has on his mind (*en noôi*)."

31 Theokritos 2.161–2 (Assyrian stranger; the local old ladies who knew spells were unable to help, 91); Vergil *Ecl.* 8.95–9 (Moeris); Lucian *Dial. Court.* 4.4–5 (Syrian herbalist, an old lady); Heliodoros *Aithiopika* 3.17, cf. 3.19; 4.5 (an Egyptian priest, pretending to be a love wizard).

32   Men aiming at women: XVIIa, XIXa, LXXXIV, CI, CVII, CVIII, CIX, O2 (PGM vol.
     2, p. 233); DT 100, 227, 230, 231, 264–71, 304; two tablets for the same agent and victim
     in SB Heidelberg 1910/2; two tablets and one ostrakon for the same agent and victim in
     Wortmann 57–84; BIFAO 76 (1976) 213–30; ZPE 24 (1977) 89–90.
     Women aiming at men: XV, XVI, XXXIX, LXVIII; DT 270, 271.
     Women aiming at women: XXXII; PSI 28, cf. F. Maltomini Miscellanea Critica (Papyro-
     logica Florentina 7 [1980] 176).
     Men aiming at men: XXXIIa, LXVI; JEA 25 (1939) 173–4.

33   Rare traces of other situations: I 98 ("fetches women and men"); IV 2089–92 ("ousia of her/
     him . . . where she, or he, dwells . . . bring her to me")—both these instances might
     equally have in view male or female lovers working the spell on a male; XXXVI 70 is
     unambiguous on this point ("brings men to women and women to men," but at 73–4 the
     client is directed to take "ousia of whatever woman you want," thus reverting to the generic
     norm); XII 364–75 is a spell to create hatred between two men, with an alternate version
     for a man and a woman.

34   Horace Epode 5 and 17, Satire 1.8; Apuleius Golden Ass 1.5–19, 2.5; Petronius Satyrica 63;
     Lucan 6.413–830.

35   In real life (or what has some claim to be such) women are charged with administering
     philtra in food or drink rather than with performing agôgai: Antiphon 1.9, 19; Aristotle
     Magna Moralia 1.16; Plutarch conj. praec. 139A.

36   A second version at IV 2643ff.; the two are written as verse and compared at PGM vol.
     2, pp. 255–7.

37   IV 1840–59; cf. the Hyperborean mage cited above from Lucian Philopseudes 13, erôtas
     epipempôn. Galen asserts that erôs is a strictly human passion, "unless of course one believes
     the tales that some people are led (agesthai) to this passion by a tiny baby-god holding
     burning torches" (Comm. in Hippoc. Prognost. I vol. XVIII/2 p.19 Kühn). Unquiet corpse:
     IV 2031–2 (nekudaimôn), 2088 (katakhthonios daimôn), cf. the related rite over a skull at IV
     1928–2005; xiv 1070 (a mummy); XXXVI 139 (demons of the darkness). The goddess: IV
     2486 (Hekate); IV 2730–6 (Hekate accompanied by troops of the shrieking untimely dead);
     IV 2907–9 (Aphrodite). Messenger: VII 884–5: Selene is asked to send a holy angel or
     sacred assistant to serve the lover in the course of this night.

38   "Drag (helke) Matrona by her hair, her guts, her psychê, her heart . . ." Wortmann 66. In
     earlier periods the iunx served to drag or draw unwilling persons to a lover's bed: Pindar
     Pyth. 4.214, Nem. 4.35, playfully at Xenophon Mem. 3.11.18 (cited above pp. 76–7).
     Hephaistos is shown making one as a torture wheel for Ixion on an Attic vase from the
     circle of the Meidias Painter—Simon 1975; Eros plays with one— Miller pl. 14, figs. 10,
     12. PGM has one poetic reference to Ixion's wheel (IV 1905–6).

39   IV 2500, 2735. Thus Cupid assumes the form of Perdica's mother and appears to him in
     a dream (Aegritudo Perdicae 77–83).

40   The victim's dreaming of the agent is explicit in XVIIa 15: enhupniazomenên, oneirôttousan.
     For the sexual implications of the latter term, see next paragraph.

41   Origen contra Celsum 2.55.

42   For wax figurines in erotic procedures, see below p. 230 n. 50.

43   du Bourguet; the text of the accompanying lead sheet is edited by Kambitsis = SEG
     26.1717.

44   laikazein, cf. Shipp, Jocelyn.

45   Martin; the text refers to itself as a philtrokatadesmos (line 8).

46   Under the heading *amatoriae* in his subject index (Index V.C, pp. 472–3) to DT.

47   DT 267–71; Boll; Wortmann 56–84; *ZPE* 24 (1977) 89–90.

48   "Give to So-and-so fighting, war, and to So-and-so contempt and hatred—such as Typhon and Osiris had," XII 372–3, 449–52 (= PDM xii 62–75, with a drawing of an ass-headed figure labeled Sêth).

49   IV 1390–495, XIXa (a prescription spell to be placed in the mouth of a dead person, lines 15–6), XIXb (a generic spell to be placed with a corpse). The witchy versions of such rites in poetry traffic in materials gathered in graveyards and from those disturbing animals that belong simultaneously to two categories, such as frogs and snakes (Propertius 3.6.27–30). The similarity of necromancy and erotic rites is the organizing principle used by Fahz.

50   Dolls in erotic operations: Vergil *Ecl.* 8.75, 80 (wax and clay); Horace *Sat.* 1.8.30–3, 43f. (wax and wool); *Epode* 17.76 (wax); PDM lxi 112–27 (wax Osiris); XCV 1–6 (uncertain material and purpose). CI, found in a pot evidently from a cemetery ("you demons who lie here"), was wrapped around what appears to be two crudely made wax figurines embracing, the male and female made of darker and lighter waxes respectively: Wortmann. With all these should be compared the dolls employed to harm enemies: Wuensch, Trumpf 1958.

51   IV.1531, XII.490 (= PDM xii.155), XVIIa.16, XXXVI.82, 113, 149, 359; DT 230, 265A.

52   Two extraordinary cases specify lengths of time: Boll—*epi e mênas;* CI 36–7, *epi chronon mênôn deka.* Eitrem takes *e* in the former text to be a five-month trial marriage (in his edition of P. Oslo II, p. 33 n.1). The latter text may refer to confirming a marriage by pregnancy, ten months being considered the normal period of pregnancy— Bergman 340–1.

53   IV 2757–60, XV 4, XIXa 53, LXI 29–30 (= PDM lxi 173); DT 266, 268. Cp. Sappho 16.

4   The Education of Chloe: Hidden Injuries of Sex

1   The text used in this essay is that of Reeve; I have also consulted Dalmeyda and Schön-berger. Most citations are given by book and chapter only; occasionally for greater precision I have added the intracapitular number as well. Translations are my own; for the general reader that of Paul Turner in Penguin is recommended. The title is variously given in the manuscripts—a normal uncertainty of ancient works; the two principal manuscripts (F and V) call it *The Pastorals [Poimenika] of Daphnis and Chloe*, though the subscript of V calls it *Aipolika,* "Goatherd (Tales)." In my text I refer to the novel as *D&C*.

2   This aspect of their calculations is made clear at 3.25.3, 26.3, 30.5.

3   There is a reminder of its significance at 2.8.4.

4   "It will by now be clear that I consider among the greatest attractions of *D&C* the very light touch with which Longus picks up and lets go all forms of literary and intellectual pretension and the skill with which this apparently simple tale seems to suggest layer after layer of meaning and resonance" (Hunter 57).

5   G. Rohde, McCulloh, Cresci, Effe.

6   Zeitlin 1989 also regards *D&C* as a theorematic work, but her emphasis is on its implied systematization of the premises of the Greek literary genres that dealt with *erôs*—romance, pastoral, and New Comedy.

7   At 2.9 we find the Greek equivalent for "homework"—*nukterinon paideutêrion,* "nightly schooling."

8   On the Greek vocabulary for rape and the legal procedures for prosecuting it, see Cole 1984a.

9   Surveyed by Reardon; Philostratos' *Lives of the Sophists* is available in English in the Loeb Classical Library edition (1921).

10 Bowie 1970. One version of this past-centered literature restricted itself, more or less, to vocabulary used by classical Attic authors. Longus' language appears to accommodate more of the post-classical (Valley 45ff.) but one should also remember that Atticist scholars sometimes regarded rural folk as representative of the purest of cultural-linguistic traditions (Philostratos *VS* on Aelian, p. 303 Wright, and more fully on p. 154 Wright).

11 Alkiphron's *Letters,* of which Book Two is "Rustic Letters," and Aelian's *Rustic Letters.* Aelian's Letter 2 is a paraphrase of Menander's *Geôrgos* 46–52; Letter 4 = Aristophanes *Akharnians* 695–8; Letter 6 is modeled on the farmers' dispute in Demosthenes 55, etc. Alkiphron is probably to be dated to not later than the first decade of the third century (B. Baldwin). Aelian, whose name is Latin and for whom Greek was a second language, flourished in the second half of the second century C.E. Other frail but cumulatively impressive arguments about Longus' date are surveyed by Schönberger 10–1 and Hunter 1–15.

12 At 2.15–7 an altercation between some wealthy city boys and Daphnis is settled by speeches in the manner of a public court. The literary style of the urban disputants is described as "clear and curt since their judge was a cowherd," implying that the youths were capable of delivering more polished pleas in the manner of Demosthenes but chose a humble, sub-Lysianic style.

13 *antigrapsai têi graphêi.* The verb can refer both to duplication (to make an exact transcription) and to competition (to rival with an answering version). Zeitlin 1989.

14 On these exegetes at shrines, see Winkler 1985a: 233–8.

15 Valley, Reeve 1971. Reeve shows that avoidance of hiatus, "a serviceable measure of literary pretensions" (537), is practised by all the novelists, a testimony to their high rhetorical education and literary ambition and a refutation of the modern view that those works were either juvenile, unimportant, or "popular."

16 Scarcella. This rural "realism" is considerably more important than the vexed question of Longus' geographical accuracy: Bowie 1985: 86–90.

17 Earlier texts and translations speak here of Tyrian pirates; "Pyrrhaian," from the Lesbian city of Pyrrha, is M. D. Reeve's convincing correction, where the two principle mss. are divided between *Pyrrioi* and *Tyrioi.* They must be Greeks of some sort, not Tyrians, because they sail in a Karian vessel "so as to appear to be barbarians."

18 Bailey, du Boulay 1976, Walcot 1977.

19 Reeve follows Castiglioni in deleting "as if slain," *kathaper pephoneumenê,* on the slim grounds that the phrase recurs at 3.20.1. But the two principle mss. have it and it should be retained.

20 And of the novel: Zeitlin 1989.

21 Aiskhylos *Seven* 753–5; *Danaids* frag. 44; Sophokles *Trakhiniai* 31–3, *Antigone* 569; Aristophanes *Peace* 566–600; Plato *Kratylos* 406B (Artemis etymologized from *aroton misei,* "she hates the plow"); [Aristotle] *Econ.* 3.2 (a wife is a plot of land to be tended); Menander frag. 720 Kock; Soranos 1.35ff.; Artemidoros 1.51, 2.24. In Boccaccio's *Decameron* 2.10 a neglected wife says to her old husband: "if you had given as many holidays to the workers on your estates as you gave to the one whose job it was to tend my little field, you would never have harvested a single stalk of wheat."

22   In Athens the shrine of Demeter Chloe was on the southwest terrace of the Akropolis: Aristophanes *Lys.* 835, IG II.[2] 1356.16, Pausanias 1.22.3; Farnell 33–4.

23   "For all his superficial *glukutês* [sweetness] Longos does not shrink from recognising as fundamental in life, and in Eros, the elements of violence, pain and contradiction," among which he includes rape (Chalk 46).

5   Penelope's Cunning and Homer's

1   Samuel Butler, *The Authoress of the Odyssey: where and when she wrote, who she was, the use she made of the Iliad, & how the poem grew under her hands* (London 2nd ed. corrected and reset 1922), here abbreviated *Authoress*, p. 1. Page numbers in parentheses in this chapter refer to *Authoress*.

2   *Authoress* 208–9. Shaw is not there named but H. F. Jones tells the same story of Shaw in his preface to the second edition, p. xviii.

3   Arthur Platt reviewed Butler's *L'Origine Siciliana dell' Odissea* (1893) and his *Ancora sull'Origine Siciliana dell' Odissea* (1894) in *CR* 9 (1895) 56–7. Butler had one enthusiastic defender in the person of Benjamin Farrington. Farrington gives special emphasis to the paradox of Penelope, "so equivocally conceived that at times she is represented in the light of a flirt, at times as the world's model of wifely fidelity. The writer cannot sacrifice either conception. . . . But who would conceive two such situations except a woman, who would attempt to combine them in the one character except a very young one?" (53–4). More recently, Butler's theory that the *Odyssey* describes Trapani has been endorsed by Pocock, his theory of female authorship by Ruyer.

4   Much the same approach, without Butler's acuity, can be found in Walter C. Perry, *The Women of Homer* (London 1898), dedicated to "Her Most Gracious Majesty Victoria *diêi gunaikôn* Queen of Great Britain and Ireland Empress of India, etc."

5   The debate over what type of social organization and political power is portrayed in the homeric epics can be followed in Calhoun, Strasburger, Donlan, and Halverson. Millett, drawing on modern comparanda, is a superb study of the predominantly peasant character of Hesiod's society.

6   Stanford 104–5; Podlecki; Austin 1972 esp. 13–7.

7   The listener might have to pay careful attention to the articulation of the first alternative, since there is only a razor's edge difference between *epe' akraanta* ("unfulfilled words") and *epea kraanta* ("fulfilled words").

8   Niese 164 suggested that in a prior stage of the *Odyssey*'s development Penelope recognized Odysseus at the foot-washing. Merkelbach 1951 developed that theory at length. Alternate analyses in Thornton 84–92, 96–108.

9   For another view altogether see Emlyn-Jones: "Penelope . . . often appears to do unmotivated or badly-motivated things" (11).

10   See Foley 1978: 9–10 is very good on Penelope's activity as a substitute king reproving the suitors, distracting them from quarreling, renewing the household's wealth, receiving and cross-examining visitors, maintaining "standards of hospitality and a network of communication in Odysseus' disrupted family." Marquardt has interesting ideas about Penelope's strategic cleverness; I do not agree with all of her analyses, but her evaluation of Penelope is the same as the one pursued here: "we do Penelope an injustice to minimize her conscious control of the situation" (46).

11   On weaving as women's household work, both for internal consumption and to supple-

ment the family's income, see Schaps 1979: 18–20; Keuls 1983. "Those textiles which men value most, therefore, being the most exacting and taking the longest time to make, were also the least understood by them" (Jenkins 114). It is not that the suitors just did not happen to notice Penelope's unweaving of Laertes' shroud each night: it would be beneath them, or outside their competence and sphere of interest, even to notice her work.

12 From the viewpoints of Hephaistos and Ares, the trick is a kind of ambush (*lochos*) such as is typically set for a *promos anêr*, "a front-line solo fighter." The Iliadic heroes who are likely to suffer ambush, as A. Edwards shows, are the swift of foot. In Demodokos' song, Ares' swiftness and Hephaistos' lameness are repeatedly emphasized, and the point of Hephaistos' trick is summed up in the comment that "the slow catches the swift" (8.329). The analogy of Odysseus : suitors : Penelope :: Hephaistos : Ares : Aphrodite makes all the more striking the reversal of expectations when Penelope's chastity is called into question only by herself, and then only as a stratagem to reassure herself of the stranger's identity.

13 The *Iliad* too takes a surprising turn in its last book, as Heubeck observes. "The events of the last book of the *Iliad* reveal characteristics of the hero which could only vaguely have been suspected from what had been told about him in the course of the epic. . . . In this regard, what we are told in the last book is no loose or inorganic appendage: without the description of the Lytra [Ransoming], the picture of Homer's hero would be incomplete; one could even go so far as to say that the portrayal of Achilles is aimed at this *telos* from the very beginning" (14).

14 Rubin emphasizes that Homer attributes to Penelope "contradictory motives and inconsistent behavior . . . which makes a reader apt to stay confused as to what Penelope desires until that moment of clarity . . . in 23.205." But she sees this as a confusion, or rather plurality of possible roles, affecting Penelope's own consciousness of herself, whereas I would want to attribute to Penelope an essentially unwavering allegiance to Odysseus' estate as long as there is any possibility of his being alive.

15 The interdependence and differentiation of male and female spheres in the *Odyssey* is superbly analyzed by Foley 1978. "It is important to note that there is a striking complementarity in [Penelope's and Odysseus'] physiological and psychological rhythms" Russo 1982: 12.

6 Double Consciousness in Sappho's Lyrics

1 English translation of *Brouillon pour un dictionnaire des amantes* (New York 1976). There are some uncritical myths in Wittig's own account of Sappho in her essay "Paradigm," in Stambolian and Marks 1979.

2 Lefkowitz 1973 and Hallett 1979 analyze the bias and distortions found in critical comments, ancient and modern, on Sappho.

3 Calder analyzes Welcker's treatise "Sappho Liberated from a Prevalent Prejudice" (1816), suggesting that Welcker's determination to prove that Sappho was not a lesbian can be traced to his idealization of the mother figures in his life (155–6).

4 This has now been done for the French tradition by DeJean.

5 My statement that this is Sappho's central topic throughout her nine books is based not merely on the few fragments (obviously), but on the ancient testimonies, especially those of Demetrios, who provided the original title of this essay (". . . nymphs' gardens, wedding songs, eroticism—in short the whole of Sappho's poetry") and Himerios ("Sappho dedicated all of her poetry to Aphrodite and the Erotes, making the beauty and charms of a

maiden the occasion for her melodies"). These and the other testimonia are collected in Gallavotti and D. Campbell.

6 The text of Sappho used here is that of Edgar Lobel and D. Page (abbreviated L-P), *Poetarum Lesbiorum Fragmenta* (Oxford 1955).

7 The evidence is found in Hephaistion *peri sêmêiôn* 138, quoted by Hooker 1977: 11.

8 As Boedeker shows for fragment 95: "a consciously 'anti-heroic' persona, specifically perhaps an anti-Odysseus. . . . The poem becomes a new personal statement of values, a denial and reshaping of epic-heroic ideals" (52).

9 Hesiod *Works and Days* 578–81. Clay suggests that the interpretation "but you bring the child *away* from its mother" could fit into a wedding song.

10 That would solve the problem felt at Theokritos 2.61, where editors emend *passô* to *massô*.

11 "The classic custom of wooing a damsel by throwing an apple into her lap still exists, though it is condemned by public opinion as improper, and is strongly resented by the maid's kinsfolk as an impertinence" (Abbott 147–8). Other literature is cited in n. 20 below.

12 E.g. J. B. Bury, ". . . while Sappho confined her muse within a narrower circle of feminine interests" (*Cambridge Ancient History* IV, 1953, 494f.) and similarly Werner Jaeger, *Paideia* (English translation, B. Blackwell, Oxford 1965) vol. 1, p. 132.

13 The comparison to gods runs throughout the Phaiakian scenes: Nausikaa (16, 105–9), her maids (18), the Phaiakians (241), Nausikaa's brothers, *athanatois enalinkioi* (7.5).

14 One could also experiment with reading the speaker's symptoms (fever, chill, dizziness) as the result of an erotic spell like those described in Chapter 3. The deadening of the speaker's tongue (so beautifully contradicted, of course, by the eloquence and precision of the poet herself) is a typical affliction brought on by a *katadesmos*.

15 Apollonios of Rhodes' Medea is conscious of love in terms drawn from Sappho (Privitera), and note especially the characteristic presentation of Medea's mental after-images and imaginings (3.453–58, 811–6, 948–55), which is the technique of Sappho 1, 16, and 96.

16 Rufinus ap. Oribasios 3.391.1, Galen 2.370E, Aetios 16.103–4 (clitoridectomy), Paulus Aigin. 6.70 (clitoridectomy for lesbians).

17 Photios *Lexikon* s.v.; Pollux 2.174, with the anagram *skairon sarkion*, "throbbing little piece of flesh."

18 For the connection of Nymphs to marriage and birth see Ballentine.

19 In her fragments 110 and 111: Kirk 1963, Killeen; fragment 121 may be "una variazione scherzosa nel nota fr. 105," Lanata 66.

20 Foster, McCartney, Trumpf 1960, Lugauer, Littlewood, Kakridis; P. Oxy. 2637, frag. 25.6; Abbott 147f., 170, 177.

21 This sense of *numphê* gives further meaning to a fragment of Praxilla, 754 in Page 1962. "Looking in beautifully through the windows, your head that of a maiden, but you are a *numphê* underneath," *ô dia tôn thuridôn kalon emblepoisa / parthene tan kephalan ta d' enerthe numpha*. Praxilla is, according to Aly's fine interpretation (RE 22 [1954] 176), addressing the moon shining through her windows (cp. Page 1962: 747, *selênaiês te prosôpon*); its mystery and elusive attraction are expressed by the image of a woman with a youthful, innocent face and a look that bespeaks deeper experience and knowledge. The physical comparison is to a woman whose face alone is visible: wrapped up under all those clothes, says Praxilla, is the body of a sexually mature woman. Page at the opposite extreme envisions a woman peeping into the windows of houses in order to attract other women's

husbands (*quae more meretricio vagabunda per fenestras intueri soles, scilicet ut virum foras unde unde elicias,* Page 1962: 754 app. crit.). This level of significance may also be relevant to Page 1962: 286 (Ibykos) and 929 e-g (anonymous).

22 Fragment 48 may be read in a similar sense: *êlthes kai m' epothêsas egô de s' emaioman / on d' ephlexas eman phrena kaiomenan pothôi,* "You came and you desired me; I searched you carefully; you stirred the fires of my feeling, smoldering with desire." *ephlexas* is Wesseling's conjecture for *phulaxas; m' epothêsas* is my conjecture for *epoêsas.* I would support this conjecture by reference back to fragment 36, which joins *poth/* and *mai/,* and by the symmetry achieved: you desired me—I felt you—you stirred me—I desired you, which we might call Sapphic reciprocity. Cf. Lanata 79.

23 "Sarebbe augurabile che nelle allusioni all'amore saffico cadesse in disuso la sgradita definizione di 'turpe amore' inventata da un moralismo se non altro anacronistico," Gentili 1966: 48 n.55. Stehle 1979 is excellent.

7 The Laughter of the Oppressed: Demeter and the Gardens of Adonis

1 The most authoritative account of Athenian festivals is still Deubner; a somewhat sketchier treatment is Parke; Simon 1983 is brief but contains the newer archaeological material. Atallah is the most detailed treatment of the Adonia.

2 In other times and places it may have been different. Pausanias mentions a temple of Zeus Savior in Argos which contains a shrine where the Argive women mourn Adonis (2.20.6), apparently incorporating him into a public sanctuary. In general, for religious festivals outside Athens, see Nilsson.

3 "Adonis appears in Greek literature and art from the beginning of the sixth century onwards, when contacts with Cyprus are certain and with Syria dubious, and all probability points to a Cyprian origin for the Athenian cult," Nock 291. "It was seen long ago that the plant-beds of Na'man . . . in Isaiah 17:10 mean 'plant-beds of Adonis,' who may be referred to under this name in Ugaritic texts. In any event, there can be no doubt that the designation Na'mân-Nu'mân-Na'môn, 'the Charming One,' was employed for Adonis by the Phoenicians. The so-called Adonis gardens enjoyed a long life in the ancient Mediterranean world and ultimately became popular Easter customs of the Greek church, where they still exist today in some places" (Albright 162). Pilitsis describes the modern Greek gardens of Adonis.

4 Apparently also once in tragedy: Euripides *Melanippe* fragment 514 Nauck.

5 Old Comedy: Plato, Nikophon; Middle Comedy: Philetairos, Antiphanes, Araros, Philiskos; New Comedy: Philippides. The older edition of comic fragments by Kock is gradually being replaced by Kassel and Austin 1983–.

6 E. L. Leutsch and F. G. Schneidewin, eds., *Corpus Paroemiographorum Graecorum* (Göttingen 1839).

7 Diogenianos' text mentions those who sow in two forms, masculine and feminine (*phuteuontes ê phuteuousai*). It may be that he used only the generic masculine and that a later hand inserted *ê phuteuousai* in an attempt to correct the false impression that men grew these gardens.

8 John Chrysostom says that the vessels were filled with "much dung," *In Epist. ad Ephes.* chap. 4, homil. 12 = *Patrologia Graeca* 62.91.

9 Of course they also provided the wherewithal for their wives' Adonia, at least nominally, and this is sometimes acknowledged in inscriptions: IG II^2 1261, 1290.

10　Aristophanes *Akharnians* 237–79, Plutarch *de cupid. divit.* 527D; Pickard-Cambridge 42–54. Plato *Republic* 475D has been taken to suggest that the Attic demes, which celebrated the Rural Dionysia, did so on various days in the month: "lovers of spectacles . . . as if they had hired out their ears to listen to every chorus, they run around to the Dionysia, not missing any, whether in the cities or in the villages." But the reference to various cities (*poleis*) shows that more than simply Attic festivals are in view, and there is nothing to tie this gibe specifically to the Dionysia in Poseideon. Still, given the great elaboration of the festival in the fourth century with tragic, comic, and dithyrambic contests, and the presumed competition for actors, it is reasonable to imagine that the Rural Dionysia was not necessarily tied to a specific date in the month.

11　The sacrifice-starved gods in Aristophanes' *Birds* complain that they are being forced to fast as if it were the Thesmophoria (1519); Plutarch refers to "the most gloomy day of the Thesmophoria, on which the women fast with the goddess" (*Life of Demosthenes* 30.5); Aristophanes' *Thesmophoriazousai* is set on the day of Fasting. The prologue of his lost *Thesmophoriazousai II* was spoken by Kalligeneia (frag. 331 Kassel-Austin).

12　Also in "The Perfumed Panther," chapter two of Detienne 1979, where he answers some of his critics. The English translation is an abridgment of the French at this point.

13　A courtesan in Lucian's *Dialogues of Courtesans* 2.1 says to her lover, "The maiden you are about to marry is not beautiful—I saw her recently at the Thesmophoria with her mother," implying that both courtesans and unmarried maidens could attend. The evidentiary value of Lucian for Athens can be doubted. Menander *Epitrepontes* 749 is another moot text. Golden 1988: 6 n.23.

Appendix Two　*Phusis* and *Natura* Meaning "Genitals"

1　Weinreich, Lenaios 4–5, Henderson 1975: 5.

2　Philemon 4.6, Anaxandrides 33.18, Alexis 240.8, Amphis 20. McLeish collects 20 examples in Aristophanes where the sense "genitals" is possible and would make a good joke, but then prefers to hold aloof from a double-entendre that is "unproven."

3　The poem, known as *diabolê* ("accusation"), is repeated later in the same handbook with some variants; *phusis* at line 2659. Preisendanz (1973–1974 = *PGM*) vol. 2, pp. 257–59 prints both as Hymn 19. Elsewhere in the magical papyri, *phusis* occurs in a generic *agôgê* (spell of erotic compulsion) at *PGM* XXXVI.150 ("Make N., daughter of N., wide awake, flighty, hungry, thirsty, sleepless, desiring me N., son of N., with a deep inner lust until she comes and glues her female *phusis* to my male one"); within similar spells of the same handbook (XXXVI.83, 114, 324) and in the title of an aphrodisiac ointment to smear on a penis—*phusikleidion* ("*phusis*-key"), line 283; and in a generic curse designed to make a woman menstruate perpetually ("Open the *phusis* and womb of N. and let her bleed night and day") at *PGM* LXII.103. A prescription erotic spell on lead: "May she touch her thigh to my thigh, her *phusis* to my *phusis*," in *Genava* 6 (1928) 56–63.

4　Bourguet 1975. The text of the lead sheet is edited by Kambitsis = SEG 26.1717. More on this image in Chapter Three (pp. 93–6).

5　Philoxenus *glossarium* (ed. M. Laistner in *Glossaria Latina* vol. 2 [Paris 1926]).

6　6th cent: codex Vossianus Latinus in Quarto No. 9, uncial, parchment, in Leiden Universitäts-Bibliothek: Piechotta (1886/7), VIII.

7　Killaktor, *Anth. Pal.* 5.45; cf. *Anth. Pal.* 11.7, *Carm. Priap.* 38.2.

Bibliography

Abbott, G. F. 1903. *Macedonian Folklore.* (Cambridge).

Abt, Adam. 1908. *Die Apologia des Apuleius von Madaura und die antike Zauberei.* (RGVV 4/2; Giessen).

Abu-Lughod, Lila. 1986. *Veiled Sentiments.* (Berkeley).

Adkins, Arthur W. H. 1970. *From the Many to the One: A Study of Personality and Views of Human Nature in the Context of Ancient Greek Society, Values and Beliefs.* (London).

Albright, W. F. 1968. *Yahweh and the Gods of Canaan.* (Garden City, N.Y.).

Allen, Thomas W. 1969. *Homeri Opera,* vol. 5. (Oxford).

Allione, Lydia. 1963. *Telemaco e Penelope nell' Odissea.* (Turin).

Alloula, Malek. 1986. *The Colonial Harem,* trans. M. and W. Godzich. (Theory and History of Literature 21; Minneapolis).

Amory, A. 1963. "The Reunion of Odysseus and Penelope," in Charles H. Taylor, ed., *Essays on the Odyssey,* 100–21. (Bloomington).

Amundsen, D. W. 1974. "Romanticizing the Ancient Medical Profession," *Bull. Hist. Med.* 48: 320–37.

Anderson, Graham. 1982. *Eros Sophistes: Ancient Novelists at Play.* (American Classical Studies 9; Chico, Cal.).

Andrewes, A. 1981. "The Hoplite Katalogos," in G. S. Shrimpton and D. J. McCargar, eds., *Classical Contributions: Studies in honour of Malcolm Francis McGregor,* 1–3. (Locust Valley, N.Y.).

Arthur, Marilyn B. 1973. "Early Greece: The Origins of the Western Attitude toward Women," *Arethusa* 6: 7–58.

Arthur, Marilyn B. 1977. "Liberated Women: The Classical Era," in Renate Bridenthal and C. Koonz, eds., *Becoming Visible: Women in European History.* (Boston).

Asmus, R. 1906. "Vergessene Physiognomika," *Philologus* 65: 415–21.

Atallah, W. 1966. *Adonis dans la littérature et l'art grecs.* (Paris).

Atkinson, J. M. 1982. "Review Essay: Anthropology," *Signs* 8: 236–58.

Aune, D. E. 1980. "Magic in Early Christianity," in *Aufstieg und Niedergang der Römischen Welt* II.23.2, pp. 1506–57. (Berlin).

Austin, Norman. 1972. "Name Magic in the *Odyssey,*" *CSCA* 5: 1–19.

Austin, Norman. 1975. *Archery at the Dark of the Moon.* (Berkeley).

Babut, D. 1969. *Plutarque et le Stoïcisme.* (Paris).

Bailey, F. G. 1971. *Gifts and Poison: The Politics of Reputation.* (New York).

Baldwin, B. 1982. "The Date of Alciphron," *Hermes* 110: 253–4.

Baldwin, K. 1985. "'Woof!' A Word on Women's Roles in Family Storytelling," in Rosan A. Jordan and S. J. Kalcik, eds., *Women's Folklore, Women's Culture,* 149–62. (Philadalphia).

Ballentine, F. G. 1904. "Some Phases of the Cult of the Nymphs," *HSCP* 15: 97–110.

Barabino, G. 1967. *P. Rutilii Lupi Schemata Dianoeas et Lexeos.* (Istituto di filologia classica e medioevale 27: Genoa).

Barnard, Mary. 1980. "Static," in *Woman Poet, I: The West,* 34. (Reno).

Barnes, J. 1984. *The Complete Works of Aristotle,* 2 vols. (Princeton).

Bartsch, S. 1989. *Decoding the Ancient Novel: The Reader and the Role of Description in Heliodorus and Achilles Tatius.* (Princeton).

Baudy, Gerhard J. 1986. *Adonisgärten: Studien zur antiken Samensymbolik.* (Beiträge zur klassischen Philologie 176; Frankfurt).

Bauer, Janet. forthcoming. *Liberation and the Veil: Women, Family, and Development in Iran.*

Behr, C. A. 1968. *Aelius Aristides and the Sacred Tales.* (Amsterdam).

Benedetto, V. di. 1973. "Il volo di Afrodite in Omero e in Saffo," *QUCC* 16: 121–3.

Bergman, J. 1972. "Decem illis diebus," in *Ex Orbe Religionum: Studia Geo Widengren oblata,* 332–46. (Studies in the History of Religions—Supplements to *Numen* 21; Leiden).

Bernal, Martin. 1987. *Black Athena: The Afro-Asiatic Roots of Greece.* Vol. 1, *The Fabrication of Ancient Greece, 1887–1987.* (New Brunswick, N.J.).

Bernikow, Louise. 1974. *The World Split Open.* (New York).

Berti, M. 1967. "Sulla interpretazione mistica del romanzo di Longo," *Studi Classici e Orientali* 16: 343–58.

Betz, Hans D., ed. 1986. *The Greek Magical Papyri in Translation including the Demotic Spells, vol. 1: Texts.* (Chicago).

Beye, C. R. 1974. "Male and Female in the Homeric Poems," *Ramus* 3: 87–101.

Blum, Claes. 1936. *Studies in the Dream-Book of Artemidorus.* (Uppsala).

Blum, Richard H. and Eva M. Blum. 1965. *Health and Healing in Rural Greece.* (Stanford, Cal.).

Blum, Richard H. and Eva M. Blum. 1970. *The Dangerous Hour: The Lore of Crisis and Mystery in Rural Greece.* (London).

Boedeker, D. D. 1979. "Sappho and Acheron," in Glen W. Bowersock, W. Burkert, and M. Putnam, eds., *Arktouros: Hellenic Studies presented to Bernard W. M. Knox on the occasion of his 65th birthday,* 40–52. (New York).

Boll, F. 1910. *Griechischer Liebeszauber aus Aegypten.* (Heidelberger Akademie der Wissenschaften, Philosophisch-Historische Klasse. Sitzungsberichte; Heidelberg).

Bolling, G. 1958. "POIKILOS and THRONA," *AJP* 79: 275–82.

Bolling, G. 1959. "Restoration of Sappho, 98a 1–7," *AJP* 80: 276–87.

Bonner, C. 1949. "KESTOS IMAS and the Saltire of Aphrodite," *AJP* 70: 1–6.

Bouché-Leclercq, A. 1879–82. *Histoire de la divination dans l'antiquité,* 4 vols. (Paris).

Bourdieu, Pierre. 1965. "The Sentiment of Honour in Kabyle Society," in Peristiany 1965: 191–241.

Bourdieu, Pierre. 1977. *Outline of a Theory of Practice*, trans. R. Nice. (Cambridge); French original *Esquisse d'une théorie de la pratique*. (Switzerland 1972).

Bourdieu, Pierre. 1979. *Algeria 1960*. (Cambridge).

Bourguet, P. du. 1975. "Ensemble magique de la periode romaine en Egypte," *La revue du Louvre* 25: 255–57.

Bowie, E. L. 1970. "Greeks and their Past in the Second Sophistic," *Past and Present* 46: 3–41.

Bowie, E. L. 1985. "Where Does Longus Set *Daphnis and Chloe?*" (Appendix I to his "Theocritus' Seventh *Idyll*") *CQ* 35: 86–90.

Brandes, S. 1981. "Like Wounded Stags: Male Sexual Ideology in an Andalusian Town," in Sherry B. Ortner and Harriet Whitehead, eds., *Sexual Meanings: The Cultural Construction of Gender and Sexuality*, 216–39. (Cambridge).

Brashear, W. 1979. "Ein Berliner Zauberpapyrus," *ZPE* 33: 261–78.

Bremmer, J. 1981. "Plutarch and the Naming of Greek Women," *AJP* 102: 425–26.

Brundage, James A. 1987. *Law, Sex, and Christian Society in Medieval Europe*. (Chicago).

Büchner, W. 1940. "Die Penelopeszenen in der Odyssee," *Hermes* 75: 146–59.

Bulkin, E. and J. Larkin, eds. 1975. *Amazon Poetry*. (Brooklyn, N.Y.).

Burkert, Walter. 1985. *Greek Religion*, trans. J. Raffan. (Cambridge, Mass.).

Bushala, E. W. 1968. "Torture of Non-Citizens in Homicide Investigations," *GRBS* 9: 61–8.

Byre, C. S. 1988. "Penelope and the Suitors Before Odysseus: *Odyssey* 18. 158–303," *AJP* 109: 159–73.

Calder, W. M. 1988. "F. G. Welcker's *Sapphobild* and its Reception in Wilamowitz," in W. M. Calder et al., eds., *Friedrich Gottlieb Welcker, Werk und Wirkung*, 131–56. (Hermes Einzelschift 49; Stuttgart).

Calhoun, G. M. 1934. "Classes and Masses in Homer," *CP* 29: 192–208, 301–16.

Cameron, A. 1949. "Sappho's Prayer to Aphrodite," *HTR* 32: 1–17.

Cameron, Averil and A. Kuhrt, eds. 1983. *Images of Women in Antiquity*. (Detroit).

Campbell, David A. 1982. *Greek Lyric. I. Sappho, Alcaeus*. (Cambridge, Mass.).

Campbell, John K. 1964. *Honour, Family, and Patronage: A Study of Institutions and Moral Values in a Greek Mountain Community*. (New York and Oxford).

Campese, S., P. Manuli, and G. Sissa. 1983. *Madre Materia: Sociologia e biologia della donna greca*. (Turin).

Cantarella, Eva. 1987. *Pandora's Daughters: The Role and Status of Women in Greek and Roman Antiquity*, trans. M. B. Fant. (Baltimore).

Carrière, J. C. 1979. *Le carnaval et le politique*. (Centre de recherches d'histoire ancienne, vol. 26 = Annales littéraires de l'université de Besançon, 212; Paris).

Chalk, H. H. O. 1960. "Eros and the Lesbian Pastorals of Longos," *JHS* 80: 32–51.

Chantraine, Pierre. 1968–80. *Dictionnaire étymologique de la langue grecque*, 4 vols. (Paris).

Chatzis, A. 1914. *Der Philosoph und Grammatiker Ptolemaios Chennos: Leben, Schriftstellerei und Fragmente*. Erster Teil. Einleitung und Text. (Studien zur Geschichte und Kultur des Altertums 7/2; Paderborn).

Chicago, Judy. 1975. *Through the Flower*. (Garden City, N.Y.).

Chicago, Judy. 1979. *The Dinner Party*. (Garden City, N.Y.).

Ciavolella, M. 1970. "La tradizione dell' *aegritudo amoris* nel *Decameron*," *Giornale storico della letteratura italiana* 147: 496–517.

Clark, Mari H. 1983. "Variations on Themes of Male and Female: Reflections on Gender Bias in Fieldwork in Rural Greece," *Women's Studies* 102: 117–33.

Clark, S. R. L. 1982. "Aristotle's Woman," *History of Political Thought* 3: 177–91.

Clay, J. S. 1980. "Sappho's Hesperus and Hesiod's Dawn," *Philologus* 124: 302–5.

Cole, S. G. 1984a. "Greek Sanctions Against Sexual Assault," *CP* 79: 97–113.

Cole, S. G. 1984b. "The Social Function of Rituals of Maturation: The Koureion and the Arkteia," *ZPE* 55: 233–44.

Collier, J. 1986. "From Mary to Modern Woman: The Material Basis of Marianismo and its Transformation in a Spanish Village," *AE* 13: 100–7.

Combellack, F. M. 1973. "Three Odyssean Problems," *CSCA* 6: 17–46.

Connor, W. R. 1988. "Early Greek Land Warfare as Symbolic Expression," *Past and Present* 119: 3–29.

Cook, B. W. 1979. "'Women Alone Stir my Imagination': Lesbianism and the Cultural Tradition," *Signs* 4: 718–39.

Cornford, Francis M. 1934. *The Origins of Attic Comedy.* (London).

Corno, D. del, ed. 1969. *Graecorum de re onirocritica scriptorum reliquiae.* (Testi e documenti per lo studio dell'antichità 26; Milan).

Corno, D. del, trans. 1975. *Il libro dei sogni.* (Milan).

Courtney, E. 1980. *A Commentary on the Satires of Juvenal.* (London).

Coward, Rosalind. 1983. *Patriarchal Precedents: Sexuality and Social Relations.* (London).

Cresci, L. R. 1981. "Il romanzo di Longo Sofista e la tradizione bucolica," *Atene e Roma* n.s. 26: 1–25.

Cronin, C. 1977. "Illusion and Reality in Sicily," in A. Schlegel, ed., *Sexual Stratification: A Cross-cultural View*, 67–93. (New York).

Dalmeyda, Georges. 1934. *Longus, Pastorales.* (Paris).

Danforth, L., ed. 1983. *Symbolic Aspects of Male/Female Relations in Greece*, in the *Journal of Modern Greek Studies* 1: 157–270.

Danforth, L. and A. Tsiaras. 1982. *The Death Rituals of Rural Greece.* (Princeton).

Davidson, A. 1987. "Sex and the Emergence of Sexuality," *Critical Inquiry* 14: 16–48.

Davies, John K. 1981. *Wealth and the Power of Wealth in Classical Athens.* (New York).

Davis, D. L. 1983. "Woman the Worrier: Confronting Feminist and Biomedical Archetypes of Stress," *Women's Studies* 10: 135–46 (special issue on Bias in Feminist Anthropology).

Davis, J. 1977. *The People of the Mediterranean: an Essay in Comparative Social Anthropology.* (London).

De Becker, Raymond. 1968. *The Understanding of Dreams.* (New York).

Decker, Friedrich. 1883. *Über die Stellung der hellenischen Frauen bei Homer.* (Programm-Pädagogium zum Kloster Unser Lieben Frauen in Magdeburg; Magdeburg).

Degani, E. 1962. "Hipponactea," *Helikon* 2: 627–9.

DeJean, Joan. 1989. *Fictions of Sappho, 1546–1937.* (Chicago).

Del Grande, C. 1959. "Saffo, Ode *phainetai moi kênos isos*," *Euphrosyne* 2: 181–8.

Denich, B. S. 1974. "Sex and Power in the Balkans," in Michelle Z. Rosaldo and L. Lamphere, eds., *Woman, Culture, & Society*, 243–62. (Stanford).

De Romilly, J. 1971. *La loi dans la pensée grecque des origines à Aristote*. (Paris).

de Ste. Croix, G. E. M. 1970. "Some Observations on the Property Rights of Athenian Women," *CR* n.s. 20: 273–8.

Detienne, Marcel. 1977. *The Gardens of Adonis: Spices in Greek Mythology*, trans. Janet Lloyd. (Atlantic Highlands, N.J.)

Detienne, Marcel. 1979. *Dionysos Slain*, trans. M. Muellner and L. Muellner. (Baltimore).

Detienne, Marcel and J.-P. Vernant. 1978. *Cunning Intelligence in Greek Culture and Society*, trans. Janet Lloyd. (Atlantic Highlands, N.J.)

Deubner, Ludwig. 1932. *Attische Feste*. (Berlin).

Devereux, G. 1957. "Penelope's Character," *Psycho-analytic Quarterly* 26: 378–86.

Dihle, A. 1957. "Der Platoniker Ptolemaios," *Hermes* 85: 314–25.

Dimen [Schein], M. 1974. "Social Stratification in a Greek Village," in A. L. LaRuffa et al., eds., *City and Peasant: A Study in Sociocultural Dynamics*, 488–95. (Annals of the N. Y. Academy of Sciences, vol. 220, article 6).

Dionisopoulos-Mass, R. 1976. "The Evil Eye and Bewitchment in a Peasant Village," in Maloney 1976: 42–62.

Dodds, E. R. 1951. *The Greeks and the Irrational*. (Berkeley).

Dodson, Betty. n.d. *Liberating Masturbation*. (B. Dodson, Box 1933, New York 10001).

Donlan, W. 1970. "Changes and Shifts in the Meaning of Demos in the Literature of the Archaic Period," *Parola del Passato* 25: 351–95.

Dornseiff, F. 1925. *Das Alphabet in Mystik und Magie*, 2nd ed. (Leipzig).

Doumanis, M. 1983. *Mothering in Greece: From Collectivism to Individualism*. (London).

Dover, K. J. 1968. *Aristophanes Clouds*. (London).

Dover, K. J. 1974. *Greek Popular Morality in the Time of Plato and Aristotle*. (Oxford).

Dover, K. J. 1978. *Greek Homosexuality*. (Cambridge, Mass.).

du Boulay, J. 1974. *Portrait of a Greek Mountain Village*. (Oxford).

du Boulay, J. 1976. "Lies, Mockery and Family Integrity," in J. G. Peristiany, ed., *Mediterranean Family Structures*, 389–406. (Cambridge).

du Boulay, J. 1983. "The Meaning of Dowry: Changing Values in Rural Greece," in Danforth 1983: 243–70.

du Bourguet, P. 1975. "Ensemble magique de la periode romaine en Egypte," *La revue du Louvre* 25: 255–7.

Dubisch, Jill. 1983. "Greek Women: Sacred or Profane," in Danforth 1983, 185–202.

Dubisch, Jill. 1986a. *Gender and Power in Rural Greece*. (Princeton).

Dubisch, Jill. 1986b. "Culture Enters Through the Kitchen: Women, Food, and Social Boundaries in Rural Greece": 195–214 in Dubisch 1986a.

duBois, Page. 1978. "Sappho and Helen," *Arethusa* 11: 88–99.

duBois, Page. 1982. *Centaurs and Amazons: Women and the Pre-History of the Great Chain of Being*. (Ann Arbor).

duBois, Page. 1988. *Sowing the Body*. (Chicago).

Duncan-Jones, R. P. 1980. "Metic Numbers in Periclean Athens," *Chiron* 10: 101–9.

Edmundsen, C. N. 1959. "A Graffito from Amyklai," *Hesperia* 28: 162–4.

Edwards, Anthony T. 1985. *Achilles in the Odyssey*. (Beiträge zur klassischen Philologie 171; Meisenheim).

Edwards, Mark W. 1987. "*Topos* and Transformation in Homer," in J.-M. Bremer, I. J. F. de Jong, and J. Kalff, eds., *Homer: Beyond Oral Poetry*, 47–60. (Amsterdam).

Effe, B. 1982. "Longos. Zur Funktionsgeschichte der Bukolik in der römischen Kaiserzeit," *Hermes* 110: 65–84.

Ehrenberg, V. 1923. "Anfänge des griechischen Naturrechts," *Archiv für Geschichte der Philosophie* 35: 119–43; repr. in his *Polis und Imperium*, 359–79. (Zürich/Stuttgart, 1965).

Eichholz, D. E. 1979. review of Detienne, *Gardens of Adonis*. *CR* 24: 232–5.

Eitrem, S. forthcoming. "Dreams and Divination in Magical Ritual," in Christopher A. Faraone and Dirk Obbink, eds., *Magika Hiera: Ancient Greek Magic and Religion*. (New York).

Emlyn-Jones, C. 1984. "The Reunion of Penelope and Odysseus," *G&R* 31: 1–18.

Epstein, Steven. 1987. "Gay Politics, Ethnic Identity: The Limits of Social Constructionism," *Socialist Review* 93/94 (= 17.3–4): 9–54.

Fahz, L. 1904. *De poetarum Romanorum doctrina magica quaestiones selectae*. (RGVV, 2/3; Giessen).

Farnell, Lewis R. 1977. *The Cults of the Greek States*, vol. 3. (New Rochelle, N.Y.).

Farrington, B. 1929. *Samuel Butler and the Odyssey*. (repr. New York 1974).

Fenik, B. 1972. *Studies in the Odyssey*. (Hermes Einzelschrift 30; Wiesbaden).

Feraboli, Simonetta. 1980. *Lisia avvocato*. (Proagones 19; Padua).

Festugière, A.-J. 1975. *La clef des songes*. (Paris).

Fetterley, J. 1978. *The Resisting Reader: A Feminist Approach to American Fiction*. (Bloomington, In.).

Finley, John A. 1978. *Homer's Odyssey*. (Cambridge, Mass.).

Finley, Moses I. 1975. "Anthropology and the Classics," 102–19 in his *The Use and Abuse of History*. (New York).

Finley, Moses I. 1978. *The World of Odysseus*, 2nd revised edition. (New York).

Fisher, N. R. E. 1976. "*Hybris* and Dishonour: I." *G&R* 23: 177–93.

Fisher, N. R. E. 1979. "*Hybris* and Dishonour: II." *G&R* 26: 32–47.

Flynn, E. A. and P. P. Schweickart, eds. 1986. *Gender and Reading: Essays on Readers, Texts, and Contexts*. (Baltimore and London).

Foley, Helene P. 1978. "'Reverse Similes' and Sex Roles in the *Odyssey*," *Arethusa* 11: 7–26.

Foley, Helene P. 1981a. "The Conception of Women in Athenian Drama," in Foley 1981b, 127–68.

Foley, Helene P., ed. 1981b. *Reflections of Women in Antiquity*. (London).

Foley, Helene P. 1982. "The Female Intruder Reconsidered: Women in Aristophanes' *Lysistrata* and *Ecclesiazusae*," *CP* 77: 1–21.

Förster, R. 1893. *Scriptores Physiognomonici Graeci*. (Leipzig).

Foster, B. O. 1899. "Notes on the Symbolism of the Apple in Classical Antiquity," *HSCP* 10: 39–55.

Foucault, M. 1985. *The Use of Pleasure* (*The History of Sexuality*, vol. 2), trans. R. Hurley. (New York).

Foucault, M. 1986. *The Care of the Self* (*The History of Sexuality*, vol. 3), trans. R. Hurley. (New York).

Fraenkel, E. 1955. "Neues Griechisch in Graffiti," *Glotta* 34: 42–7.

Frazer, James G., ed. 1931. *Ovid's Fasti*. (Loeb Classical Library; London).

Frazer, Peter M. 1969. "The Career of Erasistratos of Ceos," *Istituto Lombardo, Rendiconti, Classe di Lettere e Scienze Morali e Storiche* 103: 518–37.

Freedman, E. F. 1987. "'Uncontrolled Desires': The Response to the Sexual Psychopath, 1920–1960," *The Journal of American History* 74: 83–106.

Freud, S. n.d. *The Interpretation of Dreams*, trans. James Strachey. (Basic Books, Inc., New York).

Friedl, E. 1962. *Vasilika: A Village in Modern Greece*. (New York).

Friedl, E. 1986. "Field Work in a Greek Village," in Peggy Golde, ed., *Women in the Field: Anthropological Experiences*, 2nd ed., 195–217. (Berkeley).

Frischer, B. 1982. *The Sculpted Word: Epicureanism and Philosophical Recruitment in Ancient Greece*. (Berkeley).

Gailly, L. 1946. *Philosophes et philosophie dans la comédie grecque, I: La période antérieure à Platon*. (Thèse Liège, *non vidi*).

Gallavotti, C. 1947. *Saffo e Alceo: Testimonianze e frammenti*. (Naples).

Galt, A. H. 1982. "The Evil Eye as Synthetic Image and its Meanings on the Island of Pantelleria, Italy," *AE* 9: 664–81.

Ganschinietz, Richard. 1913. *Hippolytos' Capitel gegen die Magier*. (Texte und Untersuchungen zur Geschichte der altchristlichen Literatur 39/2; Leipzig).

Gardiner, Alan H., ed. 1935. *Hieratic Papyri in the British Museum, Third Series*. (London).

Geertz, Clifford. 1973. *The Interpretation of Cultures*. (New York).

Gentili, B. 1966. "La veneranda Saffo," *QUCC* 2: 37–62.

Geyer, A. 1977. "Roman und Mysterienritual: Zum Problem eines Bezugs zum dionysischen Mysterienritual im Roman des Longos," *Würzburger Jahrbücher für die Altertumswissenschaft* n.f. 3: 179–96.

Giannantoni. G. 1958. *I Cirenaici*. (Florence).

Gilmore, David D. 1982. "Anthropology of the Mediterranean Area," *Annual Review of Anthropology* 11: 175–205.

Gilmore, David D. 1987a. *Aggression and Community: Paradoxes of Andalusian Culture*. (New Haven).

Gilmore, David D., ed. 1987b. *Honor and Shame and the Unity of the Mediterranean*. (American Anthropological Association special publication no. 22; Washington, D.C.).

Gilsenan, M. 1976. "Lying, Honor, and Contradiction," in Bruce Kapferer, ed., *Transaction and Meaning: Directions in the Anthropology of Exchange and Symbolic Behavior*, 191–219. (Philadelphia).

Gleason, Maud W. 1989. "The Semiotics of Gender: Physiognomy and Self-Fashioning in the Second Century C.E.," in Halperin, Winkler, and Zeitlin, forthcoming.

Goessler, L. 1962. *Plutarchs Gedanken über die Ehe*. (diss. Universität Basel; Zurich).

Golden, M. 1985. "*Pais,* 'Child' and 'Slave,'" *AC* 54: 91–104.

Golden, M. 1988. "Male Chauvinists and Pigs," *Echos du monde classique/Classical Views* 32: 1–12.

Gomme, A. W. 1927. "The Athenian Hoplite Force in 431," *CQ* 21: 142–50.

Gomme, A. W. 1933. *The Population of Athens in the Fifth and Fourth Centuries B.C.* (Oxford).

Gomme, A. W. 1959. "The Population of Athens Again," *JHS* 79: 61–8.

Gordon, R. L. 1972. "Mithraism and Roman Society," *Religion* 2: 92–121.

Gould, J. P. 1980. "Law, custom and myth: aspects of the social position of women in classical Athens," *JHS* 100: 38–59.

Gouldner, Alvin. 1965. *Enter Plato: Classical Greece and the Origins of Social Theory.* (New York).

Gow, A. S. F., ed. 1952. *Bucolici Graeci.* (Oxford).

Greenblatt, S. 1986. "Fiction and Friction," in Thomas C. Heller, Morton Sosna, and David E. Wellbery, eds., *Reconstructing Individualism: Autonomy, Individuality and the Self in Western Thought,* 30–52, 329–32. (Stanford).

Guthrie, W. K. C. 1971a. *The Sophists* (Cambridge), first published as Volume III, Part 1 of his *A History of Greek Philosophy.* (Cambridge 1969).

Guthrie, W. K. C. 1971b. *Socrates* (Cambridge), first published as Volume III, Part 2 of his *A History of Greek Philosophy.* (Cambridge 1969).

Hainsworth, J. B. 1968. *The Flexibility of the Homeric Formula.* (Oxford).

Hallett, J. P. 1977. "Perusinae Glandes and the Changing Image of Augustus," *American Journal of Ancient History* 2: 151–71.

Hallett, J. P. 1979. "Sappho and her Social Context," *Signs* 4: 447–64.

Halperin, David M. 1983. *Before Pastoral: Theocritus and the Ancient Tradition of Bucolic Poetry.* (New Haven and London).

Halperin, David M. 1985. "Platonic *Erôs* and What Men Call Love," *Ancient Philosophy* 5: 161–204.

Halperin, David M. 1986. "Plato and Erotic Reciprocity," *CA* 5: 60–80.

Halperin, David M. 1989. *One Hundred Years of Homosexuality and Other Essays on Greek Love.* (New York).

Halperin, David M., John J. Winkler, and Froma I. Zeitlin, eds. 1989. *Before Sexuality: The Construction of Erotic Experience in the Ancient Greek World.* (Princeton).

Halverson, J. 1985. "Social Order in the *Odyssey,*" *Hermes* 113: 129–45.

Handman, M.-E. 1983. *La violence et la ruse: hommes et femmes dans un village grec.* (Paris).

Hansen, M. H. 1974. *The Sovereignty of the People's Court in Athens in the Fourth Century B.C. and the Public Action against Unconstitutional Proposals.* (Odense University Classical Studies 4; Odense).

Hansen, M. H. 1976. *Apagoge, Endeixis and Ephegesis against Kakourgoi, Atimoi and Pheugontes: A study in the Athenian Administration of Justice in the Fourth Century B.C.* (Odense University Classical Studies 8; Odense).

Hansen, M. H. 1981. "The Number of Athenian Hoplites in 431," *Symbolae Osloenses* 56: 19–32.

Hansen, M. H. 1983. "The Athenian 'Politicians' 403–322," *GRBS* 24: 33–55.

Hansen, M. H. 1986. *Demography and Democracy. The Number of Athenian Citizens in the Fourth Century B. C.* (Herning, Denmark).

Hansen, M. H. 1987. *The Athenian Assembly in the Age of Demosthenes.* (Oxford).

Harrison, Jane E. 1903. *Prolegomena to the Study of the Greek Religion.* (Cambridge).

Harrison, Jane E. 1912. *Themis; a Study of the Social Origins of Greek Religion.* (Cambridge).

Harsh, P. W. 1950. "Penelope and Odysseus in *Odyssey* XIX," *AJP* 71: 1–21.

Heim, Ricardus 1892. *Incantamenta Magica Graeca Latina.* (Leipzig).

Heinimann, F. 1945. *Nomos und Physis: Herkunft und Bedeutung einer Antithese im griechischen Denken des 5. Jahrhunderts.* (Schweizerische Beiträge zur Altertumswissenschaft 1; Basel).

Heiserman, Arthur. 1977. *The Novel Before the Novel.* (Chicago).

Henderson, Jeffrey. 1975. *The Maculate Muse: Obscene Language in Attic Comedy.* (New Haven).

Henderson, Jeffrey. 1987. "Older Women in Attic Old Comedy," *TAPA* 117: 105–29.

Henderson, Jeffrey. 1988. "Greek Attitudes to Sex," in Michael Grant and Rachel Kitzinger, eds., *Civilization of the Ancient Mediterranean,* 3 vols. (New York).

Hercher, R. 1855–56. "Ueber die Glaubwürdigkeit der Neuen Geschichte des Ptolemaeus Chennus," *Jahrbücher für classische Philologie* Supplementband 1: 269–93.

Herzfeld, Michael. 1980. "Meaning and Morality: A Semiotic Approach to Evil Eye Accusations in a Greek Village," *AE* 8: 560–74.

Herzfeld, Michael. 1982. *Ours Once More: Folklore, Ideology, and the Making of Modern Greece.* (Austin).

Herzfeld, Michael. 1984. "The Horns of the Mediterraneanist Dilemma," *AE* 11: 439–54.

Herzfeld, Michael. 1985a. *The Poetics of Manhood: Contest and Identity in a Cretan Mountain Village.* (Princeton).

Herzfeld, Michael. 1985b. "Gender Pragmatics: Agency, Speech, and Bride-Theft in a Cretan Mountain Village," *Anthropology* 9: 25–44.

Herzfeld, Michael. 1986. "Within and Without: The Category of 'Female' in the Ethnography of Modern Greece," in Jill Dubisch, ed., *Gender and Power in Rural Greece,* 215–33. (Princeton).

Herzfeld, Michael. 1987a. "'As in your own House': Hospitality, Ethnography, and the Stereotype of Mediterranean Society," in Gilmore 1987b: 75–89.

Herzfeld, Michael. 1987b. *Anthropology Through the Looking-Glass: Critical Ethnography in the Margins of Europe.* (Cambridge).

Heubeck, A. 1978. "Homeric Studies Today: Results and Prospects," in Bernard C. Fenik, ed., *Homer, Tradition and Invention,* 1–17. (Leiden).

Hoffmann, H. 1974. "Hahnenkampf in Athen: Zur Ikonologie einer attischen Bildformel," *Revue Archéologique.* 195–220.

Holwerda, D. 1955. *Commentatio de vocis quae est PHYSIS vi atque usu praesertim in Graecitate Aristotele anteriore.* (Groningen).

Hooker, J. T. 1977. *The Language and Text of the Lesbian Poets.* (Innsbrucker Beiträge zur Sprachwissenschaft 26; Innsbruck).

Hopfner, T. 1938. *Das Sexualleben der Griechen und Römer.* (Prague).

Hülsen, C. 1896. "Tesserae lusoriae," *RM* 11: 227–52.

Hunter, R. L. 1983. *A Study of "Daphnis & Chloe."* (Cambridge).

Jahn, O. 1855. "Aberglaube des boesen Blicks bei den Alten," *Sitzungsberichte Leipzig* 7.

Janko, R. 1988. "Berlin Magical Papyrus 21243: A Conjecture," *ZPE* 72: 293.

Jenkins, I. D. 1985. "The Ambiguity of Greek Textiles," *Arethusa* 18: 109–32.

Jocelyn, H. D. 1980. "A Greek Indecency and its Students: LAIKAZEIN," *PCPS* 26: 12–66.

Joly, R. 1962. "La caractérologie antique jusqu'à Aristote," *Revue Belge de Philologie et d'Histoire* 40: 5–28.

Jones, A. H. M. 1957. *Athenian Democracy.* (Oxford).

Jones, C. P. 1980. "Apuleius' *Metamorphoses* and Lollianus' *Phoinikika,*" *Phoenix* 34: 243–54.

Kaimakis, Dimitris, ed. 1976. *Die Kyraniden.* (Beiträge zur klassischen Philologie 76; Meisenheim).

Kakridis, Ph. I. 1972. "Une Pomme mordue," *Hellenica* 25: 189–92.

Kambitsis, S. 1976. "Une nouvelle tablette magique d'Égypte," *Bulletin de l'Institut Francqis de l'Archéologie Orientale* 76: 213–30.

Kassel, Rudolf and C. Austin, eds. 1983-. *Poetae Comici Graeci.* (Berlin).

Kelly-Gadol, J. 1976. "The Social Relation of the Sexes: Methodological Implications of Women's History," *Signs* 1: 809–23.

Kenny, E. J. 1970. "Doctus Lucretius," *Mnemosyne* ser. 4, 23: 366–92.

Kessels, A. H. M. 1969. "Ancient Systems of Dream-Classification," *Mnemosyne* ser. 4, 22: 389–424.

Keuls, Eva C. 1983. "Attic Vase Painting and the Home Textile Industry," in Warren G. Moon, ed., *Ancient Greek Art and Iconography,* 209–30. (Madison, Wis.).

Keuls, Eva C. 1985. *The Reign of the Phallus: Sexual Politics in Ancient Athens.* (New York).

Kilb, Hans. 1973. *Strukturen epischen Gestaltens im 7. und 23. Gesang der Odyssee.* (Munich).

Killeen, J. F. 1973. "Sappho Fr. 111," *CQ* 23: 197.

Kirk, Geoffrey S. 1963. "A Fragment of Sappho Reinterpreted," *CQ* 13: 51–2.

Kirk, Geoffrey S., ed. 1964. *The Language and Background of Homer: Some Recent Studies and Controversies.* (Cambridge).

Kirk, Geoffrey S. 1976. *Homer and the Oral Tradition.* (Cambridge).

Kock, T. 1880–88. *Comicorum Atticorum Fragmenta,* 3 vols. (Leipzig).

Koniaris, G. 1968. "On Sappho fr. 31 (L-P)," *Philologus* 112: 173–86.

Köster, H. 1974. "Physis" in G. Kittel and G. Friedrich, eds., *Theological Dictionary of the New Testament,* trans. and ed. G. W. Bromiley, vol. 9, 251–77. (Grand Rapids, Mich.) .

Krenkel, W. A. 1980. "Fellatio and Irrumatio," *Wissenschaftliche Zeitschrift der Wilhelm-Pieck-Universität* (Rostock) 29/5: 77–88.

Krenkel, W. A. 1981. "Tonguing," *Wissenschaftliche Zeitschrift der Wilhelm-Pieck-Universität* (Rostock) 30/5: 37–54.

Kühner, Raphael and F. Blass. 1892. *Ausführliche Grammatik der griechischen Sprache,* vol. 1, part 2, 3rd ed. (Hanover).

Kuhnert, E. 1894. "Feuerzauber," *RhM* 49: 37–58.

Lacey, W. K. 1968. *The Family in Classical Greece.* (Ithaca, N.Y.).

Lanata, C. 1966. "Sul linguaggio amoroso di Saffo," *QUCC* 2: 63–79.

Lasserre, F. 1974. "Ornements érotiques dans la poesie lyrique archaïque," in John L. Heller, ed., *Serta Turyniana,* 5–33. (Urbana, Ill.).

Laukamm, S. 1928. "Das Sittenbild des Artemidor von Ephesus," *Angelos* 3: 32–71.

Lavelle, B. M. 1986. "The Nature of Hipparchos' Insult to Harmodios," *AJP* 107: 318–31.

Lawler, L. B. 1948. "On Certain Homeric Epithets," *Philological Quarterly* 27: 80–4.

Lefkowitz, Mary R. 1973. "Critical Stereotypes and the Poetry of Sappho," *GRBS* 14: 113–23.

Lefkowitz, Mary R. and M. B. Fant. 1977. *Women in Greece and Rome.* (Toronto).

Lefkowitz, Mary R. and M. B. Fant. 1982. *Women's Life in Greece and Rome.* (Baltimore).

Lenaios, Euios [pseudonym of C. Charitonides]. 1935. *APORRHETA.* (Thessalonika).

Lerner, Gerda. 1986. *The Creation of Patriarchy.* (New York).

Levine, D. 1983. "Penelope's Laugh: *Odyssey* 18.163," *AJP* 104: 172–7.

Licht, Hans [pseud. of Paul Brandt]. 1926/7. "Sexuelle Reizmittel und Verjüngungskuren in Altgriechenland," *Zeitschrift für sexuelle Zwischenstufen* 13: 134–7.

Liddell, Henry George, R. Scott, and H. S. Jones. 1968. *A Greek-English Lexicon* (with Supplement). (Oxford).

Lippard, L. 1977. "Quite contrary: Body, Nature, Ritual in Women's Art," *Chrysalis* 2: 30–47.

Lipsius, J. H. 1908. *Das Attische Recht und Rechtsverfahren*, vol. 2/1. (Leipzig).

Littlewood, A. R. 1968. "The Symbolism of the Apple in Greek and Roman Literature," *HSCP* 72: 147–81.

Lloyd, Geoffrey E. R. 1966. *Polarity and Analogy: Two Types of Argumentation in Early Greek Thought.* (Cambridge).

Lloyd, Geoffrey E. R. 1983. *Science, Folklore and Ideology: Studies in the Life Sciences in Ancient Greece.* (Cambridge).

Loizos, P. 1975. *The Greek Gift: Politics in a Cypriot Village.* (New York).

Lovejoy, Arthur O. and G. Boas. 1935. *A Documentary History of Primitivism and Related Ideas,* vol. 1. (Baltimore).

Lowes, J. L. 1913/4. "The Loveres Maladye of Hereos," *Modern Philology* 11: 490–547.

Lugauer, M. 1967. *Untersuchungen zur Symbolik des Apfels in der Antike.* (diss. Erlangen-Nürnberg).

McCartney, E. S. 1925. "How the Apple Became the Token of Love," *TAPA* 56: 70–81.

MacCormack, C. P. and M. Strathern, eds. 1980. *Nature, Culture and Gender.* (Cambridge).

McCulloh, W. E. 1970. *Longus.* (Twayne's World Authors Series; New York).

MacDowell, D. M. 1976. "*Hybris* in Athens," *G&R* 23: 14–31.

MacDowell, D. M. 1978. *The Law in Classical Athens.* (Ithaca, N.Y.).

McIntosh, M. 1968/9. "The Homosexual Role," *Social Problems* 16: 182–92.

McLeish, K. 1977. "*PHYSIS:* A bawdy joke in Aristophanes," *CQ* n.s. 27: 76–9.

Mahaffy, John P. 1890. *Social Life in Greece from Homer to Menander,* 7th edition. (London).

Maloney, Clarence, ed. 1976. *The Evil Eye.* (New York).

Maltomini, F. 1988. "P. Berol. 21243 (Formulario Magico): Due Nuove Letture," *ZPE* 74: 247–8.

Mannebach, E. 1961. *Aristippi et Cyrenaicorum Fragmenta.* (Leiden/Köln).

Manuli, P. 1983. "Donne mascoline, femmine sterili, vergini perpetue: La ginecologia greca tra Ippocrate e Sorano": 147–92 in Campese, Manuli, and Sissa.

Marquardt, P. 1985. "Penelope POLUTROPOS," AJP 106: 32–48.

Marry, J. D. 1979. "Sappho and the Heroic Ideal," Arethusa 12: 271–92.

Martin, V. 1928. "Une tablette magique de la Bibliothèque de Genève," Genava 6: 56–63.

Mathieu, N.-C. 1978. "Man-Culture and Woman-Nature?" Women's Studies International Quarterly 1: 55–65; French original appeared in L'Homme 13 (1973) 101–41.

Meiggs, R. 1964. "A Note on the Population of Attica," CR n.s. 14: 2–3.

Merkelbach, Reinhold. 1951. "Eine orphische Unterweltsbeschreibung auf Papyrus," Museum Helveticum 8: 1–11.

Merkelbach, Reinhold. 1957. "Sappho und ihr Kreis," Philologus 101: 1–29.

Merkelbach, Reinhold. 1960. "Daphnis und Chloe: Roman und Mysterium," Antaios 1: 47–60.

Merkelbach, Reinhold. 1962. Roman und Mysterium. (Munich).

Merkelbach, Reinhold. 1988. Die Hirten des Dionysos. (Stuttgart).

Messick, B. 1987. "Subordinate Discourse: Women, Weaving, and Gender Relations in North Africa," AE 14: 210–25.

Metzger, Henri. 1951. Les représentations dans la céramique attique du IV^c siècle. (Paris).

Michelakis, E. M. 1968. "Das Naturrecht bei Aristoteles," in E. Berneker, ed., Zur griechischen Rechtsgeschichte, 146–71. (Wege der Forschung 45, Darmstadt); orig. published in Tomos Timêtikos K. Triantaphullopoulou (Athens 1959) 357–76.

Miller, S. G. 1986. "Eros and the Arms of Achilles," American Journal of Archaeology 90: 159–70.

Millett, Paul. 1984. "Hesiod and his World," PCPS n.s. 30: 84–115.

Milne, M. J. and D. von Bothmer. 1953. "KATAPUGON, KATAPUGAINA," Hesperia 22: 215–224 + plate 66.

Moreau, A. 1976/7. "L'Oeil maléfique dans l'oeuvre d'Eschyle," Revue des Études Anciennes 78/79: 50–64.

Mrabet, Mohammed. 1968. Love with a Few Hairs, translated from the Moghrebi and edited by Paul Bowles. (New York).

Murnaghan, Sheila. 1987a. "Penelope's agnoia: Knowledge, Power and Gender in the Odyssey," 103–15 in Skinner 1987a.

Murnaghan, Sheila. 1987b. Disguise and Recognition in the Odyssey. (Princeton).

Murray, Gilbert. 1912. Four Stages of Greek Religion. (New York).

Nagy, Gregory. 1974. Comparative Studies in Greek and Indic Meter. (Cambridge, Mass.).

Nauck, August, ed. 1964. Tragicorum Graecorum Fragmenta, 2nd ed. (Stuttgart).

Neuberger-Donath, R. 1969. "Sappho Fr. 1.1: POIKILOTHRON' oder POIKILOPHRON'," Wiener Studien 82: 15–7.

Newton, R. M. 1984. "The Rebirth of Odysseus," GRBS 25: 5–20.

Niese, B. 1882. Die Entwicklung der homerischen Poesie. (Berlin).

Nilsson, Martin P. 1906. Griechische Feste von religiöser Bedeutung mit Ausschluss der Attischen. (Leipzig).

Nock, A. D. 1934. Review of L. Deubner, Attische Feste, in Gnomon 10: 290–1.

Obbink, Dirk. forthcoming. "Apples and Eros: Hesiod frag. 72–75 M.-W." ZPE.

Olender, M. 1989. "Aspects of Baubo: Ancient Texts and Contexts," in Halperin, Winkler, and Zeitlin.

Osborne, R. 1985. "Law in Action in Classical Athens," *JHS* 105: 40–53.

Padgug, R. A. 1979. "Sexual Matters: On Conceptualizing Sexuality in History," *Radical History Review* 20: 3–23.

Page, Denys. 1955. *Sappho and Alcaeus.* (Oxford).

Page, Denys, ed. 1962. *Poetae Melici Graeci.* (Oxford).

Pandiri, T. 1985. "Daphnis and Chloe: The Art of Pastoral Play," *Ramus* 14: 116–41.

Parke, H. W. 1977. *Festivals of the Athenians.* (Ithaca, N.Y.).

Patterson, C. 1981. *Pericles' Citizenship Law of 451–50 B.C.* (New York).

Peacock, Sandra J. 1988. *Jane Ellen Harrison: The Mask and the Self.* (New Haven).

Peradotto, John and J. P. Sullivan, eds. 1984. *Women in the Ancient World: The Arethusa Papers.* (Albany).

Peristiany, J. G., ed. 1965. *Honour and Shame: The Values of Mediterranean Society.* (London).

Perlman, S. 1963. "The Politicians of the Athenian Democracy of the Fourth Century B. C.," *Athenaeum* 41: 327–55.

Perry, Walter C. 1898. *The Women of Homer.* (London).

Pfeiffer, Rudolf. 1968. *History of Classical Scholarship—From the Beginnings to the End of the Hellenistic Age.* (Oxford).

Phillips, C. R. III. 1986. "The Sociology of Religious Knowledge in the Roman Empire to A. D. 284." *Aufstieg und Niedergang der Römischen Welt* II.16.3, pp. 2677–773 (Berlin).

Piault, C. 1985. *Familles et biens en Grèce et à Chypre.* (Paris).

Pickard-Cambridge, Arthur W. 1968. *The Dramatic Festivals of Athens,* 2nd ed., revised by J. Gould and D. M. Lewis. (Oxford).

Piechotta, Johannes. 1886/7. "Ein anectotum Latinum," *Jahres-Bericht Des Königlichen Katholischen Gymnasiums zu Leobschütz:* VIII.

Pilitsis, G. 1985. "The Gardens of Adonis in Serres Today," *Journal of Modern Greek Studies* 3: 145–66.

Pinney, G. F. 1984. "For the Heroes Are at Hand," *JHS* 104: 181–3 + plate VIIIc-d.

Pitt-Rivers, Julian. 1977. *The Fate of Shechem, or the Politics of Sex: Essays in the Anthropology of the Mediterranean.* (Cambridge).

Pocock, L. G. 1957. *The Sicilian Origin of the Odyssey.* (Wellington).

Podlecki, A. J. 1961. "Guest-gifts and Nobodies in *Odyssey* 9," *Phoenix* 15: 125–33.

Pohlenz, M. 1953. "Nomos und Physis," *Hermes* 81: 418–38.

Pomeroy, Sarah. 1975. *Goddesses, Whores, Wives, and Slaves: Women in Classical Antiquity.* (New York).

Pomeroy, Sarah. 1978. "Supplementary Notes on Erinna," *ZPE* 32: 17–22.

Pomeroy, Sarah. 1984. *Women in Hellenistic Egypt: From Alexander to Cleopatra.* (New York).

Preisendanz, Karl. 1918. "Ousia," *Wiener Studien* 40: 5–8.

Preisendanz, Karl, ed., 1973, 1974. *Papyri Graecae Magicae,* 2nd ed. by Albert Henrichs, 2 vols. (Stuttgart).

Price, S. 1986. "The Future of Dreams: From Freud to Artemidorus," *Past & Present* no. 113: 3–37, reprinted in Halperin, Winkler, Zeitlin.

Pritchett, W. K. 1974. *The Greek State at War. Part II.* (Berkeley).

Privitera, G. A. 1969. "Ambiguità antitesi analogia nel fr. 31 L-P di Saffo," *QUCC* 8: 37–80.

Pucci, Pietro. 1987. *Odysseus Polutropos: Intertextual Readings in the Odyssey and the Iliad.* (Ithaca).

Putnam, M. 1960/1. "*Throna* and Sappho 1.1," *Classical Journal* 56: 79–83.

Rabe, H. 1971. *Scholia in Lucianum.* (Stuttgart).

Rankin, A. V. 1962. "Penelope's Dreams in Books XIX and XX of the Odyssey," *Helikon* 2: 617–24.

Raubitschek, A. E. 1981. "A New Attic Club (ERANOS)," *J. P. Getty Museum Journal* 9: 93–8.

Reardon, B. P. 1971. *Courants littéraires grecs des IIe et IIIe siècles après J.-C.* (Paris).

Reeve, M. D. 1971. "Hiatus in the Greek Novelists," *CQ* n.s. 21: 514–39.

Reeve, M. D. 1982. *Longus, Daphnis et Chloe.* (Leipzig).

Rhodes, Peter J. 1980. "Ephebi, bouleutae and the population of Athens," *ZPE* 38: 191–201.

Rhodes, Peter J. 1981. *A Commentary on the Aristotelian Athenaion Politeia.* (Oxford).

Rhodes, Peter J. 1982. "Problems in Athenian *Eisphora* and Liturgies," *American Journal of Ancient History* 7: 1–19.

Ridley, R. T. 1979. "The Hoplite as Citizen: Athenian Military Institutions in their Social Context," *AC* 48: 508–48.

Riess, E. 1894. "Volksthümliches bei Artemidoros," *RhM* 49: 177–93.

Rissman, Leah. 1983. *Love as War: Homeric Allusion in the Poetry of Sappho.* (Beiträge zur klassischen Wissenschaft 157; Königstein).

Roberts, Jennifer T. 1982. *Accountability in Athenian Government.* (Madison, Wis.).

Robertson, N. 1984. "Poseidon's Festival at the Winter Solstice," *CQ* 34: 1–16.

Robinson, David M. and E. Fluck. 1937. *A Study of the Greek Love Names.* (Baltimore).

Rogers, S. C. 1985. "Gender in Southwestern France: The Myth of Male Dominance Revisited," *Anthropology* 9: 65–96.

Rohde, Erwin. 1974. *Der griechische Roman,* ed. 5. (Hildesheim).

Rohde, Georg. 1937. "Longus und die Bukolik," *RhM* 86: 23–49 (= *Studien und Interpretationen,* Berlin 1963, 91–116).

Rubin, N. F. "Penelope's Perspective: Character from Plot." in J. M. Bremer, I. J. F. de Jong, and J. Kalff, eds. *Homer: Beyond Oral Poetry.* (Amsterdam).

Ruschenbusch, E. 1981a. "Epheben, Bouleuten und die Bürgerzahl von Athen um 330 v. Chr." *ZPE* 41: 103–5.

Ruschenbusch, E. 1981b. "Noch einmal die Bürgerzahl Athens um 330 v. Chr." *ZPE* 44: 110–12.

Russell, Diana E. H. and N. Van de Ven, eds. 1976. *Crimes Against Women: Proceedings of the International Tribunal.* (Millbrae, Cal.).

Russo, J. 1973–4. "Reading the Greek Lyric Poets (Monodists)," *Arion* n.s. 1: 707–30.

Russo, J. 1982. "Interview and Aftermath: Dream, Fantasy, and Intuition in Odyssey 19 and 20," *AJP* 103: 4–18.

Ruyer, R. 1977. *Homère au féminin*. (Paris).

Saake. H. 1971. *Zur Kunst Sapphos*. (Munich).

Sacks, K. B. and N. Scheper-Hughes. 1987. "Introduction" to *As the World Turns: Women, Work, and International Migration* (special issue of *Women's Studies* 13/3).

Safa-Isfahani, Kaven. 1980. "Female-centered World Views in Iranian Culture: Symbolic Representations of Sexuality in Dramatic Games," *Signs* 6: 33–53.

Saïd, S. 1983. "Féminin, femme et femelle dans les grands traités biologiques d'Aristote," in Edmond Lévy, ed., *La femme dans les sociétés antiques*, 93–123. (Université des sciences humaines de Strasbourg, Contributions et travaux de l'Institut d'Histoire Romaine, Strasbourg).

Sandy, G. N. 1979. "Notes on Lollianus' *Phoenicica*," *AJP* 100: 367–76.

Scarcella, A. M. 1970. "Realtà e letteratura nel paesaggio sociale ed economico del romanzo di Longo Sofista," *Maia* 22: 103–31.

Schadewaldt, W. 1936. "Zu Sappho," *Hermes* 71: 363–73.

Schadewaldt, W. 1959. *Neue Kriterien zur Odyssee-Analyse: Die Wiedererkennung des Odysseus und der Penelope*. (SB Heidelberg).

Schaps, David. 1977. "The Woman Least Mentioned: Etiquette and Women's Names," *CQ* n.s. 27: 323–30.

Schaps, David. 1979. *The Economic Rights of Women in Ancient Greece*. (Edinburgh).

Schaps, David. 1982. "The Women of Greece in Wartime," *CP* 77: 193–213.

Schauenberg, K. 1975. "*EURYMEDON EIMI*," *AM* 90: 97–121 + plates 25–42.

Schein: see Dimen.

Schneider, J. 1971. "Of Vigilance and Virgins: Honor, Shame and Access to Resources in Mediterranean Societies," *Ethnology* 10: 1–24.

Schneider, K. 1910. "Hahnenkämpfe," *RE* 7: 2210–15.

Schönberger, O. 1973. *Longos: Hirtengeschichten von Daphnis und Chloe*, griechisch und deutsch, 2nd ed. (Berlin).

Schwartz, E. 1924. *Die Odyssee*. (Munich).

Sedgwick, E. K. 1988. "Privilege of Unknowing," *Genders* 1: 102–24.

Shipp, G. P. 1977. "Linguistic Notes," *Antichthon* 11: 1–2.

Shorey, P. 1909. "*Physis, Meletê, Epistêmê*," *TAPA* 40: 190–201.

Simon, Erika. 1975. "Kratos und Bia," *Würzburger Jahrbücher für die Altertumswissenschaft*, n.f. 1: 177–86.

Simon, Erika. 1983. *Festivals of Attica: An Archaeological Commentry*. (Madison, Wis.).

Sittl, K. 1890. *Die Gebärden der Griechen und Römer*. (Leipzig).

Skeat, T. C. 1936. "A Greek Mathematical Tablet," *Mizraim* 3: 18–25.

Skinner, Marilyn B., ed. 1987a. *Rescuing Creusa: New Methodological Approaches to Women in Antiquity* (= *Helios* n.s. 13).

Skinner, Marilyn B. 1987b. "Greek Women and the Metronymic: A note on an epigram by Nossis," *Ancient History Bulletin* 1: 39–42.

Smith, Nicholas D. 1983. "Aristotle's Theory of Natural Slavery," *Phoenix* 37: 109–22.

Smither, P. C. 1939. "A Coptic Love-Charm," *Journal of Egyptian Archeology* 25: 173–4.

Snell, B. 1931. "Sapphos Gedicht *phainetai moi kênos*," *Hermes* 66: 71–90.

Sommerstein, A. H. 1980. "The Naming of Women in Greek and Roman Comedy," *Quaderni di storia* 11: 393–418.

Sorof, G. 1899. "Nomos und Phusis in Xenophons Anabasis," *Hermes* 34: 568–89.

Spelman, E. V. 1983. "Aristotle and the Politicization of the Soul," in Sandra Harding and M. B. Hintikka, eds., *Discovering Reality*, 17–30. (Dordrecht, Holland).

Stambolian, G. and B. Marks, eds. 1979. *Homosexualities and French Literature*. (Ithaca, N.Y., and London).

Stanford, W. B. 1939. *Ambiguity in Greek Literature*. (Oxford).

Stanley, K. 1976. "The Role of Aphrodite in Sappho Fr. 1," *GRBS* 17: 305–21.

Stehle [Stigers], E. 1977. "Retreat from the Male: Catullus 62 and Sappho's Erotic Flowers," *Ramus* 6: 83–102.

Stehle [Stigers], E. 1979. "Romantic Sensuality, Poetic Sense: A Response to Hallett on Sappho," *Signs* 4: 464–71.

Stehle, E. forthcoming. "Sappho and the Enclosing Goddess."

Stephens, Susan A. and John J. Winkler. forthcoming. *Ancient Greek Novels: The Fragments*.

Strasburger, H. 1953. "Der soziologische Aspekt der homerischen Epen," *Gymnasium* 60: 97–114.

Sutton, Dana F. 1984. *The Lost Sophocles*. (London).

Svenbro, J. 1975. "Sappho and Diomedes," *Museum Philologum Londiniense* 1: 37–49.

Sweet, L. E., ed. 1966. "Appearance and Reality: Status and Roles of Women in Mediterranean Societies." special issue of *Anthropological Quarterly* 40: 95–183.

Taillardat, Jean. 1967. *Suétone—Peri Blasphêmiôn. Peri Paidiôn*. (Paris).

Terian, A. 1981. *Philonis Alexandrini de animalibus*, The Armenian Text with an Introduction, Translation, and Commentary by Abraham Terian. (Studies in Hellenistic Judaism 1; Chico, Cal.).

Thimme, Otto. 1935. *PHYSIS TROPOS ETHOS: Semasiologische Untersuchung über die Auffassung des menschlichen Wesens (Charakters) in der älteren griechischen Literatur*. (diss. Georg–August-Universität zu Göttingen).

Thompson, H. A. 1936. "Pnyx and Thesmophorion," *Hesperia* 5: 151–200.

Thomsen, R. 1977. "War Taxes in Classical Athens," in André Chastagnol, C. Nicolet, and H. van Effenterre, eds., *Armées et fiscalité dans le monde antique*, 135–44. (Colloques nationaux du centre national de la recherche scientifique, No. 936; Paris 1977).

Thornton, Agathe. 1970. *People and Themes in Homer's Odyssey*. (Dunedin and London).

Tod, M. N. 1948. *A Selection of Greek Historical Inscriptions*, vol. 2. (Oxford).

Trumpf, J. 1958. "Fluchtafel und Rachepuppe," *AM* 73: 94–102.

Trumpf, J. 1960. "Kydonische Apfel," *Hermes* 88: 14–22.

Turner, P. 1960. "*Daphnis and Chloe*: an interpretation," *G&R* n.s. 7: 117–23.

Turner, P. 1968. "Novels, Ancient and Modern," *Novel* 2: 15–24.

Turyn, A. 1942. "The Sapphic Ostracon," *TAPA* 73: 308–18.

Tyrrell, William B. 1984. *Amazons: a Study in Athenian Mythmaking*. (Baltimore).

Valley, G. 1926. *Über den Sprachgebrauch des Longus*. (Uppsala).

Van Nortwick, T. 1979. "Penelope and Nausicaa," *TAPA* 109: 269–76.

Vester, H. 1968. "Das 19. Buch der Odyssee," *Gymnasium* 75: 417–34.

Vlastos, G. 1987. "Socratic Irony," *CQ* 37: 79–96.

Walcot, P. 1970. *Greek Peasants, Ancient and Modern: A Comparison of Social and Moral Values.* (New York).

Walcot, P. 1977. "Odysseus and the Art of Lying," *Ancient Society* 8: 1–19.

Wankel, H. 1988. "Die Datierung des Prozesses gegen Timarchos (346/5)," *Hermes* 116: 383–6.

Warren, Kay B. and Susan Bourque. 1985. "Gender, Power, and Communication: Women's Responses to Political Muting in the Andes," in Susan C. Bourque and Donna R. Divine, eds., *Women Living Change,* 255–86. (Philadelphia).

Weeks, J. 1977. *Coming Out: Homosexual Politics in Britain, from the Nineteenth Century to the Present.* (London).

Weill, N. 1966. "Adôniazousai ou les femmes sur le toit," *BCH* 90: 664–98.

Weill, N. 1970. "La fête d'Adonis dans la samienne de Ménandre," *BCH* 94: 591–3.

Weinreich, O. 1928. "Martial XI 43, Petron. 140,5 und Pariser Zauberpapyrus Z. 326," *RhM* 77: 112.

Weissenberger, Michael. 1987. *Die Dokimasiereden des Lysias.* (Beiträge zur klassischen Philologie 182; Frankfurt am Mein).

Wellman, Max. 1928. *Die Physika des Bolos Demokritos und der Magier Anaxilaos von Larissa.* (Abhandlungen der preussischen Akademie der Wissenschaften, phil.-hist. Klasse; Berlin).

West, M. L. 1970. "Burning Sappho," *Maia* 22: 307–30.

White, Robert J. 1975. *The Interpretation of Dreams: Oneirocritica by Artemidorus.* (Park Ridge, N.J.).

Whitehead, David. 1986. *The Demes of Attica 508/7 - ca. 250 B.C.* (Princeton).

Wikan, U. 1984. "Shame and Honour: a Contestable Pair," *Man* n.s. 19: 635–52.

Wills, G. 1967. "The Sapphic 'Umwertung aller Werte,'" *AJP* 88: 434–42.

Winkler, John J. 1980. "Lollianos and the Desperadoes," *JHS* 100: 155–81.

Winkler, John J. 1982a. "The Mendacity of Kalasiris and the Narrative Strategy of Heliodoros' *Aithiopika,*" *Yale Classical Studies* 27: 93–158.

Winkler, John J. 1982b. "Geminus of Tyre and the Patron of Artemidorus," *CP* 77: 245–48.

Winkler, John J. 1985a. *Auctor & Actor: A Narratological Reading of Apuleius' "Golden Ass."* (Berkeley).

Winkler, John J. 1985b. "The Ephebes' Song: *Tragôidia* and *Polis,*" *Representations* 11: 26–62; revised version in Winkler and Zeitlin.

Winkler, John J. and Froma I. Zeitlin, eds. 1989. *Nothing to Do with Dionysos? The Social Meanings of Athenian Drama.* (Princeton).

Wirth, P. 1963. "Neue Spuren eines Sapphobruchstücks," *Hermes* 91: 115–7.

Wolohojian, A. M., trans. 1969. *The Romance of Alexander the Great by Pseudo-Callisthenes.* (New York).

Wortmann, D. 1968. "Neue magische Texte," *Bonner Jahrbücher* 168: 56–111.

Wünsch, R. 1902. "Eine antike Rachepuppe," *Philologus* 61: 26–31.

Zeitlin, Froma I. 1981. "Travesties of Gender and Genre in Aristophanes' *Thesmophoriazousae*," in Foley 1981b, 169–217.

Zeitlin, Froma I. 1982. "Cultic Models of the Female: Rites of Dionysus and Demeter," *Arethusa* 15: 129–57.

Zeitlin, Froma I. 1985a. "Playing the Other: Theater, Theatricality, and the Feminine in Greek Drama," *Representations* 11: 63–94, reprinted in Winkler and Zeitlin.

Zeitlin, Froma I. 1985b. "The Power of Aphrodite: Eros and the Boundaries of the Self in the *Hippolytus*," in Peter Burian, ed., *Directions in Euripidean Criticism*, 52–111, 189–208. (Durham, N.C.).

Zeitlin, Froma I. 1989. "The Poetics of Desire: Nature, Art, and Imitation in Longus' *Daphnis and Chloe*," in Halperin, Winkler, and Zeitlin.

Index of Passages Discussed

Achilles Tatius: 1.3:28n.
                     2.6:80
Aelian:
nat. anim. 1.44:81
var. hist. 12.18:203
Aetios:
Placita 5.2.3:33
Aiskhines:
1:53n., 56–7, 58, 59, 63–4
2:46–7
Alexander Tralles: peri ophthalmôn, ed.
Puschmann, p. 152:183
Alkiphron: Letters of Courtesans 4:200–1
Anon. Iambl.: FVS 89.2:47n.
Antiphon Soph.: On Likemindedness FVS 87
B 49:82n.
Apollodoros: 1.30:197
Apollonios: Argonautika 3.442–58:92
Apuleius:
Apologia 90:90
Golden Ass   1.1:10
                2.32:85
                2.5:97
                3.15–8:85
                3.24:218
                7.26:218
Aristophanes:
Akh.   1071–234:52
Clouds   1083–1104.52
                1187:65
Ekkl.   1092:80
Frogs   649–61:190
Knights   425–8:62
                877–80:54
Lys.   387–96:190
                700:200n.
                885–8:7–8

Peace   607:65
                1127–90:52
Thesm.   574–6:193–4
Wasps   1456–8:65
Aristotle:
[Ath. Pol.]   18.2:51
                55.4:55
Eth. Nikom.   1116ª 12–4:83
                1128ª 13–4:52n.
                1148ᵇ 15–49ª20:69
                1160ᵇ 33–4:6, 221n3.
Gen. Anim.   728ª 3–5:50
                739ª 21–7:92
Hist. Anim.   551ᵇ 2–4:182
                581ᵇ 18:69n.
                581ᵇ 19–21:69n.
                608ª 25:224n.9
                637ª 27–8:92
                638ª 5:92
[Physiogn.]   808ª 7–11:67n.
                808ª 12–6:67
                809ᵇ 8:67n.
Pol.   1256ᵇ 20–6:70
                1259ª 37–ᵇ19:6–7
[Prob.]   3.33:81
                4.2:68n.
                4.15:68n.
                4.26:67–9
                30.1:82n.
Rhet.   1370ª 6–9:69
                1370ᵇ 32:40n.
                1374ª 13–5:48n.
Artemidoros:
Oneirokritika
    1.proem:23–4, 25
    1.1:24, 26
    1.2:25, 27, 222n.11, 223n.13

1.3:35
1.4:26
1.8:35
1.8–9:28
1.11:32n., 41
1.12:26–7, 36n.
1.45:42
1.55:34n.
1.56:34n.
1.73:34n.
1.78:34, 36, 36n., 37–8, 37n., 40–1
1.78–80:36, 210–6
1.79:34n., 42
1.80:38, 39
2.8:35n.
2.9:223n.15
2.10:34n.
2.12:26n., 34n.
2.13:34n.
2.17:34n.
2.25:34n.
2.27:34n.
2.28:29
2.32:25n., 34n.
2.33:25
2.59:29
2.66:25–6
2.69:25
3.8:41
3.16:41
3.36:208n.
3.61:25
3.66:222n.8
4.proem:31, 32, 33n.
4.1:26
4.2:29, 35
4.4:28, 36n.
4.14:28n.
4.20:31–2
4.23:32n.
4.24:30, 32n.
4.27:28
4.28:29n.
4.33:27n.
4.46:34n.
4.59:28n., 29
4.66:29
4.67:28
5.2:34n.
5.15:34n.
5.24:34
5.31:34n.

5.45:34n.
5.51:24–5
5.62:24
5.63:34
5.64:34
5.65:34n.
5.69:41n.
5.87:36n.
5.91:25
Athenaios:
    53C: 80
    63E–64B: 80
    105B: 182
    356E–F: 80
    619D–E: 83, 83n.
    670C: 94n.

Chariton: *Kallirhoe* 6.3.7: 84n., 6.7:92
Clement of Alexandria:
    Paidagôgos 3.28.3: 90
Cyril of Jerusalem:
    Catecheseis 6.33: 38

Defixionum Tabellae (DT): 230:95
                              267:97
                              271:97
Deinarchos: 1.29: 224n.3
                   1.71: 55
                   2:57–8
Demetrios: 148: 183
Demosthenes: 4.1: 225n.20
                   6.24: 66
                   10.70: 58
                   18.242: 65
                   22.30–1: 60
                   22.37: 56n., 58
                   22.53–55: 48
                   25: 65
                   25.57: 6, 221n.2
                   45.79: 57n.
                   54.7–9: 49
                   57.35: 5–6
                   [59.18]: 65
                   [59.122]: 5n.
                   Erôtikos: 65
Diktys of Krete: 6.14–5: 92
Dio Chrysostom:
    Oration   7: 21–2, 111, 111n.
                       20.19–23: 92
Diodoros of Sicily: 32.10.7: 219
Diogenianos: 1.14: 192

Dionysios of Halikarnassos:
Antiq.   20.13: 60n.
Dioskorides: Mat. Med. 3.128: 80n.
Diphilos:
    Painter Fr.42 Kassel-Austin: 200
    Theseus Fr.49 Kassel-Austin: 200

Eis Nekron Adônin: 166–7: 202
Eunapios: Lives of the Philosophers Wright
398–417:84–5

Galen: vol. 5 pp. 32–3 Kühn: 40n.
    de usu part. 15.3: 183n.
Geoponika: 80n.

Herodotos: 1.8:82
                    1.61.1: 18n.
                    2.2: 101
Hesiod:
    Erga   529–33: 184
    Theogony   120–2: 83
Hesychios: 182, 183, 189, 197n., 219
Hippokrates:
    Epid.   2.3.1: 183
    Morb.   4.3.8: 183
    Morb. Sacr.   15: 183
    Mul.   1.6: 50
Homer:
    Il.   bk.   3: 172–3, 177
                    5: 167, 170
                    13: 66
                    14: 173
                    22: 172, 175
    Od.   bk.   1: 135, 137
                    2: 134, 141, 151
                    4: 78n., 134, 136, 140,
                       141, 173
                    5: 139, 151n., 156
                    6: 110, 149n., 160, 178,
                       179, 180
                    8: 23, 134, 137, 158
                    9: 144, 184
                    10: 173
                    11: 138, 139, 141, 145,
                       147, 151, 158
                    13: 135, 136, 141, 145,
                       146, 150, 156
                    14: 154, 184
                    15: 160
                    16: 136, 137, 146, 150
                    17: 134, 148
                    18: 146, 146n., 147, 149

                    19: 24n., 136, 149, 150,
                       151, 152, 154, 156
                    20: 135, 150
                    21: 155, 160
                    22: 156
                    23: 155, 156, 157, 158,
                       161
                    24: 132, 136, 139
    Hymns   2: 184
                    5: 204
Horace:
    Epode   5.41:91
                    5.71–2: 84n.
Horapollo: 1.11: 218
Hypereides: 4.9: 56n., 59
                    4.30: 58
                    6: 74n.
                    fr. 215: 61, 225n.22

Isaios: 8.19: 197
Isokrates: 1.10: 65
                    7.38: 65
                    15.115: 65
                    15.138: 66

Julian: Symp. 329C–D: 192

Kallimakhos:
    Hymn   5.75: 204
                    5.109: 204
Kallixinos: 2: 182
Klearkhos: fr. 24 Wehrli: 94n.
Kleomedes:
    de motu circul. corp. cael. 2.1: 197
Kyranides: 1: 81, 81n., 217n.
                    2: 77, 77n., 80, 81

Longus: Daphnis and Chloe
    Proem   106, 125
    1   102, 102n., 103, 104,
                    106, 107, 108, 108n.,
                    115, 116, 116n., 118,
                    119, 124, 125, 126
    2   84n., 107, 117, 119,
                    124n., 125
    3   102, 103, 105, 108, 109,
                    115, 121, 122, 123, 124,
                    125n.
    4   108, 112, 113, 114, 123,
                    124, 125, 228n.19
Lucian:
    Dial. Meretr.   2.1: 236n.13

	8: 82	887: 92
Jup. Trag.	2: 83	888–9: 87
Kataplous	6: 83n.	889: 91
Philopseudes	13–5: 88, 88n.	913–4: 97
sch. on Lucian	275–6 (Rabe): 196–7	940–68: 78
	279–81 (Rabe): 194–5	VIII 1–63: 78–9
Lysias:	3: 49	X 36–50: 78
	14.26–8: 225n.18	XII 14–95: 79
	14.41: 225n.18	95: 174
	16: 58	107–21: 93
	19.18: 65	179–81: 78
	25.18: 65	278–9: 227n.10
	30.2: 25n.18	376–96: 95
	31: 58	397–400: 77
		XV: 96
Menander: *Samia*, 35–50: 191		XVI 5–6: 96
		XIXa: 98
Oath of Ephebes: Tod no. 204: 57		XIXb: 93
Origin: *contra Celsum* 2.55: 92–3, 229n.41		XXXIIa: 95
Ovid: *Ars. Amat.* 2.105–6: 95n.		XXXIV: 84n.
		XXXVI 69–101: 95
P. Oxy.: 1176 fr. 39 col. xiv: 82n.		75: 86
Papyri Graecae Magicae (PGM):		81–2: 86
	III 575–81: 77	83: 218
	IV 296ff: 94, 218	138–44: 89
	404: 98	142: 87
	831–2: 78	147–52: 87
	1265–74: 85	161–77: 78
	1716–870: 94	211–30: 78
	1852–9: 91	231–55: 95
	1872–926: 93	361–71: 93
	2038–41: 87	LXI 15–6: 87
	2052–3: 92	23–9: 89
	2443: 92	LXII 1–24: 86
	2445: 92	LXIV: 92
	2449–51: 95n.	CI 30–1: 98
	2466–70: 86–7	CXXIV: 95
	2471–92: 89	
	2495: 95n.	0.1 vol. 2 p. 233: 78
	2574–601: 91	(PDM)
	2597: 218	xiv 309–34: 227n.8
	2735–9: 87	528:227n.12
	2762–3: 88	1070: 92
	2767: 87	1070–9: 92
	2939–42: 87	1075: 228
	2943–66: 95	lxi 116: 87
	V 304–69: 94	Pausanias: 2.16.4: 151
	VII 191–2: 79	7.23.3: 84
	462–6: 85–6	Petronius: *Satyrica* 119.24: 218
	467–77: 95	Pherekrates: fr.170 (Kock): 190
	593–619: 86	Phidalios: FGRHist 30 F 2: 83n.
	877: 92	Philo: *On Animals*: 23

Photios: *Lexikon s.v. numphai* 182
Pindar:
Ol.   1.46: 184
Pyth.   2.35: 18n.
Plato:
Charm.   155B: 80
Gorg.   494C–E: 53
Laws   625E–626E: 49
             835B–842A: 18, 21
             836B: 84n.
             873C: 83n.
Lysis   204C: 228n.19
             211D: 225–6n.23
Phaido   62C: 83
Phaidr.   252A–B: 84n.
             276B: 192
Rep.   327B–C: 51–2
             395D: 69n.
             475D: 236n.10
             563B–C: 49n.
             571B–572B: 34, 223n.18
             571B,D: 33n.
Symp.   203D: 97
Plautus: *Truc.* 42–4: 95n.
Pliny: *nat. hist.* 10.181: 218
             11.48: 182
             22.20: 203
             27.65: 81
Plutarch:
Cicero   7.864C: 224n.8
Conj. Praec. 140B,D: 223n.21
             141B–C: 81n.
Demosth.   30.5: 236n.11
Kimon   4.3: 65–6
lat. viv.   1128E: 83n.
Lys.   9.5: 48n.
mul. virt.   244E: 74n., 182n.
             256A–C: 81
quo modo quis suos in virt. sent. prof.
             77B: 82–3n.
Theseus   26.2–5: 83n.
Poetae Lesbiorum: *fr. incert.* 16(L–P): 185
Polemo: *de physiogn. liber:* 69
Pollux: 1.25.2: 182
        2.90: 182
Praxilla: 754 (Page 1962): 234n.21
Proklos: *ad* Hesiod *Erga* 425: 182
Ps.-Kallisthenes:
Alexander: 93
Ps.-Phokylides: 187: 218

Ptolemy Chennos: *Novel History* 143, 144, 166n.

Rufus: *Onom.* 42: 182

Sappho:(L–P) 1: 167–8, 168–9
              2: 166, 186
             16: 176, 184
             31: 174, 178
             36: 185
             42: 183n.
             48: 235n.22
             51: 181
             58: 203
             94: 173–4, 185–6
             98: 166
            104a: 178
            105a: 105, 183
            110: 184
            111: 184
            132: 182n.
            140a: 205
            160: 165
            166: 184
            168: 205
          211biii: 204
Seneca: *Epistle*, 122.7–8: 21
Sophokles:
Oidipous Kol.   1192–4: 78n.
Oinomaos   fr. 474: 85
Trakhiniai   575–87: 81
Soranos: *Gynaecology* 1.18: 182
Suetonius: *Calig.* 50: 95n.

Tertullian: *de anima* 46.5: 219
Theokritos: 2.91: 90
Theophrastos:
Char.   16.11: 31
Hist. Plant. 6.6.6: 183
             9.11.6: 95n.
             9.19.3: 81
Thoukydides: 1.22: 107n.
               1.138.3: 65
               3.74: 20

Varro:
Res Rust.   2.2.14: 218
             2.4.9–10: 198n.
             2.7.8: 218
Vergil: *Ecl.* 8.108: 91

Xenophon:

[*Ath. Pol*]	1.2: 48n	*Mem.*	1.3.11: 50, 56
	1.10: 48		1.5.1: 50
Econ.	7.31: 7n.		1.5.5: 50
	12.13: 50		2.1.1: 63
Hell.	2.3.30: 65		2.6.10–3: 76n.
	5.2.29: 194n.		3.7.1: 50
Hiero	7.3: 59n.		3.11.16–8: 77
Kyr.	5.1.16: 85n.		

Zenobios: 1.49: 192

General Index

Abbott, G. F., 181, 183, 234n.11
Abt, A., 90
Achilles Tatius, 80, 105
Adolescence, erotic development in, 102–3, 104, 112, 114–5, 126n., *see also* Daphnis, Chloe
Adonia, 13, 188, 189–93, 194, 195, 198, 199, 200, 201, 202, 205
Adonis, 189, 201, 204, 235n.3; gardens of, 189–90, 191, 192–3, 202, 235n.3
Agamemnon, 132, 138, 139, 140, 145, 148n.
agôgai, 73, 85–92, 93, 95–7, 95n., *see also* magic
Aiskhines, 47, 48n., 52n., 55n., 56–7, 58, 59, 60–1, 63–4, 65
Albright, W. F., 235n.3
Alexander the Great, 30
Alexandrian scholars, 166, 168
Alkinoos, 179, 180–1
Alkiphron, 106, 200–1
Allione, L., 147
Alloula, M., 9
Amazons, 7, 221n.6
Amory, A., 153n., 155
Anagrammatism, 32n.
Anakreon, 163
Analysts, the, 155, 155n.
Anderson, G., 103
Andrewes, A., 48
Androcentrism, 5, 8, 39, 174, 179, *see also* protocols; phallocentrism; penetration; men
Andromache, 172
Animals, 113, 218; used as exempla of "nature", 22; dreamed intercourse with, 38–9, 216

Antaphrodisiacs, 79, 80, 198, 204
Anthropology, 8, 98; as methodological basis for this book, 10, 20, 104, 130, 164; Classics and, 3, 8–10, 134n.; feminist, 3, 6, 130, 142, 164; modern Mediterranean, 9, 107, 134–5, 221n.8; of cunning, 133, 145; usefulness and limitations of, for ancient world, 3, 10, 98, 113, 162
Aphrodisiacs, 75–6, 79–80, 81
Aphrodite, 12, 23, 37n., 134, 137, 157–8, 169, 188; Adonia and, 189, 190, 192; and Adonis, 204, 205, 206; in *Iliad*, 169–70; Sappho and; 167, 169–71, 173, 174, 175, 176, 178, 180, 186, 187, 203
Apollo, 23, 55, 83n., 125
Apuleius, 10, 85, 106n.
Ares, 23, 94, 134, 157, 170, 175, 202, 233n.12
Aristippos, 63
Aristophanes, 188, 190, 222n.6; *Clouds*, 19n., 51n.; *Ekkl.*, 4–5; *Lys.*, 190–1, 199–200, *see also* Comedy, Old.
Aristotle, 19, 22n., 53n., 59n., 83; on dreams, 92, 92n., 222n.11; on "nature" and desire, 67–9, 69n.; on the *oikos*, 6–7, 8
Artemidoros, 8n., 11, 20, 22, 23–44, 117n., 219, *see also* dream analysis
Artemis, 140
Astylos, 112, 113
Athena, 167, 169, 216; and Odysseus, 135, 136, 141, 145–6, 150, 156, 158n., 180; and Telemakhos, 132
Athenaios, 80, 81n.
Athens: ancient, 2, 7–8, 10, 19, 65; modern, 1–2
Atkinson, J. M., 3

Attika, population of, 47, 224n.2
Audollent, A., 94
Austen, J., 131
Austin, N., 179

Bacchis, 201
Baldwin, K., 140
Barnard, M., 162
Bartsch, S., 126n.
Baudy, G., 202
Bauer, J., 207n.
Beckett, S., 110
Bernal, M., 9
Bernikow, L., 164n.
Berti, M., 106n.
Bluffing, 4, 5, 6, 10, 54, 66, 70, 110, 207, see also duplicity, protocols
Boas, F., 9
Boccaccio, 101, 231n.21
Bolling, G., 172
Bondage, 96–7, 98, see also dominance, violence
Books in ancient world, 19, 130–1, 166
Bourdieu, P., 20, 62n., 74n., 181
Brandes, S., 138, 158n.
Brashear, W., 173
Bremmer, J., 5
Büchner, W., 146n., 147, 154
Burkert, W., 196, 199
Bushala, E. W., 49n.
Butler, S., 129–33, 143, 159
Byre, C.S., 146

Cameron, A., 167
Cameron, A., and A. Kuhrt, 3
Campbell, J., 9, 102n., 135
Canidia, 84n., 90, 91
Cantarella, E., 2
Cebes, 77
Celsus, 92
Chalk, H.H.O., 106n., 122n.
Charmides, 50
Chatzis, A., 143
Chicago, J., 182n.
Chloe, 12, 84n., 101–26; consciousness of, 103–4, 123; erotic education of, 102–3, 112–9, 233n.17; rescue by, 116; rescue of, 114, 119; violence toward, 103–4, 106, 117, 118–20, 121–2, 123, 124–6
Chrysis, 88, 88n.
Clark, M., 159, 159n.
Classics, 129, 134, 143; conservatism of, 8;

attitude toward Sappho of, 162–3, 185, 186, 206
Clay, J. S., 172
Clitorises, 40n., 181–2, 184
Cock-fighting, 49, 49n.
Cole, S. G., 6n.
Combellack, F.M., 154n.
Comedy: New, 105, 106, 112, 202; Old, 190, see also Aristophanes
Competition, 47, 47n; and sexual behavior, 11, 40n.; between social practices, 19; duplicity and, 75, 77, 78, 110; in ancient Greek society, 25, 60, 63, 74, 116; in modern Mediterranean life, 19, 27; in the Odyssey, 149, 154; kinaidos as antithetical to, 54; self-control seen as, 40n., 49–50
Connor, W. R., 48
Constraints, 110, 111, 158; affecting Chloe, 104, 117 (see also Chloe); affecting Penelope, 133, 141–3; affecting women, 12, 27, 41, 145, 189; erôs as, 83 (see also erôs); erotic magic and, 85, 94, 95, 209; this book and, 206
Convention, see Nature vs. Culture
Cook, B. W., 187n.
Cornford, F., 8, 9
Corno, D. del, 25
Courtesans, 199–202, 236n.13
Courtney, E., 54n.
Coward, R., 3
Culture, see Nature vs. Culture
Cunning, see mêtis

Daphnis, 228n.19, 231n.12; education of, 104; erotic education of, 102–3, 112–6, 120–2; kidnap of, 116; "natural" sexuality of, 114–5, 223n.17; plucking fruit, 105, 106, 107, 108; violence toward, 113–4; wedding night of, 124–5
Davidson, A., 70
Davies, J. K., 56n.
Davis, D. L., 141n.
Dawn (Eôs), 172, 202–3, 204, 205, 206
Decker, F., 132
Degani, E., 81
Del Grande, C., 178
Demeter, 12, 125, 126, 184, 189; festivals of, 188, 193, 194, 195, 196, 197, 198–9, 205, 206, see also Thesmophoria
Demeter Chloe, 126
Demetrios, 181, 182, 183
Demosthenes, 46–7, 55, 60, 61n., 65

Denich, B. S., 9n.
Desire, 57, 58n.; physical explanation for variety of, 68, 226n.36, see also erôs, see also pleasure
Detienne, M., 13, 206; phallocentrism of, 189, 199, 201, 205, 208; structuralist method of, 189, 198; view of Adonia and Thesmophoria, 193, 198–9, 200, 201, 201n.
Deubner, L., 196n., 206
Devereux, G., 153n.
diabolê, 89–90, 91, 236n.3
Dihle, A., 143
Dio Chrysostom, 21–2, 23
Diomedes, 167, 169–70, 175, 176, 180
Dionysia: city, 52; rural, 195, 236n.10
Dionysios of Halikarnassos, 166, 168
Dionysos, 49n., 106, 123, 125, 190, 194, 195
Diotima, 97
Dodds, E.R., 25
Dodson, B., 182
dokimasia 54–63, 130, 225n.11, 225n.13, see also testing
Dominance/submission: central to Greek society, 11; implied in bodily contact, 48–9; in agôgai, 83, 95–6; penetration symbolizes, 37, 37n., 39 (see also penetration); sexual propriety and, 70
Dorkon, 112, 115, 116, 120, 121; disguised as wolf, 118–9, 121
Dornseiff, F., 32n.
Dover, K. J., 19n., 45, 47, 47n., 53, 56, 59n., 69n., 74n.
Dream analysis: Artemidoros', 11, 23–36, 210–6, 222n.11; goal of, 30; sex in, 27, 36 (see also Artemidoros); Freud's, 26–7, 29, 29n.
Dreams, 24, 102, 110; erotic, 27, 33–4, 92, 211; individual souls as source of, 29, 33; cultural relativity of meanings of, 28–9, 223n.14; Penelope's, 153–4; predictive, 27, 27n., 32–3; role of in agôgai, 91–2; symbols in, 28–9, 32–3, 41, see also dream analysis
Dryas, 102, 108, 109, 110, 119
du Boulay, J., 8n., 75, 108n., 135, 138n.
Dubisch, J., 6n.
duBois, P., 177
Dumont, Margaret, 52n.

Duplicity, 75, 77; Homer's, 143–5, 156; in agôgai, 86, 89, 90, 91; in Daphnis and Chloe, 108, 108n., 109–10, 110n., 120, 122; in modern Greece, 130, 134; in the Odyssey, 130, 135–41, 144, 146, 147, 151, 152, 153, 153n., 154–9, see also mêtis, Odysseus and Penelope

Edmundsen, C. N., 200n.
Edwards, A., 143
Edwards, M. W., 143
Eichholz, D. E., 200n., 201n.
Eleusis, 188, 195, 206
Endymion, 203–4, 205
Enlightenment, the, 18, 20
Ephebes, 55, 55n.; oath of, 57
Erasistratos, 83–4
erôs, 71, 81, 85, 86, 105; adolescence and, 115–6; competitive success and, 77–9; incurability of, 84, 89, 112; invasiveness of, 73, 84, 87, 90, 106–7, 122; medical view of (ancient), 82, 83; socialization into conventions of, 119, 120–1; Sappho and woman-centered, 169, 176–8, 185–7; women and, 90, 103, 206
Erôs, 102, 103, 191; as Assistant in agôgai, 91–2; figurines of, 88, 91; involvement with Daphnis and Chloe, 79, 90, 94, 97, 102, 103, 106, 106n., 117, 118, 125
Euboulos, 194, 204
Eumaios, 134, 137, 146, 148, 159, 160
Euripides, 19, 193
Eurykleia, 146, 156, 167
Eurymedon, 51
Evil Eye, 74

Fant, M. B., 3
Feminist scholarship, 2, 3, 6, see also anthropology, feminist
Fenik, B., 143
Feraboli, S., 58
Finley, J., 9, 133, 134n.
Finley, M., 155
Fisher, N. R. E., 49n.
Fitzgerald, R., 152
Flowers, see gardens
Foley, H., 3, 126, 141n., 142n., 146, 147n.
Fotis, 85, 218
Foucault, M., 3–4, 6, 6n., 43, 45, 48, 50, 51, 53, 74
Frazer, J., 8, 76
Freedman, E., 56n.

Freud, 26, 26n., 27, 28, 29, 29n.
Friedl, E., 9, 135, 135n., 136

Galen, 40n., 84, 92
Ganschinietz, R., 80
Gardens/flowers, 123–4, 193, 203, 204; of
    Adonis, 189–92, 198, 201; Sappho's
    sexual imagery and, 180–2
Gardiner, A. H., 28n.
Gay scholarship, 3
Geertz, C., 103n.
Gender constructions, 3, 37, 224n.9, *see also*
    sexuality, constructions of
Generals, 55
Giannantoni, G., 63
Gifts, 108, 119, 146, 147, 147n., 175
Gilmore, D., 110
Gilsenan, M., 135
Glaukias, 88, 89
Gleason, M., 66
Gnathon, 112–4
Golden, M., 48n., 53, 61n., 198
Gossip, *see* rumor
Gould, J., 5, 6n.
Gouldner, A., 45, 47n., 74n.
Greece: ancient, 2, 7–8, 10, 17–8, 19, 65; mod-
    ern, 1–2, 6, 9, 66, 134, 148, 159, *see also*
    Mediterranean culture: ancient and
    modern
Greenblatt, 5, 50
Gryttos, 54, 55n., 61
gunaikes, 5, 5n., 7, 8, 11, 12, 38, 61n., 194,
    199
Guthrie, W. K. C., 63, 222n.7

Hadrian, 95
Hainsworth, J. B., 143
Hallett, J. P., 187
Haloa, 188, 194–5, 198, 206
Halperin, D., 4, 37, 40n., 46, 54, 70, 102n.,
    118n.
Handman, M.-E., 9n.
Hansen, M. H., 55n. 56, 61n.
Harrison, J., 2, 8, 9
Harsh, P. W., 148, 155
Heiserman, A., 10, 103
Hekate, 88, 95, 216, 218
Hektor, 172, 175
Helen, 92, 139, 140–1; in Sappho, 172, 173,
    177, 178, 184
Helios, 77, 78, 134
Henderson, J., 17n., 62
Hephaistion, 166

Hephaistos, 23, 134, 137, 157–8, 233n.12
Hera, 167, 169, 184n., 205, 216
Herakles, 65, 81, 125, 151
Hercher, R., 143
Hermes, 23, 139
Herodotos, 18n., 163n.
Herophilos, 33
Herzfeld, M., 2, 9, 74n., 75n., 97, 110,
    159, 159n.
Hesiod, 19, 172, 202
Hesperos, 172
hetairai, 56, 165, 223n.21
Heterosexuality, 4, 133, *see also* sexuality,
    constructions of
Hiatus, 106, 231n.15
Hippokrates, 82n., 92
Hippolytos, 80n., 110n.
Hipponax, 81
History of ideas, 10, 18, 20, 44, 222n.4
History of practices, 18–9, 45; Artemidoros
    as source for, 36, 42
Hoffmann, H., 49n.
Homophobia, 113, 162
homophrosunê (of Penelope and Odysseus),
    140, 147, 160–1
Homer, 12, 19, 25, 130, 131, 133, 137, 138,
    147, 147n., 148n., 152, 155, 158, 160,
    165, 202; duplicity of, 143–5; Sappho's
    use of, 160, 165, 165n., 166, 167, 169–80,
    186–7; used in anger-restraining spells,
    78, 78n.
——. *Iliad*, 233n.13; Sappho's use of, 164,
    167, 169, 170, 175, 176
——. *Odyssey*, 12, 110, 133, 146; duplicity
    in, 134–41; female authorship and, 190,
    131–2, 232n.3; male perspective of, 158,
    159; questions gender norms, 159–61;
    Sappho's use of, 178–80, (*see also*
    Sappho); society portrayed and, 129–30,
    133, 232n.5; women's roles in, 12, 130,
    132, 133, 164–5, but *see also* women
    characters by name, esp. Penelope, Helen
Homosexuality, 4, 36, 45, 113, *see also* ki-
    naidos; lesbianism; paederasty; sexuality;
    woman-woman intercourse
Hooker, J. T., 168
Hoplites, 45–8; antithesis of *kinaidoi*, 50, 51,
    59, 52

Incest, 37n., 38, 42, 43, 212–5, 219,
    225n.18

Isis, 39n., 87
Ixion, 18n.

Janko, R., 173
Jesus, 93, 219
Jones, A. H. M., 55
Jones, C. P., 106n.

Kaimakis, D., 77
Kallikles, 53–4, 69n.
Kalypso, 132, 139–40, 151n.
katadesmoi, see magic; erotic spells
Kessels, A. H. M., 25, 25n.
kestos, 173
Keuls, E., 2
kharis, 77–9, 227n.7, 227n.10
Kimon, 65–6
kinaidos, 34n., 45–7, 49n., 50–4, 61, 64, 67, 69, 69n., 193
Kinsey report, 33
Kirk, G. S., 133
Kirke, 132, 173
Kleis, 182n.
Kleon, 54, 61, 62, 65
kleos 130, see also rumor
Klytemnestra, 138–9
Kock, T., 49n.
Koniaris, G., 178
Korê, 194, 196, 206
Kühner, R., and F. Blass, 92
Kuhnert, E., 86

Laertes, 134, 136, 137, 149; shroud of, 141
Laios, 18, 49
Lamon, 108, 109, 110, 113, 119, 123
Lampis, 112, 123
Lanata, C., 165
Lasserre, F., 187
Laukamm, S., 30
Lavelle, B. M., 51
Lawler, L. B., 172
Leda, 184
Lefkowitz, M., 3
Lerner, G., 2
Lesbianism, 162, 187, see also Sappho; woman-woman intercourse
Lesbos, 102, 105, 106, 163–4, 168, 203
Levine, D., 146
Linos (Alexis'), 65
Lippard, L., 182n.
Lloyd, G. E. R., 22n., 67, 69, 80n.
Lobel and Page, 162–3

Lollianos, 106n.
Longus, 103, 104, 105, 108, 111, 112, 114, 116, 117, 120, 123–4, 126; differentiated from narrator, 106–7
———. Daphnis & Chloe, 11, 84, 101–26, 134n., 228n.19; structure of, 125n., violence in, 11–2, 103, see also Chloe, violence toward
Lorde, A., 182n.
Louvre figurine, 93–8, 218
Love, modern conception of, 72, 82, see erôs
Lucian, 40n., 89, 105, 194
Lykainion, 112, 120–2
Lyric poetry, 105, 165

MacDowell, D. M., 49n., 55
Magic, 72–3, 172, 173; erotic, 11, 71–7, 84, 85, 93, 94, 94n., 95; dolls used in, 94, 95, 229n.42, 230n.50; ousia used in, 86, 91, 228n.25, 229n.33; violence of, 11, 71–7, see also agôgai; Louvre figurine.
Magical papyri, 71–98, 137, 174, 236n.3
Mahaffy, J., 135–6, 153n.
Maids, 134, 148–50, 152, 153, 156
maiomai, in Sappho, 184–5, 235n.22
malakos, 50, 51, 52, 69
Malinowski, B., 9
Maltomini, F., 173
Manchus, 17n.
Mannebach, E., 63
Manoli, 75–6
Marquardt, P., 153n., 154n.
Marriage, 179, 222n.4; arranging, 108, 109, 111, 124; in Dio, 111; in Homer, 110, 133, 134, 140, 147, 152, 158n., 160–1; in Longus, 105, 108–9, 124
Marx Brothers, 52n.
Mary Magdalene, 92–3
Maximus, 84, 223n.16
Mediterranean culture: ancient, 2–3, 4, 20, 27, 73, 108, 110, 117; in Odyssey, 131, 132, 133; modern, 2, 9, 10, 19, 27, 110, 117, 148
Melantho, 149, 150
mêlon, 181, 183
Melville, H., 219n.
Men, 4, 8, 11, 19, 48–9, 138, 139, 180; and andreia, 45, 47, 47n., see also androcentrism, penetration, phallocentrism, protocols
Menander, 188, 191, 199, 200

Menelaos, 134n., 140, 141, 173
Mentes, 134
Merkelbach, R., 106n., 155n., 165
Messick, B., 208, 209
Metics, 6, 49, 224n.4
mêtis, 160; of Odysseus, 158; of Penelope, 130, 134, 138, 141, 144, 145, 150, 152–6
Metzger, H., 191
Michaelakis, E. M., 69n.
Millet, P., 47
Milne, M. J., and D. von Bothmer, 62n.
Minos, 219
Misandrism, 139–40, 205
Moralists, 22, 23, 44, 45, 60
Moschion, 191, 200
Murnaghan, S., 142, 148n., 161
Murray, G., 8–9
Muses, 78, 78n.

Nagy, G., 165
"Natural": ancient moralists' definitions of, 20–1; lover, 114–8 *cf.* conventional lover, 112–4; means conventional, 8, 17, 22, 40; sexual acts, 36, 114, 210, 214 *cf.* conventional, 36; unconventional, 37
Nature (*phusis*), 67, 68, 69, 70, 123; Artemidoros and, 41; means culture, 42, 43, 62n., 66, 116, 117, 121; moralists' appeals to, 22–3, 42, 46, 61. Variety of meanings of word: character type, 65; genitalia, 11, 34, 217–20; personal bent, 46, 65; talent, n.27
Nature vs. culture, 45, 48, 116, 160, 198; and Chloe's "education", 117; *Daphnis and Chloe* as experiment in, 102; development of the contrast, 17–8, 18n., 69; in Artemidoros' dream analysis, 35; in the *Odyssey*, 146
Nausikaa, 110, 131, 149n., 160; in Sappho, 164, 178, 179–80
Neaira, 5, 61n., 65
nomos, see Natural; Nature vs. culture
numphê, 181, 182, 182n., 183, 183n., 184
Nymphs, 106, 109, 115, 116, 120, 121, 125

Obedience, 51, 163
Obbink, D., 173
Odysseus, 12, 110, 130, 133, 134, 135, 136, 137, 138, 139, 140, 141, 142, 143, 144, 145, 147, 148, 152, 156; and Penelope,
140, 142, 143, 147, 149, 150, 153, 156; and Nausikaa, 178, 179, 184
Oidipous, 18, 49n.
Oinochoe, 51
Oral-genital sex, 37, 38, 43, 215
Osiris, 87

Paederasty, 202; ancient attitude toward, 18, 113; differentiated from *kinaidos*, 53; modern attitude toward, 18
Page, D., 162, 167, 186
Pamphile, 85, 86, 97
Pan, 106, 119, 120, 124n., 125
parasitos, 112, 114
Participant/observer: Artemidoros as, 23, 31; Polemo as, 72
Pastoral, 101, 102n., 103, 105–6, 114, 117, 118; violence at center of, 123
Patriarchalism, 199, 201, 202; organizes constraints of desire, 209; women's resistance/accommodation to, 207–8
Patrimony, 56, 56n., 225n.16
Pausanias, 84, 105
Penelope, 12, 24n., 129–61, 164–5, 232n.9, 233n.14; and Odysseus, 140, 142, 143, 145, 146, 147, 148, 149, 150, 152, 153, 155, 156; and Telemakhos, 147; as active, 142–3, 155, 232n.10; (*see also* mêtis); presentation of, 130, 132–3, 134, 137, 138, 141, 142, 151, 157
Penetration, 39, 40, 51, 121, 122, 186; in dreams, 210–21, 216, *see also* erôs, invasiveness of
Penises, 42, 79, 211, 215, 219, *see also* phallocentrism, phalloi
Peradotto, J., & J. P. Sullivan, 3
Perikles, 76
Perry, M., 132
Petronius, 223n.17
Phaido, 66
Phallocentrism, 39, 42, 117, 184, 204; of Detienne's interpretation, 189, 199, 201, 206, *see also* androcentrism; penetration; protocols
Phalloi, 195, 204, 206, 208
phêmê, see rumor
Philetas, 119, 120
Philo, 23
Philometor, 84–5, 88
Philosophy, ancient Greek attitude toward, 19, 44, 222n.6, 222n.7
Philostratos, 105

Photios, 190
phusis, see nature
Physiognomy, 66–7, 71, 226n.28, 226n.29, 226n.1
Pindar, 18n., 29
Pirates, 107, 116
Pitt-Rivers, J., 74n.
Plato, 23, 34, 97, 190, 192, 193; on paederasty, 53; *Laws,* 18, 21n., 49; *Rep.,* 18–9, 51–2
Plato comicus, 81n., 190
Playing (*Daphnis and Chloe*), 118, 120, 124
Plutarch, 222n.4
Pleasure, 53, 54, 56, 69, 98, 210; non-mutual, 37, 40, *see also* desire
Pnyx, 188, 194
Poets, authority of, 19, *see also* by name
poikilophron, 166–7
Polemarchos, 51, 52
Polemo, 71, 72, 73, 82, 83, 97
Polis, 45, 194
Politicians, competitiveness of, 62, 64; elitism of, 55, 58n., 64; sexual behavior of scrutinized, 11, 45, 56–7, 60, 61
Polyphemos, 144–5, 156, 184
Pomeroy, S., 3
Population, *see* Attika, population of
Price, S., 26
Pritchett, W. K., 48
Prostitution, 42, 56, 210; crime if by politicians, 57, 58n., 225n.18, 59, 59n., 62–3, 64; loss of citizen rights for, 55n., 62–3
Protocols, 4–5, 10, 39, 40–1, 43, 70, 71, 117, 122, 126; getting behind to unspoken, 20, 43, 70 (*see also* bluffing); hoplite personifies, 45–7; *kinaidos* goes against all, 54, *see also* androcentrism; competition; penetration, phallocentrism
Psammetikhos, 101, 102
Psappo, 170n., *see* Sappho
Psyche, 94
pteruges, 181–2
Ptolemy Chennos, 143–4, 166n.
Pucci, P., 156n.
Public/private issue, 138n.; in epic and lyric, 164, 165–6; in Sappho, 164, 174, 181

Rankin, A. V., 153n.
Rape, 48, 195, 203, 205, 224n.3, 231n.8; Chloe and, 103–5, 118, 120, 123–5;

Daphnis and Chloe's mimetic dance of, 119–20
Redford, Robert, 64
Religious festivals, women's, 12 186, 188–209, *see also* by name
rhêtores, 55–6, 58, 59, 61, 64
Rhodes, P. J., 55n., 56n.
Ridley, R. J., 48n.
Riess, E., 30
Rissman, L., 167
Robertson, N., 198n.
Robinson, D. M., and E. Fluck, 62
Rogers, S. C., 6n.
Rumor/gossip, 74, 75–6, 134, 146n., 149n., 158; role of in community, 58–9, 66
Russell, D. E. H., and N. Van de Ven, 72n.
Russo, J., 153n., 165

Saake, H., 178
Sacks, K. B., and N. Scheper-Hughes, 142
Safa-Isfahani, K., 207–8, 207n.
Sandy, G. N., 106n.
Sappho, 12–3, 84, 84n., 105, 106, 130, 162–87; as reader of Homer, 165, 165n., 167, 169–80; audience of, 165–6; Classicists' attitude toward, 162–3, 185, 186, 206; context of, 13, 163–4; double consciousness of, 12, 162–3, 164, 164n., 166–7, 169, 174–6, 179, 186–7, 188; goddesses' seizing of mortals in, 202–5, 206; lesbianism of, 162–3; sexual imagery and vocabulary in, 166–7, 168, 171, 172–4; textual problems in, 166–7, 168, 171, 172–4; treatment of Helen by, 177–8
———. Poem 1, 166–76
———. Poem 16, 176–8
———. Poem 31, 178–80
Schadewaldt, W., 180
Schaps, D., 5, 163n.
Schneider, K., 49n.
Scrutiny, public, *see* dokimasia; rumor; testing
Self-control, 33, 45, 49–50, 56, 63, 150; lack of in Gnathon, 114; women at Adonia accused of lack of, 190
Selfishness, ancient view of, 96–7
sêmata, 152
Seneca, 21, 22, 23
Sex, constructions of, 17n., 27, 41, 113; ancient Mediterranean, 20–3, 188; study

of, 3, 17; women's in male-dominated societies, 207
Sexual behavior, 40–1, 43; "conventional" and "natural", 36–7; enforcement of conventional, for politicians, 11, 45, 60; masturbation, 36, 211; non-reproductive, 21, 38, (see also kinaidos, woman-woman intercourse); positions, 42; "unconventional", 18, 18n., 37–8; "unnatural", 38–9, 43
Sexual categories (homosexuality, heterosexuality), 4, 45, 113–4
Shaw, G. B., 129
Sheikha, 201–2
Simmias, 77
Simon, 196n.
Sittl, K., 54n.
Skinner, M. B., 3, 5
Skirophoria, 196
Slaves, 48, 49, 112, 113, 199; dreamed intercourse with, 28, 36, 210–1, 215
Snell, B., 178
Sodomy law, modern, 18n.
Sokrates, 19, 63, 66, 76, 192, 228n.19; mock kidnap of, 51–2; on dreams, 34, 50; on kinaidoi, 53, 54
Solon, 19, 60, 64
Solonian law, 60, 61n.
Sommerstein, A. H., 5
Sophokles, 19, 78n., 80n.
Sosipatra, 84, 88
Souda, 190
Speakers, see rhêtores
Stanford, W. B., 144
Stanley, K., 167
Stehle, E., 182, 189, 202, 203, 205
Stenia, 188, 194, 196, 198
Stephens, S., and J. Winkler, 101n.
Structuralism, 10, 189
Suicide (and erôs), 83, 83n., 109
Supreme Court, U.S., 18n.
Sutton, D. F., 80n.
Svenbro, J., 167
Symposia, 80
Syrinx, the, 116, 124
Syrinx, 119, 120

Teasing, 52, 111, 111n., 135–6
Telemakhos, 132, 134, 136, 137, 140, 146, 147, 148, 149, 157
Testing: Chloe's of Daphnis, 116; in D&C, 108; Odysseus' of Telemakhos, 136;

Penelope's of Odysseus, 143, 146, 150–1, 153n., 155, 156–7, 158, 160, see also dokimasia
Themistokles, 65
Theokritos, 84n., 90, 102n., 172
Theophrastos, 31n.
Thesmophoria, 13, 188, 193, 202, 205n., 236n.11, 236n.13; description of, 194–8
Thompson, H. A., 194
Thomsen, R., 56n.
Thornton, A., 137, 146n.
Thoukydides, 20–1, 48n., 65, 107n.
throna, 172
thumos, 78, 165, 171
Timarchos, 53n., 55n., 56–7, 58, 59, 60, 61
Tithonos, 202–3, 204, 205
Turner, P., 101n., 122n.
Typhon, 95, 218
Tyrtaios, 19

Van Nortwick, T., 155
Vester H., 149, 155
Victimage: Chloe's innocence about own, 119; in agôgai, 72–3, 87–90, 95; of women, 104, 117; theorists, 12, 142, 155
Violence, 107, 113, 126; against women, 11–2, 93–8, 103, 104–6, 122, 122n., 126, 232n. (see also Chloe, violence toward; rape); central in Greek society, 9n., 117, 118, 118n., 123–4, 224n.5, in agôgai, see victimage
Vlastos, G., 62

Walcot, P., 75, 135, 136
Wankel, H., 56
Weaving, 149, 150, 155–6, 172–3, 208–9, 208n.
Weddings, 73, 74–6, 124–6
Weeping, 141, 141n., 151, 160, 161
Weissenberger, M., 58
Welcker, F. G., 162
Wellman, M., 80n.
West, M. L., 81
Whitehead, D., 6n.
Wills, G., 177
Wine (and sex), 195
Winkler, J., 4, 49n., 106n., 126n.
Witches, 76, 84n., 90–1
Wittig, M., 162

Woman-woman intercourse: meaningless in Artemidoros' system, 8n., 39–40; Sappho on, 181–7

Women: autonomy of, 189, (in Thesmophoria) 194, 199; centrality of (in *Odyssey*) 132–3; consciousness of, 120, 123, 142, 164–5, 165n., 169, 174, 184, 188, 208–9; essential vulnerability of, 74, 104, 117–8, 122, 227n.5; laughter of, 207–8; male representations of, 4, 50, 54, 74, 80, 81; misogynism and, 138, 139, 158; power of, 90, 97, 116, 189, 204–9; sexuality of, 163, 181–3, 207, *see also* sexuality

Xanthias, 190
Xenophon, 63, 65

Zeig, S., 162
Zeitlin, F., 4, 49n., 110n., 141, 205n., 208n.
Zeus, 53n., 55, 139, 184, 184n., 202, 205
Zôpyros, 66